D1475088

Idaho's Constitution

Idaho's Constitution

The tie that binds

Dennis C. Colson

KFI
401
1890
.A29
C65
1991
West

University of Idaho Press
Moscow, Idaho

University of Idaho Press

Moscow, Idaho 83843

© 1991 Dennis C. Colson. All rights reserved. No part of this book
may be reproduced, stored in a retrieval system, or transmitted in any
form or by any means, electronic, mechanical, photocopying, record-
ing, or otherwise, except for use in reviews, without the prior permis-
sion of the publisher.

Publication of *Idaho's Constitution: The Tie That Binds* was made
possible by the gracious assistance of the Idaho Centennial Foundation.

Design by Karla Fromm

Printed in the United States of America

96   95   94   93   92   91   5   4   3   2   1

Library of Congress Cataloging-in-Publication Data

Colson, Dennis C.

  Idaho's Constitution: the tie that binds. / Dennis C. Colson.

    p.   cm.

  Includes index.

  ISBN 0-89301-132-0

  1. Idaho—Constitutional history. 2. Constitutional conventions–
–Idaho–History. I. Title.

KFI401   1890.A29C65   1991

342.796'029–dc20

[347.960229]   90–49454

                                                        CIP

Contents

List of Tables

Preface

AT THE VERY HEART OF IDAHO are diverse, powerful, conflicting forces, social, economic, and political. Like the weather, these forces are partially created by the state's extraordinary topography: the Snake River, which drains three-quarters of the region, is unnavigable and, ironically, leaves the country it passes through a great arid plain; and the Salmon River with its great white water, which cuts through the state where the handle attaches to the pan, leaves those parts connected only by a thread called the White Bird Hill. These great landmarks produced strikingly diverse settlement patterns in the various regions of Idaho. The radical differences in topography, culture, religion, law and economics constantly push the state toward disunity rather than cohesiveness.

The Idaho Constitution is the tie that binds, the single document whose task it is to hold Idaho together. If anyone had given thought to Idaho's natural circumstances, neither the territory nor the state would have been created. However, Idaho was not created with forethought, but rather by historical circumstance and accident. Idaho Territory was formed in 1863 because it was expedient for politicians in Olympia who controlled Washington Territory. Within five years Idaho Territory was reduced by the creation of Montana and Wyoming territories because of the demands of those regions, leaving Idaho's boundaries as they are today. For the most part, these decisions were made in ignorance or in defiance of the natural features of the country. However, by 1889, when Idaho was invited to join the Union as a state, it was too late for adjustments. The country had been divided up and the lines drawn. The state needed a constitution that would bind together as one political community what fate had left to it.

This book recounts the story of the drafting of that constitution at a convention held between July 4 and August 6, 1889, in the Territorial Capitol in Boise. In order to better understand the fundamental forces at work in the Idaho Constitution, it pays particular attention to those sections that provoked great debate and controversy at the convention. Topics are arranged in the order in which they were discussed at the convention, thus recreating the experience of the convention itself. Each section on a single topic may be read by itself. Some overlap is left between the chapters and their cross references.

The common ground shared by the parts of the constitution also reveals the major influences operating at the convention, the dominant sentiment in which was anti-Mormonism. This was indeed a great irony, since no Mormons were present and virtually every delegate was anti-Mormon. The most important force was the Republican party. Even though there was a great effort to conduct convention business in a non-partisan manner, frequently the the Republican section determined that its recommended version would be adopted because they were in control. Another important force was the legal profession. Nearly half of the delegates sent to the convention were lawyers, and they frequently got their way over the objections of nonlawyers.

The conflict between the north and south was perhaps less important at Idaho's Constitutional Convention than at any time before or since. While the differences between the regions necessarily produced some conflict, it was a time of conciliation. Many other controversies were more important at the convention: the people vs. the monopolies, as typified by railroads; the taxpayers vs. the politicians; the pioneers vs. the newcomers; and local government vs. state government vs. national government.

The delegates who represented these various interests at the convention are a fascinating group, and if more were known about them they would play a larger role in western lore. The anti-Mormons included Drew Standrod from Oneida County, stronghold of the Independent Anti-Mormon Party, and William Clagett, who had been speaking against the Mormons for nearly thirty years. The powerful Republicans at the convention included Clagett, who served in the Nevada legislature and as Montana's territorial delegate to Congress. Also at the convention were William McConnell, later elected governor, Weldon Heyburn, later elected U.S. senator, and Edgar Wilson, later elected to the U.S. House of Representatives.

The most accomplished lawyer at the convention was William Clagett, the "Silver-Tongued Orator of the West," and perhaps the most well-known mining lawyer of the western territorial period. James Beatty from Alturas County, who later served seventeen years as Idaho's first federal district judge, also played a prominent role at the convention. Because the lawyer-delegates dominates the convention debates, the list of important lawyers could go on and on: Heyburn, Reid, Mayhew, Wilson, Sweet, Standrod, Vineyard, Poe, Hagan, Stull, Savidge, and others.

For twenty-eight days the delegates debated the many topics covered by the Idaho Constitution. Every important question of the day was discussed and, importantly for today, every day of the discussion was recorded. The delegates decided to record verbatim their entire proceedings and made special provision for additional stenographers to be brought from Denver for the task. The record was later transcribed and published in two volumes as *Proceedings and Debates of the Constitutional Convention of Idaho*, edited by I. W. Hart, and published by Caxton Printers, Ltd. of Caldwell in 1912.

These over two thousand pages are the richest and most detailed record of Idaho history. All too often the study of those who made Idaho what it is today is like a study of Idaho's ghost towns, both having disappeared from the record. However, there is a difference between the ghost town and the ghost, at least when it comes to the Idaho Constitution. The constitution remains basically as it was drafted one hundred years ago, so the ghosts of those who drafted it are still very much with us. The *Proceedings and Debates* offer a rare chance to meet and learn about Idaho's founders. The *Proceedings and Debates* do not offer a biography of the delegates but something more ephemeral, and ultimately more important, their ideas.

The principal purpose of this book is to describe and interpret the *Proceedings and Debates*. Its hope is to those interested gain a better understanding of the Idaho Constitution, and thus of Idaho itself. Each section attempts to put Idaho's Constitution in perspective by briefly describing the important events which created it, as well as those which have changed it during the last one hundred years. It is intended as well to be helpful to those who want to gain a better understanding of a citizen's rights and responsibilities in Idaho. It should be helpful to lawyers and judges, who constantly shape the constitution's future, and to students and scholars of Idaho history, law, and political science.

1.

Calling the Convention

1. The Genealogy of Idaho

IDAHO'S FOUNDERS CONVENED in the territorial capitol at Boise City on July 4, 1889, to write a constitution for a new state. The delegates were not brought together by the natural affinities that produce political bonding and a coherent state politic. In fact, geography, economics, politics, religion, and culture differed so radically in the northern, southeastern, and southwestern corners of the territory that statehood was unthinkable until the moment it happened. The delegates were there because suddenly it was their only choice, and a great opportunity.

Idaho Territory was created, as it were, by amputation, nearly died of fragmentation, and was saved by a shotgun marriage.[1] The amputation was the severing of Idaho Territory from Washington Territory in 1863 in order to keep the capital of Washington in Olympia.[2] The fragmentation was the dismantling of the territory, first by creating Montana Territory and then Wyoming Territory from it, and finally by the proposal to annex northern Idaho to Washington or Montana and southern Idaho to Nevada.[3] The reluctant wedlock was Idaho statehood, the wedding of the northern and southeastern parts of the state to its southwest.[4] Like most shotgun marriages, this one has often been stormy.

To understand the political forces that brought Idaho to the eve of statehood it is necessary to know something of the state's genealogy. From time immemorial, what is Idaho has been occupied by Indian nations. In the far north are the ancestral lands of the Kootenai, and just to the south of them the Kalispel and Coeur D'Alene. North-central Idaho is the home of the Nez Perce, the largest and most powerful nation in the

1

Columbia River Basin. In the south, the Snake River plains are inhabited by the Shoshone and Bannock. The most southwestern portion of the state is Paiute country.[5]

Claims of sovereignty over these lands were asserted by other nations long before they had been visited. The principle of discovery, a part of international law, permitted any nation that first discovered a river to claim all lands drained by that river. Russian fur trade and settlement had progressed across the Bering Strait and down the Pacific coast to a point south of the current United States-Canadian border. Spanish ships had begun exploration on the Pacific Coast of North America from the south. Balboa discovered the western shore of North America in 1513, Cortez visited California in 1526, Cabrillo traveled as far north as 42 degrees in 1543, and Juan de Fuca discovered the strait that bears his name in 1592. Britain's discoverers were Sir Francis Drake, who visited the California coast in 1579, and Captain Cook, who cruised the Oregon coast in 1776.[6]

Although the United States was the last nation to claim discovery rights that would affect Idaho, it made the most important discovery, the mouth of the Columbia River. In 1792, Capt. Robert Gray found an opening in the Pacific Ocean breakers and sailed through them into a large river, which he named the Columbia after his ship. Claiming that the discovery doctrine required exploration and the practical assertion of sovereignty rather than mere observation of the coast, the United States asserted Gray's discovery gave it the best title to the region between the Pacific and the Stoney (Rocky) Mountains.[7]

Despite all these claims of discovery, no European had yet travelled as far inland as Idaho. The Old World met the New in Idaho when Sacajawea led the Lewis and Clark expedition to her people in the Lemhi Valley in the summer of 1805. Their trip had been organized by President Thomas Jefferson to strengthen the claim of the United States to the region.[8] Other explorers and trappers traveled in Idaho in the years that followed. David Thompson began fur trading near Bonners Ferry in 1808; the Missouri Fur Company established Fort Henry near St. Anthony in 1810; the Astorians explored the Snake River Valley and discovered the Boise Valley in 1811; Donald Mackenzie established a trading post near Lewiston in 1812; and John Reid founded a post on the lower Boise River in 1813. Exploration and trapping increased until the mountain men exhausted the resource by the early 1830s.[9]

The next wave of immigration began in 1834 when the missionaries Henry Harmon and Eliza Spaulding established their mission in Lapwai. The Spauldings had come with the Whitmans, who established a mission near Walla Walla. Father Pierre Jean de Smet began his missionary work in 1840 and Father Point followed in 1842. Hostilities between the Whitmans and local Indians forced the Spauldings to abandon their mission in 1846. A Mormon colony was established on the Lemhi River in 1855, but was forced to withdraw in 1858, leaving Idaho with virtually no non-Indian residents.[10]

Even though there were no settlements in Idaho to govern, attempts were being made to organize a government. In 1818 the United States and Great Britain agreed by treaty that The Oregon Country should be open to settlement by citizens of either nation, but neither provided for government.[11] In 1819 Spain relinquished any claims to land in the Pacific Northwest by treaty with the United States.[12] The boundary between the two nations was set at the forty-second parallel, which is now Idaho's southern border. In 1824 Russia relinquished its claims to the region south of fifty-four degrees, 40 minutes north latitude.[13]

As American settlement, especially in the Willamette Valley, accelerated, the United States pressed England to end the joint occupancy. In 1846 the two countries agreed that the forty-ninth parallel, still the northern boundary of Idaho, should be the border between them.[14] Congress created Oregon Territory in 1848 and put all of Idaho in it.[15] Soon the population in the Puget Sound area grew and demanded to be separated from the government of Oregon in the Willamette Valley. In 1853 Congress created Washington Territory, including in it all of Idaho north of the forty-sixth parallel.[16] Oregon soon demanded statehood and Congress responded in 1859.[17] In the process the eastern boundary of Oregon was moved west. This put all of Idaho in Washington Territory and established Idaho's boundaries in the southwestern portion of the state. The Washington territorial legislature first put southern Idaho in Skamania County and the north in Walla Walla. No settlement had as yet occurred, however, and no county governments had yet been organized.[18]

Circumstances dramatically changed with the discovery of gold in the Clearwater region in 1860. Within two years there were thousands of miners in northern Idaho. In response, the Washington legislature reorganized the area by creating Shoshone, Nez Perce, Idaho, and Boise counties. The rush to Idaho was so large that discussion of moving the territorial capital east of the Cascades began. Olympia politicians sought to save their capital by cutting the new mining camps loose from the territory. The miners wanted to stay in the territory but move the capital. However, the Olympia forces managed to sever the new camps by pushing a statute through Congress and getting President Lincoln to sign it on March 3, 1863.[19] This marked the birth of Idaho.[20]

The exact origin of the word "Idaho" is uncertain. As the delegates to the Idaho Constitutional Convention were arriving in Boise in the summer of 1889, the *Boise Statesman* offered two possible explanations. Some said Col. William Craig first used the word and pronounced it E-da-Ho in an interview with Joaquin Miller in the summer of 1861 as they traveled through Nez Perce Country and gazed upon a mountain summit that appeared to glisten like a diamond or gem. There was also a steamer launched on the Columbia in the spring of 1860 by the Oregon Steam Navigation Company named *Idaho*. The word was thought to mean "Gem of the Mountains" and to be taken from a Columbia River Indian tribe.[21]

More recent scholarship has documented other early uses of the name *Idaho*.[22] In May 1860, the name was suggested to Congress by early residents of the Pike's Peak region who were organizing the territory eventually named Colorado. The city of Idaho Springs, Colorado, was organized in June of 1860. The Washington territorial legislature created the original Idaho County in 1861. Nearly all accounts of these early events conclude the name was adapted from Indians of the region. However, despite the diligent work of researchers handicapped by working long after assimilation affected the native languages, no evidence of this origin has been found. At the same time, there is no substantial evidence of another origin. There is a claim that the eccentric Dr. George M. Willing made the name up when he was sent to lobby Congress by the Pike's Peak miners. It is said that when no name could be agreed upon on the floor of Congress, Dr. Willing was approached for a suggestion because he was familiar with Indian dialects:

> One of them said: "Something round and smooth, now, with the right sort of meaning to it." Now it happened that the little daughter of one of these gentlemen was on the floor that morning with her father, and the Doctor, who was fond of children, had just been calling her to him with: "Ida, ho—come and see me."

> Nothing could be better, and the veteran explorer promptly responded with the name, "Idaho."[23]

There is little corroboration for this version, and as Idaho's centennial approached, most continued to believe the Gem State inherited its name from the original inhabitants.

Idaho had a difficult time surviving as an entity during the territorial period.[24] It was divided almost out of existence. When first created, Idaho Territory included all of modern Idaho, Montana, and Wyoming. The area was too large to govern and within one year Montana[25] and Wyoming[26] were severed. These divisions established Idaho's boundaries as they exist today. However, further division was the major political issue throughout the territorial period.

The removal of the capital from Lewiston to Boise in 1865 prompted the first proposals to sever Idaho at the Salmon River.[27] Creation of a new territory out of eastern Washington, northern Idaho, and western Montana was a popular proposal in the early years. Annexation of northern Idaho to Washington or Montana became a popular idea later. North Idaho almost had its way in 1887 when Congress agreed to annexation with Washington, but President Cleveland pocket vetoed the bill.[28]

Southern Idaho had never been anxious about losing northern Idaho, but opposition to the idea strengthened when Nevada began campaigning to annex southern Idaho. President Cleveland's veto not only discouraged those in north Idaho, it also turned back Nevada's campaign. A political stalemate thus dominated Idaho Territory as 1890 approached. Northern Idaho could not decide between annexation either to Washington or to Montana, and the national government would approve neither. If the territory were divided, south Idaho would either be annexed to Nevada or have to wait a long time for a sufficient population to justify statehood.

The "shotgun marriage," thus became acceptable. Like the father of the bride, the United States offered the north and south great incentives to forget their differences and accept their fate as a union. Statehood, with local self-governance, school land grants, representation in Congress, and full American citizenship made up the dowry. The 1888 territorial legislature encouraged reconciliation by locating the University of Idaho at Moscow and by authorizing the construction of a north-south wagon road near White Bird Hill. As with most shotgun marriages, statehood for Idaho was a rushed affair. It came about by accident. In 1888, Republicans gained control over both houses of Congress and the White House, and they were looking for more Republican territories to admit as states in order to solidify their position. As an outcome of the Mormon controversy, Idaho Territory had just become Republican and prominent Republicans sent informal invitations to join the fold.[29]

The opportunity for statehood appeared so suddenly that the normal procedures of admission could not be followed. Senator Mitchell had introduced a bill authorizing an Idaho constitutional convention in December 1888. The bill was referred to the committee on territories and reported by Senator Platt in February 1889, with major amendments. No further action was taken before adjournment (pp. 2097–3011).[30] A bill calling for a constitutional convention was also introduced in the last session of the territorial legislature, but the session was distracted by the division of Alturas County and no action was taken.[31]

The need for a convention was urgent, and the only plausible authority to issue a call was Territorial Governor Edward A. Stevenson. Stevenson was the first resident of Idaho Territory ever to be appointed as governor, and he responded to the statehood movement on April 2, 1889, by calling a convention to begin on July 4 (p.vi). He was succeeded by George L. Shoup when President Harrison, a Republican, took office. On May 11 Governor Shoup repeated the call for a convention, and elaborated the arguments in favor of statehood (pp. vii–x). The gubernatorial calls were scant authority for a convention and were unable to provide any budget, but they were adequate under the circumstances to initiate the process.

Idaho was not the first state to organize a constitutional convention without an enabling statute from Congress. In the early years of the Union, a statute was thought necessary. Ohio established the precedent by petitioning Congress for authorization in 1802. Indiana, Illinois, Alabama, Mississippi, Missouri and Louisiana all followed Ohio's example. However, between 1836 and 1848 the practice began to change. During this period, Wisconsin was admitted after first securing an enabling act, but Arkansas, Michigan, Iowa and Florida were all admitted without prior Congressional authorization. This change in procedure reflected a general policy of Congress to extend home rule to the territories. In the years that followed, both procedures were used. California, Oregon and Kansas organized without the authority of enabling acts, while Nebraska, Minnesota and Nevada all had prior authorization.[32]

The first order of business necessary to organize the convention was the election of delegates. The number of delegates and the process of selection was designed and carried out by the central committees for the Republican and Democratic parties. A total of seventy-two delegates were to be selected, from the eighteen counties in the territory. (See Appendix B.) Each county was entitled to a number of delegates determined by its proportion of the votes cast in the 1888 general election. Each delegation had party memberships in proportion to the Republican and Democratic strength in its county. The Mitchell and Platt bills introduced in Congress, the bill before the territorial legislature and Governor Stevenson's proclamation, all provided for election of delegates, but Governor Shoup authorized selection by "some other equitable method." As a result, only Custer and Owyhee counties held a popular election. In ten counties the Democratic and Republican central committees made the choices, and in six counties conventions organized by the central committees made the elections.[33] This selection process produced a group of delegates unlike any ever produced by popular election in Idaho. (See Appendix C for a roster of the delegates.)

2. Idaho's Founders

THE CONVENTION DELEGATES made up one of the most experienced and talented groups of leaders ever to convene in Idaho. Many had political experience in Idaho and elsewhere, including Oregon, Washington, Nevada, Montana, and South Carolina. Many had been educated in eastern universities, others in eastern politics, and others by life in the territories of the West. There were pioneers who had come to the Territory as part of the first gold rushes of the 1860s and there were newcomers who arrived with the mining rushes, railroads and irrigated agriculture of the 1880s. There were merchants, bankers, doctors, ranchers, farmers, miners and laborers. But, most of all, there were lawyers.[34] Forty percent of the delegates were trained attorneys.[35] According to political fashion of the day, all of the delegates were men. Ironically, many of Idaho's Founders did not die in Idaho. Just as thriving towns important at the time of statehood are ghost towns today, many leaders important in creating the new state soon disappeared from it, leaving their marks on the document of fundamental law they drafted.

These delegates shared a desire for a constitution that would create a state where none existed by unifying the territory and securing the approval of Congress. The Idaho Constitutional Convention was the process by which the people of the territory sought to discover common interests and ideals. At the same time, each delegate had the interests of his constituents in mind and fought hard for them. Given the different political cultures in the region, the delegates soon discovered they had many differences. There were miners vs. irrigators; laymen vs. lawyers; Democrats vs. Republicans; small counties vs. large; the north vs. the southeast vs. the southwest; consumers vs. railroads; the common man vs. monopolies; traditionalists vs. progressives; the people vs. the politicians; skinflints vs. spendthrifts; promoters vs. pioneers; Rebels vs. Yankees; fervent Christians vs. skeptics and virtually everybody vs. the Mormons.

The delegates did not resolve these differences, but they did establish legal and political institutions for reaching decisions about them in the process of state government. The Idaho Constitution is so extraordinarily important because it is a charter for the framework of decision. Fundamentally, the Constitution remains unchanged as its first century draws to a close, which is a testament to the wisdom of those who created it.

What follows is an introduction to the most important delegates and their role at the convention, grouped by their county delegations, beginning with the largest and moving to the smallest:

Ada County had the most delegates, nine. The delegation included *Peter J. Pefley*(D),[36] a harness-maker, who was mayor of Boise. Pefley was born June 6, 1830, in Roanoke County, Virginia. He learned saddlery and the harness trade in Ohio and lived in Oregon and California in the 1850s. He came to Idaho in 1864 and operated a stage station on the Idaho City Road before moving to Boise to open a shop in 1869. Pefley was one of only two delegates to question the strong anti-Mormon sentiment of the convention. He believed in a "wall of separation" between church and state and proposed striking any reference to God in the Preamble and prohibiting prayers in the legislative chambers. He protested the constitution by refusing to sign it, prompting another delegate to conclude he had had a falling out with his God.[37]

John Lemp (R)[38] was born in Germany in April 1838, and migrated to the United States in 1852. He first lived in Louisville, Kentucky, then at Pike's Peak in Colorado, finally arriving in Boise in 1863. He became one of Idaho's wealthiest citizens, building a brewery and pursuing real estate, irrigation development, banking and transportation interests. He built the Capital Hotel and the Schainwald block. He served many years on the Boise City Council and one term as Boise's mayor. At the time of the convention he was constructing the Lemp Building, and as a result attended irregularly. When he was there, he did not speak and so had little influence. Another delegate reported Lemp's role in the debate on prohibition, "Idaho's boss brewer, . . . becoming lost in the various motions . . . voted in favor of prohibition as often as he did against it."[39]

Isaac N. Coston (D)[40] was born in New York, September 22, 1832. He was admitted to the New York bar before moving to Walla Walla in 1862 and to the upper end of the Boise Valley in 1863. He mined for a short period, practiced law, and became a successful farmer. He served several terms in the territorial council during the 1870s. *John S. Gray* (R)[41] was a Boise lawyer who authored the first practise act in the territory. He was admitted to the bar at the first district court held in Idaho, and became one of the best known territorial lawyers. He was frequently involved in important litigation and served in the territorial legislature. He was born in Watertown, New York, moved to California in 1857, northern Idaho in 1862, and the Boise Basin in 1863. It was said that Gray "stood four square to every wind that blew and never spoke unless he has something to say." Gray, like all other Ada County delegates except Pefley, apparently had little to say at the convention for they have few recorded remarks in the proceedings.

Edgar Wilson (R)[42] was also a Boise lawyer but arrived in the territory in 1884. Wilson was twenty-eight years old and perhaps the youngest delegate at the convention. He later served two terms in Congress. Wilson spoke infrequently at the convention, but was one of the strongest advocates of an irrigation preference for water. Wilson had a tragic end. In 1913 he killed a deputy sheriff in a scuffle and was committed under the state's inebriate law. He died shortly afterwards.

William C. Maxey (R)[43] was a Caldwell physician. He was born in Wayne County, Illinois, in 1844, served during the Civil War, and moved to Caldwell in 1887. *A. B. Moss* (R)[44] arrived in the Payette Valley in 1881 with a contract to provide two hundred fifty thousand railroad ties to the Oregon Shortline Railroad. He stayed on to found the city of Payette, and became as well a banker and real estate promoter. *Charles A. Clark* (D)[45] was born in New York and had engaged in newspaper work and served in the Civil War before coming to Boise in 1885 as a representative of Bradstreet's. He later helped establish the Idaho Building and Loan Association.

Frank Steunenberg (D)[46] published the *Caldwell Tribune* with his brother. He was born in Keokuk, Iowa, in 1861, and after working as an apprentice printer in Knoxville and Des Moines, moved to Caldwell in 1887. He later became Idaho's first voting congressman and served as governor from 1897 to 1901 during Idaho's labor strife in the northern mines. He called on the U.S. Army to put down the strikes and as a result was assassinated at the gate of his home by Harry Orchard in 1905. Steunenberg never spoke at the convention, but he did report the convention's progress in a series called "The Ship of State," which appeared weekly in his *Caldwell Tribune*.

Shoshone County had the second largest, and most powerful delegation at the convention. It was led by *William H. Clagett* (R),[47] who was four-fold father to the Idaho Constitution. Just as George Washington presided over the 1787 convention that drafted the United States Constitution, William Clagett presided over Idaho's convention. Just as James Madison was the primary intellectual force behind the constitutional theories adopted in Philadelphia, William Clagett was the architect of Idaho's Constitution. Just as Edmund J. Randolph was the great orator who proposed Madison's radical ideas in the debates two hundred years ago, it was William H. Clagett who was the greatest orator and advocate during the Idaho's debates one hundred years ago. Finally, just as Luther Martin advocated states' rights at the Philadelphia convention, Clagett championed Idaho's own sovereignty.

Clagett was born in Prince George County, Maryland, in 1838, then moved with his family to Iowa where he was admitted to the bar in 1858. He moved to Nevada in 1861 and began a long career as a mining and criminal lawyer, miner, and politician. After leaving Nevada he lived in Montana, Colorado, the Black Hills and Portland, Oregon. He was one of the first to arrive in northern Idaho when gold was discovered in the Coeur d'Alenes in 1883–1884. He became known as the "Silver-Tongued Orator of the West" and had acquired enough knowledge and experience along the way to make him the most accomplished of all the delegates.

Weldon B. Heyburn (R)[48] was a conservative mining lawyer. Heyburn was born into a Pennsylvania Quaker family in 1852. He was admitted to the bar in 1876, and moved to Shoshone County in 1883–84. He and Clagett often opposed each other, both in the courtroom and on the convention floor. Heyburn represented large mining interests, including the Bunker Hill and Sullivan Mining and Smeltering Company and the Silver Tip Consolidated Mining and Smelting Company, and located the Polaris mine in 1884 with a partner. He served these clients at the convention by getting a guarantee of first priority to water for the miners in the mining districts. He also chaired the important judiciary committee and served on the elections and suffrage committee and two others. Heyburn later served as U.S. Senator from Idaho. *W. W. Woods* (R)[49], Heyburn's law partner, was also a delegate. He had served in the Civil War and lived in Salt Lake City before coming to Shoshone County in 1884.

Alexander Mayhew (D)[50] was "a fat, pudgy bachelor, scraggly of beard, careless of dress," and he was also the Democratic workhorse in Shoshone County. He was born in Philadelphia and graduated from the University of Pennsylvania before heading west to Kansas, Colorado, and Montana. He joined the rush to the Coeur d'Alenes in 1884. He practiced law, and because he "understood miners even more than the law," he enjoyed success as a mining claims speculator. At the convention he served on the judiciary and election and suffrage committees, but more importantly he chaired the public and private corporations committee which had general jurisdiction over railroads. Mayhew had a distinct dislike for railroads, perhaps because he had once been put off by the Union Pacific and forced to walk ten miles. He campaigned for the legislature in 1888 without mentioning the railroad, the most significant activity in the county at the time. The article his committee reported to the convention reflected his feelings.

G. W. King (D)[51] was the oldest delegate. He had been trained as a lawyer, but turned to prospecting and mining when his hearing failed. King was an advocate of mining interests at the convention, but his mining interests were different than those of Heyburn, and the two often disagreed about what was in the best interest of mining. *S. S. Glidden* (R)[52] from Burke was also involved in mining and other commercial activities. *A. D. Bevan* (D)[53] was a Wardner physician and *W. W. Hammel* (R)[54] was a local politician who had served as an undersheriff, a deputy U.S. marshal, U.S. commissioner of lands and superintendent of schools. He won distinction during the Civil War by taking the Bible on which Jefferson Davis had taken his oath in a raid on Montgomery.

Bingham County sent seven delegates, the most important being *John T. Morgan* (R).[55] Morgan was, along with James Beatty, the most distinguished jurist to attend the convention. He served six years as chief justice of the territorial supreme court, and eight years as a justice of the state supreme court. Morgan was born in Erie County, New York, and earned a bachelor of law degree in 1856. He practiced law, then served with an Illinois volunteer company during the Civil War before being appointed chief justice of the supreme court of Idaho Territory. As part of his duties on the supreme court, Morgan also served as the district judge for the southeastern region. Morgan established his home in Oxford, and over the years developed strong anti-Mormon sentiments. He was eventually removed from the bench, perhaps because of clashes with Mormons. Not surprisingly, he was a strong advocate of disfranchising Mormons at the convention, where he was also a strong supporter of private takings and other provisions favoring irrigated agriculture.

The Bingham delegation also included *Frank W. Beane* and *H. O. Harkness* (R),[56] a rancher and merchant from McCammon, famous for his wealth and his interest in promoting the town. *Robert Anderson* (D)[57] was a merchant and banker from Eagle Rock, now Idaho Falls. After the convention he moved to Missouri, one of the few delegates to move east after statehood. *William H. Savidge* (R)[58], from Pocatello, was a graduate of the Michigan Law School and an attorney for the Union Pacific. *Samuel F. Taylor* (A.M.-D)[59] was from Kentucky and fought in the Confederate army before coming to Eagle Rock in 1870. He was a stockraiser and was elected sheriff of Oneida and Bingham counties. *H. B. Kinport* (D)[60] was a rancher on the Portneuf River who had served in the 1888 territorial legislature.

Alturas County sent six delegates. Elmore and Logan counties had been created out of Alturas by the last territorial legislature. Had this division not occurred, Alturas County would have had the largest delegation with twelve, suggesting its importance in territorial politics during the 1880s. Even though Alturas County had been diminished, its delegation was still distinguished. The most influential member was *James H. Beatty* (R).[61] Beatty was born in 1836 in Lancaster, Ohio, and served in an Iowa regiment during the Civil War. After the war he practiced law in Missouri before moving to Salt Lake City in 1872, and the Wood River Valley in the rush of 1882. Even though he was called "Aunt Nancy" by his detractors because he was proper, and did not drink, Beatty was a central member of the "Hailey Ring," which battled with the "Boise Ring" for control of territorial offices. After the convention Beatty was appointed to the territorial supreme court, and then accepted appointment as Idaho's first federal district judge where he served for seventeen years. At the convention he chaired the elections and suffrage committee, which had the task of making certain Mormons were disfranchised. He opposed irrigated agriculture by strongly supporting a pure priority water principle, and took part in other important debates.

Lycurgus Vineyard (D)[62] also took an active part in the convention, but unlike Beatty he had little influence or effect. Vineyard was born in Missouri, attended William Jewell College, fought for the South in the war, then moved to Oregon, California and finally the Wood River Valley in 1885. He was a Jeffersonian Democrat, and came from a family of educators, serving as superintendent of schools in Oregon's early history. After the convention, he moved on to Boise and finally to Grangeville. Vineyard did not have significant committee appointments but participated in the debates. He joined with other Democrats in the argument that the legislature should not have broad authority to disfranchise Mormons, and argued riparian water rights should be written into the constitution.

A.J. Pinkham (R)[63] was born in Canada, and came to Ketchum in 1881 to practice law and represent absentee mine owners in their local dealings. He made his most important contribution to the convention by taking charge of its accounting, and after the convention served as secretary of state. *Orlando B. Batten* (D)[64] was also a mining lawyer, admitted to the bar in 1886, and a "high tariff" democrat in 1888. *J. W. Ballentine* (R)[65] was born in Pennsylvania, fought for the Union, worked as an oil refiner, and served in the Pennsylvania legislature. This was all before coming to Idaho to become a Muldoon smelter superintendent, then a rancher, then a Bellevue merchant, and finally a member of the Idaho legislature. *Patrick McMahon* (D)[66] came to Ketchum with the railroad, became a dry goods merchant, served as a delegate to the convention, and then left to become part of the Thunder Mountain gold rush.

Like Alturas County, Latah County sent six delegates, several of whom played important roles. Latah has the distinction of being the only county in the nation created by an Act of Congress, an extraordinary measure taken to separate itself from Nez Perce County. The most prominent member of the Latah delegation was *William J. McConnell* (R),[67] an Idaho pioneer and, along with James Shoup, the most significant nonlawyer in the convention debates. He was born in Oakland County, Michigan, in 1839. He went to California in 1860 and Oregon in 1862, before moving to Placerville, Idaho, in 1863. McConnell dug one of the first irrigation ditches in Idaho on the Payette and was the leader of the Payette vigilantes in the 1860s. He then returned to Oregon for many years before moving back to Idaho (Moscow) in 1886. McConnell was known as "Poker Bill" for his love of the game, and by doing business with the same enthusiasm he was able to earn and lose several fortunes. He was called the "merchant prince" of Moscow. At the convention, McConnell was important to both the education and water articles passed, and was a constant critic of the legal profession. After the convention he served as governor.

Willis Sweet (R)[68] was a young Moscow lawyer who also played an important part at the convention. He suffered misfortune while at the convention when his home in Moscow was "consumed by fire." (p. 1693). In the 1888 legislature, Sweet and *J. W. Brigham* (R),[69] a Genessee farmer and also a convention delegate, had sponsored the legislation that established the university at Moscow. Sweet was a close ally of Fred T. Dubois, the territorial delegate to Congress and the most powerful Republican in the territory. Not surprisingly, Sweet chaired the federal relations committee at the convention. Sweet was an eloquent speaker and was often chosen to speak for the Republican caucus on the floor.

H. B. Blake (D)[70] was Moscow's first physician and Latah County's first county commissioner. He was a regent of the university, and responsible for locating it on a hill at the edge of town rather than in the business district. *W. D. Robbins* (R) managed a Moscow implement company, and *A. S. Chaney* (D) was Latah's sixth delegate.

These were the delegations from the five largest counties in the territory. They selected thirty-six delegates, exactly one-half of the total. Fifteen of these thirty-six were the most accomplished lawyers in the Idaho bar. The smaller counties, however, also sent many important and influential delegates.

Custer County sent four delegates, including *James M. Shoup* (R),[71] brother of George Shoup who had been the second governor to call for the constitutional convention. Shoup and William McConnell debated actively, and prevented the convention from becoming strictly a lawyers' debate. Shoup chaired the important Declaration of Rights Committee. Shoup was joined by *Abel John Pierce* (D),[72] *Andrew Jackson Crook* (R),[73] and *O. J. Salisbury* (R).[74] Neither Crook nor Salisbury signed the constitution.

Boise County sent three delegates, led by *George Ainslie* (D).[75] Ainslie was a pioneer miner and lawyer from Missouri and chairman of the Democratic party at the time of the convention. He came to Idaho in 1862, was sworn as a member of the Idaho bar at the first district court session held in the territory, and was immediately elected to the territorial council. During the next thirty years he edited the *Idaho World*, practiced law, and served as a district attorney. He also served two terms as the territorial representative to Congress and was defeated for reelection in 1882, the first election marked by the anti-Mormon movement. Ainslie was an important spokesman for the Democratic caucus at the convention, even though he was more highly regarded for his writing than speaking. He was chosen to author the address encouraging adoption sent by the convention with the constitution.

Boise County was also represented by *Fred Campbell* (R),[76] a miner and Indian fighter who had moved to the Boise Basin in 1862, and *J. H. Meyer* (D),[77] a merchant and assayer at the time of the convention, but later a probate judge, district attorney and justice of the peace.

Elmore County's three delegates included *Homer Stull* (D),[78] a Hailey lawyer who became a resident of Glenns Ferry in Elmore County after the division of Alturas in 1888. He was appointed chair of the important manufacturing, agriculture and irrigation committee, which had jurisdiction over the water law article but left the convention early because of illness. He was replaced as chairman by another Elmore County delegate, *Frank Cavanah* (D),[79] a well-known mining engineer who was one of the first to recognize the significant mineral potential of the Wood River Valley. Cavanah fought in the Confederate army before coming to Idaho to lay out the city of Hailey. Oddly, Cavanah was also absent when the water article was debated at the convention. Also from Elmore County was *A. M. Sinnott* (Labor-R),[80] who had come to Idaho as a railroad worker, eventually becoming a lawyer, and serving as district attorney and superintendent of schools. He played an important role in the labor article, and moved unsuccessfully to grant suffrage to women in the constitution.

Idaho County selected three delegates but only *Aaron F. Parker* (D) attended.[81] Parker was born in England in 1856 and eventually became known as the "Democratic war horse from Idaho County."[82] As publisher of the *Idaho County Free Press* in Grangeville, his editorial policy was always controversial. His was one of the few papers to question ratification of the constitution. At the convention he fiercely defended private property, the rights of small counties, and the common law tradition. He also took the occasion to campaign for one of his most important projects, completion of the first north-south wagon road. He was also one of only two delegates to directly challenge the anti-Mormon sentiment of the convention.

Kootenai County elected three delegates, each with mining interests. *Judge Albert Hagan* (D)[83] arrived late at the convention but immediately became embroiled in debates defending traditional views of private property and the right to a jury trial. When the convention voted for reform, Hagan became disgusted and left. *Judge Henry Melder* (R)[84] opened his law office in the county in 1881 and served as probate judge during the 1880s. He was well-known locally, but he did little at the convention. *W. A. Hendryx* (R), a physician, did not go to the convention and was sharply criticized for his neglect.

Lemhi County sent three delegates. *N. I. Andrews* (R)[85] was a merchant and *John Hogan* (D)[86] an auditor-recorder, both from Salmon City. *Thomas Pyeatt* (R)[87] was a cattleman prominent in the upper Lemhi Valley.

Logan County sent three delegates, including *Henry Armstrong* (Labor),[88] who mined and farmed in the Broadford area and disappeared from Idaho soon after the convention. As one of two Labor delegates he was instrumental in drafting the labor article. Logan County also sent *W. C. B. Allen* (R),[89] a newspaperman who made his contribution to the convention behind the scenes as chairman of the printing committee. He had to satisfy the constant demand for immediate copies of reports and articles by enlisting the aid of any printer who would extend credit to the future state. *J.S. Whitton* (R)[90] was a Bellevue merchant with strong anti-labor sentiments.

Nez Perce County also sent three delegates, all of them lawyers. The delegation was led by *James Wesley Reid* (D),[91] a Lewiston lawyer, who was elected vice president of the convention. Reid had only recently arrived in the territory but came with experience in Congress and great oratorical skills. He, along with Ainslie, was a chief spokesman for the Democrats at the convention. He engaged constantly in arguments over convention procedure, vehemently argued in favor of Bible reading in the public schools, and strongly defended common-law principles of private property and the right to a unanimous jury verdict. Reid was accompanied by *J. W. Poe* (D),[92] a lifelong Democrat who was a prominent member of the Lewiston bar and had mining interests, and *J. M. Howe* (R),[93] one of Lewiston's earliest attorneys.

Owyhee County sent three delegates, including *J. I. Crutcher* (D),[94] a miner who came to Elk City in 1862 and later served as sheriff of Boise County and as United States marshall. With him were *Charles M. Hays* (R),[95] an attorney and local politician who came to Idaho in 1860, and *Samuel J. Pritchard* (R),[96] who was county assessor at the time.

Washington County also sent three delegates. *Solomon Hasbrouck* (R)[97] arrived in Idaho in 1861 before the territory was created. He was a miner, lawyer and merchant, one of the first Owyhee County commissioners, and for many years clerk of the state supreme court. Hasbrouck played another important role in Idaho's history in the winter of 1864–65 when he accompanied Governor Caleb Lyon on the duck-hunting trip that was actually a ruse to disguise the move of the territorial capital from Lewiston to Boise. *E. S. Jewell* (D)[98] was a merchant who served in the territorial and first state legislatures, and *Frank Harris* (D)[99] a lawyer who later served as district attorney and probate judge.

Oneida County sent only two delegates, but one of them was very important to the Idaho Constitution. *Drew D. Standrod* (D)[100] from Malad City had prosecuted Mormons while serving as prosecuting attorney in Oneida County. He became the father of Idaho water law at the convention by strongly advocating the private takings and agricultural priority sections thought necessary by those delegates promoting irrigated agriculture. After the convention he served for ten years as a district judge and then engaged in banking activities. *John Lewis* (A.M.-R),[101] who identified himself as a "Josephite Mormon," was from Malad City and spoke against the Mormons in his only speech at the convention.

Cassia County was represented by *H. S. Hampton* (R), who after the convention became a lawyer, and *J. W. Lamoreaux* (D), publisher of the *Cassia County Times*.[102]

Bear Lake County was permitted one delegate to the convention. Since Mormons had been disfranchised in the 1888 general election, few votes were cast in the county. *J. L. Underwood* (R)[103] was a freighter, who lived in Paris and then followed the railroad to Soda Springs and Montpelier.

3. *Organizing the Convention*

JULY 4. 1889, was the day chosen to convene the Idaho Constitutional Convention. The delegates gathered in the Representatives Hall of the territorial capitol which had been arrayed with "evergreens, tastefully arranged, and an abundance of the national colors."[104] They immediately began to organize by electing temporary officers: John T. Morgan as president, J. W. Reid as Secretary and Drew W. Standrod as assistant secretary. (pp. 1–3)

A credentials committee was appointed to resolve several election contests. The local selection process in Ada and Alturas counties had produced doubt about who was entitled to be admitted into the convention. William H. Clagett proposed a principle and procedure to resolve these contests. Disputes between Republicans should be settled by the Republicans, disputes between Democrats should be settled by Democrats, and disputes between Republicans and Democrats should be decided by the credentials committee.

These first organizational decisions suggest the first signs of two patterns that emerged during the convention proceedings. One was the influence of Clagett on the convention, and ultimately the constitution. The second is the nature of the cooperation between the Republican and Democratic parties. Clagett's motion could be realistically read to say that both parties wanted statehood and so would cooperate whenever possible, but that on contested points the Republicans would win because they had the majority of delegates. As a result of this general approach many important convention and constitutional decisions were made in party caucuses, away from public view and outside the historical record left by the convention.

The delegates convened on the second day to decide two important matters. The first was the report of the committee on credentials and the second the election of permanent officers. The credentials report was objected to because it did not determine the number of Republican and Democrat delegates from Ada County, so the convention decided they should be 5 and 4, respectively (pp. 7–16). The report also recommended that E. A. Stevenson be admitted as a delegate-at-large. The convention declined to seat additional delegates, but did extend honorary membership and freedom of the floor to Stevenson, as well as Governor Shoup and the justices of the territorial supreme court (p. 17). Later honorary membership was also extended to Idaho's congressional delegate, Fred T. Dubois, the attorney general, Richard Z. Johnson, and to each of the executive officers of the territory (p. 34). None of these honorary delegates participated in the convention debates.

The convention then elected permanent officers, beginning with the election of William H. Clagett as president. Many praised this choice, including the *Salt Lake Tribune*, which said Idaho had selected well, and then went on:

> Shrewd and fair and quick is Judge Claggett, and moreover, he has a fashion of stating a proposition that leaves no doubt of his meaning. When it comes to talking, he is the best between the mountains, a natural orator, that, since boyhood, has given him full command of enraptured audiences. Then, he has been in the desert for a year or two more than a quarter of century, and he knows not only the habits and wants of the people, but also of this peculiar region in which we dwell. Then he is a finished lawyer, and will take in the legal bearings of a proposition at a glance. Finally, he has courage sufficient for all emergencies. He has every attribute necessary to make him one of the best of presiding officers, not only for Idaho, but for any country. Had he gone beyond the Sierras instead of stopping on this side, his name would have been as much of a household word all over the Union as it now is in Nevada and Idaho.[105]

James W. Reid was elected vice president, and the remaining offices filled in order. These votes were recorded as amiable acclamation (pp. 19–24). However, the bitterness and rancor actually caused by them later surfaced during the debate on the Mormon question. During the intensity of the hottest debate on the convention floor, as the Republicans were forcing their anti-Mormon suffrage provisions into the constitution, Reid argued the Democratic case. He charged that the entire convention was partisan, and pointed to the election of officers as evidence. Reid claimed that as caucuses were first beginning to meet at the convention the Democrats offered a plan for selecting officers. They would concede the Republicans were entitled to the presidency, but claimed the right to elect the secretary and were willing to alternate selections after that (pp. 946–52, 985–87).

According to Clagett (pp. 977–85) and Willis Sweet (pp. 1009–11), the Republicans initially endorsed the principle of alternating, but maintained that the vice president was the second selection made. The Democrats refused the position because it had no power or prestige, and argued they should be entitled to select the secretary. Republicans were apparently willing to concede the secretary's post, but in return demanded all the remaining positions, a deal the Democrats rejected. Neither version squares exactly with the record, but the Republicans did take most of the positions. After Reid was elected vice president, Republicans elected Howard French, sergeant-at-arms, R. T. Morgan, first assistant secretary, and Rev. T. M. Smith chaplain. P. D. Canavan, a Democratic, won the doorkeeper post by an 18–16 vote. A Republican, W. R. Cartwright, was elected assistant doorkeeper, and finally two Republican and two Democratic pages were elected. Later, Republican Miss Carrie Sweet was elected second assistant secretary. In all, nine Republican officers were elected. Four Democrats won election to the least important offices (pp. 18–30).

Frank Steunenberg, a Democrat, reported these elections to his Caldwell readers:

> As the call provided for a "non-partisan" convention, the republican majority magnanimously created and conceded to the democrats an office (vice president) such an office as has never before been heard of in a body of this character, and then calmly filled the remaining offices, nine in all, from secretary to page, with republicans. Great is the republican party; but greater still is the sublimity of their nonpartisanship.[106]

The convention had difficulty getting a quorum when it convened for the third day on Saturday, July 6. Since there were 72 delegates, 37 were necessary for a quorum and only 19 were present (p. 24). Nevertheless, the convention continued to organize. Seating on the floor was determined. Some argued delegates should stay where they were, while others suggested organizing by counties. Reflecting their egalitarian sentiments, the delegates decided the final selection was to be made in a drawing by a blindfolded page (pp. 332–33, 337). Stenographers were hired (pp. 43–44), and a rules committee appointed (pp. 30–31). The committee on committees recommended 25 standing committees, and stated their charges (pp. 37–42). President Clagett announced he had determined the number of seats the Democrats were entitled to on these committees. He asked the Democratic caucus to decide who the Democratic committeemen were to be (pp. 44–45). (See Appendix D for a roster of committee appointments.)

The fourth convention session was held on Monday, July 8. *Cushing's Manual* was adopted to govern proceedings (pp. 46–55). The membership of the judiciary committee was increased from nine to fifteen, because it was thought the committee would "have more labor to perform than any other" (p. 58). The membership of the convention's standing committees was announced (pp. 64–70). (See Appendix D). The committees considered the most important and having the highest priorities were executive, legislative, judiciary, preamble and bill of rights, education, election and suffrage, and public and private corporations (pp. 70–76).

Just as the Democrats later complained about the officers elected, they were later bitter about the committee appointments at the convention. Reid complained that the Democrats chaired only three of the important committees: the executive, salaries and corporations. He was also unhappy about the most important committee of the convention, apportionment, where the Democrats held seven of eighteen seats (pp. 949, 986). Clagett rose to defend his appointments. Apparently the two men disagreed about the list of "important" committees, for Clagett claimed to have given the Democrats nine committee chairs. He also said Democrats refused four or five other unimportant committees he had offered (p. 980).

Despite this rancorous exchange, Reid and Clagett apparently parted amicably. At the close of the convention, Reid moved to thank Clagett for "his uniform courtesy, fidelity and impartiality in discharging his duties as president of the convention" (p. 2038).

The fifth session on July 9 was the shortest of the convention. J. W. Ballentine became impatient with the pace and moved to require all the standing committees to report at a given time. He thought there was ample precedent from other states for the committees and did not plan to stay at the convention longer than a week. Other delegates were more patient, and instructed the committees to report their progress as soon as practicable (pp. 84–87).

Frank Steunenberg reported to his readers the Ballentine motion had been voted down by a large majority, but thought it was a move in the right direction. Then he observed:

> A large majority of the members are lawyers, and as quibbling and priddling is a part of their training, if not of their nature, the chances of an extended session are favorable.[107]

There was a brief debate during this session about the authority of the president of the convention to administer oaths to delegates. John Morgan worried that Congress was very particular in these matters, and would prefer a Supreme Court justice to administer oaths. J. W. Poe agreed, arguing that as in business, the conservative was the wise course in creating constitutions. James B. Beatty, Orlando B. Batten and Alexander E. Mayhew were more adventurous, and they convinced the convention that the President had the necessary "inherent" power (pp. 78–82). This conclusion was predictable of a group of delegates who were themselves relying upon the inherent right of the people to write their own constitution, bolstered by the calls of Governors Stevenson and Shoup.

The delegates convened the sixth session on Wednesday, July 10, with an address calling for prohibition and women's suffrage by Mrs. Henrietta Skelton, president of the Women's Christian Temperance Union of Idaho (pp. 88–91). No session was held on Thursday to permit committee work, and the seventh session just took roll on Friday. During the eighth session on Saturday, July 13, the committee reports began coming in (p. 100). The preamble and bill of rights committee submitted a complete report which was to become the first article considered on the convention floor. The militia, legislative and public and private corporations committees also reported.

With the submission of these committee reports, the convention was finally organized and ready to begin deliberations. It had taken ten days, and eight sessions, for the delegates to choose officers, organize into committees, and begin submitting the reports. Some delegates, because of their inexperience, had come to Boise thinking the whole convention would be over within a week, but in reality, a great deal had been accomplished since the first session. The convention was large. While no more that sixty or sixty-five delegates were present at one time, this body was still two and one-half times larger than the lower house of the territorial legislature. Further, many of the delegates were strangers to each other, and were meeting to decide questions of fundamental law which most were considering for the first time in their lives.

By coincidence, the first committee reports came in on Saturday night, making Sunday, July 14, a dividing line between the organizational and deliberative meetings of the convention. But even more importantly, Sunday gave the delegates time to gather their thoughts in preparation for Monday morning and Article I.

Notes

1. A number of general history books have been written about Idaho, all containing some discussion of political history. They include: Beal, Merrill D. and Wells, Merle W. *History of Idaho*. 3 vols. New York: Lewis Historical Publishing Company, 1959; French, Hiram T. *History of Idaho*. 3 vols. New York: Lewis Publishing Company, 1914; Hawley, James H. *History of Idaho: The Gem of the Mountains*. 5 vols. Chicago: S. J. Clarke, 1920; McConnell, W. J. *Early History of Idaho*. Caldwell: Caxton Printers, 1913; Talkington, H. L. *Political History, State Constitution and School Laws of Idaho*. Lewiston: Lewiston Morning Tribune, 1911; Elliott, H. N., ed. *History of Idaho Territory*. San Francisco: W. W. Elliot & Co., 1884; Bancroft, Hubert H. *History of Washington, Idaho, and Montana, 1845–1889*. San Francisco: The History Company, 1890; Hailey, John. *The History of Idaho*. Boise: Press of Syms-York Co., 1910; Donaldson, Thomas. *Idaho of Yesterday*, Caldwell: Caxton Printers, Ltd., 1941.; Brosnan, Cornelius J. *History of the State of Idaho*. New York: Charles Scribner's Sons, numerous editions; Peterson, F. Ross. *Idaho: A Bicentennial History*. New York: Norton, 1976; and Barber, Floyd R. and Martin, Dan W. *Idaho in the Pacific Northwest*. Caldwell: Caxton Printers, Ltd., 1956.

Idaho has also received extensive treatment in several regional histories, including: Schwantes, Carlos A. *The Pacific Northwest An Interpretive History*, Lincoln: University of Nebraska Press, 1985; Johansen, Dorothy O. *Empire of the Columbia*. 2d. ed. New York: Harper & Row, 1967; Winther, Oscar O. *The Great Northwest: A History*. New York: Knopf, 1950; Pomeroy, Earl. *The Pacific Slope*. New York: Knopf, 1965; and Meinig, D. W. *The Great Columbia Plain: A Historical Geography, 1805–1910*. Seattle: University of Washington Press, 1968.

2. Wells, Merle W. "The Creation of the Territory of Idaho." *Pacific Northwest Quarterly* 40(April 1940); Hulett, Mary Lorrain. "History of the Movement for a Territorial Organization for Idaho with Special Reference to the Evolution of Idaho's Present Boundary Lines." Master's thesis, University of Idaho, 1951; "The Idaho Centennial: How Idaho was created in 1863." *Idaho Yesterdays* 7(Spring 1963):44–58.

3. Chamberlain, Lawrence H. "Idaho: State of Sectional Schisms." In Donnelly, Thomas C., ed. *Rocky Mountain Politics*. Albuquerque: University of New Mexico Press, 1940, pp. 150–88; Thomas, Benjamin E. "Political Geography of Idaho." Ph.D. diss., Harvard University, 1947; Thomas, E. Benjamin, "Boundaries and Internal Problems of Idaho." *Geographical Review* 39(1949):99–109; Burtenshaw, Claude J. "The State: Cooperation or Conquest: A Case Study of the State of Idaho." Ph.D. diss., University of Utah, 1955; Martin, Boyd A. "Idaho: The Sectional State." in Jones, Frank H., ed. *Politics in the American West*. Salt Lake City: University of Utah Press, 1969; and Wells, Merle. "Idaho: A study in Statehood and Sectionalism, 1863–1890." Master's thesis, University of California, Berkeley, 1947.

4. Gibbs, Grenville H. "Idaho Becomes a State: A Study of Territorial Political Developments, 1880–1890." Ph.D. diss., University of Utah, 1952; *Idem*. "The Idaho State Constitution." master's thesis, University of Idaho, 1949; and, Graff, Leo W. Jr. "The Idaho Statehood Movement, 1888–1890." Master's thesis, University of Idaho, 1960.

5. Walker, Deward. *Indians of Idaho*. Moscow, Idaho: University of Idaho Press, 1978.

6. Senate. "Select Committee Report on Senate Bill No. 206." 25th Cong., 2d sess.: 1–5; Hulett, "Territorial Organization for Idaho." In Talkington, *Political History of Idaho*, p. 5.

7. Select Committee Report, 5–23.

8. Moulton. *The Journals of the Lewis and Clark Expedition*. 5 vols., Lincoln: University of Nebraska Press, 1988, 5:3.

9. See the *Idaho Bluebook*, 9th ed.(Boise: Idaho Secretary of State, 1988):14–19, for a chronology of important events in the pre-statehood era.

10. McConnell, *Early History*, pp. 36–55.

11. 8 Stat. 248. The treaty was indefinitely extended in 1827, 8 Stat. 360, with the provision that either country could terminate the arrangement with 12 month's notice.

12. 8 Stat. 252.

13. 8 Stat. 302.

14. 9 Stat. 869.

15. 9 Stat. 323.

16. 10 Stat. 172.

17. 11 Stat. 383.

18. McConnell, *Early History*, pp. 161–80.

19. 12 Stat. 808.

20. Hulett, "Idaho's Present Boundary Lines;" McConnell, *Early History*, pp. 161–80; Wells, *Creation of Idaho*.

21. *Boise Daily Statesman*, 16 Jy. 1889. See also McConnell, *Early History*, pp. 301–24.

22. Ellis, Earl H. *That Word "Idaho."* Denver: The University of Denver Press, 1951.

23. *New York Daily Tribune*, 11 Dec. 1875.

24. For general discussions of Idaho politics during the territorial period see Alexander, Thomas G. "Mason Brayman and the Boise Ring." *Idaho Yesterdays* 14(Fall 1970):10–13; Blase, Fred Woodward. "Political History of Idaho Territory, 1863–1890." Master's thesis, University of California, 1925; Limbaugh, Ronald Hadley. "The Idaho Spoilsman: Federal Administration and Idaho Territorial Politics, 1863–1890." Ph.D. diss., University of Idaho, 1966; *Idem.* "Some Idaho Carpetbaggers and the Moulton War." *Idaho Yesterdays* 14(Fall, 1970):13–20; Houston, Maude Cosho. "Idaho Territory: Its Origins, Its Governors, and Its Problems." Master's thesis, University of Idaho, 1951; Pomeroy, Earl S. "Running a Territory: They Had Their Troubles." *Idaho Yesterdays* 14(Fall, 1970):10–13; "Territorial Governors of Idaho." *Idaho Yesterdays*, 7(Spring, 1963):14–23.

25. 13 Stat. 85.

26. 15 Stat. 178.

27. Bird, Annie L. "Footnotes on the Capital Dispute in Idaho." *Pacific Northwest Quarterly* 36(October, 1945):341–46. Chaffee, Eugene B. "The Political Clash between North and South Idaho over the Capital." *Pacific Northwest Quarterly* 29(1938):255–67.

28. Kingston, C. S. "The North Idaho Annexation Issue." *Washington Historical Quarterly* 21(1930):133–37, 204–17, 281–93; Wells, Merle W. "The Admission of the State of Idaho." *Secretary of State Twenty-Seventh Biennial Report* 1944:28–77; idem. "Politics in the Panhandle." *Pacific Northwest Quarterly* 46(July, 1955):79–89.

29. Gibbs, *Idaho Becomes a State*; Graff, *Idaho Statehood Movement*.

30. Hart, I. W., ed. *Proceedings and Debates of the Constitutional Convention of Idaho 1889*. 2 vols. Caldwell: Caxton Printers, Ltd., 1912. These volumes are paginated consecutively, and all page references in the text of this chapter are to them.

31. Graff, *Idaho Statehood Movement*, pp. 21–28.

32. Bakken, Gordon. *Rocky Mountain Constitution Making, 1850–1912*. Westport, Greenwood Press,1987, pp. 5–6.

33. Wells, Merle W. "The Idaho Admission Movement 1888–1890." *Oregon Historical Quarterly* 56(March, 1955):36.

34. Frank Steunenberg, a delegate at the convention, reported the following about the delegates in his *Caldwell Tribune*, 13 Jy. 1889, p. 3, col. 2: "The lawyers in the convention are in the ascendency in the point of number, there being twenty-five, or over one-third. Those engaged in mercantile pursuits come next with nine members. The mining industry has seven representatives; farmers and stock raisers, six; editors, five; doctors, three; railroaders, two; brewers, one; butchers, one; laborers, one, and twelve not classified."

35. Twenty-five of the delegates to Idaho's constitutional convention were admitted to practice before the Idaho Supreme Court: George Ainslie (1866), Solomon Hasbrouck (1871), John S. Gray (1871), Chas. M. Hays (1873), James Beatty (1884), Homer Stull (1884), Lycurgus Vineyard (1884), Edgar Wilson (1885), Orlando Batten (1886), William Clagett (1887), Weldon Heyburn (1887), Alexander Mayhew (1887), W. W. Woods (1887), Albert Hagan (1888), A. J. Pinkham (1888), W. H. Savidge (1888), Willis Sweet (1889), J. M. Howe (1891), J. W. Poe (1891), James Reid (1891), H. S. Hampton (1892), Drew Standrod (1895), John T. Morgan (1897), Robert Anderson (1899) and Frank Harris (1901). There were a total of one hundred forty-one attorneys admitted during the territorial period. Seventeen of these, or twelve percent, attended the convention. *Role of Attorneys Admitted to Practice in Supreme Court*, 18 Idaho 1911 xxxiii–xli. A number of other delegates were also trained or practised as lawyers: I. N. Coston, G. W. King, J. H. Meyer, A. M. Sinnot, and Henry Melder.

36. Wells, "Admission," p. 71; Gibbs, Grenville H. "The Idaho State Constitution: Its Origins, Framers, and Development." Master's thesis, University of Idaho, 1948, p. 32.

37. William J. McConnell, *Early History of Idaho*. Caldwell: Caxton Printers, Ltd., 1913, p. 375.

38. Davis, Rees. H. "The Land Grabber." *Caldwell Tribune* 19 My. 1894, p. 2. col. 2; Defenbach, Byron. *Idaho — The Place and its People*. 3 vols. Chicago & New York: The American Historical Society, Inc., 1933, pp. 441, 493; Hawley, *History of Idaho*, vol. 2, p 18; *Idaho Daily Statesman* 19 Jy. 1912 p. 1; *Idaho Daily Statesman*, 9 Feb. 1984, p. 5, col. 1–3; *Statesman*, 1 Jan. 1973, 8 Jan. 1973; Wells, "The Admissions of the State of Idaho," p. 68; *Progressive Men of Southern Idaho*. Chicago, A.W. Bowen & Co. 1904, pp. 70–71.

39. Steunenberg, Frank. "The Ships of State." *Caldwell Tribune*, 20 Jy. 1889, p. 3, col. 1.

40. Defenbach, *The History of Idaho*, p. 441; *Statesman*, 12 Jan. 1910; Wells, "Admission," p. 63.

41. Hawley, *History of Idaho*, vol. 1, pp. 594–95; *Statesman*, 14 Sept. 1891, p. 8; Wells, "Admission," p. 65. 42. *Evening Capital News*, 4 Jan. 1915; *Idaho Daily Statesman*, 6 Sept. 1913, p. 3, col. 5; *Idaho Daily Statesman*, 4 Jan. 1915; *Idaho Democrat*, 18 Oct. 1896, p. 3, cols. 1–3; Wells, "Admission," p. 72.

43. Wells, "Admission," p. 69.

44. Hawley, *History of Idaho*, vol. 2, pp. 384–87; Wells, "Admission," p. 70. Some twenty years after the convention, Moss, Drew W. Standrod, another convention delegate, and others loaned their name to a commercial enterprise and as a result were charged by the United States government with mail fraud. *Caldwell Tribune*, 21 Apr. 1911, p. 3, col. 3–4.

45. *Idaho Daily Statesman*, 26 Apr. 1918, p. 5, col. 4; Wells, "Admission," p. 63.

46. Wells, "Admission," p. 74.

47. *Caldwell Tribune*, 27 Sept. 1890, p. 2, col. 3; Goodwin, C. C. "The Eloquent Clagett," *Caldwell Tribune*, 1 Jl. 1910; Wells, "Admission," p. 63.; Defenbach, *Idaho*, p. 471; Stoll, William T. *Silver Strike: The True Story of Silver Mining in the Coeur d'Alenes*. Boston: Little, Brown & Co. 1932, pp. 97–101; *Illustrated History of North Idaho*. Spokane: Western History Publishing Co., 1903, pp. 1066–67.

48. Wells, "Admission," p. 67; *An Illustrated History of North Idaho*, p. 1094; Cook, R. G. "A Study of the Political Career of Weldon Brinton Heyburn Through His First Term in the United States Senate, 1852–1909." Master's thesis, University of Idaho, 1964; *Idem*. "Pioneer Portraits: Weldon B. Heyburn." *Idaho Yesterdays* 10(Spring 1966):22–26; Hawley, *History of Idaho*, vol. 4, p. 308; *Idaho Daily Statesman*, 10 Dec. 1933, vol.2, p. 4, 17 Dec., 1933, vol. 2, p. 4, 24 Dec. 1933, vol. 2, p. 2, 31 Dec. 1933, vol. 2, p. 4; Morrow, James B. "Life of Weldon B. Heyburn," *Idaho Daily Statesman*, 26 Mar. 1911, § 2, p. 11; *Idaho Yesterdays* 24(Summer 1980):2; *Idaho Yesterdays* (Winter 1981):20.

49. Hawley, *History of Idaho*, vol.4, pp. 394–97; *Illustrated History of Idaho*, p. 629; Wells, "Admission," p. 76; Stoll. *Silver Strike*. pp. 114–34.

50. *Idaho Daily Statesman*, 21 Je. 1914, § 2, p. 12; Wells, "Admission," p. 69; *Wallace Free Press* 3 Nov. 1888.

51. *Wallace Free Press*, 2 Mar. 1889, 1 Je. 1889; Wells, "Admission," p. 68.

52. Durham, N.W. *History of the City of Spokane and Spokane Country*. Spokane: S. J. Clarke Publ. Col, 1912, vol. 3, p. 498.

53. Wells, "Admission," p. 61.

54. Wells, "Admission," pp. 65–66.

55. Hawley, *History of Idaho*, vol. 3, p. 331, under "Ralph T. Morgan, son"; *Progressive Men of Southern Idaho*, pp. 28–30; Wells, Merle W. *Anti-Mormonisms in Idaho, 1872–1892*. Provo, Utah: Brigham Young University Press, 1928.

56. Elliot, *History of Idaho Territory*, p. 213; Wells, "Admission," p. 66.

57. *Illustrated History of Idaho*, p. 537; Wells, "Admission," p. 60.

58. Wells, "Admission," p. 73.

59. *Idaho Daily Statesman*, 16 Jan. 1928, 26 Oct. 1930; *Illustrated History of Idaho*, p. 406; Wells, "Admission," 74. 60. Wells, "Admission," p. 68.

61. *Caldwell Tribune*, 3 Jan. 1889, 19 Jan. 1889, p. 1, col. 7; *Idaho Statesman*, 22 Oct. 1927; Lillard, Monique. "The Federal Court in Idaho, 1889–1907." *Western Legal History*, 2(1989):35–78; Wells, "Admission," p. 61.

62. *Illustrated History of North Idaho*, p. 213; Wells, "Admission," p. 75.

63. Wells, "Admission," p. 71.

64. Ibid., p. 61.

65. Ibid., p. 63.

66. Ibid., p. 69.

67. Burke, Edward. "Minders Must Eat–William J. McConnell and the Boise Basin Gold Rush." *Latah Legacy* (Spring 1983):1–3; Hawley, James H. "Address at the Funeral of Ex-Governor Wm. J. McConnell on April 5, 1925." Latah County Historical Society Library, SC/MCC-2; *Idaho Daily Statesman*, 31 Mar. 1925, p. 1, 6 Apr. 1925, p. 1; *Idaho Daily Statesman*, 3 Je., 10 Je., 17 Je., 24 Je., 1924; *Illustrated History of North Idaho*, p. 608; McConnell, William J. *Early History of Idaho*.Caldwell: Caxton Printers, 1913; *Idem. Frontier Law: A Story of Vigilante Days*. Yonkers-on-Hudson, New York: World Book Co., 1926; *Idem*. "Idaho Inferno." *Latah Legacy* (Fall

1980):27–36; Noll, Lowell H. "Southern Idaho Vigilantism." *Pacific Northwesterner* (Spring 1958):25–32; Wells, "Admission," p. 69.

68. *Biographical Directory of the American Congress, 1774–1971*, Washington D.C.: Government Printing Office, 1971, p. 1781; *Idaho Daily Statesman*, 27 Jan., 3 Feb., 10 Feb., 17 Feb., 24 Feb., 3 Mar., 1935; Wells, "Admission," p. 74.

69. Brigham served in the territorial council and the state Senate. He was the last surviving delegate from the convention, dying on January 24, 1940, more than fifty years later. Gibbs, *The Idaho State Constitution*, p. 44; Wells, "Admission," p. 61.

70. Wells, "Admission," p. 61.

71. Wells, "Admission," p. 73.

72. *Idaho Daily Statesman*, 5 Mar. 1936; *Idaho State Historical Society Biennial Report* 1936, p. 143; Wells, "Admission," p. 71.

73. Crook was a mine superintend who served as county commissioner and was a populist nominee for governor after the convention. *Caldwell Tribune*, 3 Sept. 1892, p. 7, cols. 1–2; Wells, "Admission," p. 63.

74. Salisbury owned and operated the Bayhorse Mine as well as a stage line. Wells, "Admission," p. 72.

75. Defenbach, *Idaho*, p. 322; Donaldson, *Idaho of Yesterday*, p. 203; Hawley, *History of Idaho*, vol. 1, pp. 126, 181–82; *Idaho Daily Statesman*, 11 My. 1913, p. 9, col. 2; *Idaho State Historical Society Biennial Report* 1949–50, p. 11; *Illustrated History of Idaho*, pp. 82–84; *Progressive Men of Southern Idaho*, pp. 76–80; Wells, "Admission," p. 60.

76. Wells, "Admission," p. 62.

77. *Idaho State Historical Society Biennial Report* 1934, p. 92; Wells, "Admission," p. 70.

78. Wells, "Admission," p. 74.

79. *Idaho State Historical Society Biennial Report* 1934, p. 83; Wells, "Admission," p. 62. 80. *Illustrated History of Idaho*, p. 112; Wells, "Admission," p. 73.

81. The other two delegates were *Robert Larimer* and *T. F. Nelson*. Perhaps cost was the reason they did not attend. The convention did not have a budget, and even though the delegates eventually were paid expenses and a per diem, it was necessary for them to pay their expenses in only the hope of future reimbursement. Parker wrote the convention organizers complaining "it costs like thunder to travel."

82. Defenbach, *Idaho*, p. 430; *Idaho County Free Press*, 9 Jan. 1930; *Idaho Daily Statesman*, 6 Jan. 1930, p. 3, col. 7; *Idaho State Historical Society Biennial Report* 1930 pp. 118–20; *Illustrated History of North Idaho*, pp. 562–63; *Illustrated History of Idaho*, p. 200; Wells, "Admission," p. 71.

83. Wells, "Admission," p. 65.

84. Ibid., p. 70.

85. Ibid., p. 60.

86. Ibid., p. 67.

87. *Idaho State Historical Society Biennial Report* 1928, p. 88; *Recorder-Herald*, Salmon, Idaho, 2 Nov. 1927; Wells, "Admission," p. 72.

88. Wells, "Admission," p. 61.

89. Ibid., p. 60.

90. Ibid., p. 75.

91. *Caldwell Tribune*, 27 Sept. 1890, p. 2, col. 3; Wells, "Admission," p. 72.

92. Defenbach, *Idaho*, pp. 440–41; Wells, "Admission," p. 71. 93. Wells, "Admission," p. 67.

94. *Illustrated History of Idaho*, p. 92; Wells, "Admission," p. 63.

95. *Idaho Daily Statesman*, 15 Mar. 1917, p. 9, cols. 1–3; *Illustrated History of Idaho*, p. 549; *Progressive Men of Southern Idaho*, p. 839; Wells, "Admission," p. 66.

96. Wells, "Admission," p. 72.

97. Hawley, *History of Idaho*, vol. 1, p. 159; Wells, "Admission," p. 66.

98. *Idaho Daily Statesman*, 11 Feb. 1924; *Idaho State Historical Society Biennial Report* 1924, p. 48; *Illustrated History of Idaho*, p. 463; Wells, "Admission," p. 67.

99. Wells, "Admission," p. 66.

100. Hawley, *History of Idaho*, vol. 2, pp. 259–61; *Idaho State Journal*, 21 Je. 1982, Supp. § 5, p. 7; *Progessive Men of Southern Idaho*, p. 818; Wells, "Admission," pp. 73–74.

101. Howell, Glade F. "Early History of Malad Valley," master's thesis, Brigham Young University, 1960, p. 90; Wells, "Admission," p. 69.

102. Ibid., pp. 66, 68.

103. *Illustrated History of Idaho*, p. 635; *Progressive Men of Southern Idaho*, p. 444; Wells, "Admission," p. 75.

104. *Idaho Daily Statesman*, 5 Jy. 1889, p. 2.

105. As reprented in *Dailey Statesman*, 11 Jy. 1889, p. 1.

106. "The Ship of State," *Caldwell Tribune*, 13 Jy. 1889, p. 3, col. 1.

107. "The Ship of State," *Caldwell Tribune*, 13 Jy. 1889, p. 3., col. 2.

2.
Church and State

---

1. Temperance and Morality

WHEN THE DELEGATES left convention chambers on Saturday night, they expected to begin debating the constitution itself on Monday morning, July 25, by first taking up the declaration of rights article. But pressure from the Women's Christian Temperance Union and the prohibition sentiment of the day caused a rescheduling. As a result, the prohibition section became the first clause of the constitution to be debated. This and several other topics, including the freedom of religious conscience, the press and the Mormon question, and the preamble to the constitution will be discussed here.

In a speech given on the previous Wednesday, Mrs. Henrietta Skelton had petitioned the convention on behalf of the Women's Christian Temperance Union (WCTU) to adopt the following provisions:

Section 1. The manufacture, sale, or keeping for sale of intoxicating liquors for use as a beverage is hereby prohibited, and any violation of this provision shall be a misdemeanor punishable as shall be provided by law.

Section 2. The manufacture, sale, or keeping for sale of intoxicating liquor for other purposes than as a beverage may be allowed in such manner only as may be prescribed by law.

Section 3. The general assembly shall at the first session under this constitution, enact laws with adequate penalties for its enforcement (p. 90).[1]

The WCTU petition was referred to the election and right of suffrage committee because it also called for woman's suffrage (p. 92). James Beatty, chair of the committee, declined to accept jurisdiction over the prohibition question and referred it back to the convention floor. By a 23 to 22 vote the delegates decided to debate the question during the ninth session on Monday, July, 15 (p. 115). Because of this vote, the first section of the Idaho constitution adopted at the convention was to deal with intoxicating liquors.

There was apparently no spokesperson for the prohibition cause at the convention. Even Mrs. Skelton's address argued it only obliquely: "We only ask, dear gentlemen, that you give us a weapon whereby we may protect ourselves" (p. 90). As a consequence, in a voice vote the WCTU petition was defeated (p. 118).

Charles A. Clark (D-Ada) then proposed a substitute for the WCTU petition:

> The first concern of all good government is the virtue and sobriety of the people and the purity of the home which all legislation should further by wise and well-directed efforts for the promotion of temperance and morality (p. 118).

He observed this language was a literal transcription of the temperance plank of the most recent national Republican convention and should therefore be accepted by a majority at the convention as "emanating from the highest political authority in the land" (p. 119).

The Clark motion was not really debated, though it did provide an occasion for jesting and prognostication. When Alexander Mayhew (D-Shoshone) asked which article it was to go in, Clark drew a laugh by saying bill of rights (p. 119). The clause was eventually placed in Article III, which governs the legislative branch. When Willis Sweet (R-Latah) suggested adding the Democratic temperance plank to show the convention was nonpartisan, Mayhew said many of his Republican friends had already adopted the Democratic principle which was "the more you drink the wiser you get" (p. 120).

There is evidence Mayhew was right, at least in the Idaho legislature of the day. The *Idaho Daily Statesman* reported after the 1888 legislature adjourned, "sixty-eight whiskey flasks and bottles were found in the nooks and corners of the Capital [sic] building during the clean up that followed the adjournment of the legislature. . . . The number as well as the size of the bottles beats the record of two years ago."[2]

Mayhew also predicted the prohibition issue was becoming obsolete, and Sweet, the young Republican attorney from Moscow, agreed with him (p. 120). Their vision must have been blurred by their enthusiasm for the Democratic principle, because they were dead wrong. At the general election in 1916, Idaho citizens made it clear that the delegates had not gone far enough at the convention. Section 26 was added to Article III and provided:

Prohibition of intoxicating liquors. - From and after the first day of May in the year 1917, the manufacture, sale, keeping for sale, and transportation for sale of intoxicating liquors for beverage purposes are forever prohibited. The legislature shall enforce this section by all needful legislation.[3]

Nearly seventy-two percent of the Idaho citizens who voted favored the amendment, with 90,576 for adoption and 35,456 against.[4]

One year later, the prohibition movement had gained national support. On December 17, 1917, Congress submitted the eighteenth amendment to the United States Constitution to the state legislatures for adoption. In language similar to that proposed by Mrs. Skelton in 1889 and that adopted by Idaho in 1916, the eighteenth amendment prohibited the manufacture, sale, or transportation of intoxicating liquors for beverage purposes. Section 2 of the amendment gave Congress and the states concurrent enforcement power.[5]

The Idaho legislature was anxious to approve the amendment. At the 1919 session, the first order of business after organization in the House was Joint Resolution 1, a ratification proposal. Dr. Emma F. A. Drake, President of the South Idaho WCTU and a representative of newly-created Payette County introduced the resolution and called for unanimous assent. No voice of opposition was heard and the measure moved to the Senate.

Senator Whitcomb, president pro tem of the senate, opposed ratification and initially tried to delay consideration of the resolution. But the supporters demanded immediate consideration. On January 8, 1919, Senator Whitcomb and several others excused themselves from the roll call and the resolution was approved by another unanimous vote. Four days after the resolution was introduced in the House, Idaho became the twentieth state to ratify national prohibition, and the second state to do so by unanimous vote.[6]

On January 29, 1919, a sufficient number of states had approved the amendment and prohibition became the law of the land. The effective date was January 16, 1920, a relatively unimportant day for the already dry Idaho, except at the WCTU headquarters in Boise.

After a decade the country's enthusiasm for prohibition abated and the eighteenth amendment was quickly repealed by the twenty-first amendment. Congress submitted the repealing amendment to the states on February 20, 1933, and by December 5 a sufficient number of states had ratified it. In the meantime Congress passed the Cullen Bill which defined beer as a nonintoxicating beverage. Idaho's Senator William Borah strongly opposed the bill but the popular sentiment of the country demanded prohibition be abandoned. The Cullen Bill passed and on April 7, 1933, Americans once again could drink beer legally. At least some Americans could; Idahoans and the citizens of other states with state prohibition remained dry.

Prohibition repeal in Idaho was a slower and more divisive process, as might be expected in a state which early adopted local prohibition and quickly and unanimously endorsed national prohibitions.[7] The question was one of the first considered when the twenty-second legislative assembly convened in January 1933. Representative Troy D. Smith of Custer County introduced a bill legalizing the sale, manufacture, and possession of beer and other beverages containing less than 3.2 percent alcohol.

Wet spokesman Senator Owen Stratton of Lemhi County had been seeking total repeal and was not willing to settle for a "beer bill." Chairman of the University of Idaho Philosophy Department Dr. C. W. Chenoweth argued repeal was tantamount to "pouring poison into the necks of our children." The 3.2 percent beer bill passed the House, 32–27, and the packed gallery applauded.

The Senate was working on its own solution and without discussion indefinitely postponed consideration of the House bill. Senator Stacy from Custer County introduced Joint Resolution No. 5, which proposed a constitutional amendment repealing the Idaho prohibition provision, to be voted on at the 1934 general election. Article III, §26 was to be amended to read:

> Power and authority over intoxicating liquors.-From and after the thirty-first day of December in the year 1934, the legislature of the state of Idaho shall have full power and authority to permit, control and regulate or prohibit the manufacture, sale, keeping for sale, and transportation for sale, of intoxicating liquors for beverage purposes.[8]

Only a few dissenting voices were heard as the resolution passed both houses.

Near the session's end the legislature passed House Bill No. 337.[9] This bill authorized the governor to call a special election to determine if Idaho would repeal national prohibition. Governor C. Ben Ross had not participated in the repeal debates of the legislature. He did not mention repeal or modifying prohibition in his biennial message, and he did not seem anxious to call for the election.

Ross became the target of an intense campaign by the wet forces in the state. The legislature had adjourned without passing the beer bill, and did not guarantee an opportunity for the voters to speak until the 1934 general election, which was another eighteen months away. But Governor Ross had the corrective power of calling for a vote on national prohibition and calling a special legislative session to adopt a beer bill.

Postmaster General James Farley pressed him to legalize beer and help pass the Twenty-First Amendment. Key members of his cabinet publicly demanded at a "Beer Putsch" that the Governor yield to the popular demand for beer. He was also pressured by Idaho mayors, who threatened to legalize beer by municipal ordinance.

Despite support from the Boise Ministerial Association and the WCTU, Governor Ross finally yielded. He feared "anarchy" from the "hysterical" demand for beer, and felt compelled to call a special session of the legislature to legalize and tax beverages containing less than 3.2 percent alcohol.[10] On June 19, 1933, the session quickly accomplished its purpose by passing House Bill No. 1. Only Representative Jensen of

Franklin County argued against the bill, which passed 48–14 in the House and 35–8 in the Senate. Governor Ross signed the legislation on June 21, and beer was legal in Idaho.

Governor Ross called for the special election on the Twenty-First Amendment to be held on September 19, 1933. Thirty-three of Idaho's forty-four counties passed the Amendment. Seven of the eleven counties voting against repeal were in the predominantly Mormon area of southeastern Idaho. The other four counties voting against repeal were Latah, Canyon, Payette, and Gooding. Franklin was the driest county with over eighty-one percent voting no and Shoshone the wettest with nearly ninety percent voting yes. In total, 65,652, or fifty-eight percent, of voting Idahoans favored repeal and 40,977, or forty-two percent, opposed it.[11]

This vote was formalized on October 17 when twenty-one mostly-Democratic delegates convened in the House chambers to verify ratification of the amendment. The convention was chaired by Asher B. Wilson and the vote was unanimous, just as Idaho had earlier unanimously voted to ratify prohibition. The *Boise Capitol News* observed the convention had cost $574, while over $53,000 in beer and malt taxes had accrued to the state in the four months since beer had been legalized by the special legislative session.[12]

The amendment to repeal Idaho's state prohibition clause was passed nearly a year later at the general election of 1934. The returns were almost identical to those of the special election on the Twenty-First Amendment. Over fifty-seven percent (85,469) of the voters favored the amendment, while forty-three percent opposed it.[13] Article III, § 26 has not been amended since it was adopted in 1934, and is the primary source of legislative authority over intoxicating liquors today.

The convention's own temperance and morality section has also survived, and has recently been interpreted twice by the Idaho Supreme Court. In *Crazy Horse, Inc. v. Pearce*, 98 Idaho 762, 572 P.2d 865 (1977), Steve Biacobbi tried to get a liquor license in Ketchum. But, standing in his way, was the liquor license quota system adopted by the Idaho legislature in 1959.[14] Under this system there can be only one license for every 1,500 in population. For Ketchum at the time, that meant two licenses. In addition the quota system grandfathered all existing licenses. In Ketchum, in 1959, there were eleven licenses. These grandfathers exceeded the permissible licenses by nine and Giacobbi didn't stand a chance.

So, he brought suit alleging the quota system was an arbitrary denial of due process because it bore no rational relationship to preservation of the public good. To be rational, he argued, licensing should focus on the amount of liquor sold, not the number of licenses. The Idaho Supreme Court rejected the argument, ruling that §§ 24 and 26 of Article III give the legislature broad authority over the sale of liquor.

Article III, § 24 was also cited more recently in *Henson v. Department of Law Enforcement*, 107 Idaho 19, 684 P.2d 996 (1984). The Department was revoking the convention center liquor license of the Snake River Convention Center, claiming it had been erroneously issued. As in *Crazyhorse*, there was a quota on the number of convention center licenses that could be issued. Also as in *Crazyhorse*, the court said in Henson that quotas on the number of licenses were justified because this promoted temperance and morality.

2. Guarantee of Religious Liberty

AFTER ADOPTING THE TEMPERANCE AND MORALITY PROVISION on Monday, July 15, the convention began debate on its own committee reports during the tenth session on Tuesday, July 16. Article I, declaration of rights, was the first to be considered. Section 1 guaranteed inalienable rights, § 2 safeguarded the inherent power of the people, and § 3 pledged Idaho to be an inseparable part of the Union. All passed without discussion (pp. 128–29).

Section 4 provided for religious liberty, and for the first time the Mormon question surfaced on the floor of the convention. The tenor of this debate differed strikingly from that of the temperance and morality discussion. Humor was replaced by stern and purposeful action; and party division was replaced by unanimous agreement, a partnership of the parties.

Section 4 as reported by the declaration of rights committee provided:

> The exercise and enjoyment of religious faith and worship shall forever be guaranteed; and no person shall be denied any civil or political privilege or capacity, on account of his religious opinions; *but the liberty of conscience hereby secured shall not be construed to dispense with oaths or affirmations, or excuse acts of licentiousness or justify polygamous or other pernicious practices, inconsistent with morality or the peace or safety of the State; nor permit any person, organization or association to directly or indirectly aid or abet, counsel or advise any person to commit the crime of bigamy or polygamy, or any other crime.* No person shall be required to attend or support any ministry or place of worship, religious sect or denomination, against his consent; nor shall any preference be given by law to any religious denomination or mode of worship [emphasis added] (p. 129).

G. W. King (D-Shoshone) moved to delete the portion of the committee report italicized above. He argued this language was "utterly unnecessary" and stated, "It is absurd to think any living man would claim exemption from these crimes." He asked, rhetorically, "Could a man under either of these clauses claim to have the right to act in a manner contrary to the natural and moral law of the country?" (pp. 129–33).

King's motion was defeated and it immediately became clear the convention was interested in strengthening the language of the section rather than weakening it. From the outset, a strong, unprecedented anti-Mormon sentiment emerged at the convention.[15] George Ainslie (D-Boise) moved to declare "bigamy and polygamy forever prohibited in the state and the legislative assembly shall provide by law for the punishment of such crimes." Ainslie defended the Democratic party from the charge of being sympathetic to the Mormons. He wanted to know "if the Republicans are honest in their denunciations of bigamy and polygamy . . ." and called for the parties to join and "stamp out this twin relic of barbarism." The Ainslie motion was passed on a voice vote (pp. 133–35).

Then, Weldon B. Heyburn (R-Shoshone) suggested even stronger language. He moved to require that the section's oath or affirmation be given before "exercising the right of franchise or acquiring any portion of the public lands." Heyburn stated his objective was to constitutionalize Idaho's test oath, which had been used to disfranchise Mormon voters. Referring to *Innis v. Bolton*, 2 Idaho 442, 17 Pac. 264 (1888) and *Wooley v. Watkins*, 2 Idaho 590, 22 Pac. 102 (1889), he argued the language was necessary "in order that it may never be said in argument in the court hereafter, or elsewhere, that the makers of this constitution did not intend to except" Mormons from the protections afforded by § 4 (pp. 135–142).

The *Innis* and *Wooley* cases were prosecutions under the test oath statute passed by the 1884 territorial legislature.[16] The test oath statute permitted any voter to challenge the qualifications of another voter. If challenged, a voter was required to swear or affirm that he was not a member of the Mormon church, or in the language of the statute that he was:

> not a member of any order, organization, or association which teaches, advises, counsels or encourages its members, devotees, or any other person to commit the crime of bigamy or polygamy, or any other crime defined by law, as a duty arising or resulting from membership in such order, organization or association, or which practices bigamy or polygamy or plural or celestial marriage as a doctrine rite of such organization; that you do not either publicly or privately, or in any manner whatever, teach, advise, counsel or encourage any person to commit the crime of bigamy or polygamy, or any other crime defined by law either as a religious duty or otherwise; that you regard the constitution of the United States, and the laws thereof, and of this territory as interpreted by the courts, as the supreme law of the land, the teachings of any order, organization, or association to the contrary notwithstanding . . .[17]

Innis, a resident of the Paris precinct in Bear Lake County, challenged the oath at the election of county surveyor on November 20, 1886. He was willing to swear he was not a bigamist or polygamist, and that he did not cohabit with more than one woman, but was unwilling to swear that portion of the oath just quoted.

Bolton was judge of the election who denied the right of Innis to vote when he refused to swear the entire oath. Innis then sued in the district court for Bear Lake County alleging he had been wrongfully denied the right to vote, seeking $10,000 in damages. Bolton demurred, arguing the complaint did not state facts sufficient to constitute a cause of action. The district court sustained the demurrer and Innis appealed to the Idaho Territorial Supreme Court.

The first and most important argument Innis made on appeal was that the oath was a violation of the First Amendment to the United States Constitution, which provides, "Congress shall make no law respecting an establishment of religion, or prohibiting the free exercise thereof." Richard Z. Johnson, counsel for Innis, did not file a brief but in oral argument "strenuously argued that the oath here prescribed and required to be taken does in effect interfere with the rights of conscience in religious matters, and thereby with free exercise of religion."

The court denied Innis's appeal. Justice Broderick wrote the opinion with justices Hays and Buck concurring. After reviewing the writings of justices Story and Cooley, Justice Broderick concluded:

> Authorities might be multiplied, but the result of all is that the government must not interfere with opinion, but may with conduct. Laws are made for the government of actions, and when the conduct and actions are criminal it is no excuse to say that these things, though forbidden by the law, are done in the name of religion. . . . To permit this would make the professed doctrines of religious belief superior to the law of the land, and in effect to permit every citizen to become a law unto himself.[18]

Justice Broderick examined the oath and wrote:

> This clause is undoubtedly open to criticism, but the intention of the legislature was to withdraw the right of suffrage from persons who encourage, aid and abet those who are endeavoring, not by constitutional methods, but against all law, to overthrow a sound public policy of the government, and one that has existed from its foundation.[19]

Justice Broderick concluded his justification by emphasizing the inferior status of the right of suffrage at common law and the primacy of state sovereignty. He wrote:

> The right of suffrage is not a natural right, nor an unqualified personal right. The elementary writers do not include this right among the rights of property or persons. . . . it is a right conferred by law, and may be modified or withdrawn by the authority which conferred it . . . every government ought to contain, in itself, the means of its own preservation. . . . The only question for us to determine is purely a question of power.[20]

Wooley v. Watkins, supra, was a second challenge of the test oath statute. In early October, 1888, H. S. Wooley of Paris precinct in Bear Lake County filed a petition in the district court of Idaho's Third Judicial District. Wooley alleged that he was denied the right to vote at the general election the month before, even though he appeared at the registrar and offered to take the oath as required by the statute. He sought a writ of mandamus compelling his registration.

C. N. Watkins, the registrar, filed an answer which admitted all facts alleged, except that it denied Wooley was an elector "for the following reasons, and none others; That the said petitioner is a member of what is known as the 'Mormon church in Idaho.' "

On the same day Watkins filed his answer, H. M. Bennett filed a petition praying to be allowed to intervene on behalf of the public and people of Idaho. His petition stated the plaintiff, the defendant, and all their attorneys were members of the Mormon church, and that Watkins had registered many members of the Mormon church before denying Wooley. He finally asserted the suit was under the control of church leaders and collusively brought to procure a judgment that would aid registration of church members in violation of the law.

The district court permitted Bennett to intervene. Sitting in Bingham County without a jury, the court later took evidence and found Watkins was a member of the "Utah" or regular branch of the Mormon church, and that the Utah Mormon church doctrine encouraged and required bigamy and polygamy as a duty of membership. Based upon this evidence the mandamus sought by Wooley was denied.

On appeal Wooley argued four provisions of the United States Constitution were violated by the test oath, including the First Amendment which provides Congress shall make no law respecting an establishment of religion, or prohibiting the free exercise thereof. Chief Justice H. W. Weir wrote the court's opinion which denied all four contentions by Wooley.

Chief Justice Weir rejected Wooley's First Amendment argument for the same reasons Justice Broderick rejected Innis's. He concluded, "While Congress, and, consequently, the territorial assembly, are deprived of all legislative power over mere opinion, they are left free to reach actions which are of a criminal nature, and are in violation of social duties, and subversive of good order."[21]

Chief Justice Weir then went beyond the *Innis* opinion, and assessed the consequences of membership *alone*. He wrote:

> Orders, organizations, and associations, by whatever name they may be called, which teach, advise, counsel, or encourage the practice or commission of acts forbidden by law, are criminal organizations. To become and continue to be members of such organizations or associations are such overt acts of recognition and participation as make them *particeps criminis*, and as guilty, in contemplation of criminal law, as though they actually engaged in furthering their unlawful objects and purposes.[22]

Justice C. H. Berry filed a concurring opinion. He agreed with the *Innis* opinion and with his colleague, Justice Weir, but he wanted to go further. Counsel for Wooley had argued the provision for the "blessings of liberty" in the preamble to the United States Constitution compelled a liberal and enlarged construction of the First Amendment protection of religious freedom. Justice Berry had an opinion of the "blessings of liberty" within the Mormon church.

Justice Berry declared, "It is time to speak plainly on this subject," and wrote what is probably the strongest criticism of the Mormon church to be found in the judicial records. The Mormon book, "Doctrine and Covenants," had been introduced into evidence. Justice Berry reviewed it as a whole and quoted from three revelations which preceded the revelation on polygamy. He summarized,

> They speak of other people as "enemies," and evidently imply that their presence, their laws and institutions are to be looked upon as a "curse upon the land," which the church aspires to dominate; that in such land there is to be no government or laws, except those alone of the church—evidently the germ of that state of chronic warfare which that "church" has ever, and still does, maintain against all government save that of the church; that even the members of the "church" are not their own masters. Their individuality as freemen and citizens is denied them. Their rights of choice and of action as freemen are merged in the church. Internecine wars are welcomed as a means by which the "gentiles are to be exterminated."[23]

Both of these cases clearly held the Idaho test oath did not violate the First Amendment. Heyburn's amendment would not change existing constitutional interpretations. It was not made to change the law, but to express the anti-Mormon zeal of the convention. Heyburn is to the convention what Justice Berry was to the *Wooley* court.

While some delegates may have shared Heyburn's sentiments, others were more cautious. Alexander Mayhew (D-Shoshone) objected that the matter was within the jurisdiction of the elections and suffrage committee (p. 136). Albert Hagan (D-Kootenai) thought the convention was limited by the United States Constitution on the public lands (pp. 141–42). James H. Beatty (R-Alturas) worried that too many qualifications would cause Congress to think they were "wild" and "reject their work" (p. 137). He also feared Heyburn's amendment might restrict rather than empower the state's legislature (pp. 143–44). He cited *Whitney v. Findley*, 20 Nev. 98, 19 P. 241 (1888), which interpreted one of the few anti-Mormon statutes to ever be declared unconstitutional. In 1877 the Nevada legislature had passed a statute providing "no person shall be allowed to vote at any election in this state . . . who is a member of or belongs to the 'Church of Jesus Christ of Latter Day Saints,' commonly called the 'Mormon Church' . . ."[24]

The Nevada Constitution enfranchised all male residents over twenty-one years of age. Whitney had appealed the denial of his right to vote to the Nevada Supreme Court, which concluded, "It is not within the power of the legislature to deny, abridge, expand, or change the qualifications of a voter as prescribed by the constitution of the state."[25] Beatty warned the convention not to "tie ourselves up so that the legislature cannot from time to time add additional qualifications for suffrage so as to meet the schemes of the Mormon church" (p. 144).

In the end Heyburn's zealous amendment was defeated. But the convention was not finished strengthening the anti-Mormon flavor of § 4. Charles A. Clark moved to amend by adding, "No person shall be required to attend or support any ministry or place of worship, religious sect or denomination or pay tithes against his consent" (p. 145).

James M. Shoup (R-Custer) did not understand how one could be compelled to pay tithes by law. Clark quickly explained, "If the gentleman lived in a Mormon settlement and the water right was held by the church and he did not pay tithes and his water right was cut off, he would find a mighty strong compulsion to pay his tithes." His amendment was just as quickly adopted by a voice vote, and Article I, § 4, guaranteeing freedom of religion took its final form (pp. 145–46).

This section was the first debate on the Mormon Question, which ultimately was to occupy so much time at the convention. The language, or form, of § 4 has remained unchanged for one hundred years. But circumstances have changed, and the meaning and significance of the section have changed. Just as the convention considered the suffrage article the most important, the critical changes since the convention relating to freedom of religion can be found in the suffrage article.[26]

3. The Politics of Polygamy

AFTER AGREEING ON THE LANGUAGE for the religious freedom section, the convention quickly passed § 5 on the writ of habeas corpus and § 6 on excessive bail and cruel and unusual punishment (p. 146). Section 7 providing for the right to jury trial was read and briefly debated (pp. 146–62). The tenth session concluded in the evening with the suffrage address of Abigail Duniway, representing the National Woman's Suffrage Association (pp. 164–75). The eleventh session met briefly on Tuesday, July 17, to receive several committee reports and to approve a few changes in committee membership. After a brief discussion the convention voted to record the proceedings of its work when sitting as a committee of the whole as well as when sitting in the formal convention (pp. 175–82). The committee of the whole included all the delegates, but was a procedural device to permit more informal proceedings. Until late in the convention, each article was first considered in the committee of the whole, and then again in formal session. Since most of the convention debate took place in the committee of the whole, these proceedings were recorded. This has preserved for us the record of the creation of Idaho's Constitution (pp. 175–82).

The twelfth session opened with a second and more heated debate on the Mormon question (pp. 182–201). This time the political aspect of the question was involved rather than the principle of freedom of religious conscience. In addition, the role of free speech and the press was involved. Unlike the convention that drafted the United States Constitution, which met in closed session, the Idaho convention was open to the press. Freedom of the press came under attack because of the way the Mormon Question was being reported.

George Ainslie (D-Boise) stood on the floor of the convention on July 18 to complain about reports of the convention published in the *Salt Lake Tribune* and Boise's

Daily Statesman. On the previous Saturday the *Statesman* reported "Walter Hoge, one of the chief counselors of the Mormon Church, who has been promoted to the position of 'sack holder' . . . has been in consultation with some of the so-called leaders of the Democratic party during the past few days. It is even rumored he attended their caucus."[27] The article went on to say Hoge, who sought a constitution with no references to bigamy or polygamy, was a polygamist himself and would have been served with a warrant while in Boise had he not fled.[28]

The *Salt Lake Tribune* was Ainslie's primary target. He was willing to accept the apology of the *Tribune* reporter for saying "that I was ready to withdraw from the democratic party." That statement was "too ridiculous for denial." What outraged him was the assertion of the *Tribune* that a Bishop Hoge "is here in constant consultation with the Mormon wing of the democratic party in the interest of the Church." Ainslie vehemently claimed the statement was untrue. He claimed, "I never yet, to my knowledge, have received any letter or communication from any Mormon in regard to any political matter whatever" (pp. 184–85).

Ainslie stated he had never met Hoge until several days ago, and was then only introduced at a crowded social gathering in the Overland Hotel. He thought Hoge was a Republican, for Hoge had worked for the Republican candidate in Bear Lake County during the 1882 election for territorial delegate to Congress (pp. 184–85).

Ainslie went on to accuse the *Tribune* and Charlie Goodwin, its editor, of setting out to abuse him and the Democratic Party of Idaho. He said it was the "habit and constant practice . . . to cram the columns of the paper full of lies about democrats upon every question, nearly, that may arise touching the position of the Mormon people in this territory" (p. 184). Ainslie gave his blunt assessment of the *Tribune*: "[I]t is the most infernally filthy sheet that was ever published on the face of God's green earth, and my opinion of the conductors of the sheet is about equivalent to that of the paper" (p. 186). He demanded that the *Tribune* correspondent be "fired out of this hall" (p. 186).

Ainslie's battle with the *Salt Lake Tribune* had started eight years earlier while he was seeking reelection in the 1882 contest for Idaho's territorial delegate to Congress. Ainslie was a Southern Democrat who came to Idaho just as the territory was being created. He was an important member of the Democratic leadership that controlled territorial politics during the 1860s. When Mormons joined Idaho politics in 1872, they formed a coalition with the Democrats. This was the coalition that elected Ainslie to his first term as territorial representative. During that term there had been a dispute about the seating of George C. Cannon, a polygamist sent by Utah as its territorial delegate. Ainslie had supported Cannon, and the *Tribune* strongly opposed him for it. Ainslie was defeated in the 1882 election by a coalition between the Independent Anti-Mormon Party and the Republicans. The *Salt Lake Tribune* had been a strong voice against Ainslie. His defeat marked the end of the Democratic control over territorial politics which had been enjoyed since the earliest days of the territory. It also marked the start of a of an extraordinary period of discrimination against Mormons. While Mormons as a block held the outcome of territorial elections in their hands during the 1870s, by the end of the 1880s they were without the franchise and empty-handed.[29]

Other Democrats at the convention rose to support Ainslie and their party. Cavanah said he had read and sympathized with the *Tribune* for twelve or fifteen years, but that his "faith was a little shocked," because the reports were "unmanly" and "unfair." (pp. 186–87). Mayhew did not think it was "fair, just or honorable" to falsely brand the Democratic Party in order to bring "odium and disgrace and shame" upon it. He stated, "I don't know Bishop Hoge, I never saw Bishop Hoge, and I may say that I can express an honest sentiment when I say that I do not know that I ever saw a Mormon" (pp. 187–89). Poe did not support expelling the reporter, but thought the party had "a right to demand an absolute retraction with the same publicity that the falsehood was circulated" (pp. 189–91).

Even Republican delegates supported Ainslie. McConnell proposed a resolution, "Resolved that the correspondent of the *Salt Lake Tribune* be requested to publish a retraction of the charges against the Honorable George Ainslie or be denied the future privileges of the floor" (p. 191). Only Batten spoke against the resolution. He defended Republican honor by claiming Bishop Hoge did not belong to the party, and by speaking for Judge Goodwin's honor and honesty as the editor of the *Tribune* (p. 191–97).

Just before the vote on the resolution Cavanah moved to strike the portion that would have denied the privilege of the floor because "I don't want this convention to place themselves in as ridiculous a position as the last legislature here did and be laughed at all over the country" (p. 200). Shoup suggested a select bipartisan committee be appointed to report on the resolution, but his motion was denied and Cavanah's passed (pp. 200–1). Even though politics and the Mormon question never left the floor of the convention, the dispute between George Ainslie and the *Tribune* did not resurface.

Batten and other delegates became impatient with the slow pace of the debate and moved to limit all speeches to fifteen minutes. It was a sacrifice to attend the convention and business was pressing at home. When the motion passed, Shoup moved for a ten-minute limit, which also passed by a 38 to 18 roll call vote (pp. 203–11). The work of the convention was speeding up.

4. *Pefley's Preamble*

THE MORMON ISSUE involved the right to the free exercise of religion. The Idaho Convention also faced issues involving the establishment of religion early in the convention. Two of these were raised by Peter J. Pefley (R-Ada), champion of a wall of separation between church and state. On July 19, the thirteenth convention session, the initial work on the declaration of rights article was finished. Pefley then moved to add this additional section:

No money shall be drawn from the treasury for the benefit of any religious or
theological institution, nor shall any money be appropriated for the payment
of any religious service in either house of the legislature (p. 386).

He argued economy supported the section since it would save several hundred
dollars each legislative session. He thought the religious services were just "ostenta-
tious bosh," and claimed they had no good effect on legislators, who were "to make
laws for the country, and not to make long-winded prayers." Three-fourths of those
lawmakers, according to Pefley, "are noncommunicants of any society or sect, and take
no interest in anything which cannot be demonstrated." Progressiveness and "the blaze
of the nineteenth century" made it possible to abandon services "hoary with age and
handed down from a barbarous generation." His proposition was "to allow each man
his affinity, to invite the whole clergy to the capitol, to come and ministrate, but that
they shall not take up the hours of legislation, and that each member shall foot the bill,
because he received the benefit and not the people" (pp. 386–68).

Pefly provoked several short, strongly felt, rebuttals. Poe could not tolerate Pefley's
suggestion "in this Christian age, in the age of civilization" at a convention organized
"by the Christian people of this country" who all claimed "there is a Supreme Being to
whom we look for aid and comfort in our hours of need" (p. 388). A fellow delegate
from Ada County accused Pefley of forgetting "our fathers and forefathers, the founders
of this republic." He asked rhetorically, "Does he forget the example set to us from the
Declaration of Independence down to the present day? Does he forget that Lincoln,
Washington and Jefferson set us the example?" (p. 389).

Only Ainslie gave any support to Pefley's motion. He thought it wise not to spend
public money to support religious institutions. Pefley's proposal was rejected (pp. 390–92).

However, Pefley was not dejected. The preamble was taken up next. The declaration of rights committee had proposed:

We, the people of the state of Idaho, grateful to Almighty God for our freedom, to secure its blessings and promote our common welfare do establish
this Constitution (p. 394).

Pefley offered a substitute:

We the people of Idaho, to the end that justice be established, order maintained and liberty perpetuated, do ordain this constitution (p. 394).

Pefley had only a brief opportunity to argue on behalf of his substitute. It was so
unpopular that an immediate vote was called for. Pefley did manage to claim the committee language had "redundant, meaningless or ambiguous words in its composition."
He also claimed to rely upon the example set by drafters of the United States Constitution, "I say if they had no use for ambiguous words in the preamble of the Constitution of the United States, why should we, amateur statesmen here, far away in the

sagebrush of Idaho, undertake to improve on their work, that has been applauded all over this great universe, and is the grandest and best work that ever fell from the hand of living men?" (p. 394).

The Preamble to the United States Constitution states:

We the people of the United States, in order to form a more perfect Union, establish justice, insure domestic tranquility, provide for the common defense, promote the general welfare, and secure the blessings of liberty to ourselves and our posterity, do ordain and establish this Constitution for the United States of America.

The ambiguous phrase Pefley finds objectionable is obviously "Almighty God" which does not appear in the U.S. Preamble. When his first motion was overwhelmingly defeated, Pefley offered another substitute which replaced "Almighty God" with "the Constitution of the United States" so the preamble would read:

We, the people of the state of Idaho, grateful to the Constitution of the United States for our freedom to secure its blessings and promote our common welfare do establish this Constitution. (p. 395).

There was no support for Pefley's second substitute either. In fact, there was outrage. On the following morning Cavanah moved to have Pefley's motions expunged from the minutes (pp. 405–6). Pefley rose to defend himself, claiming he was not an infidel for introducing language taken from preambles of other states. Ainslie interrupted him as he was saying, "the idea of expunging anything of that kind from the minutes appears to me ridiculous, and could only emanate from a man who was not in his right–" (pp. 405–6).

Ainslie's interruption was a point of order, and gave Clagett an opportunity to rule that debate on the motion to expunge out of order. The motion was never debated, and Pefley was never able to defend himself. He tried to bring the motion to the floor the following day but the chair ruled against him. The same thing happened again on the last day of the convention. Pefley never wavered in his opposition to the preamble, and was the only delegate to vote "Nay" when it was formally approved (pp. 1700–1).

Pefley's separation of church and state put him at odds with all the other delegates on the Mormon question too. He was the only delegate to speak out against the anti-Mormon sections of the constitution. As the convention was about to empower the legislature with the power to forever disfranchise Mormons, Pefley rose to protest. He argued "American citizenship is the highest work that can exist," characterized by "equality of all men and universal suffrage." He said the convention was starting to grant "unheard of powers to the legislature in order to regulate the right of suffrage to suit the republican party and keep it in power forever." He lamented, "Political and religious persecution are supposed to have died at the termination of the revolution; but it appears that Idaho is again an exception, and that the bloody history of two hundred years ago is about to repeat itself, in sentiment at least, with all its hideousness in this state, which should be one of the most liberal, tolerant and enlightened in the American Union" (pp. 1014–18).

Another delegate at the convention said that Pefley had "a falling out with his God."[30] He apparently also had a falling out with his colleagues, the amateur statesmen in the sagebrush. He was the only delegate in attendance at the signing of the constitution who refused to endorse it. His refusal prompted Cavanah to move to withhold any payment of a delegate's expenses until he signed. Pefley then made his last convention speech, saying: "I came here . . . not expecting to get any pay, and I suppose every man in this convention came in the same way. I do not ask any pay, and I would not have it . . ." (p. 2043).

Notes

1. Hart, I. W., ed., *Proceedings and Debates of the Constitutional Convention of Idaho*. 2 vols. Caldwell: Caxton Printers, Ltd., 1912. These volumes are paginated consecutively, and all page references in the text of this chapter refer to them.

2. *Idaho Daily Statesman*, 9 Mar. 1889, p. 3, col.1.

3. I *Idaho Code* 157.

4. "Abstract of Votes cast in the Several Counties of the State of Idaho at the General election held November 7th, 1916," Secretary of State Geo. R. Barker.

5. I Idaho Code p. 26.

6. Putnam, Edison. "The Prohibition Movement in Idaho, 1863–1934." Ph. D. diss., University of Idaho, 1979.

7. Quinn, Larry. "The End of Prohibition in Idaho." *Idaho Yesterdays* 17(Winter, 1974):6–13.

8. I Idaho Stat. p. 157.

9. H.B. No. 337, ch. 179, 1933 Session Laws, p. 328.

10. Malone, Michael P. *C. Ben Ross and the New Deal in Idaho*. Seattle: University of Washington Press, 1970, pp. 65–66.

11. "Abstract of Votes." Idaho Secretary of State, Election Division.

12. *Boise Capitol News*, 17 Oct. 1933, p. 1, col. 7; p. 2, col. 3.

13. "Abstract of Votes." Idaho Secretary of State, Election Division.

14. S.B. No. 89, ch. 118, 1959 Session Laws, p. 254.

15. For the anti-Mormon experience in Idaho see: Thompson, Dennis L. "Religion and the Idaho Constitution." *Pacific Northwest Quarterly* 58(October 1967):169–78; Wells, Merle W. "The Idaho Anti-Mormon Movement, 1872–1908." Ph.D diss., University of California, Berkeley, 1950; Lyman, E. Leo. "A Mormon Transition in Idaho Politics." 20 *Idaho Yesterdays* 20(Winter 1977):2–11, 24–29; and Christensen, Michael E. "Footnote to History: Charles W. Nibley and the Idaho Test Oath." *Idaho Yesterdays* 22(Fall 1978):19–20. The national anti-Mormon experience is described in Arrington, Leonard J. *Great Basin Kingdom*. Cambridge: Harvard University Press, 1958, pp. 353–79.

16. For a more thorough discussion of these cases see chapter 8 below.

17. 1885 Idaho Terr. Sess. Laws 106.

18. 2 Idaho 442, at 449, 17 P. 264, at 267–68.

19. Ibid. at 450, at 268.

20. Ibid. at 442, at 268.

21. 2 Idaho 590, at 601, 22 P. 102, at 105.

22. Ibid. at 601, at 106.

23. Ibid. at 609, at 109.

24. St. Nev. 1887, p. 107, §1.

25. 20 Nev. 98, 19 P. 241.

26. See chapter 8 below.

27. *Idaho Daily Statesman*, 13 Jy. 1889, p. 2.

28. Walter Hoge was born in Northumberland, England, in 1842. He sailed from London to Vancouver Island in 1862 and for several years roamed the Northwest working as a miner, butcher, logger, and construction worker. In 1867 he hired on at a Mormon sawmill near Logan, Utah, and by the spring he had joined the church. He was called by Brigham Young to settle in the Bear Lake Valley, and he became active there in political affairs. He served as sheriff, deputy of the U.S. Court, a member of the first Paris city council, and representative to the Idaho territorial legislature. He married Amelia Smith, and then married Sarah Beck polygamously. Peterson, F. Ross; Haddock, Edith Parker; and Matthews, Dorothy Hardy, eds. *History of Bear Lake Pioneers*. Bear Lake County, Idaho: Daughters of Utah Pioneers, 1948.

29. Wells, Merle W. "The Admission of the State of Idaho." *Secretary of State of Twenty-Seventh Biennial Report* (1944).

30. McConnell, William J. *Early History of Idaho*. Caldwell: Caxton Printers, Ltd., 1913, p. 375.

3.

The Right to Jury Trial in Idaho

1. Idaho's Original Intention

ARTICLE 1, § 7 of the Idaho Constitution guarantees the right to a jury trial for Idaho citizens. The section adopted by the constitutional convention provided:

> The right of trial by jury shall remain inviolate; but in civil actions, three-fourths of the jury may render a verdict, and the legislature may provide that in all cases of misdemeanors five-sixths of the jury may render a verdict. A trial by jury may be waived in all criminal cases not amounting to felony, by the consent of both parties, expressed in open court, and in civil actions by the consent of the parties, signified in such manner as may be prescribed by law. In civil actions and cases of misdemeanor the jury may consist of twelve or any number less than twelve upon which the parties may agree in open court.[1]

The history of this section is one of reform, similar to that of other Rocky Mountain states where prolonged litigation had been a problem in mining and irrigation areas.[2] The common-law jury right was as secure in Idaho Territory as any place in the Union. Juries were made up of twelve, verdicts were unanimous and every civil litigant or criminal defendant was entitled to one. Idaho the state has been as committed to jury reform as the territory was to the jury right. Today, juries are often made up of fewer than twelve, verdicts need not be unanimous, and parties are often not entitled to the decision of their peers.

43

William H. Clagett (R-Shoshone), the "Silver-Tongued Orator of the West," almost single-handedly engineered Idaho's jury trial innovations. To him, the true principle was the Scottish system of majority control rather than the common-law tradition of unanimous verdicts. Clagett made a career out of mining law and politics. He started with the Comstock Lode in Nevada in the early 1860s, moved to Montana Territory in 1866, to Deadwood in the Black Hills in 1877, then to Portland, with a short stop in Butte. He stampeded into the Coeur d'Alene region during the winter of 1883–84, and built the first cabin in Murray after the rich strikes were made on Pritchard Creek. By the summer of 1889, Clagett had been in the mining frontiers for nearly thirty years and along the way had tried some of the most important mining law cases in the history of the west.[3]

Clagett had considerable power as president of the convention, and he appears to have used it to further reforms that especially interested him. He originally introduced his proposal for majority verdicts to the judiciary committee, which rejected it. The proposal then was taken to the declaration of rights committee, which agreed to recommend the innovation in civil, but not criminal trials. Securing a committee recommendation gave Clagett a recommendation for change, and an important procedural advantage in getting its passage. Section 7 of the Committee's Report first came to the convention floor on Tuesday, July 16th, the tenth day in session. J. W. Reid (D-Nez Perce) was the first to object. He suggested the committee language be amended by adding "by consent of the parties" (p. 146).[4] Weldon B. Heyburn (R-Shoshone) moved a substitute for the Reid motion. He suggested everything after the first phrase of the committee report be struck, so that it would read, "The right of trial by jury shall remain inviolate" (p. 152). Reid welcomed the support of a prominent Republican, and accepted the substitute.

This clash between Clagett and Heyburn was only one of many. Clagett's daughter, Ida, later reported his view of Heyburn, "Father despised him for there was nothing he would not stoop to to gain his end. He used to say that Mr. Heyburn had at his disposal all the gamut of legitimate action to run through, plus the gamut of trickery, which gave him a mean advantage. Father would not stoop to dishonesty, nor would he take a case unless he thought he was in the right."[5]

Reid tried to defeat Clagett's reform by referring it to the judiciary committee, which had already refused to endorse it (p. 210). A final effort was made to derail the Committee's (and Clagett's) proposal by John T. Morgan (R-Bingham). He suggested amending it so that the legislature had authority to experiment by adding: "The right of trial by jury shall remain inviolate, *but the legislature may provide that* in civil cases three-fourths of the jury may render a verdict" (emphasis added) (p. 212). This would have delayed reform, but still create its possibility. Morgan thought he had a majority committed to this compromise during one of the breaks in the debate, but in the end his amendment, like all attempts to amend Clagett's proposal for reform, was rejected by the delegates. There were sixty-three delegates present when the civil jury reform vote was taken as the last item of morning business, and only eleven supported Morgan's amendment (p. 234). So, by a 5 to 1 margin the convention adopted Clagett's innovation in jury trials, as the delaration of rights committee had recommended.

However, Clagett was not satisfied with the civil trial provision alone. After the lunch break, wanting to push further than the declaration of rights committee had been willing to go, Clagett moved to amend by adding, "And the legislature may provide that in all criminal actions, except for capital offenses, five-sixths of the jury may render a verdict" (p. 235).

When the convention refused to support him, Clagett moved to except those cases "where punishment is death or may extend to imprisonment for life" from the five-sixths verdict provision (p.254). When that was defeated, he offered yet another amendment: "And the legislature may provide that in all cases of misdemeanor, five-sixths of the jury may render a verdict" (p. 259). It is difficult to determine whether the delegates were convinced of the need for reform, or merely tired of Clagett's persistence, but by a 31 to 21 vote this language was adopted, and Idaho became the first state in the union to begin the reform of the common law tradition of unanimous verdicts in criminal cases.

This chapter first describes the debate over jury reform. Clagett offered common sense, justice, history and progress to support his majority verdicts. His opponents relied heavily upon the jury's power to protect the weak, tradition and the United States Constitution in their opposition. The discussion concludes by surveying jury trial developments during Idaho's first one hundred years.

2. *Common Sense and Better Justice*

PRESIDENT CLAGETT was a skillful advocate and eloquent spokesman for his causes. A contemporary of Clagett recalled, "I suspect it was that faculty of winning the sympathy for the cause he advocated, that gave the chiefest charm to his eloquence."[6] Clagett first argued that common sense dictated reform. After observing that the majority vote controls in the legislature, on the bench, and in the board room, he asked rhetorically about the unanimous verdict rule, "Does not the common sense of the business community, does not the common sense of the public, does not the common sense of every individual man reject it . . . ?" (p. 156).

James N. Shoup (R-Custer), one of the few delegates to assist Clagett in the debate, offered the same argument in the form of a business proposition. He supposed a property dispute between neighbors. A friend suggested the two submit the dispute to a jury of twelve neighbors, and let three-fourths of them decide the case. Shoup asserted, "Now, wouldn't any fair-minded or sensible business man that wanted to do what was right agree to such a proposition? But if a man was dishonest and wanted to take advantage of his neighbor, he would say, 'No, sir. I want the whole twelve to decide the thing' " (p. 219).

In another line of argument Clagett contended that majority rule produced better and more efficient justice than a unanimity rule. He spoke from "observation and pretty long practice" and had concluded there were two types of jury deliberations: those about which there was "practically no dispute" and those in which there was a "decided difference of opinion" (p. 149).

In cases of no dispute, the unanimity requirement was irrelevant. In the case of the difference of opinion, "the verdict of the twelve is less apt to be right than the verdict of the nine out of the twelve; for the simple reason that wherever there is a controversy of that kind in the jury box the verdict is inevitably the result of a compromise which gives neither the plaintiff nor the defendant what he is entitled to as a matter of law" (p. 150). From these observations Clagett concluded a three-quarters verdict produced purer justice.

Clagett also argued the unanimity requirement was expensive and inefficient. In his experience with mining litigation, the rule of unanimous verdicts too often produced hung juries which caused expensive retrials, tied up property interests and impeded development. He said: "In civil cases where large sums of money and valuable property are involved, it is almost an absolute certainty that you will have from one to two jurors upon the jury who have been bought to hang it, on the one side or the other; or, if they have not been bought, they are influenced by personal or private considerations of such a character as practically disqualifies them to sit as jurors . . ." (p. 150).

Finally, Clagett cited a common strategy of lawyers to support his indictment of the unanimous verdict requirement. He observed, "It is an axiom in the legal profession that whenever you have no right, demand a trial by jury, and stand upon a verdict of twelve, for the reason that where you have no case, you have a chance at least to secure some one or two persons to hang the jury" (p. 148).

3. Protection for the Weak

BECAUSE THE DECLARATION OF RIGHTS COMMITTEE had recommended a majority control rule, a heavy burden of persuasion shifted on the convention floor to those favoring the old unanimous verdict. These delegates first argued the unanimous verdict was an essential protection for the weak in society. Even though Albert Hagan (D-Kootenai) had given strong support to civil jury reform (pp. 226–29), he just as strongly opposed reform of criminal juries and argued, "I appeal upon the ground of the weak against the strong" (p. 240). J. W. Poe (D-Nez Perce) argued, "It is a maxim of law that it is better that ninety-nine guilty men should go unpunished than that one should suffer for a crime of which he is not guilty" (p. 242). He concluded, "I appeal to you in your magnanimity to consider the many thousands who have suffered ignominious death upon the scaffold or who have eked out a miserable existence in the prison cell" (p. 242). Weldon Heyburn argued, "It is the strong arm of the law that stands between the weak and the strong, between rich and poor, between oppressed and oppressor" (p. 153).

John S. Gray (R-Ada) added a new twist to the argument: the hanging jury. He said, "It is almost taking away from the criminal that charity which is extended to him by the law of presumption of innocence. I have seen communities when a poor, unfortunate man has been indicted and brought before the court, and from the reading of the indictment five-sixths of that community would have hung him then without a bit of evidence further than the reading of the indictment" (p. 245).

Clagett not only challenged the assertion that the weak needed help in 1890 American criminal law, he asserted it was the prosecution that was weak. In his view, because old English prosecutions were conducted by the king through the sheriff who controlled the jury, "The crown was the stronger, and all the safeguards which grew up under the common law were designed for the express purpose of mitigating this strength so that it should not be exercised tyrannically" (p. 250). Did these conditions prevail in the United States? Clagett observed here the sheriff has no power except to summon jurors chosen by others, the defendant has the benefit of reasonable doubt, the defendant has double the number of peremptory challenges as the state, once acquitted the defendant cannot be tried again, the judge has the power to suspend the verdict, and the governor has the power of pardon. He described "abuses which have grown up under the changed conditions and circumstances of society" (p. 151). He concluded, "Now I ask whether all these things . . . do not constitute too much advantage on the part of the defendant, and whether the strong arm of the state . . . whose function is to protect the people, is not paralyzed by this system of a unanimous verdict" (p. 251).

Clagett not only rebutted the hanging jury argument but turned it to his favor. He admitted to having seen hanging juries, but claimed they were the result of a unanimous verdict requirement. He explained, "The reason [for your hanging jury] . . . is very simple. . . . Under your requirement of unanimous verdict, term after term and year after year goes by without any practical enforcement of the criminal law, until crime multiplies and criminals increase to such an extent that the whole people rise up . . . in a revolutionary movement, and . . . they will convict—almost going to the point of convicting innocent men" (p. 249).

Clagett often mentions "revolutionary methods . . . of an indignant populace" in the debates. He cited the acquittal in Portland of a notorious criminal named Olds, and read a newspaper article advocating "the system requiring unanimous verdict of the jurors be suspended for the more sensible method - the Scotch method - a majority being necessary to decide a trial" (p. 238). Finally, Clagett reminded the convention, "In Cincinnati there was a riot in which many men were killed and hundreds were wounded, where the people rose up in arms and undertook to sack the jail, and hang the prisoners there confined. Why? Because under the constitution of the state of Ohio requiring this unanimous verdict, public justice had become a mockery" (p. 157).

In less sweetened language, and more in keeping with Idaho's heritage, Clagett was talking about vigilante justice which was so popular in frontier communities.[7] Ironically, William J. McConnell (R-Latah) Idaho's most famous vigilante, was present at the convention the day jury reform was discussed (p. 125), but he did not enter the debate. As Captain of the Payette Vigilante Committee he led the effort to establish law and order in the Boise and Payette valleys during the 1860s. While he did not speak to the jury issue at the Convention, he described in another place the jury system of the Payette Vigilantes – a jury of seven, majority controls, with a verdict that was final.[8]

Another delegate also had experience with vigilante justice in Idaho, but for understandable reasons did not bring it up. In the fall of 1862 George Ainslie (D-Boise) had just arrived in Lewiston and was requested by friends of Dave English and William Peebles, who had been arrested for robbing gold from the Berry brothers, to represent them. Here is the rest of the story:

> He [Ainslie] was then a young man of twenty-four. He had been admitted to the bar in Missouri about two years before. He consented to act as counsel for the defense and went to the temporary jail to have a talk with his clients. The guards there courteously but firmly told him that he could not see the men until next morning. . . . The next morning Ainslie went back to the jail and found the building surrounded by a crowd but no guards in sight, and going through the door to make his promised call, he discovered his clients hanging from the joists of the unfinished building.[9]

It is clear that Clagett himself knew how to read and use the passions of a community and a jury drawn from its members. In the spring of 1886 he defended Noah S. Kellogg, Philip O'Rourke, Con Sullivan and others in a fight over what was to become the Bunker Hill and Sullivan mine, one of the world's richest. O. O. Peck and Dr. J. T. Cooper alleged they had grubstaked Kellogg with a three-dollar jackass that roamed around Murray and seventeen dollars worth of groceries and therefore were entitled to a half share of the fantastic new discovery. Cooper and Peck were represented by W. B. Heyburn and his partner, W. W. Woods, both of whom later served as delegates to the Idaho Constitutional Convention.

Cooper and Peck brought an action in equity, where there is no right to a jury under the common law. As the trial began Clagett moved the court to empanel a jury to assist the court because "the issue at stake . . . involving, as it does, millions, is of such importance, both to my clients and to the Territory of Idaho, that the decision should rest with men, rather than one man. . . ."[10] Cooper and Peck were tight-fisted commercial men in Murray and greatly disliked by the miners. On the other hand, Kellogg, and especially O'Rourke, were popular, particularly in the bars where O'Rourke spent monies he received from leasing his share of the mine buying whiskey and support from miners in the months before the trial. As Clagett expected, the jury deliberated a few minutes for the sake of formality and returned a verdict in favor of Kellogg and the other defendants.

However, the jury's verdict did not stand for long. Judge Buck began his opinion by noting that on the testimony of Kellogg himself the plaintiffs should win. He found no evidence to support the jury's verdict and said, "Since time out of mind it has been the boast of all English speaking peoples that their courts have stood as impregnable barriers against waves of passion and prejudice; and I would feel recreant to my bounden oath, my duty, and my conscience, were I not entirely to disregard the findings of the jury."[11] Even though unpopular, Judge Buck's opinion was accepted and Clagett's ploy to use the jury's passions was thwarted.

4. Tradition or Progress?

THE DUTY TO FOLLOW TRADITION was the argument most passionately and frequently raised by Clagett's opponents. Weldon B. Heyburn opposed jury reform because he did not believe "in the wisdom of changing entirely the system that is as old as government itself, that no man shall be deprived of his rights, of his liberty or his life, except by a unanimous verdict of a jury of his fellow citizens. . . . This principle has been deemed so important that at one time the demand that man should be protected by right of trial by jury revolutionized the civilized world" (p. 152).

James W. Reid pleaded, "I appeal to this convention to be careful in adopting innovations. We have a great empire here, a glorious territory; . . . We have the great principles of government under which the eastern states have prospered and profited. Let us follow experience" (p. 160). Reid's colleague from Nez Perce County, J. W. Poe (D-Nez Perce), reverently added, "When I behold the wisdom that has been manifested by our statesmen of the past I bow with humble reverence to that wisdom" (p. 232). Poe went on to declare "I am not one of those who is of the opinion that the world is growing physically weaker but mentally stronger. I find giants in the days of the past that equal anything I find in the days of the present" (p. 232).

John T. Morgan put the argument in terms the lawyers at the convention could understand. "Why is it that we have this library, Sir, here in this building? Simply that we may have the crystallized genius of the past, of the greatest men the world has ever produced before us, so that we can follow in the precedents they have laid down for us" (p. 233).

The reformers quickly rose to rebut the tradition argument. Clagett first denied his proposal was an innovation with respect to the civil jury, pointing out that Nevada had adopted a similar provision in 1862 and California in 1879, and that Montana was putting such a provision in its constitution then being drafted (p. 149). Clagett conceded there was no precedent, however, for the criminal provision. For this reason he merely wanted to authorize the legislature to experiment with the idea in the future rather than constitutionally require five-sixths verdicts.

The jury reformers also argued progress should prevail over tradition. James H. Beatty (R-Alturas) championed the progressive attitude. "I do not concur that because a thing is old and venerable that therefore it is right. If our forefathers lived in log cabins, that is no reason why we should not live in palatial homes; or if our ancestors were monkeys, that is no reason why we should persist in being monkeys still. If we can be men, if we can improve upon the past, I am in favor of doing it . . ." (p. 223).

Albert Hagan was more direct, if less eloquent, when he said in frustration, "Not one single reason has yet been given by any of them why a jury should remain twelve. Not one reason has been given. The reason of the opposition to the change is only based upon the ground of its antiquity. Now let us consider this in the light of the fact that we are seeking to change a rule for some reason" (p. 219).

The conflict between tradition and progress was particularly troubling to the lawyers at the convention. In the heat of the debate Clagett turned his rhetoric against a segment of the profession and drew applause. He charged, "I have seen all of these same old, ancient stick-in-the-bark legal propositions and sacrifices of substantial justice to mere legal technicality. I have seen the members of the legal profession, who ought to be the leaders in all matters of practical reform . . . fighting step by step and stage by stage, every effort to change or modify any one of these ancient traditions, hoary with time . . . until at last there has come to be a widespread conviction throughout the United States that the legal profession itself . . . constitutes one of the things that needs the greatest reformation" (p. 154).

James H. Beatty went further in criticizing the bar and argued money was at the heart of the dispute, "It is the lawyers who benefit by this heathenish system. It is by this system that we have repeated trials and new trials because juries often fail to agree. Now then, that is an advantage to the lawyers" (pp. 223–24).

The lawyers opposing reform rose to defend their tradition and their honor. John T. Morgan said of lawyers, "I believe they ought to be conservative. I believe it is right to be conservative, and I believe it is necessary that we should all be conservative in this convention in order to preserve the rights of the people" (p. 213).

James W. Reid disputed the need to reform the legal profession, and cited Clagett's own appointments at the convention as evidence. "The people of Idaho do not think so; out of this body representing Idaho, I am proud to say that nearly one-half are lawyers. In naming the twenty-five committees which my friend (Mr. Claggett) formed here, I am glad to say he did not carry out this theory, because such was his unbounded confidence in his brother lawyers that at the head of those 25 committees he put sixteen lawyers" (p. 160).

Clagett's final counter to the tradition argument was that he, not his opponents, had the best claim to being faithful to history. He offered this history, "I am not now talking about the common law as it was perverted after the Norman conquest; I am going back to the very roots of the common law as it was established by the ancient customs of our Saxon forefathers, and before the principles and ideas of the law which were brought in by the Norman Conquest had perverted to any degree whatever the English jurisprudence. What was the old common law practice with regard to trial by jury? . . . the jury should consist of twenty-three persons . . . and a verdict of the majority was the verdict of the jury" (p. 155).

Clagett explained the perversion of this ancient Saxon custom of majority rule into the common-law unanimous verdict requirement, "A unanimous verdict is itself a perversion of the old common law and came historically around in the following way. As time went on, it was found that the cases multiplied in the court. . . . It was found that a jury of twenty-three was too large and too expensive and it was cut down to sixteen, and afterwards to twelve, as a mere matter of economy. In the meantime the phrase 'It takes twelve men to make a verdict,' in other words, that it takes a majority to make a verdict, had gone into the lawbooks . . ." (p. 155).

Reid challenged Clagett's history. "The gentleman argues this question and states that the jury system had its origin in England and forgets that even in the Dicasteria of Athens this system prevailed. . . . It was in vogue in England, and not only there, but way back even to the time Cadmus invented letters, almost; because in Athens we had it; we had it in the Comitia of Rome, by the Dane, through the Scandanavian [sic] the system has been improved as experience and use suggested it, thence on down, all through the nations, before the Conqueror came to England, Edward the Third had it—in the states of Germany they had it; our American colonies inherited that great system in jurisprudence which the old world had adopted . . ." (pp. 220–21).

J. W. Poe emphasized the customary nature of the right to jury trial, "So it came down to you under their practice; that system of jurisprudence was adopted in the United States; the common law of England was the law of the land. . . . The law of custom and the common law, and the practice of the people under that law" (p. 230–31).

Whose history is right? We cannot know, for the origin of the jury trial and the use of unanimous verdicts predates known history. In many world cultures, the jury right was in practice before the art of written language developed.[12] As Reid said, the right goes "way back even to the time Cadmus invented letters."

5. The Sixth and Seventh Amendments in Idaho

THE UNITED STATES CONSTITUTION as written in 1787 guaranteed a jury trial in all criminal cases except for impeachment and mandated that the trial be held in the state where the crime occurred.[13] This right was strengthened from 1788 through 1790 by ratification of the first ten amendments, commonly known as the Bill of Rights. The Sixth Amendment provides in part, "In all criminal prosecutions, the accused shall enjoy the right to a speedy and public trial, by an impartial jury of the state and district wherein the crime shall have been committed. . . ." The Seventh Amendment spoke to the right to jury trial in civil cases. "In suits at common law, where the value in controversy shall exceed twenty dollars, the right of trial by jury, shall be preserved, and no fact tried by a jury, shall be otherwise re-examined in any court of the United States, than according to the rules of the common law."

While these sections guarantee a "jury trial" and an "impartial jury," they do not expressly provide for the number of jurors needed to make up a jury or to render a verdict. When these and other questions about the right to a jury trial have been raised in the United States Supreme Court, the justices have looked to the common-law right to a jury trial as it existed in 1787 for answers. The belief in the right to a unanimous verdict was so widespread that neither Congress nor the territories experimented with the requirement for the country's first one hundred years. At about the time of Idaho's Constitutional Convention, Utah Territory authorized a three-fourths verdict in civil cases, but the Supreme Court declared the statute unconstitutional, writing, "Now, unanimity was one of the peculiar and essential features of trial by jury at the common law. No authorities are needed to sustain this proposition."[14]

The opponents of jury reform at Idaho's convention argued these federal principles were the best system, and that the new state was bound to adhere to them in drafting its own constitution. James W. Reid, who headed up the Democratic delegates at the convention and was one of their strongest orators, gave the most impassioned argument: "Does the gentlemen [sic] remember that in 1787, when our fathers met in Philadelphia and framed the constitution of the United States, they left out the right of trial by jury in a civil case, and did not guard the right of trial by jury in criminal case particularly? What was the result? . . . the people cried out that this great right, which came down to them sacred and hallowed through the centuries, wrung from King John on the plains of Runnymeade, and which was declared one of the reasons why they separated from the mother country, and sealed their declaration with their blood for eight long years, should be put in the fundamental law, the constitution of the land" (p. 252).

J. W. Poe argued it was the "spirit and intention of the framers of the constitution of the United States" (p. 231) that every man should be guaranteed the common-law right of a jury trial. Albert Hagan said, "I do not believe in a criminal case we should touch one single hair of his head, around whom the safeguards of the constitution have always been placed—that he should be convicted without a unanimous verdict of his countrymen" (p. 240). Hagan also cited cases where it was held the right to jury trial could not be waived, and he suggested other cases. "Hasn't the Supreme Court of the United States decided that no state law can be passed where the verdict is rendered in a case where the party is charged with an infamous crime without a unanimous verdict?" (p. 244).

George Ainslie, Idaho's most well-known pioneer attorney, explained the common-law history of the jury right, and urged its merits. "The common law of England has never been adopted by the Congress of the United States, but the understanding has been that trial by jury under the constitution of the United States comprehends the common law doctrine of a trial by jury. Now if that is the meaning of the constitution, the law-makers and law givers who have presided over the inception of the laws of this nation for a century have not seen proper to adopt any amendment or legislation looking to convicting persons by a jury of less than twelve, or five-sixths, as proposed by the gentlemen here; and that is a very worthy example for us minor statesmen to imitate" (pp. 256–57).

Clagett, the champion of jury reform, took the floor to boast of the power of state sovereignty by referring to the Tenth Amendment, and to rebut his detractors. "The constitution of the United States is the organic law of the nation in a national capacity, and these amendments to the federal constitution which have been referred to here are mere limitations upon the powers to be exercised by Congress, but every power which is not specifically delegated to Congress by the national constitution, or which in the national constitution is not specifically prohibited to the states, is reserved to the states respectively or to the people by the language of that instrument itself. There is in the constitution of the United States no prohibition against a state having any such legislation as this . . ." (p. 254–5). Finally, to make his point, Clagett asserted it was as far beyond the power of the Supreme Court to interfere with Idaho's Constitution as it was "for the Shah of Persia to undertake to interfere with the Pope's decree" (p. 248).

The votes cast by the delegates make it clear that Clagett and Idaho's inherent state sovereignty won the day on the convention floor. The proposal to authorize five-sixths verdicts in misdemeanor cases passed 31 to 21, and the entire section, including the mandatory three-fourths verdict in civil matters, passed by such a wide margin, a vote count was not called for. (pp. 259–60).

6. *One Hundred Years of Experience*

IRONICALLY, one hundred years of experience has proven both Clagett and his opponents to be half wrong and half right about the effect of the Sixth and Seventh Amendments in Idaho. Today, it is commonplace for the Shah of Persia (United States Supreme Court) to interfere with the Pope's decree (Idaho's Constitution). However, even though the Supreme Court has required states to generally guarantee the right to jury trial in its courts, it has not required strict adherence to every detail of the common-law right. Reid, Poe, Hagan, and Ainslie would be disappointed to discover that the right to a unanimous verdict has become one of the details of the common-law right on which states have been permitted to experiment.

The Fourteenth Amendment provided the constitutional authority for the United States courts to insist states guarantee to their citizens most of the rights set out in the first eight amendments. The Fourteenth Amendment was ratified in 1868 as the middle of three amendments produced by the Civil War. The first sentence of the Fourteenth defines citizenship, "All persons born or naturalized in the United States . . . are citizens of the United States and of the state wherein they reside." The second sentence of the section compels states to honor the rights of United States citizens. "No state shall make or enforce any law which shall abridge the privileges or immunities of citizens of the United States; nor shall any state deprive any persons of life, liberty or property, without due process of law, nor deny to any person within its jurisdiction the equal protection of the law."

Since the earliest days of the republic, the individual rights specified in the first eight amendments guaranteed citizens' rights in dealings with the United States government. Those who drafted and debated the Fourteenth Amendment were unable to agree upon how many of these rights were to be guaranteed by state governments.[15]

This disagreement produced the general language of the amendment, which first secures the "privileges and immunities of citizens," and then guarantees "due process of law" and "the equal protection of the law."

The task of finally deciding which rights are guaranteed by the Fourteenth Amendment has fallen to the United States Supreme Court.[16] The court had its first opportunity to interpret the amendment in 1873 in *The Slaughter-House Cases*.[17] A New Orleans ordinance requiring all butchers to buy a license and do their butchering in prescribed places was challenged. Some alleged the ordinance took from them their right to make a living, a right guaranteed by the privilege and immunities clause of the Fourteenth Amendment. The court rejected the challenge and sustained the ordinance, holding the amendment was primarily concerned with the newly emancipated slaves and avoiding an interpretation that would make the court "a perpetual censor upon all legislation of the states."[18]

By the turn of the century the Court increasingly abandoned its timid, early interpretation and began to censure state laws. The most well-known case of the era is *Lochner v. New York* (1905)[19] where a state law setting 10-hour daily maximum and 60-hour weekly maximum for bakers was invalidated. From *Lochner* to the present, the court has selectively incorporated the Bill of Rights. Those rights which are so fundamental they are "implicit in the concept of ordered liberty"[20] or are "fundamental to the American scheme of justice"[21] have been incorporated. Three of the exceptional rights the Court has refused to incorporate bear directly upon Idaho's Article I § 7. The Seventh Amendment right to trial in civil cases has not been incorporated.[22] The right to a grand jury in criminal matters in the Fourth Amendment has not been incorporated.[23] Finally, the right to a unanimous verdict in criminal cases has not been incorporated.[24]

The path of the incorporation of the requirement of a unanimous verdict has been a zigzag one. Early cases held the Sixth Amendment jury right was not incorporated,[25] but *Duncan v. Louisiana* (1968)[26] rejected them and held the jury trial in criminal cases "is necessary to an Anglo-American regime of ordered liberty," and therefore guaranteed by the Fourteenth Amendment. *Duncan* and other incorporation cases decided shortly thereafter suggested all the Sixth Amendment rights, including a jury of twelve and a unanimous verdict, would be incorporated.

However, the cases that followed practiced a more selective incorporation. In *Williams v. Florida* (1970)[27] the court decided six-person state juries did not violate the Sixth and Fourteenth Amendments. In *Apodaca v. Oregon* (1972)[28] the court sustained convictions based on 11–1 and 10–2 verdicts, refusing to incorporate the requirement for a unanimous verdict. In the most recent test of these principles, *Williams* and *Apodaca* were combined. The defendant in *Burch v. Louisiana* (1979)[29] challenged a Louisiana statute that provided for conviction by five-sixths of a six-person jury for misdemeanors punishable by greater than six month's imprisonment. Justice Rehnquist, later appointed Chief Justice, wrote the opinion of the Court, which declared the statute unconstitutional. "Undoubtedly, the State has a substantial interest in reducing the time and expense. . . . But that interest cannot prevail here. . . . [V]erdicts by such juries sufficiently threaten the constitutional principles that led to the establishment of the size threshold that any countervailing interest of the State should yield."[30]

Justice Rehnquist observed that twenty-five states allowed six-person juries, but only Oklahoma and Louisiana provided for conviction by five-sixths of a six-person jury. In a warning to limits on Idaho's § 7, Rehnquist noted, "The Constitution of the State of Idaho allows, but does not require, nonunanimous six-person juries in certain circumstances; however, the Idaho criminal rules appear to require verdicts of six-person juries to be unanimous."[31]

Even though the Fourteenth Amendment has become important as a guarantee of citizens' rights in dealing with their state government, it was never mentioned on the floor of Idaho's Convention. This was no doubt because of the narrow Supreme Court interpretations of the amendment which prevailed in the summer of 1889. There is, however, an interesting reference to the broader issue of state's rights that accompanied the Civil War. George Ainslie, the Missouri Democrat who had been a party leader in the territory from the earliest days, chided Clagett for his expansive conception of state sovereignty. "We are told by all the republican newspapers and by all the republican statesmen that the state's right doctrine was a heresy and state sovereignty was politically dead. I am glad to see some leading lights of the republican party residing in this territory like prodigal sons return to the fold . . . they are in the position of trying to revive a political corpse and infuse the breath of life into by this amendment" (pp. 358–59).

Idahoans have amended the right to a jury trial guaranteed in Article I § 7 of their constitution three times during the first century. Each of these amendments has carried the state farther along the road to reform and away from tradition, the path first chosen by the delegates at the 1889 convention.

The original § 7 permitted use of a jury of fewer than twelve in misdemeanor and civil trials, *if the parties agreed in open court*. The section was amended in 1934 to require a jury of six in all misdemeanor trials and in civil actions involving not more than five hundred dollars.[32] In 1966 the section was amended to expand the category of civil trials, which required six-person juries to include all actions within the jurisdiction of courts inferior to the district court.[33] Finally, in 1982 the section was amended to permit waiver of the right to jury trial in all criminal actions; the original section had permitted waiver only in cases not involving a felony.[34]

The jury trial guarantees in § 7 have been before the Idaho Supreme Court on several occasions. In *State v. Jutila*[35] (1921) the defendants were charged with robbery. The trial court instructed the jury that five-sixths of them could convict of simple assault, an included offense, and the defendants appealed alleging a violation of Section 7. The supreme court held the statute did not authorize the instruction, and avoided the constitutional interpretation. *State v. Conner*[36] (1939) interpreted the 1934 amendment which made six-person juries mandatory for all misdemeanors. The supreme court rejected the defendant's contention that he was charged with a serious misdemeanor and therefore entitled to a jury of twelve, pointing out the amendment drew no distinction between major and minor misdemeanors.

The three-quarters verdict in civil cases has most recently been interpreted by the court in *Tillman v. Thomas*[37] (1978). Tillman brought an action against a hunting ranch and its employee for personal injuries suffered when his horse reared while crossing a boggy area during a hunting trip. In response to a special verdict form, nine jurors found the employer not liable. A different nine jurors found the employee not liable, and Tillman appealed arguing he was denied his right to a jury trial unless the same nucleus of nine jurors decided each material issue in the case. The Idaho Supreme Court reviewed the proceedings of Idaho's Constitutional Convention and concluded, "It is evident that the founders of the Idaho Constitution recognized that practical considerations concerning delay, retrials, hung juries, are important considerations in arriving at justice. . . ."[38] The court observed requiring the same nucleus of jurors would plainly result in burdensome retrials in multi-issue cases, and ruled against Tillman.

The Idaho Supreme Court has had many opportunities to define Idahoans' right to a jury trial on issues that were not raised in the constitutional convention. The earliest case was *Christensen v. Hollingsworth*[39] (1898) where the court held the section "must be read in light of the law existing at the time of the adoption of the constitution," and that the section was "not intended or designated to extend the right of trial by jury, but simply to secure that right as it existed at the date of the adoption of the constitution."[40] The court also held the right to trial by jury did not apply to equitable cases.

The most recent cases have been the most important, and the most difficult. The defendants in *State v. Creech*[41] (1983) and *State v. Sivak*[42] (1983) alleged their rights to a jury trial under the Idaho Constitution were violated when they were sentenced to death for murder by a district judge, with no participation by the jury. Justices Huntley and Bistline agreed in both cases. They stated that Idaho's Constitution should be construed to apply as it existed at the time of constitution's creation. After reviewing the relevant statutes and cases, they decided the "right of trial by jury as it existed at the time our constitution was adopted provided for jury participation in the capital sentencing process."[43] During all of the territorial period and until 1973 Idaho juries decided whether a defendant was guilty of murder in the first or second degree. In the early years the death penalty was automatic for a first-degree conviction, but in later years the jury had the option of imposing life imprisonment.

However, a majority of the court, Justices Bakes, Shepard and Donaldson, thought the section was not violated. They had a very different understanding of the historical role of the jury. In their view, the jury's decision on first or second degree had only an "incidental effect" on the sentence, and therefore the jury was not "an integral part of the sentencing process." They said the argument of Huntley and Bistline "basically misconstrues the distinction between the factfinding function of determining the degree of crime . . . and the sentencing function."[44] Justice Bistline described the majority's analysis as "pure sophistry at its best," accused the majority of not having read his opinion, and said, "It cannot in good conscience be argued that . . . it was not the jury which made the life and death decision."[45]

More recently, in *State v. Bennion*[46] (1986) the court was asked to declare a section of the Idaho Traffic Infractions Act, which defined an "infraction" as "a civil public offense . . . for which there is no right to a trial by jury . . . ,"[47] unconstitutional because it violated the guarantee in § 7 that "the right of trial by jury shall remain inviolate. . . ." Justice Huntley, writing for the court, noted the statute did not violate the Sixth Amendment of the U.S. Constitution because the Sixth Amendment does not apply to petty crimes or offenses. The most important factor in determining whether an offense is petty is the severity of the penalty, and the maximum penalty involved in the offense before the court was a fine of $100. However, Sam Bennion, who had been charged with running a red light, argued the Idaho Constitution provided greater protection than the Sixth Amendment.

According to conventional rules of interpretation, Sam Bennion was right. The Idaho Constitution creates only criminal and civil actions in the courts and "infraction" is clearly defined as criminal.[48] Over the years the court has frequently stated § 7 preserved the right to jury trial as it existed in the common law and under the territorial statutes when the Idaho Constitution was adopted. The court has also noted that it had "a duty to protect the people's rights as enumerated in the Idaho and United States Constitutions from legislative encroachment,"[49] and that "the right to a jury trial is a fundamental right, and must be guarded jealously."[50] Since territorial statutes were revised in 1887 on the eve of statehood and clearly provided for a jury trial in every criminal offense, felony or misdemeanor, it appeared Sam Bennion had a right to trial by jury.[51]

However, unlike his opinions in *Creech* and *Sivak*, Justice Huntley failed to jealously guard Bennion's fundamental right from legislative encroachment. While the idea of a living, changing constitution has generally been used to argue for expansion of individual rights, Justice Huntley used it to argue for their contraction. He cited the well-known comment by Justice Holmes that a constitution is "an organism" and that each case had to be decided "in light of our whole experience and not merely in that of what was said a hundred years ago."[52] Huntley then held that time had created a class of petty offenses where no right to a jury trial was guaranteed. The court stated summary proceedings were permissible if the sanction had been decriminalized. Imprisonment is always to be considered criminal, and fines may be if the the legislature had a punitive intent. Punitive intent is to be determined by the size of the fine, the loss of other privileges, the stigma and the potential for arrest and detention. The court concluded the one hundred-dollar fine facing Bennion was reasonable and remedial rather than punitive. He had, therefore, no right to a jury trial.

The *Bennion* case is but the last chapter in Idaho's one hundred years of jury reform. Writing the first chapter of this reform was one of William H. Clagett's most enduring contributions to Idaho's Constitution. Clagett would be pleased that Idaho citizens have perpetuated his great enterprise by amending their constitution, and that Idaho courts have strengthened it through their interpretations.

Notes

1. 1 Idaho Code 78.

2. Bakken, Gordon Morris. *Rocky Mountain Constitution Making, 1850–1912.* Westport, Conn.: Greenwood Press, 1987, pp. 25–28.

3. *Illustrated History of North Idaho.* Spokane: Western Historical Publishing Company, 1903, pp. 1066–67; Goodwin, C.C. *As I Remember Them.* Salt Lake City: Special Committee of the Salt Lake Commercial Club, 1913, pp. 137–39; Moxley, W. A. "Builders of the West–A Human Interest Story of Incidents in the Life of Wm. H. Clagett, Related By the Late Frank W. Beane." *Daily News-Times and Democrat* (Goshen, Indiana) 18 Feb. 1935; Stoll, W. T. *Silver Strike; The True Story of Silver Mining in the Coeur d'Alenes.* Boston: Little Brown, 1932. Reprint edition, Moscow: University of Idaho Press, 1991; Wells, Merle W. "The Admission of the State of Idaho." *Twenty-seventh Biennial Report* (1944), p. 63.

4. The debates at the Idaho Constitutional Convention are reported in Hart, I. W., ed. *Proceedings and Debates of the Constitutional Convention of Idaho 1889.* 2 vols. Caldwell: Caxton Printers, Ltd., 1912. These volumes are paginated consecutively, and all page references in the text of this chapter are to them.

5. Ida Clagett to C. J. Brosnan, University of Idaho Special Collections, Brosnan Collection, Group 18, Box 1, Clagett file.

6. Goodwin, C.C. *As I Remember Them,* p. 137.

7. Brown, Richard M. "Legal and Behavioral Perspectives on American Vigilantism." In Kermit L. Hall, ed., *Crime and Criminal Law.* New York: Garland Publishing Co., 1987; Caughey, John W. "Their Majesties the Mob: Vigilantes Past and Present." *Pacific Historical Review* 26(1957):217–34; Dimsdale, Thomas J. *The Vigilantes of Montana.* 3rd ed. Helena: State Publishing Co., 1940; Gard, Wayne *Frontier Justice.* Norman: University of Oklahoma Press, 1949; Jordan, Philip D. *Frontier Law and Order.* Lincoln: University of Nebraska Press, 1970; Valentine, Alan *Vigilante Justice.* New York: Reynal, 1956.

8. McConnell, William J. *Early History of Idaho.* Caldwell: Caxton Printers, Ltd., 1913, p. 207.

9. Hawley, James H., ed. *History of Idaho.* Chicago: Clarke Publishing Co., 1920, vol. 1, p. 126.

10. Stoll, W. T. *Silver Strike,* p. 92.

11. Ibid., p. 151.

12. Devlin, Patrick Baron. *Trial by Jury.* London: Sweet & Maxwell, Ltd., 1956; Frankfurter & Corcoran, "Petty Federal Offenses and the Constitutional Guaranty of Trial by Jury." *Harvard Law Review* 39(1926):917; Forsyth, William. *History of Trial by Jury.* Los Angeles: J. W. Parker & Son, 1852; Thayer, J. *A Preliminary Treatise on Evidence at the Common Law.* Boston: Little Brown & Co., 1898; Wells, Charles L. "The Origin of the Petty Jury." *L.Q.Rev.* 27(1911):347.

13. Art. 3, §2, cl. 3.

14. *American Pub. Co. v. Fisher,* 166 U.S. 464, p. 468 (1897).

15. For the argument that the drafters of the Fourteenth Amendment did not intend to include all of the Bill of Rights see Fairman, Charles. "Does the Fourteenth Amendment Incorporate the Bill of Rights?" 2 *Stanford Law Review* 5(1949). The argument for intent to incorporate all of the Bill of Rights has been just as forcefully made in Crosskey, "Charles Fairman, Legislative History and the Constitutional Limits on State Authority." 22 *University of Chicago Law Review* 1(1954).

16. See generally Tribe, L. *American Constitutional Law.* Mineola, N.Y.: The Foundation Press, 1988, pp. 546–87.

17. 83 U.S. (16 Wall.) 36 (1873).

18. Ibid. at 78.

19. 198 U.S. 45, 25 S.C. 539, 49 L.Ed. 937 (1905).

20. *Palko v. Connecticut*, 302 U.S. 319, 325 S.Ct. 149, 82 L.Ed. 288 (1937).

21. *Duncan v. Louisiana*, 391 U.S. 145, 88 S.Ct. 1444, 20 L.Ed.2d 491 (1968).

22. *Minneapolis & St. Louis R.R. Co. v. Bombolis*, 241 U.S. 211, 36 S.Ct. 595, 60 L.Ed. 961 (1916); *Melancon v. McKeithen*, 345 F.Supp. 1025 (E.D. La. 1972), aff'd 409 U.S. 943, 93 S.Ct. 289, 34 L.Ed.2d (1973).

23. *Hurtado v. California*, 110 U.S. 516, 4 S.Ct. 111, 28 L.Ed. 232 (1884).

24. *Apodaca v. Oregon*, 406 U.S. 404, 92 S.Ct. 111, 28 L.Ed.2d 184 (1972).

25. *Maxwell v. Dow*, 176 U.S. 581, 20 S.Ct. 448, 44 L.Ed. 597 (1900); *Palko v. State of Connecticut*, 302 U.S. 319, 58 S.Ct. 149, 82 L.Ed. 288 (1937); *Snyder v. Commonwealth of Massachusetts*, 291 U.S. 97, 54 S.Ct. 330, 78 L.Ed. 674 (1934).

26. 391 U.S. 145, 88 S.Ct. 1444, 20 L.Ed.2d 491 (1968).

27. 399 U.S. 78, 90 S.Ct. 1893, 26 L.Ed.2d 446 (1970).

28. 406 U.S. 404, 92 S.Ct. 1628, 32 L.Ed.2d 184 (1972).

29. 441 U.S. 130, 99 S.Ct. 1623, 60 L.Ed.2d 96 (1979).

30. Ibid., p. 139, 99 S.Ct. at 1628, 60 L.Ed.2d at 104.

31. Ibid., fn. 12, p. 138, 99 S.Ct., p. 1628, 60 L.Ed.2d p. 104.

32. 1933 Idaho Sess Laws 468, S.J.R. No. 1, ratified at the general election in November 1934.

33. 1965 Idaho Sess Laws 952, S.J.R. No. 6, ratified at the general election in November 1966.

34. 1982 Idaho Sess Laws 931, S.J.R. No. 112, ratified at the general election in November 1982.

35. 34 Idaho 595, 202 Pac. 566.

36. 59 Idaho 695, 89 P.2d 197.

37. 99 Idaho 569, 585 P.2d 1280.

38. Ibid. at 572, p. 1283.

39. 6 Idaho 87, 53 P. 211.

40. Ibid. at 93, p. 212.

41. 105 Idaho 362, 670 P.2d 463.

42. 105 Idaho 900, 674 P.2d 396.

43. 105 Id. 362, p. 376, 670 P.2d 463, p. 477.

44. 105 Idaho 900, at 904, 674 P.2d 396, at 400.

45. Ibid. at 909, p. 405.

46. 112 Idaho 32, 730 P.2d 952 (1986).

47. Idaho Code 49–3401(3).

48. "[T]here shall be in this state but one form of action for the enforcement or protection of private rights or the redress of private wrongs, which shall be denominated a civil action; and every action prosecuted by the people of the state as a party, against a person charged with a public offense, for the punishment of the same, shall be termed a criminal action." Art. V, § 1.

49. *Thompson v. Hagan*, 96 Idaho 19, at 24, 523 P.2d 1365, at 1371 (1974).

50. *Farmer v. Loofbourrow*, 75 Idaho 88, at 94, 267 P.2d 113, at 116 (1954).

51. 1887 Rvsd. Stat. § 7358.

52. *Missouri v. Holland*, 252 U.S. 416, at 433, 40 S.Ct. 382, at 383, 64 L.Ed. 641 (1920).

4.

Eminent Domain and
Private Property

1. The Course of the Debate

PRIVATE PROPERTY is the legal right to use and dispose of property according to the wish of its owner. Eminent domain is the power of government to appropriate private property for public use by paying just compensation, regardless of the wish of the owner. Article I, § 14 of the Idaho Constitution attempts to balance the two ideals.

The section came to the floor of the Idaho Constitutional Convention for debate late in the afternoon on July 18, the twelfth session. The morning had been spent fighting out the innovative jury provisions championed by William H. Clagett. The declaration of rights committee then presented the convention with an even more radical innovation.

The committee recommended expanding the power of eminent domain so that it could be used for *private* as well as public purposes. The committee proposed the following language:

> Private property shall not be taken or damaged for public *or private* use without just compensation. Such compensation shall be ascertained in such manner as may be prescribed by law, and until the same shall be paid to the owner, or into the court for the owner, the property shall not be needlessly disturbed nor the proprietary rights of the owner divested. *Private property*

shall not be taken for private use, unless by consent of the owner, except for private ways of necessity and for reservoirs, drains, flumes or ditches on or across the lands of others, for agricultural, mining, milling, domestic or sanitary purposes (p. 295)[1] (emphasis added).

This proposal to expand eminent domain and diminish private property by authorizing private takings was contrary to the principles that had governed American constitutional law from colonial time. In 1889 it was the general understanding of common-law principles that private takings were not permitted under state constitutitons or the Fifth Amendment to the United States Constitution.

States and territories in the arid West tried to except themselves from this tradition. Colorado had provided in its 1876 constitution for private takings of easements to aid mining and irrigation development; California passed a similar statute, which was later declared unconstitutional; and, Idaho Territory had provided for limited takings pursuant to authority granted by Congress. The Idaho declaration of rights committee borrowed Colorado's language for § 14. The first and last sentences of the proposed Idaho section were taken verbatim from §§ 14 and 15 of Article II of the Colorado Constitution.

Three amendments were proposed as soon as the committee's section was read to the committee of the whole. Aaron F. Parker (D-Idaho) proposed the first amendment when he rose to defend private property. He prefered to authorize takings of any sort only by the consent of the owner. He argued that Article I, § II, which guaranteed the right to possess and enjoy property, was all that was needed to insure the individual property rights of Idaho citizens. His motion drew little support and was defeated by voice vote (pp. 291–93; 308).

Albert Hagan (D-Kootenai), another defender of private property, was willing to concede property could be taken for public purposes, but there drew the line. As a second amendment to the committee report, he proposed to strike that portion of the report which authorized private takings, arguing that private takings were antirepublican and would be disastrous to the miners. After a brief debate his motion was passed 32 to 7 (pp. 288–91, 294–307).

While both Parker and Hagan were openly critical of the committee for failing to protect private property, Drew W. Standrod (D-Oneida) thought private property was too secure and proposed a third amendment. He argued the committee did not go far enough in expanding the power of eminent domain. He wanted to expand the purposes for which private takings could be used, and to declare private takings a public purpose. Historically, courts had limited takings by insisting the purpose be public. By declaring private takings public uses, Standrod hoped to disarm the courts and render them unable to protect private property.

After passing the Hagan amendment, the convention turned to Standrod's proposal. Suddenly, there was a radical change in the direction of the debate. After a brief discussion Willis Sweet (R-Latah) suggested the section be referred to the irrigation committee because he thought they might be able to propose "some arrangement by which the lands can be irrigated and not interfere with the industries and the right of property in the state" (p. 310). Other delegates claimed the mines and mining committee had an interest in the question, so Sweet moved to refer the matter to a joint meeting of the mines and irrigation committees. The convention passed the motion and adjourned for the day so the two committees could meet (p. 313).

Although we have no record of the joint committee meeting, an idea of what happened can be inferred from comments made on the convention floor the following morning. Drew W. Standrod was probably the most dominant figure in the joint committee meeting. Standrod was born in Rockcastle, Kentucky, in 1859 and moved to Malad with his father in the mid-1870s. He was admitted to the bar in 1880 and elected district attorney of Oneida County in 1888. After the convention he served as district judge for the fifth district from 1891–99. He was defeated in his campaign for the supreme court in 1898 and for governor in 1900. In 1895 he moved to Pocatello, where he became a prominent banker.[2] Standrod, the first delegate to call for expanding the eminent domain power, was on the mining committee, and he was chosen by the joint committees to present their proposal to the convention. Standrod was also a strong supporter of the preference for irrigation over manufacturing that was recommended by the irrigation committee. For this work he must be recognized as the legal father of irrigation in Idaho.

The joint committee meeting appears to be the most important work of the mines and mining committee. Except for Standrod, no prominent convention delegates sat on the Mines Committee even though mining interests were undoubtedly the second most powerful economic group present, next to lawyers. Approval of private takings in the constitution was essential for continued mining development. Miners were also very concerned about the principle of taxation to be applied to mines, which was within the jurisdiction of the revenue and finance committee (pp. 1707–69). The strategy of the mines and mining committee was to get the provisions it needed inserted in the articles of other committees. As a result, this committee was the only one that did not report an article to the convention (p. 1603).

The mining delegates at the convention were divided on the eminent domain vs. private property controversy. Albert Hagan said, "as a representative of the mining interests of the territory, it is my duty to speak out" (p. 304) and, referring to the section, argued that "the mining interests of this country would be damaged by it and embarrassed in every regard" (p. 289).

On the other hand, there were many influential mining delegates just as adamantly in favor of a strong eminent domain power. William H. Clagett (R-Shoshone), who had been a mining lawyer for thirty years, argued, "We have an immense mining interest here that has got to be protected, and we need the incorporation of some such provision . . . in order that they may have mining easements upon their placer ground and condemn them when necessary" (p. 310). Clagett said the section "was absolutely necessary for the miners, and for the poorer miners rather than the richer ones" (p. 1619). Weldon B. Heyburn, another advocate for the section, had arrived in the Coeur d'Alenes in the winter of 1883 about the same time as Clagett. In 1884 he and others recorded the Polaris, Southern Cross, and Omega lode claims. He was one of several who represented Cooper and Peck in the Bunker Hill and Sullivan lawsuit and in 1892 represented the Mine Owners' Association by getting an injunction against union activities.[3] While Heyburn quibbled with the language of the section, as he often did at the convention, in the end he supported expanded private takings and wanted to make certain mining was clearly included (pp. 325–26; 346–50). James H. Beatty (R-Alturas) spoke for the Wood River mining region and also supported private takings because he thought it was essential for development of the mining interests in the territory (p. 1614).

Perhaps the split in the mining delegates reflects a more fundamental division of delegate sentiment on the private takings question. The champions of private property were the mining pioneers from the small owner-worked placer mines discovered in the territory's streambeds in the 1860s and, to a lesser extent, the '70s. The champions of eminent domain were newcomers to the territory. They were engaged in quartz mining, which required great capital and development to be productive.[4] Large-scale irrigation development, which was just coming into Idaho, was the other source of strong support for private takings. The controversy between private property and private takings was a conflict between entrepreneurial pioneers and capitalist newcomers.

Willis Sweet entirely ignored the declaration of rights committee in his proposal for a joint meeting, despite the fact that the section was within its jurisdiction and later appeared in the declaration of rights article. Not surprisingly, the irrigation and mining committees resolved the conflict between private property and the need for development by ignoring private property. The shield of protection for private property that had been proposed by the declaration of rights committee was hammered into a sword of power for the state. The language reported from the joint committee meeting shifted the focus of the section from a protection of rights to an authorization of power. It stated:

> The necessary use of lands for the construction of reservoirs, or storage basins, for the purpose of irrigation, or for rights of way for the construction of canals, ditches, flumes or pipes, to convey water to the place of use for any useful, beneficial or necessary purpose, or for drainage; or for the drainage of mines, or the working thereof, by means of roads, railroads, tramways, cuts, tunnels, shafts, hoisting works, dumps or other necessary means to their complete development, or any other use necessary to the complete development of the material resources of the state, or the preservation of the health of its inhabitants, is hereby declared to be a public use.

> Private property may be taken for a public use, but not until a just compensation, to be ascertained in the manner prescribed by law, shall be paid therefore (pp. 317–18).

Once this provision had been worked out by the committees, it had the support of the most powerful delegates and was destined to become part of the constitution. Standrod introduced the new section at the opening of the thirteenth session on July 19 and made a long argument on its behalf. Clagett and John T. Morgan (R-Bingham) also argued on its behalf. In strong opposition to the proposed section, the defenders of private property made several attempts to limit the new language. They proposed to strike the broad "or any other use" language and limit the takings to "necessary" takings. But neither attempt was successful, and the report of the joint committees was adopted (pp. 317–68).

This argument before the committee of the whole was replayed when the section came before the convention. Orlando B. Batten (D-Alturas) moved to substitute the original declaration of rights committee language for that of the joint committees. James W. Reid (D-Nez Perce) sought to narrow the section by striking "for any useful, beneficial or necessary purpose." George Ainslie (D-Boise) tried to narrow it by striking "or any other use necessary to the complete development of the material resources of the state." However, all these proposals were rejected and the section written by the joint committee meeting was adopted (pp. 1596–1633).

There was one important difference between the arguments that took place before the committee of the whole and in the convention. Albert Hagan from Kootenai county was not in the convention session to argue against private takings. Orlando Batten reported that after the vote of the committee of the whole, Hagan "left in voicing the spirit of disgust . . . and said he could not approve of the constitution with any provision like this embodied in it." James Beatty suggested Hagan had gone home to go fishing, but Alexander Mayhew quickly seconded Batten, reporting Hagan said "he did not care about being a member of a constitutional convention that had this provision in it" (p. 1597). Whether disgusted or fishing, Hagan did not return to the convention and did not sign the constitition (p. 2090). Given the strong support in favor of private takings, his absence did not matter in the end.

Section 14 was the third novel section put into Article I of the Idaho Constitution. Each innovation, the guarantee of religious liberty in § 4, the right to a jury trial in § 7 and the private takings in § 14, diminished the rights of the individual and expanded the power of state government. In each case, the Idaho Convention went farther than any previous state convention.

2. Private Property's Advocate

AARON F. PARKER was private property's greatest advocate on the convention floor. Parker was born in Wells, England, in 1856 and went to sea at a young age. He came to Idaho in 1876 from San Francisco and edited newspapers in Lewiston and the Coeur d'Alenes before establishing the *Idaho County Free Press* in Grangeville in the summer of 1886. Parker had mining interests, promoted railroads and real estate, and was the leading proponent of the first north-south wagon road to link the state. His proposed road had been approved by the 1888 territorial legislature, even though the Constitutional Convention was unwilling to grant his request that the road be built into the constitution.

Parker's proposal that "private property shall not be taken or damaged for public or private use, unless by consent of the owner," if passed, would have nearly extinguished the power of eminent domain. Land for roads and other public projects would have been difficult to acquire, except at exhorbitant prices. For Parker the controlling principle was in § 1 of the declaration of rights article which proclaimed, "All men are by nature free and equal and have certain inalienable rights, among which are enjoying and defending life and liberty, acquiring, possessing and protecting property, pursuing happiness and securing safety." Parker argued the proposed § 14 took away from these rights, and accused the convention of being "in the position of a cow which gives a bucket of good milk and then kicks it over" (p. 291). Parker sought to "curb the omnipotence of the state" and to protect what a person has earned by his own labor so that he "is not the subject of arbitrary power, nor ought he to be the victim of a majority." If the state took property only as a matter of convenience to private business, it was "departing from its true sphere of action, and transcending its lawful authority" (pp. 292–93).

Parker cited Cooley's *Blackstone's Commentaries* (4th ed.) to support his argument (pp. 292–93). However, Parker's reliance was misplaced. Blackstone did not endorse his contention that property can be taken only with the consent of the owner. In fact, Blackstone clearly recognized that the power of eminent domain, properly exercised, is superior to the right of the property owner to refuse to sell. Perhaps Parker should be excused for mis-citing Blackstone because he had just arrived at the convention the morning of the debate on § 14 and stated he had not "not had time to collect my ideas" (p. 291).

However, even with more time Parker would have found no authority in the common law for his proposition that a sovereign could take private property only with the consent of the owner. The power to take private property for public use has always been a given, the right to compensation has been the issue. The phrase "eminent domain" apparently first appeared in print in *De Jure Belli et Pacis* by Hugo Grotius, published in 1625. Grotius wrote, "The property of subjects is under the eminent domain of the state, so that the state or he who acts for it may use and even alienate and destroy such property . . . for ends of public utility . . . the subject ought to receive, if possible, a just satisfaction for the loss he suffers, out of the common stock."[5] William Clagett summarized the history of the doctrine for the convention when he said, the state "may take the private lands of individuals for public use without compensation; that is the original theory of the law of eminent domain" (p. 328).

Passage of the Fifth Amendment did a great deal to secure the right to just compensation. The amendment states, in part, "nor shall private property be taken for public use, without just compensation." Even though common-law courts generally required just compensation,[6] only Massachusetts and Vermont included compensation clauses in their state constitutions. Compensation clauses were rarely included in colonial charters. Even though no state had mentioned a compensation clause during the ratification debates concerning the Bill of Rights, James Madison included one in the draft submitted to Congress on June 8, 1789. Even though Madison's "reasons for proposing it have never been satisfactorily explained"[7], his proposal became the Fifth Amendment.

Although the right to just compensation had become much more secure by the summer of 1889, nobody thought the property owner could frustrate the sovereign's eminent domain power by withholding consent, and Parker's proposal was defeated by voice vote (p. 308).

3. Neccessity vs. Tradition

THE PROPONENTS OF THE PRIVATE TAKING PROVISION § 14 were in no better position than Parker when it came to finding precedent to support their plan for private takings. No case law supporting private takings existed, and the reference to "public use" in the Fifth Amendment incorporated the common-law doctrine, which prohibited private takings. The United States Supreme Court condemned private takings as early as 1798 when Justice Chase wrote in *Calder v. Bull* that no statute could be constitutional that attempted "to take property from A and give it to B."[8] A popular treatise on eminent domain widely used in 1889 stated, "As between individuals, no necessity however great, no exigency however imminent, no improvement however valuable, no refusal however unneighborly, no obstinacy however unreasonable, no offers of compensation however extravagant, can compel or require a man to part with one inch of his estate."[9] Albert Hagan summarized this precedent on the floor of the convention when he said, "I do not know any state in the Union that has any such provision, that private property—my property, shall be taken for the benefit of my neighbor" (p. 288).

The private takings proponents did have a few examples to point to. The declaration of rights committee had based its recommendation upon Article II, §§ 14 and 15 of the Colorado Constitution. In addition, the California legislature had authorized private takings by statute, but the California Supreme Court struck down the law in *Consolidated Channel Co. V. Central Pac. R. Co.* (1876).[10] Congress also permitted some territorial experiments with private takings to aid mining development when it enacted an early mining law in 1866. It stated, "The local legislature of any state or territory may provide rules for working mines involving easements, drainage, and other necessary means to their complete development."[11] Pursuant to this authority, the Idaho territorial legislature authorized the exercise of eminent domain for a broad list of public purposes, including: "canals, ditches, flumes, aqueducts and pipes, for public transportation, supplying mines, and farming neighborhoods with water."[12]

None of these earlier experiments were as far-reaching or comprehensive as the proposal of the mines and irrigation committees. These committees proposed to make eminent domain available to any industry that would aid development of the new state. The committees also would greatly expand the types of easements and property interests that could be taken; and finally, they sought to declare them all a public use to avoid review in the courts. Even though its section was inspired by Colorado's, Idaho went its own way on the question of judicial review. Idaho omitted the last phrase of Article II, § 15, of the Colorado Constitution which states, "The question whether the contemplated use be really public shall be a judicial question, and determined as such without regard to any legislative assertion that the use is public."

Standrod and his supporters were not deterred by the absence of precedent. They conceded the power proposed was novel and extraordinary, but felt necessity compelled it. John L. Morgan represented Bingham County, where irrigation was most developed. He argued, "It is an extraordinary power, I grant it, and we should be careful in granting extraordinary powers, but it is a necessity which exists in this country and without which the country cannot exist. We must give this country up and let it go back to desert unless we can do this very thing. If we can't do it, then this country as a country cannot exist" (p. 344).

Clagett added his support, "This provision . . . is absolutely necessary, unless we want to leave the whole domain of this state practically undeveloped" (p. 296). Standrod agreed, "This country has got to be irrigated. A man has to have his ditches and flumes in order to procure water. I do not believe there is a gentleman here but would willingly admit that there must be some law providing for this necessity" (p. 296). Perhaps John S. Gray (R-Ada) summarized best the committee's argument, "I think the law must yield,—even the stubborness of the law must yield, for the necessities of a country like this" (p. 299).

Orlando Batten tried to rebut the contention that they were living under a condition of things that required invading private rights. He said, "It is a flimsy argument because it is not grounded upon anything solid or substantial. It is an argument . . . – *ex necessitate rei*–from the necessity of the thing; and this sort of arguments [sic] are negative arguments, not grounded upon anything firm or solid that will appeal strongly to the reason of man." In his view eminent domain was not the best solution, and he concluded, "What we seek to attain by this section can be equally attained, just as effectively attained, by the old method of an understanding with your neighbor–an agreement with him" (p. 1599).

The interplay between tradition and the necessity of conditions in the development of law on the frontier has been of great interest to observers of western legal history.[13] Some have seen the physical and social conditions on the frontier as the distinctive force in legal developments. For example, James H. Beatty, a convention delegate, wrote as a member of the territorial supreme court shortly after the convention, "When, from among the most energetic and enterprising classes of the east, that enormous tide of emigration poured into the west . . . the new inhabitants were without law, but they quickly recognized that each man should not be a law unto himself. . . . They established their local customs and rules for their government in the use of water and land. They found a new condition of things."[14]

Frederick Jackson Turner is no doubt the best-known advocate of the frontier thesis, the notion that necessity and innovation on the frontier prevailed over tradition.

His paper "The Significance of the Frontier in American History," read to the American Historical Association in 1893, remains today the beginning point for discussion. Turner said there, "The peculiarity of American institutions is, the fact that they have been compelled to adapt themselves to the changes of an expanding people–to the changes involved in crossing a continent, in winning a wilderness, and in developing at each area of this progress out of the primitive economic and political conditions of the frontier into the complexity of city life."[15]

Many writers have accepted Turner's general thesis and sought to accumulate evidence. Roscoe Pound, an important American legal scholar, confirmed the influence of the frontier on civil and criminal procedure and upon the liberty of contract.[16] Frederick L. Paxson qualified his opinion but agreed with Turner in his *History of the American Frontier*,[17] while Walter Prescott Webb detailed the influence of the arid plains on water and land law in *The Great Plains*.[18] Other scholarship has examined the development of range law,[19] criminal justice,[20] mining law[21] and water law in Colorado.[22]

On the other hand, a number of observers have examined Turner's thesis, found the evidence lacking, and concluded that tradition and precedent were the prevailing influences in legal development in the West. William Wirt Blume did extensive reserach on legal developments in Michigan during its territorial period and concluded the critical influences were "the various schemes of colonial government" and not frontier conditions nor the pioneer spirit.[23] Blume joined with Elizabeth G. Brown to study the Turner thesis in the territorial courts. They concluded, on balance, that tradition was the most important influence, but did find evidence of the influence of the frontier on mining and water law and court procedures. The studies also found tendencies to favor codifications and adaptation of laws rather than adherence to precedent because of a superstitious respect.[24] Other scholars have found little support for Turner's emphasis upon the influence of the frontier in the old Northwest, particularly Indiana and Illinois,[25] and in the new Southwest.[26] Finally, research on criminal justice on the frontier has tended to diminish the role of the frontier. The subjects studied have included the court of common pleas in Wayne County, Michigan,[27] law enforcement in general,[28] "Wild Bill" Hickok in particular,[29] and vigilantism.[30]

The 1890 census marked the end of the frontier for Frederick Jackson Turner.[31] It is not an accident that that same year marks the end of the territorial period for Idaho and five other states in the west. So, what can be said of Turner's frontier thesis in light of the debates at the Idaho Constitutional Convention?

On the face of it, adoption of Article I, § 14 is an obvious example of the influence of frontier conditions. The convention approved an innovative and extensive private takings clause, known to be in violation of traditional common-law principles, but thought to be necessary because of the arid conditions within the territory. Upon closer examination, however, § 14 is actually the exception that proves the general rule. Loyalty to tradition was the greatest difficulty that had to be overcome by those promoting the innovation, and it was the animating force behind most sections adopted at the convention. With a few exceptions, like § 14, Idaho's founders did not reinvent, or even forge, a new constitutional wheel. They looked, rather, to the constitutions of other states, and of the United States. In the end one must conclude, "The degree of innovation and modification in the region was greater than postulated by anti-Turnerians but was not as sweeping as Turner claimed."[32]

4. People, Courts, and Monopolists

THE POWER OF EMINENT DOMAIN enjoyed first by the king and then the independent states of the Union has become more and more limited during the course of common-law development. These limitations have expanded citizens' rights to enjoy and dispose of private property. The courts have been instrumental in this development. Eminent domain had been limited by courts, requiring due process of law and compensation long before those rights became embedded in charters, statutes or constitutions. Throughout the nineteenth century, after the rights to due process and just compensation became recognized guarantees in the federal and state constitutions, courts continued to review and confine the plans and schemes of legislative and executive branches who wished to appropriate the property of citizens under the power of eminent domain.

Drew Standrod's proposal was a bold exception to this principle. Both his amendment and the one he brought back from the joint committee meeting sought to declare private takings public uses. By doing this, he hoped to make the convention and not the courts the arbiter in the struggle between eminent domain and private property.

A number of delegates questioned the authority of the convention to define "public use." None stated the question more succinctly than G. W. King (D-Shoshone). King was a lawyer who had turned to mining when he lost his hearing, and the oldest delegate at the convention. He asked, "What I want to understand from these learned men is, who is to determine what is a public use. . . . Some of these men learned in the law may tell me if they will what is a public use and who decides what is a public use, whether it is the courts or whether it is the people of the state in their convention" (p. 350).

In the end the learned men were unable to answer King's question because they differed both in their answers and their theories. Standrod, Heyburn, Clagett and Morgan claimed the convention had the power to define "public use." Standrod introduced his amendment stating his purpose to "declare what a public purpose is, in order to settle it in the courts." In his view, the courts refusal to allow private takings had "given rise to more litigation and more trouble in trying to irrigate lands in sections of the country such as this, than anything else" (pp. 295–96). His argument relied upon bold assertion rather than reason and explanation. He challenged, "It certainly will not be contended that this convention has not the power—that the state has not the power to prescribe or define what a public use is.. . " (p. 324). Heyburn's claim was similar, "I believe that this convention and that the people of this state represented in this convention, have the right to say that private property may be taken for these uses" (p. 349).

Clagett's approach was more metaphysical. For him the issue was not whether the property was owned by the public and put to a public use, but whether an amorphous "public interest" was being secured. He denied there was a taking of private property for anybody's private benefit. "It is simply the subjection of private property to public control, in the interest and for the purpose of promoting the development of the state and securing the welfare of its people; that is all" (pp. 332–33).

The power of railroads to condemn right-of-ways provided the controlling principle and example. Clagett suggested the railroads were the agents of the state, and that their power to condemn derived from the public benefit to be derived, not the public purpose to which the property was being devoted. Clagett argued rhetorically, "Why is it a public use to take a man's land and give the use of it to a railroad corporation for transporting passengers? Is it because all men may ride on it as they choose? Not at all. It is because thereby the public interests will be provided for and the public benefit secured" (p. 332).

Clagett had an equally abstract answer to the question of who had the authority to determine whether a particular use benefited the public. In Clagett's view, there was a "sovereign power of the state" embodied in the constitution. He answered King, "as to in whom is lodged the power to determine what is a public use, I will say that it is lodged in the sovereign power of the State" (p. 353). When questioned by Heyburn, "Can the state delegate that power to the judiciary?," Clagett explained, "The powers of every state . . . are divided up between three co-ordinate departments. When you speak of regulation by the state, you speak of regulation by legislative authority. The functions of the judiciary are merely interpretative. They neither can make laws nor limit laws; they interpret the law as they find it. The constitution of the state tells the legislature how far they can go and what they may do. In pursuance of that power that is delegated by the sovereign to the legislature, laws are passed. . . Of course the people can abolish the legislative department altogether if they choose . . ." (p. 354).

Morgan offered a different theory of the power to declare public uses. He explained the federal constitution was one of enumerated powers, "a grant by the sovereign people of all the states to the federal government to do certain things." By contrast, state constitutions assumed inherent rather than enumerated powers. He explained, "the constitution of the state is a limitation of power; the power resides in the people. The legislature of the state can do anything unless it is restrained by its constitution." Like Clagett, Morgan argued, "All power resides in the people of the state; within the sovereignty of the state, the state can do anything," unless restrained by the constitution (p. 343).

Five other learned men in the law took the convention floor to argue that only the courts, and not the convention, had the authority to define public use. They were Ainslie, Beatty, Hagan, Batten and Woods. The five complained about the deceitful and misleading character of the language proposed for § 14. Ainslie complained that calling a private taking a public use was "nothing but a sugar-coated pill" (p. 358) or like saying "two and two make two, instead of two and two make four" (p. 294). Beatty questioned, "Can you by any declaration make a thing different from what it is" (p. 309). Hagan said the language amounted to gilded pills, "They give us a dose of medicine; they expect, because they gave it with some covering, that we can't taste it; at present we have not taken the medicine" (p. 338). Batten accused the convention of passing a pious fraud, declaring, "The primary object of this scheme is really to deprive a man of his . . . property . . . under the specious pretext that it is being taken for a public use. Now that to my notion is tantamount to the old idea of pious fraud" (p. 356).

Beatty challenged, "Can you by saying that this property which is actually taken – private property taken for private use – by declaring that it is a public use, change the facts? . . . Can you by any declaration make a thing different from what it is? . . . I cannot conceive that it does . . ." (p. 309).

Both those supporting and those opposing proposed § 14 accused their opponents of aiding monopolies, to the detriment of the people. Clagett argued for § 14, saying "No man should be permitted to stand like a dog in a manger, simply because he happens to have possession of adjoining property . . . and levy blackmail upon the industries of the country" (p. 298). On another occasion Clagett said, "If you do not put such a provision as this in the constitution, you will be hung up by the holidays, so far as the complete development of all the resources of this state is concerned. Under the old constitution of the state of California they had that provision, prohibiting the taking of private property for anything except public uses, and what was the result? We saw how the monopolies grew up . . ." (p. 333). In support of Clagett, John S. Gray said, "a stubborn man upon the head of a stream can prevent the settlement of thousands and thousands of acres of land" (p. 299).

George Ainslie rebutted these allegations and argued against the proposed § 14. "I don't propose to put the property of every citizen in Idaho Territory to the hazard of being taken for the benefit of a lot of scattering settlers who are engaged in farming. It may work a hardship in some cases, but we propose to legislate for the public good of the people of the whole territory, and not for one class of individuals" (p. 295). On another day Ainslie said, "There is a provision of law well known to lawyers and probably to many laymen, that is recognized throughout the civilized world wherever the law is enforced, that he who is first in point of time is first in right. Now are we going to reverse all the laws of every civilized country? . . . We should carefully guard and protect the rights of the individual as against the encroachment of monopolists . . ." (pp. 359–60).

Albert Hagan, in strong protest, complained, "State constitutions have gone into the business of supporting railroad corporations and public corporations, until the poor men of the country are now subject to have their lands confiscated. . . . The excuse that it is for public use has gone far enough – it is time to call a halt" (pp. 305–6). Hagan left the convention in disgust when the convention refused to call a halt and constitutionalized private takings (p. 1597).

5. The United States Constitution

PERHAPS THE STRONGEST ARGUMENT made by those who opposed private takings was that such takings violated the United States Constitution. The last clauses of the Fifth Amendment of the United States Constitution guarantees no person shall "be deprived of life, liberty, or property, without due process of law; nor shall private property be taken for public use, without just compensation." From comments on the floor of the Idaho convention, it appears the argument that the Fifth Amendment was a limitation was most forcefully put forth in the joint committee meeting for which we have no record. However, parts of the discussion carried over into the convention debates. For example, Reid argued "[T]he constitution of the United States is my political Bible, and I do not propose to be sneered at. . . ." He charged that the proponents of private takings had "lived on this coast too long," and "forgotten . . . parts of the Constitution of the United States, which is above all these state constitutions" (pp. 335–36).

Reid closed his argument with this plea, "I insist upon my rights guaranteed me by the Constitution of the United States. And, Mr. President, if I am to go into this Union without the barriers thrown around the protection of my rights and my liberties that the Constitution of the United States guarantees, then I don't want to go into a Union of that sort. I want its safeguards . . . that old flag, those great principles that I am trying to stick to now, that gave us liberty and freedom" (p. 337).

Albert Hagan argued a similar theme. "[W]hen you tell me that a private individual can take my property for his private use as he may see fit and say it is a public use, you deprive me of a constitutional privilege that is guaranteed by the constitution of the United States itself, and you seek to do that which no state in this Union has ever sought to do" (p. 341).

When the thirteenth session convened on July 19, the morning following the joint committee meeting, Standrod took the floor to argue that his proposal did not violate the United States Constitution. After reading the new draft, Standrod read from a series of opinions, beginning with *Twitchell v. the Commonwealth of Pennsylvania*[33] (1868) and ending with *Barron v. Baltimore*[34] (1833). *Barron* is the landmark opinion written by Chief Justice John Marshall which analyzes the effect the Bill of Rights had upon states in the period before the Civil War. Barron owned a docking facility that was filled with silt and made unusable because of public improvements made by the city of Baltimore. The Supreme Court denied his claim that the city's actions violated the Fifth Amendment. The opinion concludes, "We are of the opinion that the provision of the fifth amendment to the Constitution, declaring that private property shall not be taken for public use without just compensation, is intended solely as a limitation on the exercise of power by the government of the United States, and is not applicable to the legislation of the states."[35]

Only James Reid attempted a rebuttal of Standrod's cases. He challenged, "Why not come down to a latter day, and present to this convention . . . some decisions of recent date from this court, where they passed upon these very constitutional provisions" (p. 336).

Clagett reinforced Standrod's cases with a theoretical explanation of states rights. He explained, "A state possesses the power of eminent domain; a state is a sovereign with the exception of such limitations as are contained in the Constitution of the United States and the national character of the few prohibitions which are specifically there laid upon state action. With these exceptions and limitations the state is a sovereign power, which is possessed of the same degree of power as the most despotic nation on this earth. It may take the private lands of individuals for public use without compensation; that is the original theory of the law of eminent domain" (p. 328).

George Ainslie responded to Clagett's description of states' rights. Reflecting upon the debate that occurred during and after the Civil War, he chided, "We are told by all the republican newspapers and by all the republican statesmen that the state's rights doctrine was a heresy and state sovereignty was politically dead. I am glad to see some leading lights of the republican party residing in this territory like prodigal sons return to the fold. . . . They are in the position of trying to revive a political corpse and infuse the breath of life into it by this amendment" (pp. 358–59).

Apparently the delegates were able to breathe life back into the doctrine of states' rights and convince themselves their power was independent of that of the United States Constitution. They adopted the radical proposal put forward by Standrod and the irrigation and mining committees. At the same time, they breathed life into Idaho's future development by abandoning tradition and Idaho's pioneers and creating a right of private eminent domain for newcomers to the state.

6. One Hundred Years of Private Takings

ONE HUNDRED YEARS AGO, the United States Supreme Court was adamant in insisting that takings be for a public purpose, and kept a watchful eye on legislatures who tended to exceed their powers. For example, in *Missouri Pacific Rw. v. Nebraska* (1896) the Court held Nebraska could not compel a railroad to grant an easement to a group of farmers who wanted to build an elevator alongside the track. The Court stated broadly, "The taking by a State of the private property of one person or corporation, without the owner's consent, for the private use of another, is not due process of law, and is a violation of the Fourteenth Article of Amendment of the Constitution of the United States"[36]

The *Missouri Pacific* ruling suggested trouble for Idaho's private takings. However, this broad principle wilted in the United States Supreme Court just at it did in the sun of the arid western states. The question was squarely before the Court in *Clark v. Nash*[37] (1904), a case arising in Utah. The plaintiff sought to widen a neighbor's irrigation ditch a foot to get water to his property. Utah statutes authorized a private taking of that sort, and the Utah Supreme Court held that the plaintiff was entitled to the easement. The U.S. Supreme Court agreed. Utah was a territory at the time so the Fifth Amendment was directly involved, rather than operating through the due process clause of the Fourteenth Amendment.

The Court emphasized the factual nature of deciding the public use and expressed a strong inclination to defer to the local court on such issues. The court denied "approving of the broad proposition that private property may be taken in all cases where the taking may promote the public interest . . ."[38] However, finally, the Court surrendered to necessity, "The rights of a riparian owner in and to the use of the water flowing by his land are not the same in the arid and mountainous states of the West that they are in the States of the East. . . . This court must recognize the difference of climate and soil, which render necessary these different laws in the States so situated."[39]

The United States Supreme Court today adheres to the permissive takings doctrines that first appeared in *Clark* and other cases from the first third of the century. The Court has held that it is a legislative function to determine whether a particular taking is or is not for a public purpose.[40] In *Berman v. Parker* [41] (1954) the court upheld a statute that authorized government to take private property and sell it to private management to be redeveloped for improved private use. Most recently, in *Hawaii Housing Authority v. Midkiff* [42] (1984) the court upheld the Hawaii Land Reform Act, which used the power of eminent domain to allow homeowners with long-term leases to buy the lots on which they lived. Public purpose was defined broadly as "coterminous with the scope of a sovereign's police power."[43]

While the U.S. Supreme Court has been permissive with private takings in the West, the Idaho Supreme Court has been enthusiastic. The first case to reach the court was a condemnation of a private roadway constructed only days after statehood was declared. John T. Morgan, who attended the convention from Bingham County and argued in favor of a broad private takings clause, wrote the opinion for a unanimous court. It sustained the condemnation and the statute under which it was carried out.[44] When the timber industry began to develop, the supreme court made room for it under § 14. In 1906 Potlatch Corporation was permitted to condemn private land to construct a reservoir on the Palouse River so that logs could be floated to its mill during the dry season. Justice Isaac N. Sullivan, who wrote several eminent domain opinions strongly supporting private takings, wrote in the *Potlatch* case emphasizing the conditions in the Gem State. "In Idaho, owing to the contour of the country, its mountain fastnesses and the great difficulty of preparing and constructing means and modes of communication and transportation, and also owing to the arid conditions of the state, the necessity for irrigation in the development of the state's agricultural resources and in the development of its boundless mineral wealth, it was considered a necessity to complete development of the material resources of the state to enlarge and broaden the power of eminent domain in the state. . . ."[45] Later, the upstart timber industry was even able to acquire a temporary railroad easement over an established mining property.[46] The condemnation authority of electric power companies was also confirmed.[47] These broad readings of § 14 in the early years have discouraged landowners from challenging the authority for private takings. As a result there are few reported opinions during the last half of Idaho's first century.

Only once in the first fifty years did the court find a private taking impermissible. In *Marsh Mining Co. v. Inland Empire Mining and Millings Co.*[48] a mining company that had extracted $500,000 worth of ore sought to condemn three acres of surface land owned by another mining company that had spent $20,000 but had not yet marketed any ore. Two justices concluded Section 14 did not authorize a taking when the same use was going to be made of the land by the competing landowners. Justice Sullivan dissented, arguing the possible future use by an inactive owner should not deprive a developing company from taking the land.

Observers of Idaho's political culture have noted that private property has been highly valued in Idaho tradition. For example, it has been written, "The concept of private property has played a crucial role in the development and maintenance of political culture in Idaho."[49] Whether or not this assessment is generally fact or myth, Idaho's Convention is clearly not an example of loyalty to the principle of private property.[50] As their debates indicate, Idaho's founders knowingly discarded important common-law property rights. They did so in the name of private development, something quite different from private property. From the private property perspective, "the delegates opted for a form of socialism that allowed the taking of private property in state courts under the authority of the state constitution. The method might be termed 'privatization' rather than 'nationalization,' since ultimate ownership was with the private developer. From the viewpoint of the condemnee there was little difference."[51]

Section 14 has obviously had a great impact on Idaho's development. It has been suggested the section has been so fully used it has exhausted its life: "An observer would think the state to be fully developed or even verging on overdevelopment. Though the practice of instituting condemnation actions for essentially private purposes has not been totally abandoned, such lawsuits are seldom used. The need for them no longer exists."[52]

Idaho's experience in drafting and interpreting § 14 suggests otherwise. The circumstances have not changed in the last one hundred years. Idahoan's descend "from among the most energetic and enterprising classes of the east," and by nature are given to development. Idaho is still a country, just as it was a hundred years ago, of "mountain fastnesses and arid conditions." Whether or not this enterprise earns a profit has always depended upon markets outside the state. These conditions do not change, but change still occurs. Idaho's founders, debating in the summer of 1889, never foresaw Idaho's timber industry and rarely mentioned timber harvest. Nevertheless, within twenty years the timber industry had a major impact on Idaho.[53] Demands and opportunities for Idaho's products have continued to change as the state developed through its first century, and it is certain that changes will continue during the second century. Whenever the pace of development shifts or quickens, § 14 will be resurrected to live another day.

Notes

1. Hart, I. W., ed. *Proceedings and Debates of the Constitutional Convention of Idaho.* 2 vols. Caldwell: Caxton Printers, Ltd., 1912. These volumes are paginated consecutively, and all page references in the text of this chapter are to them.

2. Wells, Merle W. "The Admission of the State of Idaho." *Twenty-Seventh Biennial Report* (1944), pp. 73–74.

3. Cook, Rufus George. *A Study of the Political Career of Weldon Brinton Heyburn Through His First Term in the United States Senate 1852–1909.* Master's thesis, University of Idaho, 1964, pp. 2–6.

4. For the general history of mining development in the West see Greever, William S. *Bonanza West.* Reprinted Moscow, Idaho: University of Idaho Press, 1986; Paul, Rodman W. *Mining Frontiers of the Far West.* New York: Holt, Rinehard & Winston, 1963; Smith, Duane A. *Rocky Mountain Mining Camps.* Lincoln: University of Nebraska Press, 1974, reprint of 1967 edition; Spence, Clark C. *Mining Engineers and the American West.* New Haven: Yale University Press, 1970. For mining influence in other Rocky Mountain constitutions see Bakken, Gordon Morris. *Rocky Mountain Constitution Making 1850–1912.* Westport, Conn.: Greenwood Press, 1987, pp. 51–64.

5. See Gelin, Jacques B. and Miller, David W. *The Federal Law of Eminent Domain.* Charlottesville: Michie Co., 1982, p. 3.

6. The cases are collected at Mills, Henry E. *The Law of Eminent Domain.* St. Louis: F.H. Thomas, 1879, p. 2, n.4.

7. Ackerman, Bruce A. *Private Property and the Constitution.* New Haven: Yale University Press, 1977, p. 192, n. 10. See also Dumbauld, Edward. *The Bill of Rights and What It Means Today.* Norman, Oklahoma: University of Oklahoma Press, 1957, pp. 173–205.

8. 3 U.S. (3 Dall.) 386, 388 (1798) (seriatim opinion).

9. Mills. *The Law of Eminent Domain,* p. 24.

10. 57 Cal. 269.

11. Sec. 5, 14 U.S. Stat. at Large, p. 252.

12. Section 5210 (3) of 1887 Rvsd. Statutes, p. 576. Subsection (4) went on to list as public uses: "Roads, tunnels, ditches, flumes, pipes and dumping places for working mines; also, outlets, natural or otherwise, for the flow, deposit, or conduct of tailings or refuse matter from mines; also, an occupancy in common by the owners of possessors of different mines of any place for the flow, deposit or conduct of tailings or refuse matter from their several mines."

13. For a recent survey of the literature see August, Raymond S. "Law in the West A History of the Origins and Distribution of Western America Law." Ph.D. diss., University of Idaho, 1987, pp. 1–40; and Bakken, Gordon M. *The Development of Law on the Rocky Mountain Frontier.* Westport, Conn.: Greenwood Press, 1983, pp. 9–19.

14. *Drake v. Earhart,* 2 Idaho 750, at 753, 23 P. 541, at 542 (1891).

15. Frederick Jackson Turner, *The Frontier in American History.* New York: Holt, Rinehard and Winston, 1962, reprint of 1920 ed., p.2.

16. Pound, Roscoe *The Spirit of the Common Law.* Boston: Marshall Jones Co., 1966, reprint of 1921 ed.; *Idem.* "The Pioneers and the Common Law." *West Virginia Law Quarterly* 27 (1920):1–19; *Idem.* "The Development of American Law and Its Deviation from English Law." *Law Quarterly Review* 67(1951):49–66.

17. Paxson, Frederic L. *History of the American Frontier*. Cambridge, Mass.: Houghton Mifflin Co., 1924; *Idem.* "Frontier Influence in the Development of American Law." *Proceedings of the State Bar Association of Wisconsin* 13(1921):477–89.

18. Webb, Walter Prescott. *The Great Plains*. New York: Houghton Mifflin Co., 1931.

19. Scott, Valerie Weeks. "The Range Cattle Industry: Its Effect on Western Land Law." 29 *Montana Law Review* 29(1967):155–83; Davis, Rodney O. "Before Barbed Wire: Herd Law Agitations in Early Kansas and Nebraska." *Journal of the West* 6(1967):41–52.

20. Gard, Wayne. *Frontier Justice*. Norman, Oklahoma: University of Oklahoma Press, 1949; Dimsdale, Thomas J. *The Vigilantes of Montana*. Virginia City, Mt.: D. W. Tilton & Co., 1866; Rogers, James Grafton. "The Beginnings of Law in Colorado." *Dicta* 36(1959)111–20; Valentine, Alan. *Vigilante Justice*. New York: Reynal, 1956.

21. Marshall, T. M. "The Miner's Laws of Colorado." *American Historical Review* 25(1920):428.

22. Dunbar, Robert G. "The Origin of the Colorado System of Water-Right Control." *Colorado Magazine* 27(1950):262.

23. Blume, William Wirt. "Civil Procedure on the American Frontier." *Michigan Law Review* 56(1957):161–224, 206. See also *Idem.* "Probate and Administration on the American Frontier, A Study of the Probate Records of Wayne County–N.W. Territory, 1796–1803; Indiana Territory, 1803–1805; and Michigan Territory, 1805–1816." *Michigan Law Review* 58(1959):209–46; *Idem.* "Chancery Practice on the American Frontier, A Study of the Records of the Supreme Court of Michigan Territory, 1805–1836." *Michigan Law Review* 59(1960):49–96; *Idem.* "Legislation on the American Frontier: Adoption of Laws by Governor and Judges–Northwest Territory, 1805–1823." *Michigan Law Review* 60(1962):317–72.

24. Blume, William Wirt, and Brown, Elizabeth G. "Territorial Courts and Law." *Michigan Law Review* 61(1962):39–106, 497–538. 25. Philbrick, Francis S. *The Rise of the West*. New York: Harper & Row, 1965; *Idem.* "Law, Courts, and Litigation of Indiana Territory (1800–1809)." *Illinois Law Review* 24(1929):1–19, 193–219.

26. Hamilton, William B. "The Transmission of English Law to the Frontier of America." *South Atlantic Quarterly* 67(1968):243–64.

27. Brown, Elizabeth Gaspar. "Frontier Justice: Wayne County 1796–1836." *American Journal of Legal History* 16(1972):126–53.

28. Prassel, Frank R. *The Western Peace Officer*. Norman, Oklahoma: University of Nebraska Press, 1972.

29. Dykstra, Robert R. "Wild Bill Hickok in Abilene." *Journal of the Central Mississippi Valley American Studies Association* (Fall, 1961), pp. 20–48.

30. Brown, Richard Maxwell. "Legal and Behavioral Perspectives of American Vigilantism." In Donald Fleming and Bernard Bailyn, eds., *Perspectives in American History*, 5 vols. Cambridge: Little, Brown Co., 1971, 5:95–144; *Idem.* "The American Vigilante Tradition." In Hugh David Graham and Ted R. Gurr, eds., *Violence in America*. Washington, D.C.: Bantam, 1969, 1:121–80.

31. Turner explained 1890 marked the end of the frontier because of this statement in a superintendent of the census bulletin: "Up to and including 1880 the country had a frontier of settlement, but at present the unsettled area has been so broken into by isolated bodies of settlement that there can hardly be said to be a frontier line. In the discussion of its extent, its westward movement, etc., it can not, therefore, any longer have a place in the census reports." Turner. *The Frontier in American History*, p 1.

32. Bakken, Gordon Morris. *The Development of Law on the Rocky Mountain Frontier*. Westport, Conn.: Greenwood Press, 1983, p. 16.

33. 74 U.S. (7 Wallace) 321, 19 L.Ed. 223 (1868).

34. 32 U.S. 242, 8 L.Ed. 672 (1833).

35. Ibid. at 250, 8 L. Ed. at 675.

36. 164 U.S. 403, at 417, 41 L.Ed. 489, at 495, 17 S.C. 130, at 135 (1896).

37. 198 U.S. 361, 49 L.Ed. 1085, 25 S.C. 676 (1904).

38. Ibid. at 369, 49 L.Ed. at 1088, 25 S.C. at 678.

39. Ibid. at 370, 49 L.Ed. at 1088-9, 25 S.C. at 678-9.

40. 327 U.S. 546, 90 L.Ed. 843, 66. S.C.715 (1946).

41. 348 U.S. 26, 99 L. Ed. 27, 75 S.C. 98 (1954).

42. 467 U.S. 229, 81 L.E.2d 186, 104 S.C. 2321 (1984).

43. Ibid. at 240, 81 L.E.2d at 197, 104 S.C. at 2329.

44. *Latah County v. Peterson*, 3 Idaho 398, 29 Pac. 1089 (1892).

45. 12 Idaho, 769, 785, 88 P.426, 431 (1906).

46. 28 Idaho 556, 155 P.680 (1916), appeal dismissed, 244 U.S. 651, 61 L.Ed.2d 1372, 37 S.C. 744 (1917).

47. 19 Idaho 595, 115 P. 682 (1911).

48. 30 Idaho 1, 165 P. 1128 (1916).

49. Blank, Robert H. *Regional Diversity of Political Values: Idaho Political Culture.* Washington D.C.: University Press of America, 1978, p. 26.

50. Both Robert H. Blank and Scott W. Reed characterize section 14 as a vindication of private property. pp. 69–70. This essay reads the debates differently than Robert H. Blank in several other important respects as well. The debate did not follow "the line of division between the mining and irrigation interests." The mining and irrigation committees met in joint session early in the debate and were united thereafter. The lines of division were between the pioneers and the boomers or developers, and between progressives and those loyal to tradition. The object of the section was not to "guarantee the sanctity of private property." The original version of section 14 submitted by the declaration of rights committee might be described as attempting to guarantee private property, but the version produced by the mining and irrigation committees hammered the shield into a sword. The object of the joint committee proposal was to strike down private property rights, so that they would not stand in the way of private development. The final wording did not limit eminent domain to the taking of private property "only for public use," it authorized a private taking where none had been possible before.

51. Reed, Scott W. "New Law For a New State–The Legal Impetus to Development of the Material Resources of Idaho." *Idaho Yesterdays* 25(1981):55.

52. Ibid.

53. A part of this story is told by Keith Peterson in *Company Town: Potlatch, Idaho, and the Potlatch Lumber Company*. Pullman, Washington: Washington State University Press, 1987.

5.
The Legislative Branch

1. The Legislative Issues

THE CONVENTION, sitting as committee of the whole, finished its work on the declaration of rights article late in the afternoon on Friday, July 19. It quickly passed Article XIV on the militia and adjourned for the day (pp. 397–400).[1] The delegates reconvened the next morning, the fourteenth day in session, and approved Article IV on the executive department (pp. 411–34) and Article X on public institutions (pp. 434–54) with little debate. They were then ready to take up Article III establishing the legislative department. It took the remainder of Saturday, including an evening session, for the delegates to reach a consensus on the legislative branch (pp. 456–556). Even then, the article was back on the convention floor a week later and debate was carried on for another half day (pp. 1192–1237).

The committee on the legislative department proposed an article with twenty-five sections. The first section created a bicameral legislature with a senate and a house of representatives. Sections two through five established the number of legislators in each house, and how the new state was to be divided into districts for their election. Section six established the qualifications of the legislators, seven granted them immunity from arrest or civil process during legislative sessions, twenty-three provided for compensation and twenty-five was an oath. Sections eight through eighteen, and section twenty-two, provided for biennial sessions and established the powers of both houses and legislative procedures. Finally, three sections set limits on the exercise of legislative power. Section nineteen prohibited many types of local and special laws, Section twenty prohibited authorization of any lottery or gift enterprise, and Section twenty-four, the prohibition section, urged the legislature to promote temperance and morality (pp. 2052–56).

The legislature was the only branch of government under local control during the territorial period. While the Organic Act empowered the president to appoint the governor, secretary, justices of the supreme court, attorney and marshall,[2] members of the legislative assembly were chosen by the electors of the territory.[3] The twenty-five years of territorial legislative experience were often tumultuous.

Idaho's territorial legislature met for fifteen sessions. Annual sessions were held in the earlier years but Congress changed them to biennial in the late 1860s. A number of recurring issues occupied these bodies. There was always a conflict between the locally elected legislature and the nationally appointed governor. Taxpayers constantly fought to prevent the legislators from creating public offices with good salaries. The legislature frequently produced controversy by intervening in local affairs, creating counties, moving county seats, and passing other special and local legislation. Finally, there was the perpetual struggle for power between the political parties.[4] These controversies provided the starting point for the convention.

A number of the twenty-five sections proposed by the committee on the legislative department sparked short, intense debates. Section 1 proposed to vest the legislative power in a senate and a house of representatives. G. W. King (D-Shoshone) moved to entirely do away with the senate, and delivered an impassioned indictment of that institution. King started with the history of the senate, which he traced to the English House of Lords. In King's view, the English system was "essentially an artistocratic government," (p. 456) and the House of Lords was what made it possible for the artistocrats to maintain their control. King claimed creation of the senates in the United States and state constitutions was "done in the interest of a class of men who have by law secured rights and powers and privileges inconsistent, in my opinion, with the privileges that should be conferred by a nation that professes to regard all men as equal" (p. 457). He concluded, "I do not look upon this system of the senate as founded upon anything but a desire to increase the wealth of the privileged class, to increase their power and their patrongage" (p. 462). The delegates were not persuaded by King, no doubt in part because many had served in the territorial council, and as subsequent history revealed, just as many had ambitions to serve in the Senate after statehood.

When Section 12 requiring the business of the legislature to be conducted in open session was under discussion, there was a disagreement about whether the Senate should be able to meet in closed session to consider nominations for appointment by the governor. Aaron F. Parker (D-Idaho) strongly favored compelling all legislative business to be open, "I am opposed to dark lantern matters, I am opposed to star chambers or Jack Shepard methods of doing business at all. I am in favor of turning the electric light of publicity upon every act of the legislature" (p. 1222). Edgar Wilson (R-Ada) agreed with Parker, "I think that more abuses have grown up under this rule of a secret session in the matter of confirmations than any other matter that comes before a legislative body. I think here in Idaho we have had some evidence of it" (p. 1218). James M. Shoup (R-Custer) thought the voters had a right to know everything, "[w]hen a member is elected to the legislature or to the United States senate, either one, he should say nothing nor cast any vote but what everybody and especially all of his constituents should know just how he voted, and every word he said" (p. 1217).

Other delegates thought there had to be an exception for confirmations. J. W. Brigham (R-Latah) said, "I do not see how anyone who has ever been in a legislature could place this restriction upon the senate. . . . There are times when the names of individuals may be sent in for confirmation, when perhaps their reputation and ability should be discussed" (p. 1217). William H. Clagett (R-Shoshone) carried Brigham's argument one step further and said since the governor could conduct secret proceedings on nominations, "If you desire to preserve the power of the senate as a co-ordinate body in the matter of appointments you must necessarily allow their sessions to be held secretly" (p. 1220). Clagett concluded, "It seems to me that the wisdom which has dictated this matter so frequently everywhere in all the states and in the constitution of the United States, indicates that there are some reasons for it" (p. 1221). John S. Gray (R-Ada) predicted the consequences of an open meeting requirement, "the result will be that it will be made a party matter in the confirmation or ratification of nominations" (p. 1224).

The proponents of open meetings were unpersuaded. Alexander Mayhew (D-Shoshone) said, "I don't think the executive of the territory would ever send a person's name in whose reputation and character could be questioned" (p. 1218). J. W. Poe (D-Nez Perce) argued, "If any man's character is so checkered that he is afraid to have it analyzed and presented before the world in all its hideousness, let him not seek a position where he will be subject to having it revealed to the world" (p. 1221). Solomon Hasbrouck (R-Washington) declared, "I cannot for the life of me see why, if a man is to procure his office by appointment, he shall object or be less criticized than the man who procures it by election" (p. 1224). In the end, the advocates of open sessions prevailed.

These debates, and others, like the discussion of local and special legislation, slowed progress on the legislative article. But the major issue was apportionment. Apportionment involves dividing and distributing the power of the legislature, which is the inherent political power of the state, among the citizens. It involves determining how many members the Senate and House of Representatives are to have, and drawing the lines of the districts those members represent.

2. The Apportionment Debate

THE STATUTE CREATING IDAHO TERRITORY stipulated the territorial legislature was to be apportioned according to a population principle, with roughly equal populations in each district so that each voter ultimately had equal representation in the legislature. There was to be a Council and House of Representatives. The first Council was to have seven members and the House thirteen. The territorial legislature was authorized to increase these numbers up to thirteen and twenty-six, respectively, as the population increased. The territorial governor was to conduct a census and apportion the territory for the first election. Thereafter, apportionment was to be done by the legislature itself. The legislative districts were to be created so that each district was to have representation in the ratio of its number of qualified voters.[5] It is almost impossible for apportionment principles to prevail in apportionment decisions made by legislatures because of a basic conflict of interest. The legislators who must decide apportionment questions are the same persons whose personal political fortunes are at stake. Experience in Idaho, and elsewhere, has proven political fortunes frequently prevail over political principles when apportionment is at issue.

There was considerable controversy about the first territorial census and election because of the "Laramie fraud," the invention of three or four hundred voters on the far eastern border of the territory.[6] In response to these difficulties, Congress amended the Organic Act to authorize the governor to reapportion the territory for election of the legislative assembly.[7] This power was never exercised, but the legislature frequently reapportioned itself to keep up with the many population shifts and the politics of the day. In addition, Congress reduced the maximum number in the Council to twelve and in the House to twenty-four.

The committee on the legislative department submitted a Report which significantly altered this apportionment scheme by making the counties a central feature in the system, at the expense of the population principle. Section two of the report provided for the election of one senator for each county. The first house of representatives was to have twice the number of senators, with the legislature authorized to increase the number in the future, with an upper limit of three times the number of senators (p. 464). Under Section 3, senators were to serve four year terms, staggered so that half would be elected every two years, and representatives were to serve two-year terms (p. 474). The report provided for a census to be conducted in 1895, and every ten years thereafter (p. 485). Representatives were to be elected from districts, each of which was to have roughly the same population (p. 486). Counties were finally emphasized in the report by a requirement that no county could be divided in creating legislative districts, and that when a district included more than one county, the counties had to be contiguous (p. 505).

A very unusual event occurred when this report came to the floor of the convention. The chairman of the committee, Republican John T. Morgan from Bingham County, made a series of amendments which significantly altered the committee's principles. Morgan undercut the role of the counties in apportionment by proposing a scheme that apportioned according to population. Instead of guaranteeing each county a senator, Morgan proposed continuing the territorial scheme by having twelve in the senate and twenty-four in the house (p. 465). Further, he proposed the counties be divided into legislative districts according to the number of votes cast in the most recent election rather than according to population.

Several arguments were offered against Morgan's proposals. Alexander Mayhew argued twelve senators and twenty-four representatives was too few. He said, "We are going out of this colonial form of government into state government, and my own opinion always has been . . . our representative apportionment by the organic act of Congress has been too small, and my experience has been that the larger the representation, so long as it is not a burden to the people, the better laws we have enacted and better men get into the legislature" (pp. 466–67). J. W. Reid (D-Nez Perce) agreed, arguing, "Our senate should be larger than twelve, so as to have representation for the entire territory and its diversified interests" (p. 469).

George Ainslie (D-Boise) tried to avoid the question, and put the matter in the hands of the apportionment committee created by the convention. He argued, "Now I insist this belongs to the committee on Apportionment, and we have the largest committee of the convention to consider that subject. I say . . . let them report that matter" (pp. 468–69).

J. W. Poe objected to Morgan's proposals because they slighted the sovereignty of the counties. He said, "I take it that each county of this territory is a sovereign within a sovereign, and that the people within that sovereign have rights in legislative bodies, and they are entitled, before any of those rights can be taken away from them, to a representation in that body. . . . Now the idea is fair that the representative shall be a senator . . . . we, in every state of the Union have prospered under this theory of two senators from every state in the Union. The least state in population, according to the size of its representation in the senate of the United States is the greatest; and it was recognized as being according to the justice of the thing . . ." (pp. 471–72).

James Reid saw the question as a controversy between large and small counties. He said small counties "have large wants, they need to be developed, they need some one here to stand up for them and tell the legislature their wants and interests . . ." (p. 481). He was afraid Morgan's proposal would concentrate too much power in two large counties, namely Ada and Shoshone (p. 475).

Mayhew agreed that too much power would be placed in the hands of the two largest counties, and shared with the convention his experience with apportionment in the territorial legislature. "Now I say . . . that any legislature in the world that has the power they have themselves, acts the king . . . they will if possible prevent a change in that representation . . . I don't believe you will change their political ambition to work for the different sections they represent and to hold political power in the way of representation" (p. 477).

In the face of these strong objections, Morgan was supported by prominent delegates at the convention. President William H. Clagett rose to speak against representation by the counties. "We are now laying the foundation of the political power of the state; I am not talking about power in the abstract, but the political power. . . . And if it be true that all power is of right derived from the people, and if it be further true that the majority of the people should govern and express the will of the whole, then it is perfectly plain . . . that equality of representation should be the controlling factor . . ." (p. 470).

Weldon B. Heyburn (R-Shoshone) made an even more direct attack on the counties. Referring to their sovereignty he said, "No such character can be attached to the existence of a county. We have heard of state sovereignty, but I never heard of county sovereignty. I suppose next we will have township and village sovereignty . . . It seems to me it is so manifestly unjust upon the face of the statement, that a county that only casts a hundred or two legal votes, should have the same power in the councils of the state as a county that casts several hundred. It is un-American, it is a violation of the principles that underlie our government of equal representation to all the people, based upon the number of people themselves" (pp. 473–74).

In his enthusiasm for the representative principle, Heyburn misspoke. He and Morgan did not really want voting strength measured by population, but rather by the number of qualified voters. Clagett explained shifting from population to electors was necessary to prevent those counties with significant Mormon populations from gaining too much power in the legislature (p. 471).

On the face of it, this was a contest between the principles of county sovereignty and representation according to population. But the real conflict was one of party politics. Those who argued the county sovereignty principle were Democrats from the smaller counties. Those who argued the population principle were Republicans from the larger counties.

Morgan claimed his amendments were his own proposals formulated after talking with other delegates. But Mayhew claimed, "You can see politics sticking out of this question so plainly and strongly that it must arouse the condemnation of every man in this convention" (p. 473). Charles A. Clark (D-Ada) was even more blunt in his assessment. He supported the committee's original proposal, but said, "After the iron hand of the caucus is in action, why make motions, and why make speeches? . . . There is some power behind this throne, or no doubt this change would not have been agreed to by such a vote as this . . . the side of my democratic friends will go down as rapidly as the snows of winter go under the summer's thermometer" (p. 484).

The action of the Republican caucus is even more interesting because the nine-member committee on the legislative branch was dominated by large-county Republicans. Several standards can be used to determine the largest counties. One is the number of delegates sent to the convention, which in turn was based on the number of votes cast for the territorial delegate to Congress in the 1888 general election. Judged in this manner, the five largest counties were Ada (9), Shoshone (8), Bingham (7), Alturas (6) and Latah (6). These counties had six of the nine members on the committee, but still the committee reported in favor of the smaller counties.

A very different list is created if the counties are measured by the 1890 census. Judged in this manner, the five largest counties were Bingham (13,575), Latah (9,173), Ada (8,368), Oneida (6,819) and Bear Lake (6,057). The difference between the number of delegates and the census figures was due to the disfranchisement of Mormon voters.

Despite the iron hand of the Republican caucus witnessed by Clark, the convention took an erratic course in making the apportionment decisions, and in the end compromised between the population principle championed by Morgan and the county prinicple in the legislative committee report. At the end of the first debate on Section 2, the delegates adopted Morgan's proposal 31 to 20, and rejected a motion by Clark to guarantee each county a representative (p. 474).

Section 3 proposed two-year terms for representatives and four-year terms for senators. J. W. Reid immediately moved to reduce the senate terms to two years. He complained that under Morgan's proposal to have only twelve senators, the two largest counties could control the senate. He pointed to the representation in the convention itself and concluded, "We have in this body to-day [sic] about one-third of the representatives of the territory coming from Shoshone and Ada counties . . ." (p. 475). Applying this ratio to the senate, he concluded Shoshone and Ada counties would have four of the twelve seats, and when combined with four-year terms, "will practically put the political power of this new state in the hands of two counties" (p. 474).

Alexander Mayhew agreed with Reid and cited his experience as a member of the 1886 and 1888 territorial legislatures as evidence. He said in 1886 Bingham County joined with Ada "and prevented the other counties from having a just representation" (p. 477). About the 1888 session he said, "They wrangled, fought and abused one another to that extent that men became so disturbed in their political sentiments that they had no communication with one another" (pp. 477–78). He finally charged that the senators' concern "only goes to the extent by which they can maintain political power in their hands, and not that the people shall be well represented" (p. 478).

Morgan gave a token argument in favor of four-year terms. He observed, "This is a very common provision in the constitutions of nearly all the states in the Union" and gave this justification, "One-half of the number go out every two years, so that a portion of the body all the time may be men of experience" (p. 476).

Clagett rose to rebut Reid's argument about the power of Shoshone and Ada counties in the convention, and in the new senate. Clagett pointed out there were sixty-nine delegates at the convention, and sixteen of them were from Ada and Shoshone. Reid said, "Isn't 16 nearly about one-third of 69?" Clagett shot back, " O, no sir, no sir; it is one-third of 48; between 48 and 69 there is a difference of 21 votes. My friend had better go to school and learn addition and subtraction" (p. 482). According to Clagett's calculation, it would take five counties to control the convention, or the senate. James H. Beatty (R-Alturas) agreed with Clagett, but phrased it differently. "The members of the smaller counties have the control in the aggregate, and it is utterly impossible that two of the larger counties can make such a combination as to control the legislature, unless by the consent of the smaller counties" (p. 478).

Reid's motion to reduce the terms to two years passed 29 to 17 (p. 485). Perhaps Beatty was right, and the smaller counties saw four-year terms as a threat to their aggregate control so they reduced the terms. The convention next struck down the committee's proposal for a state census in 1895 and every ten years thereafter because it was too expensive (pp. 485–86). Attention was then turned to how the House should be apportioned. The committee recommended apportionment on the basis of population, with districts of roughly equal population (p. 486). Chairman Morgan again immediately moved to amend by apportioning on the basis of the number of votes polled at the last general election for delegate to Congress (p. 487). Morgan explained he was personally opposed to his own amendment because his county would not be allowed to count the 2,000 Mormons who could not vote, and their representation would therefore be reduced. However, he had concluded there was not enough support in the convention to pass the section as originally presented (p. 489). Morgan was right, because his amendment passed (p. 493).

Not only did Morgan read the sentiments of the convention, so did Reid. Reid moved to amend Morgan's motion by adding, "Provided that each county shall be entitled to one representative" (p. 488). This same motion had earlier been made by Clark and rejected, but the delegates had reconsidered. When it became apparent there was support for Reid, Willis Sweet (R-Latah) became concerned that since it had already been decided there were to be only twenty-four members in the House, and it would take eighteen of those if every county had one member, the more populous counties would not be adequately represented. He said if Reid's motion passed, he would move to reconsider how many were to be in the legislature under Section 2 and increase the senators to eighteen and the representatives to thirty-six. The convention passed Reid's motion with 35 votes in favor and those opposed not recorded (p. 493). The convention then decided to reconsider the number of legislators (p. 495).

James W. Reid was a tenacious and skillful advocate for his causes and saw another opportunity to strengthen the position of the small counties. As soon as the convention agreed to reconsider the number of legislators, Reid moved to amend by substituting the original committee report, which would have provided each county with a senator (p. 496). Morgan, Clagett and Beatty all objected that Reid's motion went beyond the motion to reconsider the number of legislators. Beatty accused Reid of "taking advantage of what many members understood, and we have acted in good faith" (p. 503). Clagett pointed out the object of Reid's motion. "You are proposing not only to turn over one branch but both branches of the legislature to a minority of the people, and you can figure it from now until the day of doomsday, and that is precisely what this motion amounts to . . . the whole rule of majorities is stricken down in that way" (p. 500).

Reid claimed the real improprieties in the matter were Morgan's motions, changing a report "supported unanimously by a committee representing both sides of the house – if there are two sides, that is, by the republicans and the democrats" (p. 496). Reid offered to withdraw his previous motion, which guaranteed each count a representative, a motion the convention had already adopted, if his present motion to give each county a senator was itself adopted. But, the delegates were not swayed and rejected Reid's motion 20 to 27 (p. 504). They then went on to set the number of senators at eighteen and the number of representatives at thirty-six, also providing those numbers could be increased to twenty-four and sixty, respectively (p. 505).

The legislative department article came on the convention floor one week later, and the same debate was replayed. Weldon Heyburn, joined by other conservative forces, moved to extend the terms of senators from two to four years, arguing, "The object of the senate is that it shall be a worthy body and shall not be subject to those repeated and constant changes that prevail in the other body of the legislature" (p. 1193). Delegates from small counties who were to be joined together to form senatorial districts, like Solomon Hasbrouck, objected, "I hail from a county where my constituents are in such a minority that we shall only get an occasional senator under the apportionment, and that being the case, I want a chance occasionally, and so do my constituents, to vote for a man that is nominated from our own county; and I do not see any other way of getting it than to have them elected every two years" (p. 1197). Others argued the governor and other elected officials were to serve terms of two years, and so should senators (p. 1195). Gray explained his notion of why there would still be a rapid turnover of senators, "A good many of them who are elected senators will want to get rid of it as soon as possible if they are good ones, and if they are not good ones, we will want to shut them out as fast as we can" (p. 1194). The delegates agreed and defeated Heyburn's motion.

Then George Ainslie tried to improve the position of the small counties by moving to amend Section 4 to provide a senator and representative for each county. He argued, "It is nothing more than fair and right that each county should have a voice in the permanent selection of the nominees of the governor" (p. 1203). Delegates from large counties protested. Heyburn said, "I am opposed to Bear Lake county, with its legitimate votes of less than a hundred or two, having the same representation in the senate of the state as the counties of Ada or Shoshone or Bingham or any other of the populous counties. It is manifestly a violation of every rule of representation based upon the people and the voting strength of the people" (p. 1202). Other delegates agreed with Heyburn but none was more indignant than William H. McConnell (R-Latah), who said he did not suppose "any county in Idaho would have the gall to come here and say they should have a senator and representative in the legislature of this coming state regardless of the population they had" (p. 1209).

Ainslie's motion was defeated 21 to 26. He then moved to amend by providing each county with a senator rather than a representative, but that was also defeated 22 to 27 (pp. 1210–11). A. S. Chaney (D-Latah) described the issue in this fashion, "I think it is simply a question between the large counties and the small counties; not a political question, and it ought not be considered as such. It is a question between right and wrong" (p. 1207). A roll call vote was taken on Ainslie's motions so it is possible to determine whether Chaney was correct. Of the twenty-one delegates voting in favor of Ainslie's first motion, seventeen were Democrats and four Republicans, and fifteen represented small counties and six large counties (the delegates thought of Ada, Shoshone, Bingham and Latah as populous counties). The four Republicans were all from small counties and the six large-county delegates who voted with the small counties were Democrats. Of the twenty-six delegates voting against Ainslie's first motion, twenty-three were Republican, two Democrats and one Labor, while twelve represented small counties and fourteen large counties. One of the two Democrats was from a large county, and eleven of the twelve small county delegates to vote against were Republicans.

Stating this another way, six large-county Democrats were willing to vote with the small counties and their party, while eleven small-county delegates were willing to vote with the large counties and their party. A total of seventeen delegates were willing to place party loyalty over loyalty to counties of a similar size. On the other hand, only five delegates were willing to vote against their party and with similar sized counties. This voting pattern suggests the issue was primarily a struggle between the parties and secondarily between the large and small counties. How many of these delegates saw this issue as a question of right and wrong? It is possible, though not likely, that all of them did. A. J. Pierce from Custer County certainly did, for he was a Democrat who voted with the Republicans and a small-county delegate who voted with the large counties.

In the end, the convention compromised between the committee's report and the Republican caucus command. Idaho's convention apportioned with a combination of population and county sovereignty theories. Each county was guaranteed a representative in the House, but not a senator. The number of senators was set at eighteen and the representatives at thirty-six with possible increases. The requirement that no county be divided in the creation of legislative districts was left intact.

3. Apportionment of the First State Legislature

IDAHO'S CONSTITUTIONAL CONVENTION appointed a Legislative Apportionment Committee (p. 67) with one delegate from each county and charged the committee with the task of apportioning the first state legislature (p. 39). It was the largest committee of the convention and was chaired by Republican James M. Shoup from Custer County. There were ten Republicans and eight Democrats on the committee.

In passing the legislative department article, the convention had set the number of senators at eighteen and representatives at thirty-six. To distribute these representatives throughout Idaho's eighteen counties, the apportionment committee created sixteen senatorial districts and twenty-two districts for the House. The distribution of representatives to the various counties can be seen in Table A.

The legislative apportionment committee report did not come before the convention until Monday morning, August 5, the twenty-seventh day in session. This was the last real working day of the convention and the delegates worked into the evening to complete their tasks. The convention was in a hurry and decided to bring the report directly on the floor of the convention rather than consider it as a committee of the whole (pp. 1898–99). Three delegates moved to amend the report because of the way their own counties were handled. But, of course, the major controversy was caused by another motion by the persistent James Reid to elect one senator from each county for the first state legislature (p. 1906–7).

James Shoup objected to the motion and asked that it be ruled out of order because it was "in opposition" to the legislative department which had already been adopted (p. 1907). Clagett, sitting as president, ruled the motion out of order but Reid immediately appealed to the convention to overrule Clagett. By a 28 to 26 vote the delegates overruled the president (p. 1909). The vote was on nearly straight party lines. Voting to sustain Clagett were twenty-five Republicans and the one Labor delegate at the convention. Voting to overrule him were 25 Democrats and 3 Republicans. Of the three Republicans, Sinnott from Elmore County and Whitton from Logan County chose to vote with the small counties rather than with their party, and inexplicably, Republican A. S. Chaney from Latah voted with the Democrats and small counties.

Reid no doubt saw a last chance for victory for the Democrats and small counties, and argued his amendment on its merits after Clagett had been overruled (pp. 1910–11). But William McConnell would have nothing of it and called the Republicans to rally. He said, "Of course, there is no politics in this, oh no; this is purely a nonpartisan measure. . . . This is purely a partisan measure. I had hoped we would get through the last few days of this session without drawing party lines; but the time has come when it is precipitated upon the republicans to stand by the report of this committee" (pp. 1911–12).

Weldon Heyburn moved for a call of the house so that Republican delegates who were not on the floor could be rallied to turn back Reid's challenge. His motion caused an extended parliamentary debate about how to vote on a call of the house (pp. 1913–18). Heyburn did not get his call of the house, but by the time it was decided, McConnell thought he had gotten the votes he needed and moved to table Reid's amendment.

During the procedural debate the Republicans had explained the matter to Chaney, and he was ready to switch his vote. In addition Harkness and Lemp arrived. This gave them a total of twenty-nine votes. The Democrats started with twenty-eight votes on the motion to overrule Clagett. They managed to get three more delegates on the floor, but they had lost Chaney, who switched, and for some reason Meyer left the floor. So they too had twenty-nine votes. Of course Clagett, sitting as president, broke the tie by voting with the Republicans and Reid lost by one vote his dream of establishing county sovereignty as the primary consideration in Idaho apportionment (pp. 1918).

Aaron F. Parker was one of those delegates who complained about the representation of his county under the committee report. Idaho County had been joined with Nez Perce to elect a senator. Parker said, "I come from a county, sir, that is once and a half times as large as the state of Massachusetts. How big it would be if it was spread out flat, I don't know. . . . My county polled at the last election 675 votes; the only democratic county in the territory. Taxes and Idaho county are the only things that are left of the democratic party. . . . Now I see counties that only polled forty or fifty votes more than my county are given a whole senator, and my county only half a one" (p. 1912). Parker argued the small counties needed representation to develop. "All those great counties, Mr. President, have their resources developed, and their population, while these little counties, like mine, for instance, and Nez Perce, which are hampered with reservations, have all their resources yet to be developed. There the matter stands today; counties that need legislation for their development are practically deprived of it" (p. 1913). In the end Parker was the only delegate from Idaho County and he could do nothing about the committee report.

James Beatty also complained about the manner in which Alturas County was being represented. Beatty and the other Alturas delegates were still smarting from the division of Old Alturas county and the creation of Elmore and Logan counties in the 1888 legislature.[8] Beatty brought that old fight onto the floor when he complained, "It requires 889 1/2 votes to entitle any county to a senator. . . . Alturas by this report is entitled to one senator. She has 1,031 votes. She has 141 votes more than enough to entitled her to a senator, while Elmore county as about 141 less than enough to entitle here to a senator. . . . Now that is an unjust apportionment." Beatty's solution was to leave Alturas with its one senator, and to attach it to Elmore for election of another.

Homer Stull (D-Elmore) was quick to answer Beatty. He explained the line dividing Elmore from Alturas followed the line of the Camas Prairie, cutting many districts in half. The number of voters cited by Beatty included only those precincts which remained intact after Alturas was divided. So Stull concluded, "The present territory comprised in the county of Elmore cast a considerable number of votes that are not included and are not shown in these statistics" (p. 1902). Stull reminded the delegates that putting the two counties together "would not be conducive to the harmony for which our chaplain has so eloquently prayed" (p. 1902).

Frank P. Cavanah, also an Elmore Democrat, agreed with Stull. "The gentleman from Alturas says there was no animosity between the two counties. There is not, except polygamy; and I guarantee that if there was a vote taken in Elmore county today, there would not be ten votes in favor of going to Alturas county." Cavanah concluded by pointing to another important difference between the counties, "Alturas county is full of politicians, and there isn't one in Elmore county. They want voters; that is all they want" (p. 1906). Beatty was unable to persuade the convention, but there was one change made in the committee report involving an adjustment between the southern-most counties (pp. 1899, 1920).

Table A makes possible an assessment of the fairness of the apportionment done at the convention, as well as in other apportionments through 1891. Column 1 is the apportionment of the 1888 territorial legislature (Council & House), column 2 is the convention itself, column 3 is the 1890 legislature apportioned by the convention, and column 4 is the legislative apportionment bill passed by the first state legislature. The counties are listed according to the number of votes cast in the 1888 election for territorial representative to Congress, beginning with the largest. The first number in each

Table A.

Number and Percentage of Representatives by County, 1888–1891

County	1888 Terr.Leg.		Const.	1890 St. Leg.		1891 Statute*	
	Council	House	Conven.	Senate	House	Senate	House
Alturus	2 (16.7)	4 (16.7)	6 (8.3)	1 (5.5)	2.3 (6.4)	1.5 (9.4)	2.5 (6.8)
Ellmore	–	–	3 (4.2)	1 (5.5)	1.5 (4.2)	0.5 (3.1)	1.5 (4.1)
Logan	–	–	3 (4.2)	1 (5.5)	2.3 (6.4)	0.5 (3.1)	1 (2.7)
Shoshone	0.5 (4.2)	1.5 (6.2)	8 (11.1)	2 (11.1)	4 (11.1)	2 (12.5)	4 (10.8)
Ada	1.5 (12.5)	3 (12.5)	9 (12.5)	2 (11.1)	3.5 (9.7)	2 (12.5)	4 (10.8)
Latah	0.5 (4.2)	1 (4.2)	6 (8.3)	2 (11.1)	2.5 (6.9)	1.5 (9.4)	4 (10.8)
Bingham	1.5 (12.5)	2.5 (10.4)	7 (9.7)	1.3 (7.2)	3.3 (9.2)	1.8 (11.2)	3.5 (9.5)
Boise	0.5 (4.2)	1 (4.2)	3 (4.2)	1 (5.5)	2 (5.5)	1 (6.2)	2 (5.4)
Custer	0.5 (4.2)	1 (4.2)	4 (5.6)	1 (5.5)	2 (5.5)	1 (6.2)	1.5 (4.1)
Lemhi	0.5 (4.2)	1 (4.2)	3 (4.2)	1 (5.5)	2 (5.5)	0.5 (3.1)	1.5 (4.1)
Washington	0.5 (4.2)	1 (4.2)	3 (4.2)	1 (5.5)	2 (5.5)	1 (6.2)	2 (5.4)
Idaho	1 (8.3)	1 (4.2)	3 (4.2)	0.5 (2.8)	1.5 (4.2)	1 (6.2)	1.5 (4.1)
Nez Perce	0.5 (4.2)	2 (8.3)	3 (4.2)	1 (5.5)	1.5 (4.2)	1 (6.2)	1.5 (4.1)
Bear Lake	0.3 (2.5)	1 (4.2)	1 (1.4)	0.3 (1.7)	1 (2.8)	0.3 (1.9)	1 (2.7)
Kootenai	0.5 (4.2)	0.5 (2.1)	3 (4.2)	0.5 (2.8)	1.5 (4.2)	1 (6.2)	2 (5.4)
Owyhee	0.5 (4.2)	1 (4.2)	3 (4.2)	0.5 (2.8)	1 (2.8)	0.5 (3.1)	1.5 (4.1)
Cassia	0.3 (2.5)	1 (4.2)	2 (2.8)	0.5 (2.8)	1 (2.8)	0.5 (3.1)	1 (2.7)
Oneida	0.8 (6.7)	1 (4.2)	2 (2.8)	0.3 (1.7)	1 (2.8)	0.3 (1.9)	1 (2.7)
	12	24	72	18	36	16	37

*An Act Providing for the Apportionment of the Legislature, 1890–91 Idaho Sess. Laws, pp.195–96.

column is the number of representatives apportioned to that county, and the second number, in parentheses, is the county's percentage of the total representation.

By comparing the shifts in percentage of representation from each county it is possible to determine which counties gained influence during the adjustments to statehood. The biggest winner was Shoshone County, which increased its percentage in the Senate by 8.3 percent and in the House by 4.6 percent between 1888 and 1891, for a total increase in legislative representation of 12.9 percent. Latah county was another winner and managed to increase its share of the legislature by a total of 11.8 percent Kootenai increased by 5.5 percent, Boise and Washington by 3.2 percent and Custer by 1.9 percent. The obvious big loser was Alturas County, which sent 16.7 percent of the delegates to the last territorial legislature, but less than half that under the 1891 statute. This loss was caused largely by the creation of Logan and Elmore counties, but also because of declining population. Oneida lost 6.3 percent in its share of the total representation, and Bingham, Lemhi, Idaho, Nez Perce, Bear Lake, Owyhee and Cassia all suffered small losses. Ada County sent roughly the same proportion of the delegates to the last territorial legislature as under the 1891 act, but its share of the total dipped in the middle during the convention and in the 1890 legislature.

The fairness of the apportionment of these various representative bodies can be judged by the four standards set out in the columns of Table B: (1) equal representation of each county; (2) the number of votes cast in the 1888 election of the territorial delegate to Congress; (3) the number of votes cast in the 1889 ratification of the Idaho Constitution; and, (4) the 1890 census. The first number in each column is the tally of votes cast in that county, and the second number, in parentheses is that county's share of the total.

The four standards correspond to the convention debates. Equal county representation is what Reid fought so tanaciously for, especially in connection with the senate of the first state legislature. Under Reid's plan, each county was entitled to 5.5 percent of the Senate. Under the plan actually adopted, 8 counties received exactly 5.5 percent, including Reid's own county of Nez Perce. Just as Reid had predicted, the big winners were Shoshone, Ada, Latah and Bingham counties, which held 11.1 percent, 11.1 percent, 11.1 percent and 7.2 percent, respectively, of the delegates rather than the equal share of 5.5 percent. The big losers were the three most southern, and Mormon, counties. Bear Lake and Oneida counties each held only 1.7 percent of the first Senate, while Cassia had 2.8 percent. In the north, Idaho and Kootenai were also both losers because their delegations made up only 2.8 percent of the total.

From these figures it is possible to calculate the difference to the political parties between apportioning equally between the counties or on the basis of the 1888 votes. Ten counties at the convention were represented by Republican delegations.[9] Four of these counties would have had the same representation under either alternative. Latah, Ada, and Shoshone as a group would increase their percentage of representation by a total of 16.8 percent if the 1888 census was used. Two Republican counties suffered a loss of 5.4 percent, but the aggregate Republican gain was 11.4 percent Eight counties at the time of the convention can be described as Democratic.[10] Four of these counties

Table B.

Number of Votes by County, 1888 and 1889, and 1890 Census

County	Equal	1888 Election	1888 Ratif.	1890 Census
Alturus	1 (5.5)	2,747 (17.1)	341 (2.4)	2,629 (3.1)
Elmore	1 (5.5)	–	821 (5.8)	1,870 (2.2)
Logan	1 (5.5)	–	399 (2.8)	4,169 (4.9)
Shoshone	1 (5.5)	1,805 (11.2)	1,862 (13.2)	5,382 (6.4)
Ada	1 (5.5)	1,670 (10.4)	1,774 (12.6)	8,368 (9.9)
Latah	1 (5.5)	1,442 (9)	2,640 (18.7)	9,173 (10.9)
Bingham	1 (5.5)	1,416 (8.8)	887 (6.3)	13,575 (16.1)
Boise	1 (5.5)	849 (5.3)	619 (4.4)	3,342 (4)
Custer	1 (5.5)	797 (5)	510 (3.6)	2,176 (2.6)
Lemhi	1 (5.5)	763 (4.8)	920 (6.5)	1,915 (2.3)
Washington	1 (5.5)	763 (4.8)	615 (4.4)	3,836 (4.5)
Idaho	1 (5.5)	713 (4.4)	336 (2.4)	2,955 (3.5)
Nez Perce	1 (5.5)	635 (4)	215 (1.5)	2,847 (3.4)
Bear Lake	1 (5.5)	614 (3.8)	83 (0.6)	6,057 (7.2)
Kootenai	1 (5.5)	613 (3.8)	1,056 (7.5)	4,108 (4.9)
Owyhee	1 (5.5)	472 (2.9)	425 (3)	2,021 (2.4)
Cassia	1 (5.5)	414 (2.6)	222 (1.6)	3,143 (3.7)
Oneida	1 (5.5)	340 (2.1)	374 (2.7)	6,819 (8.1)
	18	16,053	14,109	

were also unaffected by the choice. But, four others lost a total of 13 percent of their representation. Bingham County gained nearly 2 percent, but the Democrats were still short the roughly 11 percent the Republicans had gained.

The 1888 votes in the congressional delegate election were used to apportion the constitutional convention and the first legislature. As a result, the percentages from each county correlate closely. Still, Ada County, and to a lesser extent Bingham, enjoyed a slight overrepresentation in the convention at the expense of Bear Lake and Boise. Bingham, Nez Perce and several other counties managed a slight overrepresentation in the first state legislature, again at the expense of Bear Lake, Idaho, and several other counties.

Using of the 1890 census to assess apportionments makes a dramatic difference because it includes the Mormon population in the formula. This was the standard originally proposed by the legislative committee, but the 1888 voting numbers were substituted at chairman Morgan's request. The extent of the underrepresentation of Mormon counties at Idaho's convention can be measured by comparing the percentage of population from the 1890 census with the percentage of representation at the convention. Bingham County had 16.1 percent of the population and 9.7 percent of the convention delegates. Bear Lake had 7.2 percent and 1.4 percent, Oneida 8.1 percent and 2.8 percent, and Logan 4.9 percent and 4.2 percent, respectively. Latah and Kootenai counties were also underrepresented by this standard because of the large immigration occurring at the time. The advantage of the underrepresentation was distributed evenly between the remaining counties. As measured by the census, Alturas County was overrepresented by 5.2 percent at the convention, Shoshone by 4.7 percent, Custer by 3 percent, Ada by 2.6 percent, Elmore by 2 percent, Lemhi by 1.9 percent, and several other counties by smaller amounts. The underrepresentation in the first state legislature was not quite as extreme.

The Idaho Constitutional Convention decided to apportion on the basis of the 1888 vote rather than population or by treating each of the counties as an equal sovereign. As a result, Republicans gained 11 percent of the first senate over the Democrats, the large counties gained 18.5 percent over the small counties,[11] and the non-Mormon counties gained 16.5 percent over the Mormon counties.[12] These three figures neatly summarize the forces that ruled Idaho apportionment at the time of statehood.

4. Idaho's Apportionment Tradition

THE IDAHO LEGISLATURE'S long and tumultous history of apportionment legislation began in its first session with the passage of An Act Providing for the Apportionment of the Legislature on March 13, 1891.[13] The legislature had earlier created Alta and Lincoln out of Alturas and Logan counties, with some boundary adjustments,[14] and the apportionment statute reflected these changes. The Alta and Lincoln act was subsequently found unconstitutional because the legislature did not allow the counties to vote on the division.[15] This ruling, in turn, lead to a challenge of the apportionmment act. It was alleged the state's first apportionment act was unconstitutional in total because it named Alta and Lincoln counties which did not exist and failed to give representation to Alturas and Logan counties which did exist.

The Idaho Supreme Court agreed in *Ballentine v. Willey*.[16] Those wanting to sustain the statute argued the legislature had the power to entirely deprive a county of representation, except for the one representative required by the constitution, so that it did not matter that Alturas and Logan were not mentioned. One of the most important passages from the court's opinion is the answer it gave to this contention:

> One of the very foundation principles of our government is that of equal representation, and the legislature is prohibited from enacting an apportionment law which does not give to the people of one county substantially equal representation to that given each other county in the state. . . . The reservation of rights by the people is broad enough to prohibit the legislature from passing an apportionment act which is manifestly unequal and unjust to the people of any portion of the state."[17]

No authority was cited by the court, because none really existed. The Idaho Constitution did not expressly require apportionment according to population. Article III, § 4 states only that the legislature is "to be apportioned as may be provided by law."

A few months after its first apportionment statute was struck down, the Idaho legislature had occasion to try again while creating Fremont and Bannock counties out of Bingham County. The statutes attached each county to the tenth senatorial district, which was Bingham County, but said nothing about representation in the House.[18] Bingham County claimed the statute creating Bannock County was unconstitutional, in part because Bannock County was not entitled to elect a representative. The Idaho supreme court disagreed, and upheld the statute. The court put the entire emphasis upon apportionment according to population, and ignored entirely the role of counties in apportionment under the Idaho Constitution. It said, "The voting population was the basis of representation under the constitutional apportionment, – not the county."[19] Since the representation of the *voters* of Bannock County did not change, the act was sustained.

The legislature passed another general apportionment act in March 1895[20] and began traveling the opposite direction from the court. The statute emphasized counties in apportionment by creating twenty-one senatorial districts, one for each county. The number of representatives was increased to forty-nine, and they were to be elected by a scheme which did not combine any two counties. County sovereignty was clearly a coprinciple of population in the act. This scheme was amended in 1899 to reflect the creation of Blaine and Lincoln out of Alturas and Logan counties.[21] In 1901 some adjustments were made in the apportionment of the House. The number of representatives was reduced to forty-six, and a formula for new counties was included. Each new county was to constitute a senatorial district and elect one representative.

The legislature passed an apportionment bill nearly every session for the next twenty years. In 1903[22] and 1909[23] adjustments were made in the House apportionment. Statutes were passed to include new counties and make related adjustments in the House in 1907 (Bonner and Twin Falls),[24] 1911 (Adams, Bonneville, Clearwater and Lewis),[25] and 1913 (Franklin, Gooding, Minidoka, Power, Jefferson, Madison and Valley).[26] Finally, in 1917 the legislature devised a formula for apportionment which made it unnecessary to consider a bill every session.[27] Each county would continue to be a senatorial district, and in addition would elect one representative for each 2,500 votes and an additional representative if another 1,000 votes were cast for governor in the last general election. The secretary of state was empowered to certify the number of representatives for each county and to make the necessary apportionments when new counties were created.

The legislature provided for each county to elect its own senator in all this legislation, except in the 1911 bill. The constitution put the maximum number of senators at twenty-four, which created a problem for the legislature in the spring of 1911 because it wanted to create Adams, Bonneville, Lewis and Clearwater counties but already had twenty-four senators. The counties were created and in the short term combined with other counties into senatorial districts. For a long-term solution the legislature proposed to amend Article III, § 2, to read, "The senate shall consist of one (1) member from each county."[28] Idaho voters ratified the amendment in November 1912 and the legislature returned to its policy of apportioning the senate by counties. This was, of course, what James W. Reid had proposed, and the other delegates rejected, in the summer of 1889.

The 1917 formula was revised in 1933[29] to provide for calculation of each county's representation on the basis of population rather than votes cast in the most recent governor's election. Since the Mormons had regained the franchise in the 1890s,[30] there was no longer a reason to use votes cast rather than population. Each county was to get one representative for every ten thousand of its population, and another one thousand for a remaining fraction of five thousand or more. It was revised again in 1951[31] to allow one representative for each seventeen thousand population and one for a remaining fraction of three thousand or more.

By the early 1960s county sovereignty had become established as the most important principle in apportionment of the Idaho legislature. The Senate was apportioned strictly by the counties. The House apportionment was based upon population, but even here county sovereignty played an important part. Each county was guaranteed a representative regardless of population. The House election districts were based upon county lines with no two counties combined. The legislature had followed these prinicples consistently since 1895, and the constitution had been amended by the people to endorse its policy.

Then, the world began to change, and the first sign was a lawsuit filed by George O. Caesar, an Ada County resident.[32] Caeasar alleged it would violate both the United States and Idaho constitutions to apportion Idaho after the 1960 census under the 1951 statute. He complained that the requirement of one representative per county and the low minimum number of persons needed for an additional representative enabled 15.2 percent of the population living in counties with fewer than 8,500 people to control 35 percent of the representation in the House. He also complained that Elmore County with a population of 16,719 would have one representative just like Clark County with a population of 915. The district court agreed with Caesar, found the 1951 statute produced an arbitrary and capricious apportionment, and ordered apportionment under the 1933 statute. In a three-two decision the Idaho supreme court reversed on appeal in March 1962. The majority thought the cases interpreting the Fourteenth Amendment of the U.S. Constitution permitted states to take into account county lines and factors other than equal representation. It also found disproportionate representation permissible under the Idaho Constitution because, after all, it is that constitution that requires one representative per county.

The 1963 legislature passed a reapportionment statute,[33] but Walter R. Hearne from Pocatello and Stanley E. Whitman from Ada County filed suit, this time in federal district court, seeking a declaration that the 1962 elections were invalid because they violated the Fourteenth Amendment.[34] In January of 1964, a three-judge district court panel held, as the Idaho supreme court had, in a split decision, that the apportionment of the 1962 legislature was constitutionally permissible.

Even though Idaho's traditional apportionment withstood these first two attacks, in the spring of 1964 the United States Supreme Court held in *Reynolds v. Sims*[35] that the Fourteenth Amendment required both houses of state legislatures be apportioned according to a population principle. Several state apportionment schemes were before the Court, including Alabama's, whose apportionment looked very much like Idaho's. Chief Justice Earl Warren wrote for the Court, " Simply stated, an individual's right to vote for state legislators is unconstitutionally impaired when its weight is in a substantial fashion diluted when compared with votes of citizens living in other parts of the State."[36] In light of *Reynolds*, the Supreme Court summarily reversed the district court in the *Hearne* case.[37]

In response to *Reynolds* and *Hearne*, Idaho called an extraordinary session of the legislature to consider reapportionment and other matters.[38] The legislature responded by reapportioning the Senate according to a scheme designed to appear based on population while still actually dominated by counties.[39] Nine senatorial districts were created. Each district included several counties, and was entitled to elect one senator for each county. Even though every voter in the district voted for each of the senators in the district, one senator came from each county. The House was also reapportioned among twenty-seven representative districts.[40]

One year later the governor responded with another call for an extraordinary session.[41] On its second try, the legislature abandoned the traditional principle of apportionment by counties and declared its objective to comply with the United States Constitution and to form legislative districts of approximately equal population with one senator and two representatives to be elected from each district. The counties were divided and combined in various ways to form the districts, which were described in great detail by precincts in the statute.

After the 1970 census, another extraordinary session to reapportion was called,[42] and the legislature made some adjustments in the 1967 statute.[43] H. Dean Summers and others challenged this statute in federal district court,[44] alleging the legislature had failed to adhere to the population principle because the districts ranged from 18,207 to 22,162 persons per legislator, or in other terms, from 10.62 percent overrepresentation to 8.79 underrepresentation. The court upheld the apportionment finding "the Legislature made a conscientious and good faith effort to create districts of equal populations as near as practicable," and held it was permissible to take into consideration "existing county, natural and historical boundary lines so as to create districts with similar economical and community interests."[45] Without stating its reasons, the court also said the legislature "could not and was not required to comply with the Idaho Constitutional prohibition against dividing counties."[46]

The court also observed a small part of the statute was improper because districts included precincts that were not contiguous, as required by the Idaho Constitution, and suggested this problem be corrected. The legislature made the corrections, and some other changes in the spring of 1972 and all appeared well.[47] But not for long. Summers appealed to the United States Supreme Court which vacated the district court's sanction of Idaho's statute and sent the case back for further consideration in light of three apportionment decisions it had rendered during the 1973 term.[48] There was a strong dissent which argued the population deviations were caused by population shifts and geography, not from the influence of counties, and therefore was permissible. The 1974 legislature responded by appointing a nonpartisan committee to prepare a plan for reapportionment,[49] and later adopting a statute which made the population in every district more nearly equal.[50]

The 1980 census caused even more apportionment controversy. The legislature was convened in a special session in July 1981, but the bill they passed was vetoed. The first reapportionment bill passed in 1982 was also vetoed, but on the third try the legislature and governor were able to agree and a statute was passed.[51] But not everyone was happy. One month later William and Gretchen Hellar and others filed a complaint in state district court alleging the statute violated Article III §5 because it divided counties. They sought to enjoin the 1982 primary and general elections. The district court judge was unwilling to stop the elections, but he did rule the statute violated the Idaho Constitution, because it was possible to apportion Idaho in a manner that complied with both the U.S. and Idaho constitutions. The plaintiffs had submitted five plans that would satisfy both, including using multi-county and floterial districts, which would make all districts nearly equal. The judge went on to order that if the legislature did not reapportion itself in the fall of 1982, and hold a special election during 1983, he would enter an order redistricting the legislature. The legislature ignored the order, and that is where matters stood when the Supreme Court rendered its judgment on the appeal from the district court in June of 1983.[52] The Supreme Court unanimously agreed the right to equal protection under the United States Constitution made the prohibition on dividing Idaho counties invalid only if there were no possibility of compliance with both. However, the court avoided the difficult task of devising a remedy and remanded the case to the district court for further proceedings.

On remand, the district court again ruled Idaho's apportionment statute was invalid because it divided counties. The court was unwilling to enjoin the 1984 elections which were approaching because of expense and other difficulties, and also ruled the legislature elected in 1984 could lawfully sit even though it had been ruled in advance that it would not be lawfully elected. However, the court did rule that further legislative elections would be held pursuant to a court-imposed apportionment, which established thirty-three districts with forty-two senate seats and eighty-four representatives. The plan used six multi-member districts and seven floterial districts. The largest district under the plan had a population of 23,748 people, and the smallest 21,576. In a 4–1 decision,[53] the Idaho supreme court upheld the district court in every particular except one. The court again invited the legislature to pass a constitutional apportionment plan to replace the judicially imposed plan.

The legislature was caught on one hand between the United States and Idaho constitutions, and on the other between its own interests in apportioning. The first two attempts failed, but during the last hours in session in the spring of 1984 a bill was passed.[54] No counties were divided, but the plaintiffs in the *Hellar* case immediately petitioned the Idaho supreme court asking it to find that the statute failed to comply with the U.S. Constitution because the populations in the districts varied too much. In April 1984, in a 3–2 decision,[55] the court declared the statute unconstitutional and ordered that the 1984 elections would be held under the apportionment plan devised by the district court. Not only did the majority and dissenters disagree on whether the statute complied with the Fourteenth Amendment, in a crass breach of judicial decorum the justices impugned each other's character and criticized their conduct of the case.

The legislature also sought to solve its problem by amending the Idaho Constitution. In 1984 it proposed Article III § 5 be amended so that counties could be divided in creating legislative districts.[56] The measure was not approved by the voters. The legislature became reconciled to live temporarily with the judicial plan but to try amending the constitution again so that it could recapture and exercise its own authority to apportion after the 1990 census. In 1986 the legislature proposed amending Art III § 1 so that after 1990 the Senate would have between thirty and thirty-five members and the House up to two times as many representatives.[57] At the time, the section still required the Senate to be apportioned by counties even though that practice had been abandoned in 1967. The legislature also proposed to amend Article III § 5 by prohibiting use of floterial districts and by dividing counties, but "only to the extent it is reasonably determined by statute that counties must be divided to create senatorial and representative districts which comply with the constitution of the United States."

Idaho voters approved these two amendments in the fall of 1986, and on the eve of Idaho's centennial the principles of county sovereignty and population have found a new equilibrium in their continual struggle. While in every era the self-interests of the legislators are evident, during the territorial period the population principle was the prevailing norm. County sovereignty was strongly advocated in the Idaho Convention, and within twenty years had captured a dominating influence, especially in the Senate but also in the House. There was a complete reversal in the late 1960s, and the influence of counties in apportionment almost completely vanished. County sovereignty made a strong comeback in the 1980s, finally being accorded a status equal to the population principle of the U.S. Constitution. But the 1986 amendments seriously compromised the role of counties in apportionment, so that as Idaho heads into its second century their influence is but a ghost of the past. But the controversy continues, and a workable consensus is often hard to find. Harsh words have sometimes been spoken, and they will no doubt be spoken again, because, as Justice Huntley of the Idaho supreme court observed, "Did anyone ever believe that either legislators or jurists could maintain decorum and a sense of humor while undergoing reapportionment proceedings?"[58]

Notes

1. The debates at the Idaho Constitutional Convention are reported in I.W. Hart, ed., *The Proceedings and Debates of the Idaho Constitutional Convention*. Caldwell, Idaho: Caxton Printers, Ltd.,1912, 2 vols. These two volumes are paginated consecutively, and all page references in the text are to them.

2. Section 11, 12 Stat. 808.

3. Ibid., section 4.

4. These sessions are briefly reviewed in Hawley, James H., ed., *History of Idaho*. 5 vols. Chicago: S. J. Clarke Publishing Co., 1920, 1:149–95.

5. Section 4, 12 Stat. L. 808, ch. 17.

6. Beal, Merrill D. and Wells, Merle W. *History of Idaho*. 3 vols. New York: Lewis Historical Pub. Co., 1959, 1:341–42.

7. Act of June 20, 1864, ch. 141, 13 Stat. 142.

8. McCleod, George A. *History of Alturas and Blaine Counties Idaho*. Revised edition. Hailey: *The Hailey Times*, 1938.

9. Eight counties sent delegations where the Republicans outnumbered the Democrats: Kootenai, Latah, Lemhi, Custer, Ada, Owyhee, and Logan. Bear Lake sent one Republican because of Mormon disfranchisement, and it should properly be considered a Democratic county at the time of the convention. To these obviously Republican delegations should be added Shoshone and Alturas. Even though the delegations from these two counties were divided equally between the parties, the Republican members of each delegation were obviously dominant at the convention.

10. Six counties sent delegations where the Democrats outnumbered the Republicans: Nez Perce, Idaho, Washington, Boise, Elmore, and Bingham. Bear Lake should be added to this list on the basis of its territorial history. In addition, even though Oneida and Cassia sent delegations evenly divided between the parties, they should also be considered Democratic counties for the same reason.

11. The large counties were Latah, Ada, Shoshone and Bingham. The small counties who suffered the loss were Kootenai, Owyhee, Idaho, Bear Lake, Cassia and Oneida.

12. This would be the amount if Bingham, Bear Lake and Oneida were considered Mormon counties.

13. 1890–91 Idaho Sess Laws 195–96.

14. An Act to Create and Organize the Counties of Alta and Lincoln, 1890–91 Idaho Sess Laws 120–24.

15. *People ex rel. Lincoln County v. George*, 3 Idaho 72, 26 P. 983 (1891).

16. *Ballentine v. Willey*, 3 Idaho 496, 31 P. 994 (1893).

17. Ibid. at 997.

18. An Act to Create and Organize the County of Fremont, 1893 Sess. Laws, 97; An Act to Create and Organize Bannock county, 1893 Idaho Sess. Laws 173–74.

19. *Sabin v. Curtis*, 3 Idaho 662, at 668, 32 P. 1130, at 1132 (1893).

20. An Act to Provide for the Apportionment of the Legislature, 1895 Idaho Sess Laws 52–54.

21. An Act to Provide for the Apportionment of the Legislature, 1899 Idaho Sess Laws 132–33.

22. Canyon, Fremont, Nez Perce, and Oneida each gained one representative, while Boise, Lemhi, and Owyhee lost one. An Act to Provide for the Apportionment of the Legislature, 1903 Idaho Sess Laws 220–22.

23. Bonner, Canyon, Kootenai, Lincoln, Shoshone, and Twin Falls counties all gained one representative. An Act Defining the Apportionment of the Senate and House of Representatives, 1909 Idaho Sess Laws 106–08.

24. Bonner, Twin Falls, and Nez Perce each gained one representative, while Oneida and Shoshone each lost one. An Act to Provide For a New Apportionment of the Legislature, 1907 Idaho Sess Laws 472–74.

25. Adams, Bonner, Bonneville, Lewis, and Oneida all gained one representative, while Bingham, Canyon, Idaho, and Nez Perce all lost one. An Act Relating to the Apportionment of the Senate and House of Representatives, 1911 Idaho Sess Laws 730–31.

26. An Act Relating to the Apportionment of the Senate and House of Representatives, 1913 Idaho Sess Laws 622–24.

27. An Act Relating to the Apportionment of the Senate and House of Representatives, 1917 Idaho Sess Laws 493–94.

28. 1911 Idaho Sess Laws 788, J.J.R. No. 13.

29. An Act Providing for Reapportionment of the Members of the House of Representatives of the State of Idaho, 1933 Idaho Sess Laws 125.

30. See chapter 8 below, subheading 4.

31. An Act to Provide for Reapportionment of the Members of the House of Representatives of the State of Idaho, Regular 1951 Idaho Sess Laws 88.

32. *Caesar v. Williams*, 84 Idaho 254, 371 P. 2d 241 (1962).

33. 1963 Idaho Sess Laws 145.

34. *Hearne v. Smylie*, 225 F.Supp. 645 (1964).

35. 377 U.S. 533, 84 S.Ct. 1362,

36. 84 S.Ct. at 1385.

37. *Hearne v. Smylie*, 378 U.S. 563, 84 S.Ct. 1917, 12 L.Ed.2d 1036 (1964).

38. 1965 Idaho Sess Laws, Extraordinary Session, pp. 3–4.

39. An Act Creating Seantorial Districts, 1965 Idaho Sess Laws 16–17.

40. An Act Providing that Representatives of the House Shall be Elected From Twenty-Seven Representative Districts, 1965 Idaho Sess Laws 19–20.

41. 1967 Idaho Sess Laws, Third Extraordinary Session, pp. 3–4.

42. 1971 Idaho Sess Laws, Extraordinary Session, pp. 3–4.

43. An Act Providing for Legislative Districts, 1971 Idaho Sess Laws 18–24.

44. *Summers v. Cenarussa*, 342 F.Supp. 288 (1972).

45. Ibid.

46. Ibid. at 290.

47. An Act Relating to Legislative Districts, 1972 Idaho Sess Laws 250–56.

48. *Summers v. Cenarrusa*, 413 U.S. 906, 93 S.Ct. 3037, 37 L.Ed2d 1018 (1973).

49. A Concurrent Resolution Authorizing and Directing a Committee to Prepare a Plan for Reapportionment of the Idaho Legislature, S.C.R. No. 132, 1974 Idaho Sess Laws 1850.

50. An Act Relating to Legislative Districts, 1974 Idaho Sess Laws 1083–90.

51. An Act Relating to Legislative Districts, 1982 Idaho Sess Laws 473.

52. *Hellar v. Cenarrusa*, 104 Idaho 858, 664 P.2d 765 (1983).

53. *Hellar v. Cenarrusa*, 106 Idaho 571, 682 P.2d 524 (1984).

54. 1984 Idaho Sess Laws 414–19.

55. *Hellar v. Cenarrusa*, 106 Idaho 586, 682 P.2d 539 (1984).

56. H.J.R. No. 5, 1984 Idaho Sess Laws 691.

57. H.J.R. No. 4, 1986 Idaho Sess Laws 869–70.

58. *Hellar v. Cenarussa*, 106 Idaho 586, 617, 182 P.2d 539, 570 (1984).

6.
Education

1. Public Indebtedness

THE CONVENTION DELEGATES reconvened on Monday morning, July 22, for their fifteenth session, and many believed it would be their last week in session. The majority (Republican) and minority (Democratic) reports of the suffrage committee, which included the critical sections on the Mormon question, had been printed and were on the desks of the delegates when they arrived. The Republicans wanted to take up the suffrage article immediately, so James H. Beatty (R-Alturas), chair of the committee, moved to dispense with the regular order of business in order to do so. The convention rejected his suggestion, however, and it instead took up the public indebtedness and subsidies article (pp. 557-660).[1]

After the lunch recess Beatty once again made his motion to take up the suffrage article. He argued that since suffrage is covered in the second article of most state constitutions, and since it was important for the convention to deliver completed articles to the committee on revision in order to adjourn within a reasonable time, it was necessary to take up his committee's report (pp. 557–58). In addition, Beatty claimed many delegates had told him they were leaving at the week's end, "While a large majority of the convention is present . . . by the end of the week the convention will be largely scattered" (p. 630).

Democrats protested loudly. James W. Reid (D-Nez Perce) claimed that in most constitutions, the legislative, executive and judicial articles follow the declaration of rights article (pp. 607-8). Alexander Mayhew (D-Shoshone) wanted to continue the business under consideration at the morning's end, and complained, "It is nothing more than fair, it is nothing more than legitimate, it is nothing more than parliamentary to consider the matter as unfinished and continue the sitting upon that question until it is disposed of" (p. 611). George Ainslie (D-Boise) charged that taking up suffrage out of order would violate the rules of the body (pp. 608–9).

The Democrats tried a whole series of procedural motions to disrail Beatty's proposal (pp. 609–21). They began by accusing the Republicans of being partisan. J. W. Poe (D-Nez Perce) charged that "the object and the intention of this convention is to take up something out of order in order to get political advantage, it seems to me" (p. 621). George Ainslie stated that the Democrats had not had a caucus on the suffrage reports and urged that "every democratic member of this convention . . . remain silent and not vote and leave the republican party of this convention without a quorum" (p. 619). Mayhew argued that "If there was any haste in this—if the republicans were going to lose some of their members as the democrats have by getting leave of absence, I would not then be astonished at their anxiety to consider the subject, but I see they are more anxious to remain here than the democrats are, because the latter are going away very rapidly" (pp. 628–29).

Finally, Ainslie offered to compromise by suggesting the suffrage article be set as a special order of business to be taken up on Friday. Beatty refused, and insisted on Wednesday at the latest. The delegates adjourned for twenty minutes, and then reported back an agreement to set the article for Thursday morning. The main bout had been scheduled.

Sandwiched between these partisan skirmishes on the Mormon question was the article on public indebtedness and subsidies. The committee was chaired by Judge Albert Hagan (D-Kootenai), who by this time had left the convention in disgust over the private takings power that had been included in the declaration of rights article. As a result, the report of the committee had not been carefully worked out. Orlando B. Batten (D-Alturas) was the real sponsor of the bill, even though he had submitted it to Hagan for his review (p. 567). At one point William J. McConnell (R-Latah) complained, "I think the committee did not carefully and fully consider this question. I am a member of the committee myself; the chairman was absent nearly all the time, but we brought in this report, so that the convention can take it up and consider it themselves" (p. 567). The public indebtedness committee brought in a report that adopted a policy of closely restricting the ability of state and local governments to incur debt, and it recommended five sections to tie the hands of government officials.

Section 1 prohibited the legislature from creating any general indebtedness that would "exceed the sum of one per centum upon the assessed value of the taxable property in the state" (p. 651). Special indebtedness could be incurred for a single project, if a fund was created for retiring the debt within twenty years, and if the voters approved at a general election.

There was bipartisan objection to the committee's theory. McConnell moved to raise the limit to one and one-half percent (p. 561). Mayhew wanted to raise it to two percent, or two and one-half percent (p. 563). Batten, who wrote the report, suggested excluding territorial indebtedness, so that the state government could incur more liability (p. 573). Sol Hasbrouck (R-Washington) wanted an absolute limit of $250,000 for ten years, after which a percentage limit would become applicable (p. 581). William H. Clagett (R-Shoshone) thought that was a good idea, but wanted a limit of $500,000 (p. 583).

The debt limit was the source of considerable confusion during the debate. A number of delegates, like Charles M. Hays (R-Owyhee), thought the power to levy an annual tax was at issue, and complained that the debt limit would not permit a large enough budget to meet the annual expense of government. McConnell continually explained that, "No, it is not in regard to levying taxes; it is in regard to the future indebtedness of the state.. .. It is a question of future taxation for the present; it is not a question of present taxation" (pp. 570–71). Ainslie stated the territory had property valued at a total of $48 million (p. 562), but Mayhew quickly corrected him, and it was generally agreed that according to the report of a territorial official, the total property valuation was less than $22 million (pp. 563–64).

While these delegates were confused on the details, they were certain about the need to increase the niggardly debt limit in the committee report. McConnell did the arithmetic, and pointed out that the one percent limit on the $22 million worth of property would allow a maximum of $220,000 in debt. Since the territory was already $200,000 in debt, and the state would have to assume that debt, only $20,000 remained for those things necessary after statehood (p. 566). McConnell pointed out the necessity of building a penitentiary, and that the warrants were still outstanding for the salaries of the last territorial legislature. W. C. B. Allen (R-Logan) was worried about the need to issue bonds for constructing irrigation canals, and Aaron F. Parker (D-Idaho) was concerned about "radical road improvements," by which he meant the wagon road near White Bird hill that had been approved in the last territorial legislature (p. 569). Ainslie worried about paying a "contingent indebtedness for the state university at Moscow" (p. 575).

In a rather sudden vote that is no doubt not fully reported in the convention proceedings, the delegates decided to exclude territorial indebtedness from the limitation, and to raise the limit to one and one-half percent of the assessed property valuation (p. 584). They then adopted § 2 which prohibited extension of the state's credit on behalf of any private interest, and took up § 3. Section 3 severely limited the capacity of counties to incur indebtedness by prohibiting any debt beyond current revenues, unless a special election was held to approve it and a tax established to retire the debt. Just as there were immediate objections when limits were proposed for the state government, there was outcry about putting such strong limits on the counties.

H. S. Hampton (R-Cassia) was worried that ordinary expenses could not be paid, and moved to strike the section (p. 584). Weldon Heyburn (R-Shoshone) and Drew Standrod (D-Oneida) explained that one-third of their counties' revenues were from licenses, which varied greatly, sometimes five or six thousand dollars a year, which made necessary incurring temporary indebtedness, beyond the current revenues. Therefore, it did not make sense to pay "eight or nine hundred dollars – for the purpose of determining whether or not you should issue $500 worth of warrants" (pp. 590–91).

Peter Pefley (D-Ada), who had recently served as Mayor of Boise City, thought cities and counties should be able to incur debt "in contingencies [emergencies] to abate them immediately," and told of his concern that the streams and canal in his city might "break away and run down through the city" (p. 592). J. M. Howe (R-Nez Perce), another opponent of limitations, wanted to limit government by limiting expenditures rather than revenues (pp. 592–93).

Clagett moved to exclude from the § 3 limitation any ordinary indebtedness created under the general laws of the state (p. 586). Clagett explained the operation of county finances under territorial law. "We all know that in the practical administration of county government, that there sometimes will be extraordinary expenses, I mean extraordinary expenses in the ordinary administration of affairs." He stated that witness fees were routinely paid with scrip, and that the proposed section would require the commissioners to hold a special election to pay witness fees (p. 588).

Orlando Batten, who had been flexible on the limitation to be put on the legislature, staunchly defended the county restrictions in his bill. He argued, "If we are going to restrict any state or municipal indebtedness, let's restrict it. Let's not do as did Rip Van Winkle when he made a resolution not to drink anything–keep on drinking and say each drink did not count." Batten claimed Clagett's proposal would "eat the whole life out of the matter, deprive it of its very meaning," and argued that his proposal was supported by his committee and the municipal corporations committee, and that it was based on provisions in the California Constitution, and other states (p. 589). Batten's defense was not persuasive, however, and Clagett's exception to the limitation was approved.

The convention then considered Batten's next proposed limitation. Section 4 of the committee report limited the total amount of indebtedness that any unit of local government could incur to five percent of the assessed valuation. This limitation received the same reception as Batten's other proposals. Edgar Wilson (R-Ada) protested the limitation on behalf of Boise City, and laid the city's finances on the table in presenting his argument. He explained that Boise had $40,000 in floating debt, between eleven and twelve hundred thousand dollars of assessed property, and desperately wanted to build a water and sewer system. This would require incurring an additional $150,000 of debt, which could not be done under the committee report. Wilson, who thought the only city in the territory with over two thousand residents was Boise, moved to permit cities with two thousand inhabitants to raise the limit to fifteen percent by special election (pp. 594–95).

It was clear the delegates did not support Batten's miserly proposals. Wilson rather eloquently stated the prevailing conceptions on wise local government, "As you all know, these western towns cannot grow except by contracting a large indebtedness. There has not been a western town within the last ten years that has increased to any extent unless they incur large indebtedness. I think, as well shown by writers on political economy, that municipal indebtedness is absolutely necessary for municipal prosperity and . . . I make the assertion that with indebtedness the debtors are those who make vastly more wealth" (p. 595).

In his usual manner, Weldon Heyburn made a similar objection, but more bluntly. He started by saying that if the proposed section was not stricken, "as far as the members of this convention from Shoshone County are concerned, they can just go home." He explained Shoshone County had a bonded indebtedness of $150,000, a floating indebtedness of $65,000, and an assessed valuation of only a little over $1 million. He asked rhetorically on behalf of Shoshone County, "They have now an indebtedness of several times the limit that is allowed by this provision and what are they going to do?" (pp. 599–600). His solution was to strike the entire section and the rest of the delegates agreed (p. 602).

When the public indebtedness article came back to the delegates sitting in convention, William Clagett proposed a plan to get local governments on a cash basis that would discourage accumulation of debt. Under territorial law, counties levied taxes for a series of special funds like hospital, road, and education, all in addition to a general levy. Clagett suggested eliminating all special funds except education, and replacing them with a system where all funds collected, from whatever source, first went to pay current expenses and then were used to retire outstanding debts (pp. 1466–67). Clagett explained that he had sponsored and secured approval of a similar bill passed in the Nevada legislature thirty years earlier, and as a result Storey County had been able to retire a $2 million debt in two years (p. 1475). Similar statutes had also been passed by Idaho's territorial legislature, with application limited to particular counties (p. 1464).

Numerous objections were made to Clagett's suggestion. Heyburn claimed it would make it impossible for counties to keep roads and bridges in repair, or to take care of indigent people in the communities (p. 1468). Aaron Parker liked the idea of operating on a cash basis, but said that it was impossible in Idaho County because "the circulating medium is so scarce" (p. 1471). James Reid predicted it would lead to a depreciation in the value of county warrants, and a windfall to speculators (p. 1472). A special committee was finally appointed to work out the details of the proposal, but in the end the whole plan was rejected (pp. 1492–93, 1541–42).

Idahoans have frequently amended the public indebtedness and subsidies article, always for the purpose of taking on greater indebtedness. Section 1 limiting state indebtedness to one and one-half percent of the assessed property was amended in 1910 to exclude a new capitol building.[2] The section was amended again two years later to exclude other expenditures by the eleventh legislature, and the limitation of one and one-half percent was changed to a limitation of $2 million.[3] Section 2, which prohibited extension of the state's credit to private interests, was amended in 1920 to state, "except the state may control and promote the development of the unused water power within this state."[4]

Section 3, requiring an election and sinking fund for any indebtedness of local governments, has been amended six times—more than any section of the Idaho Constitution except one.[5] In 1950 cities and villages were authorized to build water, sewage and public parking facilities with revenue bonds.[6] In 1964 the time for payment of bonds was extended to thirty years, and port districts were empowered to issues revenue bonds, without approval of the voters in the district.[7] Cities were authorized to build public recreation facilities with revenue bonds in 1966,[8] and to build air and navigation facilities in 1968.[9] Voters made it easier to construct water and sewer projects in 1972 when the vote required in the special election was reduced from two-thirds to a majority.[10] Finally, in 1976, local governments were authorized to rehabilitate existing electrical generating facilities with revenue bonds approved by a majority of the voters.[11]

In addition to amending Article VIII frequently, Idaho voters have added three sections to it. In 1974 voters approved § 3A which authorizes environmental pollution control facilities to be built with revenue bonds not secured by the full faith and credit of the government.[12] A similar section was passed for port districts in 1978.[13] Most recently, in 1982, voters authorized the legislature to create public corporations authorized to issue nonrecourse revenue bonds for industrial development facilities, solid waste disposal, recreation, and energy facilities.[14]

Apparently, Idaho citizens in recent years have come to agree with Edgar Wilson's philosophy. He said at the convention, "[T]hese western towns cannot grow except by contracting a large indebtedness," and "I make the assertion that with indebtedness the debtors are those who make vastly more wealth" (p. 595).

2. Public School Lands

LATE IN THE AFTERNOON of Monday, July 22, the delegates finally scheduled the debate on the all-important Mormon question for Thursday. The next order of business was Article IX, covering education and school lands. O. B. Batten, who by default had become chairman of the public indebtedness and subsidies committee, was appointed to chair the the education committee. Batten had as much difficulty getting approval for his education article as he had with the public indebtedness article. Four sections were stricken from the article Batten proposed, and several sections were amended.

Discussion of the education article by the committee of the whole began late on July 22 and continued all day on the 23rd, the sixteenth day in session. The delegates took time from their work after the lunch recess on the 22d to receive a United States congressional delegation touring the West. The delegation was chaired by Senator Dorsey from Nebraska, and included Congressman Burrows, who was expected to become the next Speaker of the House. The various congressmen addressed the convention, and they had a common message: make your constitution as anti-Mormon as you can. They had just visited Salt Lake City, and Burrows warned the delegates he had privately learned the Mormons were planning a large immigration, "to such an extent as to absolutely dominate . . . civil affairs" (p. 719). Despite this warning, Senator Stewart from Vermont expressed his confidence that "it is not possible that the ignorance and the superstition of the narrow minded emmissaries from Utah or anywhere else will reconvert this state into a Mormon state" (p. 722).

Burrows went on to explain that polygamy must be prohibited, but that it was not the real problem. He described a sermon he had heard in the great cathedral where a church leader said, "We are loyal to the constitution of the United States, we are loyal to its flag, but I will be frank with you and state that when we receive a revelation from on high that is in conflict with either of those, we will follow the revelation to the death" (p. 720). Burrows was outraged by this claim of divine revelation and drew applause when he declared, "No body of people in this country can dominate, either in the state or in the nation that acknowledges a higher power than the power of the government in civil affairs" (p. 720). These warnings and admonitions from congressional leaders no doubt made a strong impression on the delegates as they looked forward to their debate on Mormon suffrage, only two days away.

By the time the committee of the whole finished its work on the education article during the morning of Wednesday, July 24, it had adopted eleven sections. Section 1 ordered the legislature to create a general, uniform, and thorough system of public, free, common schools, and § 2 created a board of education. Section 4 defined the public school fund, § 3 required it to remain inviolate, and § 11 provided for its investment. Section 5 prohibited appropriations to sectarian schools, § 6 prohibited religious teaching and testing in the schools, and § 9 established compulsory attendance. Section 8 governed the location and disposition of public lands and § 7 created a state board of land commissioners to carry out the policy. Finally, § 10 created a board of regents for the University of Idaho and confirmed the location of the university at Moscow.

The education article was the subject of three extended debates at the convention. The first and most lengthy controversy concerned public school lands.[15] The United States government had a long tradition of supporting public schools, dating back to the Ordinance of 1787, by granting school lands to new states upon admission to the Union.[16] Following this tradition, Congress reserved sections 16 and 36 of every township for educational purposes in the Idaho Territory's Organic act.[17] In 1883 Congress approved a special grant of seventy-two entire sections for the establishment of a university.[18] The convention had to decide what should be done with these lands.

The education committee report recommended the lands be sold and the proceeds invested as a permanent endowment, with the interest to be used to support the public schools. Section 4 stated the public school fund should include the "proceeds of such lands . . . granted by the general government." Section 7 created a board of land commissioners and entrusted to it "the direction, control and disposition of the public lands of the State." Section 8 further detailed the powers of the board, including the power to provide for the "sale . . . for the maximum possible amount." Section 8 also authorized the state legislature to "provide for the sale of such lands from time to time."

Many thought disposal of school lands a ruinous policy. Aaron Parker immediately moved to amend the report by providing "the title to all school lands shall remain forever vested in the state, and said lands shall never be encumbered by lien or mortgage for any purpose whatsover." In addition, the permanent school fund was not to be made up of "proceeds." Rather, "revenues derived from the lease or rental" was suggested (p. 649).

Parker argued that "[a] stable republican form of government depends upon our educational interests." Apparently, all at the convention agreed. Parker then went further and declared, "I hold that congress gave us these lands not for ourselves, but for our children and our children's children and for generations of posterity yet unborn" (p. 649). But not everyone at the convention agreed with this. J. W. Poe represented the claims of the living. He argued, "There is a present generation that requires aid from this school land. . . . They have had to strive . . . in almost abject poverty. . . . They had to pay the taxes out of their hard-earned money, which absolutely almost took bread from their mouths, to educate their children and provide for the public schools. . . . Shall we keep it intact for future generations and deprive ourselves?" (pp. 656–57).

Poe also argued that renting agricultural land was not the best policy. "Whenever you lease that land to an irresponsible person, a person who cares for naught so far as the preservation of that land is concerned, only that he may for the time being reap the greatest profit out of the use of it, he will care not what the condition may be that he leaves it in. . . . It will grow up in wild oats and other obnoxious substances . . ." (p. 657).

Clagett supported Parker's leasing idea. This is an odd tandem, the leading Republican at the convention joining with perhaps the most die-hard Democrat there. Clagett stated that in eastern Washington, nearly half the land was settled by renters, and that they paid one-half of their gross crop as rent. He also assumed the state would draft leases which would have conditions in them requiring the renter to maintain and preserve the land (pp. 664–65).

Heyburn, Chaney (D-Latah), Maxey (R-Ada), McConnell and others argued against renting agricultural lands. Chaney stated that in northern Idaho many prefer to let land lie idle than to rent it, because "if they rent them or lease them, in three or four years they become so foul with wild oats or cockle seed that they are no account any more" (p. 659). Heyburn related that in Spokane Falls he knew of the lease of a valuable quarter of school lands with the board of land commission for only $10. He also argued, "men will not stay on them who lease them, and they will be blots upon the surface of an otherwise prosperous country, and the men who lease them will lease them for the simple purpose of cropping them and wearing out the soil . . ." (p. 655).

Those who wanted to lease the school lands, like Parker and Clagett, were from the northern region of the territory. They met strong opposition from those in the south, such as W. C. B. Allen from Logan County. Allen argued, "The character of our lands is that they are sagebrush lands, and when once cultivated they are very much more valuable from year to year by that fact of cultivation." Sol Hasbrouck from Washington County asked, "Who is going on there to clear the sagebrush and get water rights on that land and fence it, and lease it and pay anything for the lease?" (p. 661). James Shoup (R-Custer) warned that, "nine-tenths of the school land of this territory will now be arid land" (p. 664). Dr. Maxey from Ada County pointed out, "this is a peculiar country and a peculiar soil, and the soil particularly is not adapted to leasing or renting" (p. 661). For him, the question was clear. "It simply amounts to this: The man that is tilling the land is not interested in the land, and it runs down" (p. 662).

Those who favored sale of school lands rather than leasing contended that speculators and waste could be controlled by attaching a minimum sale price, limiting the amount sold to each individual, selling at public auctions, and other devices. Minimum price provisions were commonly put in statehood acts by Congress. A minimum price of ten dollars had been included in a statute that would have authorized an Idaho constitutional convention which was introduced but not passed by Congress in 1889 (p. 2107). A minimum price of $2.50 per acre was set by Congress for the university lands Idaho received when the University of Idaho was created.[19]

Aaron Parker's absolute prohibition on sale was ultimately defeated, but his motion had its effect. The debate produced a compromise policy. Section 8 of the article as finally passed authorized disposal, but with conditions. The amount sold could not exceed twenty-five sections in any one year, it could not be sold for less than $10 per acre, it was to be sold at public auction, and it was to be sold in subdivisions not to exceed one hundred sixty acres to any one individual, company, or corporation.

Over the years, Idaho citizens have decided the convention did not go far enough in disposing of the school lands. In 1916 Section 8 was amended to raise the maximum sections to be sold in any one year from 25 to 100, and to permit sales of 320 acres to each entity.[20] In 1942 the minimum price was reduced from $10 to $5 per acre,[21] and then raised back to $10 in 1952.[22] Section 8 has also been amended to allow consolidation of lands by exchanges of school lands for land owned by the United States.

In carrying out these policies during the last century, Idaho has disposed of the bulk of its school lands.[23]

3. Bible Reading in the Public Schools

THE EDUCATION COMMITTEE REPORT addressed church and state involvement in education in two sections. Section 5 of the report prohibited any appropriation or transfer of real or personal property by the state to aid any religious or sectarian organization or its purposes.

There had been one extraordinary attempt to aid sectarian education with public monies during the territorial period. It is reported that the fourth territorial legislature, in session from December 3, 1866, until January 11, 1867, authorized an issue of $30,000 in territorial bonds. The bonds were to be redeemed by the sale of section 36 of the school lands. The proceeds of the issue was to be paid to F. N. Blanchet, the Catholic archbishop of Oregon. This bill was passed over the veto of the territorial governor but later invalidated by congress. A young George Ainslie, just beginning his long career, presided over the council during the session.[24]

The other section of the committee report touching on religion in the public schools was § 6, in which the education committee proposed, "No religious test or qualification shall ever be required of any person as a condition of admission . . . either as a teacher or student . . . and no teacher or student shall be required to attend any religious service whatsoever. . . ." The last sentence of § 6 concluded, "No sectarian or religious tenets or doctrines shall ever be taught in the public schools."

This last clause relating to sectarian or religious tenets was part of the territorial law.[25] Its development can be traced back through federal statutes governing territories, and ultimately to the First Amendment of the United States Constitution. That amendment states in part, "Congress shall make no law respecting an establishment of religion."

Shortly before the Idaho Convention, the territorial superintendent of public instruction had ruled that Bible reading in public schools violated the territory's prohibition on sectarian teaching. The superintendent further ordered that if a teacher continued Bible reading, and anybody in the community objected, that teacher forfeited pay.

The delegates at the convention recalled two versions of this territorial ruling. Edgar Wilson stated: "I know the decision, if I recollect it right, to which the reference has been made, was made for the purpose of excluding the book of Mormon from the public schools, and not the Bible" (p. 697). J. H. Meyer (D-Boise) disagreed, "It was sent up from the superintendent of Boise County to the superintendent of the territory, . . . but I dare say there is no book of Mormon within the precincts of Boise County" (p. 697).

Charles Clark (D-Ada) wanted to reverse the superintendent's ruling, and constitutionalize Bible reading in the public schools. He moved to add this language to the committee report, "Provided, that nothing therein contained shall be construed to forbid the reading of the Bible in public schools in any commonly received version, nor to enjoin its use" (p. 684). He told the convention he "would simply like to get back to where we were before that decision was rendered; that is, leave the matter entirely within the hands of the people" (p. 685). The other delegates who supported Clark argued in favor of local majority control. McConnell said: "I think where a neighborhood is religiously inclined, where the patrons of the school believe in reading of the Bible, where the trustees are willing, it should be read" (p. 686). Dr. Maxey also supported Bible reading: "If people want the Bible read, let them read it; if they do not want it read, let them keep it out" (p. 688). John Morgan also argued, "I am in favor in this country of the majority ruling" (p. 686).

Many opponents of Bible reading opposed local majority control of the question because of the disharmony it would create. John Gray said, "The use of the Bible, which I will say as for myself I would have no objections to, but I have seen schools even broken up for that reason and that reason alone" (p. 686). Aaron Parker agreed, "In a territory like this we have a large and cosmopolitan population, and I ask you, suppose we had a school district composed on an equal number of Mormons, Catholics, Jews, and Protestants? . . . What is going to become of your school system then?" (p. 695). Some delegates also challenged the right of the majority to control all affairs. Edgar Wilson stated sharply, "I believe in the majority ruling all temporal affairs, but I do not believe in the majority rule in spiritual affairs" (p. 696).

J. W. Reid was Clark's most adamant supporter, and he took the argument beyond a simple matter of local control. He claimed the Bible was the origin of American government. In refering to the committee reports of the Idaho Convention he said, "There is not one principle of sound law, one principle of right, one principle of liberty, that they have not taken from that very book" (p. 687). He continued, "It is because the Bible is read, preached and taught in the schools that this country is great and glorious, and for one I do not want to see any constitution adopted that has not in it a recognition of Jehovah" (p. 687).

To support his claim, Reid recounted a famous incident from the Philadelphia Convention that drafted the United States Constitution: "When the constitutional convention of 1787 had groped for two or three weeks, and were about to come to a disagreement on important matters of fundamental government which they were considering, and it seemed that the contentions of conflicting interests could in no way be harmonized, one of the greatest and best men of this country, the great philosopher Franklin, rose in that convention and announced the fact that he had always perceived that God governed the affairs of men in the affairs of nations as well as those of individuals, and he moved then and there that the convention proceed no further without daily invoking the aid of Jehovah in their considerations of government. From that time full light broke upon the intellects of those men, and they were able to agree and frame a constitution which has been the pride of the whole world."

Franklin was prompted to make his motion because the delegates had come to an impasse in the struggle between the large and small states over representation in Congress. Reid's account is stirring, even if it is misleading, because he left the impression the delegates agreed with Franklin, and adopted Franklin's motion. It is reported that Alexander Hamilton and others expressed their apprehensions about the motion, saying that it might have been proper at the beginning but not then, and suggesting that it might alarm citizens outside the hall about the impasse within. Williamson observed that the real reason no prayers were given was that they had no funds. Dr. Franklin defended his motion, but "[a]fter several unsuccessful attempts for silently postponing this matter by adjourning, the adjournment was at length carried, without any vote on the motion."[26] The Philadelphia delegates apparently had too much respect for Franklin to vote his motion down, but rather simply refrained from voting at all.

Partisan politics took the back seat when theology was involved on the floor of the Idaho Constitutional Convention. George Ainslie, next to Reid perhaps the most important Democrat at the convention, indignantly rebutted Reid's contention that the U.S. Constitution drew its inspiration and principles from the Bible. He said, "The statement has been made that this is a Christian nation. I deny the proposition in toto. I deny that Christianity has anything to do with the government of this country, any more than has Mormonism or Mohamedanism [sic] or any other religion. And while a majority of the people of the United States are no doubt of the Christian faith, it is not through any indorsement of the constitution of the United States or any enactments of the legislature. I believe, sir, in keeping religion and state as far apart and separate as possible" (pp. 699–700).

Clark's opponents defended the decision of the territorial superintendent, and argued the Bible was in fact a sectarian book, and should not be constitutionally read in

Idaho's public schools. Clagett defined sectarian in this manner, "The Bible is a composite book. It takes first the history of the Jewish race and the religion of the Jews. It takes in what is called the new dispensation. To this extent it may be regarded in a large sense as a sectarian book. It is not a sectarian book as between the different denominations of the Christian religion, but it is a sectarian book as applied as between the Christian religion as a whole and any other of the great religions of the earth" (p. 692).

Those supporting Bible reading couldn't accept Clagett's argument. Poe said, "This is the first instance in my life where I have ever heard it intimated that the Bible was sectarian" (p. 688). Reid was even more indignant, and said "I do not want the day to come when my children and those of my neighbors cannot read the Bible, the Bible as it is; not the book of Mormon nor the Hebrew Bible, but always the one Bible. Talk about versions! It is the Bible that was given to us in Sinai and handed to us on Olivet and preached to us, the Bible that all recognize" (p. 688).

Inevitably, the tone of the debate became more contentious and mean spirited. Reid accused Parker of speaking with "scorn and contempt" about his suggestion to include Jehovah in the constitution (p. 687). Reid also referred to an earlier attempt by Peter J. Pefley to remove the reference to God Almighty from the preamble (p. 695). James Shoup from Custer County was offended by the righteousness of Reid's arguments and declared, "But I do not think . . . members should get up and make long and eloquent speeches and references in regard to their mothers . . . or that any member on this floor should be condemned for anything he believes right and proper. I do not propose to have any such whip lash cracked over my head" (p. 699).

Edgar Wilson challenged the sincerity of Bible-reading advocates. He accused, "I think this discussion has developed more hypocrits [sic] upon this floor than anything else before the convention . . . I have heard men advocate that the Bible be read in the public schools who know more about draw poker than they do about the Bible, to my certain knowledge" (p. 696).

William Clagett made a proposal which was both a compromise, and an entirely different approach from any suggested thus far. He explained that he wanted to keep the Bible out of the schools because he feared "bigoted genetlemen" would use it to teach Christianity. On the other hand, Clagett thought the students should "have an opportunity of learning the moral lessons which are contained in that Bible" (p. 693). Clagett's compromise was to propose the section be amended to provide "nothing herein shall be construed to prevent the reading in the public schools of those portions of the Bible as inculcate lessons of morality" (p. 692).

As precedent for his proposal Clagett pointed to Ireland. He told of conditions there approximately forty years earlier that made it impossible to establish a sound school system. In search of a solution, Bishop Cullen of the Catholic church and Archbishop Wately of the Episcopal church "got together and threw aside everything of a controversial or denominational nature, and agreed to select those portions from the Bible and made it a text-book upon which not only all Christians but all people who believed in morality and decency combined and united" (p. 693).

It was of course James Reid who righteously argued against Clagett's proposal. He questioned, "Who is to decide what portions of the Bible inculcate morality? Some of the most beautiful lessons of morality are contained in the very portions he would have to exclude. . . . And then there are some of us who do not want any Catholic bishop or Episcopal bishops either to dictate what portion of the Bible we shall read . . ." (p. 694).

The debate finally ran its course, and the motions were put to a vote. Clagett's suggestion was so overwhelmingly rejected no vote count was needed (p. 702). Clark's motion to constitutionalize Bible reading in the schools was then rejected, 25 opposed, 23 in favor. Then a motion by Sol Hasbrouck was voted upon. Hasbrouck had made his motion at the outset of the debate, but it was not read (p. 684). It was moved to add, "No books, papers, tracts, or documents of a political, sectarian or denominational character, shall be used or introduced in any schools established under the provisions of this article, nor shall any teacher or any district receive any of the public school moneys in which the schools have not been taught in accordance with the provisions of this article" (p. 701).

Hasbrouck stated that his purpose was "to make it stronger than the section now appears," and regarding the meaning of his proposal said, "It is perfectly clear" (p. 701). Nevertheless, when Reid asked whether the proposed language would authorize the superintendent to exclude the Bible as sectarian, Hasbrouck replied, "I don't think it would" (p. 701). Whatever the answer to that question, the delegates liked Hasbrouck's stronger language and passed it by a vote of 25 to 22.

When the section came before the convention itself, Reid and Willis Sweet (R-Latah) tried again to get approval for Bible reading. Reid offered the Clark amendment again, and demanded a roll call vote in order to register for all the world to see the sentiments of each delegate. Most of the argument he offered was an attack on the word "political," included in the Hasbrouck motion. Reid complained that under the provision one could not teach politcal economy or the science of politics or government (pp. 1438–39). Willis Sweet agreed and cited the problem of whether to teach free trade or protection at his alma mater (p. 1439).[27]

Edgar Wilson defended the section as it was written, and claimed that political economy was not a political work, any more than astronomy or geography or chemistry. Regarding free trade, Wilson went on to say, "It is a notorious fact that every college and university of the United States of any standing at all . . . teaches the theory of free trade absolutely, but Cornell University presents both sides" (p. 1440).

When the roll call was taken on Reid's motion, only eighteen delegates would permit the Bible to be read. Twenty-five would not (p. 1443).

Despite the decision of Idaho founders to expel the Bible from the classroom, the Idaho legislature readmitted it in 1925 by passing a statute that provided in part:

Be It Enacted by the Legislature of the State of Idaho: . . . Sec. 2. That teachers employed in [public schools] shall, at the opening of each morning session . . . read, without comment or interpretation, from twelve to twenty verses from the standard American version of the Bible, to be selected from a list of passages designated from time to time by the State Board of Education. . . .[28]

This statute went unchallenged until 1963 when Rev. and Mrs. Jack Adams of Moscow filed suit in federal district court alleging it violated the First Amendment of the United States Constitution and the Idaho Constitution. This challenge came in the wake of *School District of Abington Tp., Pa. v. Schempp*,[29] which had been decided the previous year by the U.S. Supreme Court. *Schempp* involved a challenge to a Pennsylvania statute and a Baltimore ordinance, which like Idaho's statute, required reading from the Bible as part of the opening exercises each school day.

The majority opinion in *Schempp* reviewed the history of the First Amendment and the cases interpreting it and concluded that a "wholesome neutrality" was required. The Court said, "The test may be stated as follows: what are the purposes and the primary effect of the enactment? If either is the advancement or inhibition of religion then the enactment exceeds the scope of legislative power . . . there must be a secular legislative purpose and a primary effect that neither advances nor inhibits religion."[30] The trial court in *Schempp* had found the Bible reading and recitations involved were religious, not educational, in purpose and effect. A majority of the Supreme Court agreed and struck down the statute and ordinance.

The Supreme Court in *Schempp* anticipated the allegation that its decision would create a "religion of secularism" in the schools. The majority wrote, "it might well be said that one's education is not complete without a study of comparative religion or the history of religion and its relationship to the advancement of civilization." The opinion continued, "The Bible is worthy of study for its literary and historic qualities."[31] While the Court did not specifically mention teaching morality, its approach to the problem is strikingly similar to that of Clagett one hundred years earlier at the Idaho Constitutional Convention. In contrast to the Court in *Schempp*, the Idaho delegates rejected Clagett's proposal.

The Idaho federal district court, which heard the Adams' suit against Idaho's statute, would like to have followed the example of the Idaho delegates, but its sworn duty was to the United States Constitution and not the people of Idaho. The court wrote, "While members of the court may have personal reservations, we unanimously agree that the issue is settled by the United States Supreme Court ruling in . . . *Schempp*."[32] The court then declared the Idaho statute void and unenforceable.

Since the opinion in *Adams* was based upon the First Amendment, there was no reason to interpret Article IX, § 6, of the Idaho Constitution. There has, however, been an important interpretation of § 6, and § 5 which is closely related. In 1970 the Idaho legislature required that school districts should provide transportation for students to public *and private* schools. The state superintendent of public instruction and the state board of education refused to allocate funds for transportation to private schools and were sued in *Epeldi v. Engelking*.[33] In defense, the superintendent and board argued the statute violated Article I § 5 of the Idaho Constitution which prohibits "any appropriation or . . . anything in aid of any church or sectarian, or religious society, or for any sectarian or religious purpose. . . ."

The district court upheld the statute, interpreting § 6 by using the tests from *Schempp* and other cases interpreting the First Amendment. One of those cases, *Board of Education of Central School Dist. No. 1 v. Allen* (1968),[34] held that state busing of children to church schools did not violate the First Amendment. The Supreme Court had concluded, "As with public provision of police and fire protection, sewage facilities, and streets and side-walks, payment of bus fares was of some value to the religious school, but was nevertheless not such support of a religious institution as to be a prohibited establishment of religion within the meaning of the First Amendment."[35]

However, in contrast with the United States Constitution, the superintendent and board argued the Idaho Constitution was more restrictive than the First Amendment, and the cases decided under it. The Idaho supreme court agreed. It was persuaded by the language of § 6 which prohibited "anything in aid" and wrote, "By the phraseology and diction of this provision it is our conclusion that the framers of our constitution intended to more positively enunciate the separation between church and state than did the framers of the United States Constitution."[36]

Idah's convention delegates expressly rejected Clagett's suggestion that Bible reading be permitted for the secular purpose of teaching morality, a proposal very similar to the the prevailing interpretation of the First Amendment today. They adopted the motion of Sol Hasbrouck, which made the separation between church and state even stronger. Whether the Idaho Constitution will also be interpreted as more restrictive in cases involving prayer in the public schools, purchasing textbooks for church schools, release time for attending church seminary, and similar questions remains to be decided during the state's second century.

4. Investing the School Fund

THE FINAL DIFFICULTY caused by the education article at the Idaho convention was deciding the investment philosophy that should control the state's education fund. The education committee defined the public school fund in § 4 as the proceeds of dispositions of the school lands, and property or money received from various other sources. In § 3 the public school fund was made inviolate. In what eventually became § 11, the committee recommended that the education fund be invested only in improved agricultural property.

A number of delegates had different ideas. George Ainslie suggested that instead of investing only in improved farm lands, investment be made in improved real estate, as long as the property was within the state (pp. 773–74). James Reid thought that investment in Idaho state bonds should also be permitted (p. 774). Robert Anderson (D-Bingham) was worried that if all monies collected for educational purposes had to be invested, there would be no money for current expenses (pp. 775–76). On the other hand, Clagett worried that Anderson was suggesting all monies collected be spent, including the proceeds of school land sales (pp. 776–77). Tired and confused, the delegates adjourned for the day.

When they convened the next morning, Wednesday, July 24, the seventeenth day in session, the delegates were more certain of what they wanted. William McConnell proposed a substitute which stated, "The principal of all educational funds belonging to the state shall be loaned on first mortgage on improved farm lands within the state, or on state bonds . . ." (p. 779). Weldon Heyburn supported the proposal but wanted to extend investments to United States bonds and to any first mortgage security in improved land within the state, limited to one-half the value of the land (p. 779). Clagett was willing to loan on any land within the state, but wanted to limit loans to one-quarter of the value (p. 784). James Reid wanted to prohibit the sale of all coal lands.[37]

McConnell was the strongest advocate of limiting investments to improved farm property. He appears to have taken over as spokesman for the committee in the absence of Batten (p. 1300). He relied upon his own experience, and related, "My first experience in loaning money in this territory was in the town of Placerville, six months after I placed that mortgage on that property there I could not have got two bits on the dollar for it, and I never did get a cent out of it" (p. 774). He also stated that the Oregon school fund had been depleted by similar investments. John Morgan verified McConnell's testimony. "Ten years ago I knew lots in this territory worth $1,000 to $1,500, and people were quarreling over them and cheating one another for the purpose of getting title . . . that could not today be sold for $5 apiece" (p. 782). John Gray testified, "I have seen this town of Idaho City, where I will say I have rented the bare ground for $100 a month, twelve foot front, without a thing on it, that is not worth a dollar today, not a dollar" (p. 786). A. S. Chaney described Silver Cliff, Colorado, where "town lots sold for five and six hundred dollars. In three years, to my certain knowldege, you could not get ten dollars for those lots" (p. 786).

McConnell was also worried about political influence with the school fund. "It has been my experience in the loaning of school funds that during the seasons when we have political elections, that the privilege of loaning these monies for the state has been and always will be used as a political leverage to obtain power" (p. 785). No one at the convention could speak with as much authority on this question as McConnell, who had taught school and been active in Idaho and Oregon politics since the early 1860s.

McConnell also spoke about the compulsion of state government to distribute benefits evenly. "While it may be desirable to distribute this money around in different parts of the country where there are not good farm lands to be found, as a matter of justice to the children we should pass upon this very cooly and intelligently" (p. 775). William Clagett, from Shoshone County, of course, had a different perspective. "Miners will object to this. They do not care whether they receive any part of the school fund or not, but they do not want anything put in the constitution which is an advertisement to the world at large that they consider mining property of uncertain value" (p. 784). Clagett added, "I object to any kind of plan that throws into the hands of a few bankers, scattered here and there through the agricultural regions, the exclusive handling of the school fund of the state" (p. 787).

Clagett argued that a better rate of return could be earned from short-term loans on city properties. He said, "Although farm lands as a rule are much better security on long loans than other forms of real estate, they do not begin to be as good security on short loans, and nowhere is a farming community as good and prompt in the payment of loans and debts as they are in a live, growing and progressive city" (p. 788). The reason city loans were better was that farmers only market their crops once a year, and then pay their debts. Clagett also complained farmers were receiving preferential treatment. He charged, "it is class legislation under the guise of security for the school fund" (p. 789).

McConnell did foresee a day when there might be secure real property investments other than farm land. He said, "There might be on some business street, particularly in a city like Boise, or in some of the towns in agricultural districts, loans that will be all right, but it will be many a year before that time will arrive . . ." (p. 775). John Morgan shared McConnell's vision. "There are very few towns where any man can say in the near future, within ten or fifteen years, whether the security shall be good or not . . ." (p. 783).

McConnell without question had the most cautious investment policy. At one point he said, "it is not wise for our citizens in these towns to borrow money on their town lots" (p. 785). Ironically, he suffered greatly in the next financial depression to visit the state.[38]

When it came time to vote, the committee of the whole disapproved of Heyburn's and Clagett's proposals, and adopted McConnell's (pp. 790–91). Clagett then moved to amend the proposal to limit the loans on farm lands to one-quarter of the value. He pointed to the practice of the bankers in the territory. "Practically the highest they will go, when they are doing a prudent and conservative business, is to advance one-third of the value of the land at the time of the loan" (p. 791). Edgar Wilson suggested raising the limit to one-third the value (p. 798). McConnell resisted the amendments, arguing that the legislature had the authority to set these limits. In the end, however, the delegates voted to limit the loans to one-third of the value (p. 804).

Before the article was approved by the delegates sitting in formal session, there was another debate and more uncertainty about the investment policy. Willis Sweet worried that § 11 conflicted with the statute granting the state university lands, which stipulated that proceeds from sales were to be invested in United States bonds (p. 862). As a result, it was decided to delay consideration of the section until some time in the future (pp. 866–67). When that time arrived, Weldon Heyburn again tried to authorize investments in any land, not just farm land. There was also another attempt to raise the amount of the loan from one-third to one-half. However, the delegates were unwilling and McConnell's original amendment was adopted (pp. 1287–1304). One reason for McConnell's success was his dogged advocacy. At one point Alexander Mayhew said to McConnell, "My God, you are like a goat; I can't get my word in at all" (p. 1300).

Over the years, Idaho citizens have decided McConnell's investment policy was just too restrictive. In 1900, investment in school district bonds and state warrants was authorized.[39] In 1928 county, city and village bonds were added to the list.[40] McConnell and the other delegates who had such great confidence in the security of farm loans, did not forsee the effects of the Great Depression. And after Idaho citizens had experienced it, they removed farm lands from the list of authorized investments.[41] State bonds were added to the list in 1946.[42]

Finally, in 1968, Idaho citizens decided that they no longer wanted to directly control the investment of their school funds through the constitution, and adopted an amendment that turned matters over to the legislature. In this last amendment of the century, loans are authorized "on such other investments as may be permitted by law."[43]

Notes

1. The debates at the Idaho Constitutional Convention are reported in I. W. Hart, ed., *The Proceedings and Debates of the Idaho Constitutional Convention*. Caldwell, Idaho: Caxton Printers, Ltd., 1912) 2 vols. These two volumes are paginated consecutively, and all page references in the text of this chapter are to these volumes.

2. 1909 Idaho Sess Laws 447, H.J.R. No. 3, ratified in November 1910.

3. 1911 Idaho Sess Laws 787, S.J.R. No. 16, ratified in November 1912.

4. 1919 Idaho Sess Laws 622, H.J.R. No. 13, ratified in November 1920.

5. Article XVIII, § 6, providing for county officers has been amended twelve times. Article IX, § 8, regulating the location and disposal of public lands has been amended five times.

6. 1949 Idaho Sess Laws 598, H.J.R. No. 9, ratified in November 1950.

7. 1963 Idaho Sess Laws 1149, H.J.R. No. 5, ratified in November 1964.

8. 1966 Idaho Sess Laws, 2nd Ex. ratified in November 1966.

9. 1967 Idaho Sess Laws 1577, H.J.R. No. 7, ratified in November 1968.

10. 1972 Idaho Sess Laws 1251, H.J.R. No. 73, ratified in November 1972.

11. S.J.R. 109 (S.L. 1976, p. 1269), ratified in November 1976.

12. S.J.R. No. 114 (1974 Idaho Sess Laws 1888), ratified in November 1974.

13. S.J.R. No 102 (1976 Idaho Sess Laws 978), ratified in November 1978.

14. 1982 Idaho Sess Laws 933 H.J.R. No. 17, ratified November 1982.

15. The other two issues were Bible reading in the public schools and the investment policy for the school fund. See §§ three and four of this chapter.

16. The Ordinance declared: "Religion, morality and education being necessary to good government and the happiness of mankind, schools and means of education shall forever be encouraged." Laws of the United States of America, 1789–1815, Vol. I, Chap. 32, pp. 563–69.

17. 12 Stat. 808, Ch. 117, § 14.

18. U.S. Stat. at Large, 1879–1881, Ch. 61, p. 326.

19. Ibid.

20. 1915 Idaho Sess Laws 396, H.J.R. No. 3, ratified in November 1916.

21. 1941 Idaho Sess Laws 484 S.J.R. No. 3, ratified in November 1942.

22. 1951 Idaho Sess Laws 658, H.J.R. No. 6, ratified in November 1952.

23. Dienst, Charles Franklin. *The Administration of Endowments with Special Refernce to the Public Schools and Institutional Trust of Idaho*. New York: Teachers College Press, 1933.

24. Hawley, James H., ed. *History of Idaho*. Chicago: Clarke Pub. Co., 1920, 1:165.

25. 1887 Id. Rvsd. Stat., Title 3, ch. 9, § 705.

26. Elliot, John. *Elliot's Debates*. Philadelphia: J. B. Lippincott Company, 1836, 5:253–55.

27. Sweet's alma mater was the University of Nebraska. Wells, Merle W. "The Admission of the State of Idaho." *Secretary of State Twenty-Seventh Biennial Report*. 1944: 74.

28. 1925 Idaho Sess Laws, 48–49.

29. 374 U.S. 203.

30. Ibid. at 222.

31. Ibid. at 225.

32. *Adams v. Engelking*, 232 F.Supp. 666, at 667 (1964).

33. 94 Idaho 390 (1971).

34. 392 U.S. 236.

35. Ibid. at 242.

36. Ibid. at 395.

37. Reid's suggestion could only have been made by a newcomer to the state who had immigrated from a coal region. The delegates, of course, did not pass his motion (pp. 791–93).

38. McConnell, W. J. *Early History of Idaho*. Caldwell: Caxton Printers, Ltd., 1913.

39. 1899 Idaho Sess Laws 330, S.J.R. No. 12, ratified in November 1900.

40. 1927 Idaho Sess Laws 589, H.J.R. No. 10, ratified in November 1928.

41. 1939 Idaho Sess Laws 670, S.J.R. No. 5, ratified in November 1940.

42. 1945 Idaho Sess Laws 402, S.J.R. No. 4, ratified in November 1946.

43. S.J.R. No. 4, 1968 Idaho Sess Laws (2nd Ex. Sess.) 69, ratified in November 1968.

7.

Public and Private Corporations

1. The Corporations Issues

ARTICLE XI OF THE IDAHO CONSTITUTION is titled "Corporations, Public and Private."
This caption is a misnomer, or perhaps a misrepresentation, when viewed in light of
the policies in the article, the sentiments of committee chairman Alexander Mayhew
(D-Shoshone), and the arguments on the convention floor. A more apt title would have
been "Railroad Code," or for some of the delegates, "Railroad Indictment."

The corporations article as reported by Mayhew's committee contained nineteen
sections. Six of those sections applied specifically to railroads; five of the six were
adopted by the convention. In the committee report, § 5 declared railroads to be public highways and subjected the rates charged to legislative control. Section 6 guaranteed to each citizen an equal right of transportation and freedom from unreasonable
discrimination. Section 11 required local approval before any railroad could be built
within an incorporated area. Section 12 prohibited the legislature from passing any
retroactive law for the benefit of a railroad or any law which imposed a new liability for
past transactions with railroads. Section 14 claimed jurisdiction over the property of
any Idaho railroad that consolidated with a foreign corporation. The section not adopted
by the convention prohibited the combination or consolidation of parallel or competing
railroads.

The striking thing about these six sections as a group is that they are all hostile to
railroads. With one exception, each of the sections is devoted entirely to controlling or
regulating the railroads. That exception is the last part of § 5 which grants the right to

construct railroads and connect with other railroads in the state, all under regulations prescribed by the legislature.

Another six sections in the proposed corporations article continued this hostile policy. While these sections did not name railroads, the convention debates indicate railroads were their target. Section 1 declared all existing corporate charters invalid unless the grantees had organized and commenced business. Section 2 prohibited creation of corporate charters by special legislation, but did authorize the legislature to pass a general incorporation statute. Section 3 authorized alteration of charters, provided no injustice was done to the incorporators. Section 7 required all existing corporations to file an acceptance of the Idaho Constitution with the secretary of state. Section 8 preserved the power of eminent domain and the police power over corporations. Section 10 subjected all foreign corporations doing business within the state to the same rules and regulations as Idaho corporations. Finally, § 18 prohibited corporations from combining to fix the price or production of commodities. Only § 13, which granted the right to construct and maintain telegraph or telephone lines within the state, gave any authority or aid to corporations.

The corporations article reported to the convention reflected the sentiments of the committee chairman, Alexander Mayhew.[1] Mayhew was generally known as "Honest Alex" because of his frank and forthright manner. However, the debate over Article XI suggests that "Honest Alex" was not always an open book. Early in the discussions Mayhew confessed a lack of experience and knowledge. He said, "[S]o far as I am concerned and understand this railroad business—I was not as familiar with it as I would like to be, and depended solely upon . . . members of the committee that were railroad attorneys and men connected with the railroads" (p. 879).[2]

By the middle of the debate, Mayhew's attitude had changed from inexperience to indifference. In defending one section of the committee report he said, "If this constitutional convention desires to cut this out, I don't think I am going to go crazy over the subject; but I think it is important, and hence put it in here" (pp. 1093–94). Finally, in the heat of the last debate over the article, the chairman's real views became apparent. Mayhew revealed, "My individual views would go . . . to the extent to place a larger and more extended restriction upon these corporations. . . . I am jealous of their rights, and I think it is prudent and necessary in our legislative bodies to throw such a safeguard around the people that they may not be imposed upon in any manner or form by corporations" (p. 1098).

There were friends of railroads and corporations at the convention. When Mayhew's article reached the convention floor, they objected, and several spirited debates followed. As a group, the delegates at the Idaho Constitutional Convention were caught in a love-hate (or need-fear) relationship with railroads. William Clagett (R-Shoshone) argued the need for railroads. "We are a young country, and what we want of all things is local lines of railway . . . what we want to do is encourage railroad building in the state" (p. 882). James Beatty (R-Alturas) agreed, and asked rhetorically, "Is there a man living in the uttermost parts of this territory that does not want a railroad to reach his home?" (p. 886). On the other hand, George Ainslie (D-Boise) and others repeatedly pointed to the evils of corporations. "We all know that when competition arises there are some hogs that want to get everything. We have Jay Gould, who gobbled up a railroad and telegraph line, and the telegraph line is like a devil fish, gobbling up everything within its reach, and outraging the people by its charges" (pp. 883–84).

The conflicting attitudes brought to Boise by the delegates produced two major debates on the floor of the convention. The first was a section that prohibited consolidation of parallel lines. The second debate involved sections that required corporations to accept the constitution, and prohibited the legislature from enacting retroactive legislation for their benefit. This chapter describes these two debates in §§ 4 and 5, after first describing the debates on the labor article at the convention (§ 2) and the territorial railroads (§ 3).

2. The Labor Article

WHILE THE IDAHO CONVENTION was strongly opposed to corporations, namely railroads, it was not particularly sympathetic to labor. The delegates were regulating railroads on behalf of rate-payers, or consumers, and were not interested in aiding labor. Mayhew's corporations committee did recommend one pro-labor provision. It sought to declare invalid any contract clause releasing employers from liability for personal injuries suffered by workers. Edgar Wilson (R-Ada) and John Morgan (R-Shoshone) objected, claiming that the law already declared those clauses void, and that adopting the section would amount to putting "buncombe" in the constitution. Wilson said, "I think that is the general rule of law both in England and in this country. I had occasion to look it up before I came here this morning." Mayhew was equivocal, "I will say that I have seen some dissenting opinions . . . I cannot say positively that the courts have held that they are null and void." He urged that putting the clause in the "organic act" of the state "settles for all time that question of litigation." Mayhew was unable to convince the delegates, and the section was stricken by a vote of 22 to 17 (pp. 1104–06).

A labor article was also adopted by Idaho's Constitutional Convention. Even though labor conflict was destined to be a bloody fight during Idaho's first decade of statehood, the territorial period had been quite peaceful. Large capital interests were just beginning to come into the region; as a result labor and capital had not yet crossed swords and came to the convention in a spirit of cooperation. The committee that drafted the labor article was chaired by Henry Armstrong (Labor-Logan), a railroad employee. However, Weldon B. Heyburn (R-Shoshone), the most forceful spokesman for capital and corporate interests at the convention, was also on the committee. The result was a report that was supported by both labor and capital because it didn't address the issues that divided the two.

Section 1 of the labor committee report recommended a bureau of labor and statistics charged with collecting "information upon the subject of labor, its relation to capital, the hours of labor and the earnings of laboring men and women, and the means of promoting their material, social, intellectual and moral prosperity" (pp. 2077–78). Several delegates objected, stating that they saw no reason or benefit from such a bureau since labor could always present these statistics by petition. William Clagett predicted Idaho's future and gave the strongest argument supporting the section: "[W]e will very soon be confronted with problems of a very difficult nature relating to labor in its various forms of employment and various exactions that may be imposed upon it, and the various exactions imposed by it upon capital. As a basis to enable the legislature to act wisely with regard to many different forms of legislation . . . it is necessary that all the information upon the subject . . . be gathered together and reported . . ." (p. 1374).

Heyburn gave the labor bureau the endorsement of capital interests. He observed there had been no labor difficulties in the territory. "We have not recently had any very serious question between labor and capital in this territory. We may not have in years to come, and yet we may have at any time. Those difficulties are constantly arising." Because of the constant threat, Heyburn thought the reports of the bureau would "be a very useful source or a valuable source of information from which to draw statistics and facts and details for our legislature . . ." (pp. 1375–76). These endorsements were able to overcome objections to a labor bureau, but they were not able to prevent amendments. The convention amended the section by making the labor bureau a labor *and immigration* bureau.

The second section recommended by the labor committee stipulated not more than eight hours labor should constitute a lawful day's work on state and municipal projects. At the time, labor was paid according to a daily rate, and a day's labor was considered ten hours. It was objected that getting paid a day's wages for working only eight hours would amount to a bonus. Supporters of the eight-hour day argued that there was a similar provision under the federal law, and that the section dealt only with hours and not wages (pp. 1370–80). H. S. Hampton (R-Cassia) explained, "I take it that one object of this section is or should be a sort of entering wedge, as it were, to enforce or bring about the custom of eight hours of labor among laboring people. I believe this is enough for any man to work hard . . ." (p. 1380). The question was then called, and the section passed.

The third section recommended by the labor committee sought to confine convicts to the state prison so that they would not compete with the local labor market. Two objections were raised to the section as written. Some delegates worried that local chain gangs would be prohibited. It was a practice in the local courts of the day to fine and assess costs against petty criminals, and then order the amounts to be paid by working on the streets. James Reid from Lewiston explained. "Sometimes persons are incarcerated for the costs, and may be released on working them out, paying them in that way. Frequently that is the judgment of the court, and in our city we frequently work them on the streets to work out costs and fines"(p. 1381).

The second objection was that the proposed section would not permit convicts to work on public projects, such as building canals on state owned land or building a new prison. I. N. Coston (D-Ada) pointed out, "[T]he present condition of our prison is very crowded. We shall need in the early history of the state, if we are so fortunate as to become a state, greatly enlarged accommodations" (p. 1384). As a result of these objections, the section was amended so that it applied only to the state prison and so that convict labor could be used on public projects.

Section 4 of the labor committee report prohibited children under fourteen years of age from working in the mines. Not a single objection was raised. The Committee's final section prohibited employment of noncitizens on state and municipal projects. Edgar Wilson worried the section might interfere with Ada County road improvements. "I rise to inquire whether that would not prohibit Chinamen from working out their road tax. I want to know, because we work 400 Chinamen working out their road tax on the street" (p. 1388). Nobody responded, and the delegates answered Wilson by passing the section.

James Reid (D-Nez Perce) then moved to add two sections to the article. The first required the legislature to provide a mechanics and laborers lien on the property they improved. There was a similar provision in Idaho's territorial statutes,[3] and the section quickly passed. Reid's second proposed section authorized the state legislature to create a board of arbitration that would have the power to decide all differences and controversies submitted to it by laborers and their employers. Reid explained his proposal was similar to one that had passed the House of Representatives several years earlier when he was a member of that body. He also explained the section did not provide present solutions but only possibilites for the future because the legislature was only authorized and not required to create the boards, and the boards would only hear controversies the parties voluntarily submitted to it. Without much discussion, the section passed (pp. 1389–95, 1484–86).

The modest and noncontroversial nature of Idaho's labor provisions can be seen by comparing them to those of Wyoming, which was drafting its constitution at the same time. Wyoming delegates established an inspector of mines, provided for proper ventilation and drainage of mines, outlawed female and child labor in the mines and passed a wrongful death statute for laborers killed in mine accidents. Wyoming also prohibited legislative limits on wrongful death actions and adopted an eight-hour work day for mines as well as public works.[4]

As a result of the philosophy of the convention delegates, Idaho's Constitution has not been significant in labor relations in Idaho. The article has been infrequently litigated and amended only twice. In 1902 the legislature was empowered to "pass laws to provide for the health and safety of employees in factories, smelters, mines and ore reduction works."[5] It is unclear what additional power this conferred upon the legislature, since the general understanding was that the legislature had any power not forbidden it, and nothing in the original constitution forbade legislation of this sort. In 1912 the restrictions on convict labor were repealed.[6] Perhaps the best indication of the relative insignificance of the labor article is the fact that in 1974 the Idaho legislature, by statute, stripped the bureau of immigration, labor and statistics of its constitutional status, and made it a branch of the executive department.[7]

3. Idaho Territorial Railroads

IDAHO'S TERRITORIAL RAILROADS[8] had a tremendous impact upon Idaho's Constitutional Convention, beginning with the first rail laid in late 1873 by the Utah Northern Railroad. Utah Northern's story began with the Golden Spike Celebration at Promontory Summit on May 10, 1869, marking the completion of the first transcontinental railroad in the Unted States. The road had been run north of the Great Salt Lake, and thus did not go through Salt Lake City. Brigham Young was disappointed in the route decision, but quickly organized the Utah Central to connect Salt Lake City with the main line. Between 1869 and 1882, the Utah Central, Utah Southern, Utah Western and Utah Eastern were built. The four railoads had over 300 miles of track, all built with Mormon church sponsorship by those who lived along the routes.

The Utah Northern was organized and started construction in August 1871. John. W. Young, son of Brigham Young, was president and superintendent. William B. Preston from Logan was vice president. The plan was to join the Utah Northern to the Central Pacific near Brigham City, go north through Logan, then to Franklin, Idaho, and on to Soda Springs where the organizers had property interests.

Logan was reached by January 1873, and Franklin by May 1874. However, the building of Idaho's first track coincided with the panic of 1873 in the nation's financial circles. It also coincided with hard times caused by drought and grasshopper infestations in the farm communties along the track. As a consequence, construction came to a halt and the assets of the railroad were sold at a foreclosure sale. Jay Gould, the same devil fish described by George Ainslie on the convention floor, was there to buy the assets at forty cents to the dollar. Along with Sidney Dillon and other Union Pacific owners, Gould took over the Utah Northern. It was renamed the Utah and Northern, and John W. Young resigned. In March 1878 the Utah and Northern began construction again, planning to take the line north to the mine fields near Helena, Montana. The Idaho-Montana border on the Rocky Mountain Summit at Monida Pass was reached on May 9, 1880, and the line completed to Garrison, Montana in 1882.

Plans for Idaho's second railroad began in 1879 when the Union Pacific decided to build a branch from Granger, Wyoming, to Huntington, Oregon, following the route of the old Oregon Trail across the Snake River Plain in southern Idaho. This was the Oregon Short Line. Construction began in Granger and reached the Wyoming-Idaho line on June 16, 1882. It took over two years for the railroad to make its way across Idaho, and the Idaho-Oregon border near Huntington was reached in November of 1884. Along the way a branch line was built into the Wood River Country. In all, 434 miles of Oregon Short Line track were built in Idaho.

The only other railroad in southern Idaho before statehood was a 20-mile line from Nampa to Boise called "The Stub." It was built by the Idaho Central Railway during 1887 and absorbed by the Oregon Short Line in 1889, about the time the convention was in session.

In northern Idaho, the Northern Pacific had crossed by 1890. This line was first proposed in the 1840s by Asa Whitney, a wealthy Boston entrepreneur. The Civil War interrupted, and organization did not begin until the 1860s when Josiah Perham, another wealthy Yankee, organized The People's Pacific Railroad. Failures and reorganizations occurred during both the 1860s and 1870s. Construction finally began in February 1870, near Duluth, Minnesota. By building from both east and west, the nation's second transcontinental railroad was completed at Hellsgate Canyon on August 23, 1883.

Because the Pacific Northern crossed a very narrow strip of the Idaho panhandle, it was necessary to build branch lines into other regions of the territory. The Spokane Falls and Idaho Railroad connected Coeur d'Alene Lake to the mainline. In addition, the Spokane & Palouse Railroad traveled 112 miles from Spokane to Genesee, Idaho.

There was a second transcontinental railroad perched on northern Idaho's borders on the eve of the constitutional convention. James Jerome Hill, beginning in 1879, had blasted and cut his Great Northern into the high passes and river gorges of the Rocky Mountains by 1889. Construction reached the western border of Idaho in the spring of 1892, and Hill completed his line the following year.

It is impossible to overstate the tremendous influence the construction of these railroads had upon Idaho during the late territorial period. Each railroad brought its own people and culture to the territory. The Utah and Northern was the critical factor in the Mormon colonization of the upper Snake River Valley and consequently in the development of Idaho irrigation. This 1882 message from Mormon President John Taylor to William B. Preston illustrates church policy. "Go into the Snake River Country, found settlements, care for the Indians, stand upon an equal footing and cooperate in making improvements. Gain influence among all men, and strengthen the cords of the Stakes of Zion."

Members of the church were the laborers who built the Utah Northern, and much of the Utah and Northern after the acquistion by the Union Pacific interests. Perhaps this laborer's statement best describes the culture that came with Idaho's first railroad. "Yes sir, we took and went to work and got the job done."

The impact of the other railroads was just as significant. The Union Pacific brought to the Snake River plain a tough and hard-drinking work force that was Republican and strongly anti-Mormon. The Northern Pacific was built by Swedes and Irishmen, and by the first large group of Chinese laborers brought into the territory. James J. Hill said of his crews, "Give me enough Swedes and whiskey, and I'll build a railroad to Hell." Each of these groups was an important force in Idaho territorial politics at the time of statehood.

Even more importantly, the railroads were the keys that opened Idaho to immigration so that mining, ranching, irrigation, and commercial communities could grow throughout the 1880s. Of course, the traffic flowed both ways, and it became possible for Idaho's economy to develop by shipping natural resources to manufacturing and other markets outside the territory. A territory's population and assessed property were two of the most important factors in qualifying for statehood. Railroad development made it possible for Idaho to claim sufficient population and property by the summer of 1889. The railroads contributed to Idaho's growth so that when the political opportunity presented itself, Idaho was ready to join the Union.

4. Parallel Lines

THE FIRST SECTION of the Corporations Article to be discussed at any length by the convention was § 5, which declared all railroads public highways and railroad companies to be common carriers subject to legislative control. The section went on to provide, ". . . the legislature shall have power to regulate and control by law, the rates of charges. . . ." William H. Savidge (R-Bingham), legal counsel for the Union Pacific, proposed this verson, " . . . the legislature shall have power to establish by law, reasonable rates of charges . . ." (p. 870).

Mayhew, as chair of the committee, objected to the amendment because " 'regulate and control' have a stronger and more extended meaning than the word 'establish' " (p. 870). George Ainslie also opposed the amendment. He complained the amendment would make it impossible for the legislature to create a board of commissioners with authority to regulate rates, and further explained, "it appears to me it would prevent the legislature, after passing one bill, from ever regulating the matter afterwards" (p. 871).

The convention refused to accept the Savidge amendment, but it was willing to make clear that established railroads had a priority over newcomers. Section 5 of the committee report granted to any railroad the right to intersect, cross or connect with any other railroad in the state. Savidge wanted to make it clear new railroads could take advantage of this right only "under such regulations as may be prescribed by law, and upon making due compensation" (p. 871). The vote was 20 to 20. The chair favored it, breaking the tie, and Savidge secured one advantage for his employer.

The first section of Article XI to provoke significant disagreement on the convention floor was § 6 of the committee report, which prohibited parallel or competing railroads from combining. The section had two strong supporters, Chairman Mayhew and George Ainslie. The two first argued the section produced competition and thus lower fares. Mayhew said, "Where there is competition in all trades, there we find articles cheaper, manufactures cheaper, travel cheaper, . . . What the people want in this section of the country is cheap rates, if they can obtain them, over these railroads, and cheap fares traveling over the roads" (p. 887). Ainslie made a similar argument. "If there are competing lines they will both compete for business, and the public will receive the benefit of the competition. If you allow competing lines to consolidate, then the big fish eat up the little ones, and the rates are crowded up to the maximum allowed by the legislature" (p. 883).

Ainslie offered a second reason to support the section. The people of the state needed to act early to protect themselves from the corporations to come. Ainslie said,

"Now, I say, is the time for the people to stand on guard against the encroachments of these powerful corporations, and not leave themselves at the mercy of them" (p. 884). Mayhew carried on with this theme, "[N]ow is the time at the very infancy of our statehood when we are about to bud into statehood and take our place in the Union as other states – it is now the time we should have these safeguards thrown around the people . . . to prevent an evil that has grown up, that we should have prevented in its incipiency" (p. 888). He also noted that the proposed section was taken from Colorado's Constitution, and that other territories drafting constitutions were considering similar provisions (p. 889).

A. J. Pinkham (R-Alturas), the only Republican to speak in support of the committee's proposal, offered another justification. Pinkham claimed to be an authority on the subject. "I have had occasion in former years to examine into the workings of this system and study well what the intention and purpose of the legislature was that enacted laws under the sections of the state constitution" (p. 879). In Pinkham's view, the intention and purpose of the section was "to prevent pooling, and prevent two parallel lines of railroad from pooling and discriminating in their charges against one local point in favor of another local point" (p. 880).

Opponents of the section had two principal arguments. The first was that the constitution provided for rate regulation, and beyond that corporations should be left alone. Going beyond rate regulation was an interference with private property. John S. Gray (R-Ada) stated, "Railroads can do what they have a mind to do. We can control by legislation the amount they may charge . . . . But as to how they can control their own property, I do not think it is our business to attempt in the constitution to control their business or their property" (p. 876). Willis Sweet (R-Latah) agreed, and said ". . . so long as the state has control of the tariff, I do not see that we gain anthying by it" (p. 878). James M. Shoup (R-Custer) also argued, "I don't think we have any right to legislate to whom any man shall be forced to sell his property or to whom he shall not be allowed to sell his property; and I think it is bad policy to have any such section in the constitution of our state" (p. 877).

The second principal argument was that the section would prevent the railroads from building the lines the citizens so desperately wanted. John Morgan argued, "The great need in this country, it seems to me, is railroad lines, and whether they are competing lines or not, I do not care, so we can get the railroads" (p. 880). William Clagett agreed, and argued, "We are a young country, and what we want of all things is local lines of railway. We do not care whether they are competing lines or not competing lines" (p. 882). James Beatty also stated the need for railroads. "We are legislating, in my humble opinion, in a way to keep out of this territory the very thing we need" (p. 886). Beatty was also concerned about the effect the section would have upon capital investment. "Every sensible man sees at once that if we have railroads built here it will not be by our own people; we haven't the money; the money has to come from abroad. We all know how timid capital is . . ." (p. 885).

Chairman Mayhew tried to rebut these arguments by pointing out the powerful influence and danger of corporations: "[W]e can see that not only these large and stupendous corporations have control of states and great interests of the state, but we can see they have almost got control of the United States" (p. 889). He finally warned again, "I, for one, Mr. Chairman, think it is necessary to protect ourselves against a railroad corporation" (p. 889).

Mayhew and Ainslie had to be thinking of the Great Northern, which was preparing to cross northern Idaho on a route roughly parallel to that of the Northern Pacific, even though they never mentioned it in their arguments on the convention floor. The two were not able to persuade their fellow delegates and the section prohibiting consolidation of parallel railroads was struck by a vote of 27 to 15 (p. 890). Even though Mayhew and Ainslie were unpersuasive, they did predict the development of railroads in northern Idaho. Within a decade after statehood James J. Hill had acquired the Northern Pacific and the parallel lines became merged under a single ownership.

5. Corporate Acceptance and Retroactive Laws

AFTER THE CONVENTION DELEGATES struck the committee's proposal relating to parallel lines, they routinely approved a series of sections until § 12 was read:

> The legislature shall pass no law for the benefit of a railroad, or other corporation, or any individual, or association of individuals retrospective in its operation, or which imposes on the people of any county or municipal subdivision of the state, a new liability in respect to transactions or considerations already passed.

J. W. Poe (D-Nez Perce) moved to strike the section entirely (p. 1062). Clagett moved to replace "retrospective" with "retroactive" (p. 1063). Then Weldon B. Heyburn made an objection that sent the delegates into a clamorous debate. Heyburn accused the delegates of being inconsistent. He alleged the convention itself had just passed a retroactive law when it approved § 7 of the committe report, which provided:

> No corporation shall have the benefit of any future legislation, without first filing in the office of the secretary of state an acceptance of the provisions of this Constitution in binding form.

As Heyburn often did, on this occasion he used caustic irony in his argument and contended § 12 should be stricken because the legislature should have the same power to pass retroactive laws as the convention had.

Heyburn chided the delegates. "A constitutional convention should have some conscience. It should not do that which it says is incompetent or wrong for the legislature to do, because we are simply legislating a primary law. . . . If we do it, it would be hard to find a reasonable excuse for it as a moral principle" (p. 1066). From this point on, §§ 12 and 7 were debated together.

Heyburn gave an example of the injustice to be done by § 7. He pointed out that there were "in Northern Idaho perhaps twenty or twenty-five very considerable mining corporations" organized so that a simple majority of the stockholders could control action of the company. Since the convention was establishing a new rule that required an overwhelming majority to control a corporation, and since existing corporations had to accept the constitution or receive no future benefits, the current stockholders were going to lose control of their corporations and suffer an outrage.

James Beatty supported Heyburn's objection to § 7. He thought the section would sacrifice a corporation's right to litigate. He said, "[I]f I read it right, if a railroad company or a mining company or any other company, is convinced that it has a right which it ought to litigate in court, you bind them by this section to waive that right; you bind them to come in and submit to the laws passed here, whether right or wrong, and as a penalty, if they do not submit to those laws, they shall have the benefit of no future legislation" (pp. 1073–74).

Edgar Wilson also wanted to strike the section because he thought ". . . that we have enacted fundamental law, which . . . would be retroactive in its nature, so far as some corporations or perhaps so far as all corporations are concerned, and it would probably impair the obligation of contracts" (p. 1078). Savidge added his opposition because ". . . sections appear in this constitution that will put great hardships upon corporations, and prevent or discourage them from coming into this state" (p.1079). J. W. Poe questioned, "Is not this in the nature of class legislation . . . ?" (p. 1081)

Many delegates defended §§ 7 and 12 from these attacks by claiming they had nothing to do with each other. For example, William Clagett looked at § 12 and argued, "It is aimed at retroactive legislation for the benefit of some particular person. That is one thing. But when you come to section 7 it deals with a subject that is altogether different" (p. 1080). Clagett claimed, "[S]ection 7 does not take away one single right which any corporation or any person has at the time the consititution is adopted." As he read the section, it simply ". . . imposes upon the corporation a thoroughly reasonable and necessary restriction" (p. 1080). Clagett finished with a flair. "[T]his section is aimed exactly at those autocratic powers, persons, individuals, firms and corporations, who claim the benefit of all the laws while repudiating the obligation of the laws" (p. 1081).

Alexander Mayhew also defended the committee's proposals. He began by distinguishing between the rights of a natural person and the rights of an artifical person. "The gentlemen seem to forget that corporations are artifical persons. . . . As it is laid down by all text writers, there are two kinds of persons, one a natural person, the other an artificial person. What are the artificial persons? Corporations" (p. 1093). Mayhew thought that because corporations were "creatures of the law, creatures of a creation of law giving them certain powers and immunities and privileges that individuals do not have," they could be required to file an acceptance of the constitution while individuals could not (p. 1093).

As the debate developed, Heyburn tried again to torpedo the committee's proposal. He moved to amend § 7 so that all persons, corporations and natural, would have to file an acceptance of the constitution. Heyburn pushed his satirical argument, "I desire to have harmony throughout this state, and that this constitution shall be ratified by a unanimous vote; and I cannot see any better way to do it than simply to put a penalty on the man who votes against this constitution and who is not in favor of it, by excluding him from the benefits of all future legislation. . . . I think it would result in obtaining for the constitution a unanimous ratification" (p. 1086).

When the votes were finally taken, the corporations and railroads lost the day. The motion to strike § 7 requiring corporations to file an acceptance of the constitution was defeated by a vote of 14 in favor, 26 against (p. 1103). A similar motion to strike § 12 failed by a vote of 14 in favor, 20 against (p. 1076).

The convention did decide to adopt Clagett's proposal to change "retrospective" to "retroactive" in § 12. Clagett explained the need for retroactive laws by recalling that early in the territorial period, even though the law required transferring mining properties by a deed under seal, "Nevertheless, miners went to work and transferred their properties, involving the whole mining section of the country around here, by bills of sale that did not comply with the law." Clagett then asked rhetorically, "What did the legislature do," and provided his own answer: "Came in and validated those past defective interests . . ." (p. 1070). The point was made clear to the delegates, and they adopted the amendment overwhelmingly.

Idaho citizens have been happy with the corporations article drafted by the convention. Of course, there have been many cases litigated under the article, but its eighteen sections have been amended only three times. All three amendments have pertained to voting rights of shareholders. Section 4 of the original article made cumulative voting of shares mandatory. An amendment in 1972 required that nonvoting stock be clearly designated.[9] In 1982 the section was amended to provide that the legislature and not the constitution should govern shareholder voting rights, except that cumulative voting cannot be prohibited.[10] Section 9 of the original constitution required the approval of all voting shares before a class of shares could be increased. In 1966 the section was amended so that approval is only required from the class of shares being increased.[11]

Notes

1. Mayhew had a reputation of being hostile to railroads in Shoshone County. He had campaigned for the territorial council at a time when the railroad was the biggest event in the community without once mentioning it. It was thought that he had been put off a railroad in Montana for some reason, and forced to take a long walk to his destination.

2. Hart, I. W., ed. *Proceedings and Debates of the Constitutional Convention of Idaho 1889.* 2 vols. Caldwell: Caxton Printers, Ltd., 1912. These volumes are paginated consecutively, and all page references in the text of this chapter are to them.

3. If the owner of the property who contracted for the work to be done refused to pay, the lien enabled the mechanic or laborer to cause the property to be sold and the proceeds used to pay for the services. *Revsd. Statute*, 1887, §§ 5125–39.

4. Bakken, Gordon. *Rocky Mountain Constitution Making, 1850–1912*. Westport, Greenwood Press,1987, pp. 80–81.

5. 1901 Idaho Sess Laws 311, H.J.R. No. 2, ratified at the general election in November 1902.

6. 1911 Idaho Sess Laws 791, H.J.R. No. 24, ratified at the general election in November, 1912.

7. 1974 Idaho Sess Laws 1023.

8. For the story of railroad development in Idaho, see Beal, Merrill D. and Wells, Merle W. *History of Idaho*. 3 vols. New York: Lewis Historical Publishing Company, 1959, pp. 494–552.

9. H.J.R. No. 63, S.L. 1972, ratified at the general election in November 1972, p. 1250.

10. 1981 Idaho Sess Laws, S.J.R. No. 110, p. 930, ratified at the general election in November 1982.

11. 1965 Idaho Sess Laws, H.J.R. No. 10, p. 958, ratified at the general election in November 1966.

8.
Suffrage

1. Suffrage Guaranteed

THURSDAY, July 25, finally arrived. It was the date set for consideration of the report of the suffrage committee. Although this was the eighteenth day in session, the Mormon question had throughout been foremost in the minds of the delegates. There had been many preliminary skirmishes, such as George Ainslie's motion to expel the reporter from the *Salt Lake Tribune* and the debates over Article I, § 4, guaranteeing freedom of religion.[1] In addition, an important congressional delegation traveling through the West had addressed the convention and further excited the anti-Mormon sentiments. Mormon suffrage was the main question, the one of most intense interest.

Before getting to the Mormons, however, the convention had to consider the rights of others to vote. The first section of Article VI declared "an absolutely secret ballot is hereby guaranteed" and instructed the legislature to carry the section into effect. This guarantee was accepted by the delegates without comment (p. 904).[2] However, an earlier article contained voting guarantees that had been more controversial. Those guarantees appear in the declaration of rights article.

Article I, § 19 guarantees that no civil or military power shall interfere with exercise of the right of suffrage. Article I, § 20, as recommended by the declaration of rights committee, provided that no property qualification should ever be required to vote or hold office. J. W. Reid (D-Nez Perce) moved that in addition to no property qualification, there should be no educational qualification. He argued, "I have seen some of the best men in the country that had to sign their names with a cross-mark, and they were just as safe depositories of the business of the state as the graduate of a university . . ." (p. 375). Reid was especially worried about an education requirement in the territories where, unlike the eastern states, there were often no schools and little educational opportunity (p. 378).

Reid's colleague, J. W. Poe (D-Nez Perce), supported him. "There are many persons in this territory who have never had the opportunities of some of the gentlemen who oppose this, good citizens, men who know what is right and what is wrong as well as the learned gentlemen who oppose it. . . . I believe it to be an absolute wrong for us at this time to deny any American citizen the right of suffrage on account of his ignorance" (p. 377). Poe also was concerned that an educational requirement would prevent Indians from voting, even though they were entitled to if they had abandoned their tribal ways.

Willis Sweet (R-Latah) objected to Reid's proposal, and to Poe's example. He said, "[S]uppose two or three reservations are opened[3] here, and a thousand Indians are permitted to vote at once, without any knowledge whatever of the laws of this country . . . Now I say it is no more than right that they be required to know a little something about our government and our people . . ." (p. 379). While Sweet did not think it was necessary at present to have an education requirement, he did not want to restrict the power of the legislature to do so in the future. He cautioned, "We do not know what class of people may become citizens of this state, how many of them or where they may come from, and it may be very desirable some time to require this qualification, to insist that the voter know something about the fundamental principles of state government and that he can read the fundamental law . . ." (p. 376). James Beatty (R-Alturas) agreed, "The emergency may arise when we may want to say that we value and encourage education in this territory" (p. 376). He asked rhetorically, "Would it not be an inducement to an ignorant population, to come in here instead of intelligent people?" (p. 380).

John S. Gray (R-Ada) encouraged the delegates to trust the legislature. "Let them take care of that when the proper time arises" (pp. 279–80). He pointed out Reid's amendment would interfere with the requirement in the judiciary article that judges be learned in the law. John T. Morgan (R-Bingham) took Gray's argument further, and complained that a superintendent of public instruction or the clerk of the district court could be elected, even though they could not read or write (p. 381).

Weldon Heyburn (R-Shoshone) not only opposed Reid, he supported an education requirement, and argued, "I would be rather inclined to favor a provision that would require that in ten years no person should be allowed to vote who could not read and write, to compel these people to learn to read and write who have been here so many years that they have had time enough." He also wanted to be able to prevent Indians from voting when the reservations were opened. He concluded, "If this law was made in the northwestern states where public school books are in Norwegian and Swedish, that would compel them to learn to read the English language and it would be so much better for the nation" (p. 382).

John Lewis (A. M. R-Oneida) analyzed the education requirement with the Mormon question in mind. He alleged, "It is a well known fact that in the Mormon church a very large percentage of the members of that church in this territory today are unable to read or write, and the source of their strength is the fact that in their ignorance they have absolute control of all their material affairs." He offered to prove it was the position of the Mormon church to avoid any restrictions on the right to vote (pp. 382–83).

Reid's amendment was defeated by a "loud chorus of noes." James N. Shoup (R-Custer) then made a second motion to amend § 20. He proposed to allow property qualifications in school elections and elections creating indebtedness. His motion passed without discussion (p. 386), and the suffrage guarantees in the Idaho Constitution were fixed.

These suffrage guarantees were upheld on several occasions during Idaho's first century. When irrigation districts were first organized, these principles were contrary to the manner in which irrigators wanted to do business. The Idaho supreme court struck down a statute which provided that each voter in an irrigation district was to vote with a ballot marked by the number of acres and inches of water used because it violated the right to a secret ballot.[4] Statutes requiring that voters had to own property to vote in irrigation districts[5] and drainage districts[6] were also declared unconstitutional because they violated the guarantee of no property qualifications. The problem was eventually solved when Article I, § 20, was amended by adding the following language to the section: "or in irrigation district elections, as to which last-named elections the legislature may restrict the voters to land owners."[7]

The Idaho delegates created two exceptions. They permitted property qualifications for elections creating indebtedness and for school elections. In 1970 the United States Supreme Court held that property qualifications in general bond elections are inconsistent with the United States Constitution.[8] As a result, Idaho's first exception is now gone. However, the Idaho supreme court has held that school elections were not affected by the federal case,[9] so that during Idaho's centennial year, property qualifications are impermissible except in school and irrigation district elections.

2. Suffrage Granted

AFTER DECIDING who should be guaranteed suffrage, Idaho's Constitutional Convention turned its attention to who should be granted suffrage. The suffrage committee recommended that the right to vote be extended to every male citizen of the United States who was twenty-one years old and a resident of the territory. The section went on to provide that "women who have the qualifications prescribed in this article, may continue to hold such school offices and vote at such school elections, as provided by the laws of Idaho territory," until the legislature provided otherwise. This recommendation reflects the evolution of the right of suffrage during the territorial period.

Idaho's first legislature granted the right to vote to white male residents over twenty-one years of age.[10] In March 1870 the Fifteenth Amendment to the United States Constitution was ratified. This amendment prohibited the United States, or any state, from denying the right to vote "on account of race, color, or previous condition of servitude." Four years later the eighth session of the Idaho territorial legislature removed the requirement that voters must be white.[11]

Women's suffrage was addressed by Idaho's territorial legislature before Negro suffrage was. Wyoming Territory extended suffrage to women in 1869, and Utah in 1870. Following the lead of Idaho's neighbors, in January 1871 Dr. Joseph Williams Morgan introduced a suffrage bill in the House of Representatives. The *Idaho Tri-Weekly Statesman* reported Dr. Williams' argument, "He took the position that the female represented a distinct individual member of the Government; that she ranked as a person, a citizen, and as such being affected by the laws of the country, it was in accordance with democratic teachings that she be allowed a voice in the making of those laws." Williams was opposed by W. H. VanSlyke, a thirty-one-year-old bachelor Republican who had immigrated from New York and lived in Silver City. VanSlyke argued, "Woman rules us through her love, and her chiefest power over us is through her graceful impulsiveness of heart and fancy, well enough around the fireside, but dangerous guides in the halls of legislation." In a roll-call vote on the third reading the House deadlocked at 11 to 11, and the bill was defeated.[12]

Women's suffrage, like virtually every issue during the last half of Idaho's territorial period, was strongly affected by the Mormon question. At the time, some thought women's suffrage was a plan of the Mormon church to gain political influence. Williams was a Welsh physician who immigrated to Salt Lake City, and then to Malad. Mormons in Malad were particpating in territorial politics in 1870, even though Mormons in other Idaho communities still viewed themselves as part of Utah. Beverly Beeton wrote, "There were, however, those who feared that if women were enfranchised it would give the Mormons in the territory disproportionate political power since there were many more women proportionately in the Mormon settlements than in the rest of the territory."[13] Extending suffrage was also a way for the church to counter the downtrodden image of Mormon women, and thus stem the tide of anti-polygamy legislation.

Whatever his motives, Williams had started women's suffrage in Idaho on its course. The next year an Idaho lawyer named Carrie F. Young delivered the first lecture on women's suffrage by a woman, arguing that "frivolity and extravagance among women could be remedied by making them responsible for their own debts and support."[14] Suffragettes and their supporters had their first success in Idaho in 1879 when a bill permitting unmarried women who were taxpayers to vote at school tax elections was passed.[15] Another small gain was made in 1885, when women were extended suffrage in all school elections, and in addition were permitted to hold elected school offices.[16] The *Boise City Republican* explained the justification for this extension, "Women being naturally gifted as teachers, we see no reason why they should not be competent to judge the qualifications necessary for teaching, which is the only matter which the law intrusts [sic] to the sole judgement of the Superintendent."[17] In 1889 the territorial legislature endorsed the election of female county school superintendents.[18]

The committee on suffrage at the constitutional convention took the conservative approach and only recommended that the existing territorial privileges be extended into statehood. However, two women came to address the convention to demand full suffrage. The first was Mrs. Henrietta Skelton, President of the Idaho Christian Temperance Union. The WCTU formed its first union in Boise in 1883, and held its first state convention there in 1887. It was also holding its annual meeting while the Idaho Constitutional Convention was in session, so it was convenient for the group to petition the convention for the right to speak. Mrs. Skelton asked the convention for two clauses in the constitution. The first provided, "no discrimination on account of sex shall be made; but citizens of both sexes, possessing the necessary qualifications, shall be equally eligible as electors;" and the second that: "The manufacture, sale, or keeping for sale of intoxicating liquors for use as a beverage is hereby prohibited . . ." (p. 90).

Mrs. Skelton made a relatively short speech in support of the WCTU requests, and made it clear temperance was their real concern. Suffrage was a means to that end. She told the delegates, "We come to you with a new voice today of the motherhood, of the sisterhood, of the womanhood, asking you to place in that constitution something which shall be a weapon to the dear women of the land to protect our homes. . . . We also ask you to help to build a wall around this state,—put out strong drink . . ." (p. 89). Mrs. Skelton lamented, "If only Wyoming had as many women voting as men voters, Wyoming today would be free from everything that demoralizes manhood; but unfortunately Wyoming has only one woman voter for forty men voters, and Wyoming is not able to do what it should do" (p. 89).

Even though Mrs. Skelton did once mention the right of women to participate in government as taxpayers, her basic strategy to persuade the delegates was to flatter them, and appeal to their sentiments and largesse.

> We only ask what every one who loves his home and its fireside and the rising generation must today ask for. . . . I appeal to you and to all Idaho. There was a mother once who held you at her knee. There was a mother once who placed into your life all that which is noble and good. If that mother is alive, she must be proud of her boy who helps to lay the foundation for a grand work today in Idaho. If she is dead, her angel spirit will certainly hover around you today and will be there when you frame that constitution. There is a dear wife at home. She is one of our sisters (p. 90).

Mrs. Skelton concluded by presenting a bouquet to the convention, and another WCTU member invited the delegates to an ice cream social in their reading rooms.

Abigail Scott Duniway[19] was the second woman to petition the convention for women's suffrage, and a more striking contrast to Henrietta Skelton could not have been found. While Skelton had been interested in women's suffrage for a year, Duniway had been an outspoken advocate of suffrage for twenty years. In 1871 she established a weekly newspaper, *The New Northwest*, which was devoted to women's rights and distributed throughout the Northwest, including Idaho. Duniway also made frequent lecture tours, and was active in national suffrage organizations. In her speech to the Idaho Convention she described recent conventions in Minneapolis and Washington,

D.C., where she had met with Bessie Isaacs, Lucy Stone, Julia Ward Howe, Isabella Beecher Hooker, Harriet Beecher Stowe, and others (pp. 172–73).

Duniway gave a long and fiery speech, by many criteria the best oration of the entire convention. The Duniway family had recently acquired a ranch in Custer County, so she spoke as a resident of the territory as well as a suffrage advocate. She began her speech by observing that "women seem destined not to be left much behind in the race . . . onward and upward toward liberty." She also thought that while women "differ very much as women, sometimes, as to the methods and aims of public work," she assured the delegates, "in a multitude of counselors there is wisdom" (p. 164). Duniway also addressed other differences between women and men later in the speech. "You say we must fight if we vote, forgetting or pretending to forget that life's hardest battles everywhere are fought by the mother of men in giving existence to the race" (pp. 169–70). She maintained there was an inherent difference between "the right to bear arms which nature accords to man, and the still more perilous right to bear armorbearers, which the same inexorable power assigns to woman" (p. 169).

Duniway elaborated the principles upon which women's suffrage was based. She began by saying she was proud to be from the West, because "the people who lived beyond the Rocky Mountains and beyond the valley of the Mississippi formed newer and better conceptions of the fundamental principles of liberty under the plastic conditions of their then new environment than had ever been dreamed of by their ancestors." She thought that people from the West had a "broader and more practical conception of life," gained through "struggles in the far, free West." She declared, "The freedom-loving spirit of the west has long passed into a proverb" (p. 171). Then Duniway reminded the delegates that "governments derive their just powers from the consent of the governed," and that "taxation and representation are co-existent factors in all just governments." She commended the work of the convention on the three branches of government, and joined in the strong anti-Mormon sentiment of the convention (pp. 164–66).

After these preliminaries, Duniway turned to her real mission which was to attack the argument of Henrietta Skelton that suffrage and prohibition were twin issues. Duniway wanted to separate the two, and set about to persuade the delegates. She began with a scathing attack on the women who worked in the prohibition movement. She challenged the sincerity of the prohibitionists, charging "they have sought the first avenues that opened to them for making money in which they may work and travel and receive pay and the plaudits of men, while at the same time conforting their consciences by the feeling that they are serving God and doing good." She also argued that the pushing of prohibition by the press and the pulpit and women's need to earn money "so stimulated woman's long-repressed and naturally emotional sensations that it was not difficult for political cranks, the one-idea men, who had been kicked out of the old parties, to secure their catspaw services in raking chestnuts for themselves from the fires of political controversy" (pp. 164–65). Duniway concluded her attack by saying the delegates should not be concerned about her harsh criticisms of women, because men just as eagerly sought wealth and recognition.

Duniway's experience had taught women the danger of prohibition being a "boomerang against their ballots." Washington Territory had extended suffrage to women who then adopted prohibition. In response, the men of the territory rescinded suffrage. Duniway told the delegates Washington women had "unwisely yielded to the counsels of women from the east who sought them out, on a handsome salary, to induce them to use their newly found ballots as catspaws in the hands of idealists and cranks." She praised Wyoming, where "the women have been voters long enough to learn wisdom before the prohibition rage became the fashion" (p. 168).

After attacking the prohibitionists, Duniway offered her own philosophy on prohibition. She assured the delegates, "women are quite as much opposed to drunkenness in husbands as men are opposed to drunkenness in wives" (p. 169). However, she also maintained that any thinking person came to only one conclusion. "Coercion or any species of arbitrary law never yet restrained any man in his vices so long as he was not constrained in his liberty. Give a man who desires to indulge a vice the liberty of locomotion, and depend upon it, he will find the opportunity to indulge . . . That is human nature" (p. 167). It was Duniway's view that "Liquors are sold because men buy them, and the river of intemperance flows because it was a perennial fountain in the desire of the consumer. . . . the river is always flowing, flowing. You may obstruct it here and viaduct it there, but you cannot stop the flow" (p. 171). As several delegates did on the convention floor, Duniway confidently predicted, "Clearly the prohibition movement is dying out" (p. 167).

Duniway offered her solution to the problem. "Tax whiskey and all other intoxicants as heavily as the traffic will bear, not so heavily as to amount to prohibition, for experience proves that the ends of justice are thus defeated for then the dealers will sell and pay no tax at all" (p. 171). She encouraged the delegates to "Regulate what you cannot destroy. Confine the stream to a limit as narrow as will contain its flow and keep the dikes high and in order." She assured them, "Give us the levee, gentlemen, and oh, give woman the ballot with which to build it high and strong and we will help you build right royally" (p. 172).

Duniway offered the convention delegates two proposals for extending women the ballot. The first was, "The right of suffrage shall not be prohibited to any law abiding person, if a taxpayer, or person of good moral character, on account of sex, provided always that such person be able to read, write and speak the English language." While this would have brought women into the political community, it would have excluded those who did not pay tax and the uneducated, which the delegates had included. Duniway's alternative did not immediately extend suffrage to women, but created a better possibility in the future. It provided, "Nothing in this chapter shall be construed to prohibit the legislature from extending the elective franchise to women" (p. 174).

When § 2 of the committee report came before the convention, James Reid moved to strike "until otherwise provided by the legislature" in the last clause granting women suffrage in school elections (p. 905). He explained, "I want to fix it in the constitution so that they will be allowed to vote, whether the legislature desires it or not, for school officers" (p. 905). William Clagett (R-Shoshone), was the first to object to Reid's motion. He declared its effect would be to "enfranchise every woman in this territory on all subjects, and Mrs. Duniway has her day" (p. 906). John Gray and James Beatty argued against Reid's proposal from the opposite direction, contending they wanted the legislature to go further in the future in granting women's suffrage, and that Reid's motion would not make that possible (pp. 907–10). Weldon Heyburn wanted legislative authority left in the section because he did not think it was appropriate for a woman superintendent of public schools to sit on the land commission as provided in the education article. He summed up, "I think we ought not to deprive the legislature of the power to regulate this, if there is any possibility of finding ourselves with a lady commissioner of lands on hand" (p. 911).

Reid's motion was defeated by voice vote. Then, A. J. Pierce (D-Custer), Frank Harris (D-Washington), G. W. King (D-Shoshone) and A. M. Sinnot (R-Logan) all moved that women be extended full suffrage (p. 912). Only King offered this short argument before the question was called, "I firmly believe that a majority of the women of this territory, or in any state of the Union, are just as well qualified for the right of suffrage as the average man. And there are thousands, tens of thousands and hundreds of thousands of women, ten thousand times better qualified than one-half of the men that vote in these United States" (p. 913). While King drew applause, he only drew twenty votes and thirty-six votes were cast against him. The other amendments quickly suffered the same fate.

There were several controversies at the convention where the delegates were out of step with the voters of the day. Women's suffrage was one of those. Wyoming carried its territorial policy of women's suffrage into statehood, and became the first state in the Union to do so. Colorado was the second in 1893 and Utah third in early 1896. Idaho became the fourth state in November 1896, when its constitution was amended to enfranchise every "male or female citizen."[20] This was nearly a quarter of a century before the Nineteenth Amendment to the United States Constitution was ratified in 1920, extending suffrage to women in all national and state elections.

3. Suffrage Denied

SECTION 3 of the suffrage committee report expressly denied the right to vote to three classes of people: idiots, criminals and Mormons. James Shoup immediately moved to add two more to the list, "Nor shall Chinese, or persons of Mongolian descent, not born in the United States, nor Indians not taxed who have not severed their tribal relations and adopted the habits of civilization, either vote, serve as jurors or hold any civil office" (p. 914). James Beatty, chair of the committee, accepted the amendment, and the convention added the language without debate.

Given the widespread discrimination against Chinese during the territorial period, it is surprising the committee report had not denied them the franchise. Idaho had a substantial Chinese population from the earliest territorial days. The 1870 census counted 4,272 Chinese residents, second among the states and territories only to California. The first territorial legislature had denied Chinese residents the right to vote by extending suffrage only to "white" males. Beyond being denied political rights, Chinese residents were also often denied civil rights. They were subject to special legislation and prosecution by public officials, and vigilante terror by self-proclaimed officers of the law.[21]

Congress preempted local legislation by passage of the Chinese Exclusion Statute in 1882, which provided, "That hereafter no State court or court of the United States shall admit Chinese to citizenship; and all laws in conflict with this act are hereby repealed."[22] Since this statute was in effect until 1943, the exclusion in Idaho's Constitution was legally superfluous, even if a strong expression of local prejudice. After the Exclusion Statute was repealed in 1943, however, Idaho's denial of citizenship to Chinese not born in the United States became important. Nearly twenty years later, in 1962, § 3 was finally amended to remove foreign-born Chinese from the list of those denied citizenship in Idaho.[23]

By denying citizenship to "Indians not taxed, who have not severed their tribal relations, and adopted the habits of civilization," Idaho was following traditional U.S. policy. From the earliest days of the country, Indians were given a choice of remaining tribal or assimilating into the white culture and becoming U.S. citizens. The United States Constitution in apportioning representation in the House of Representatives had excluded "Indians not taxed" from the enumeration.[24]

Idaho's Convention coincided with a very important change of policy towards Indian citizenship in the national government. The Dawes Act (General Allotment Act), which opened the reservations, also conferred citizenship on Indians once an allotment was received. The Nez Perce Reservation allotment was in progress when the Idaho Constitutional Convention was being held.[25] The convention delegates were obviously opposed to these new citizens, and with the constitution took away what the federal statutes had granted.

By 1924 the United States government had changed its policy on the terms of Indian citizenship. In that year the Indian Citizenship Act was passed, which extended citizenship to all Indians born in the United States, but did not demand that they abandon their tribes to obtain it.[26] Idaho, however, persisted in denying citzenship to Indians. Finally, in 1950, Idaho amended its constitution to remove Indians from the list of those explicitly disfranchised.[27] As a result, Idaho Indians today bear the burdens and enjoy the benefits of being citizens of three sovereigns, first their tribe, then the United States, and finally, the state.

Even though there were no debates about adding Chinese and Indians to the list, there were delegates who objected to the committee's harsh treatment of criminals. The committee proposed to disfranchise anyone ever convicted of treason, felony, embezzlement of public funds, buying and selling votes, or other infamous crimes, as well as anyone in prison at the time of the election. Judge John Gray proposed to add "and who has not been restored to the rights of citizenship" so that criminals once convicted would not forever be disfranchised. He argued, "If he has been so restored, I say it is our duty to recognize him and lend a helping hand to help this poor man. . . . let us take him as a man and try him again, not crush him and keep him down all his life" (p. 919). He repeatedly expressed his confidence in the judgement of the pardon authorities and summed up, "Punishment is not alone for the purpose of torture, but for reformation" (p. 922).

William Clagett wanted to disfranchise criminals who were convicted of treason or bartering to sell their vote, and he wanted to fix it so these would never be able to vote again. He emphasized, "When it comes down to a man assailing the purity of the ballot, then we are reaching a question which does call for some action on the part of the convention." He warned, "If there is any one danger from which republican institutions have good cause to fear today it is . . . the corruption of the ballot" (p. 925).

James Beatty was unwilling to accept these amendments. He pointed out some of those included in the section "have been convicted of polygamy; a great many more may be" and stated, "I do not believe those men, even if they should be pardoned out, would be worthy of the franchise." He also testified from his experience. "It is a very common custom in some sections of the country, that they pardon a man out a day before his term of imprisonment expires, for the very purpose of giving him the right of franchise, and that is often done for a political reason" (p. 920). Beatty's opposition was not entirely successful, and Gray's amendment to restore suffrage to some convicted felons found its way into the constitution (p. 928).

The last group to be disfranchised by the suffrage committee were Mormons. The committee did not mention Mormons directly, of course, but in a wordy and convoluted clause accomplished its purpose. The section disfranchised bigamists and polygamists, those who in any manner taught, advised or aided bigamy and polygamy, and finally, anyone who was a member of or contributed to the support of any order or organization that taught patriarchal or plural marriage, or taught that the state laws prescribing rules of civil conduct were not the supreme law. This clause was similar to the language already included by the convention in Article I., § 4, as a qualification upon freedom of religion, which in turn was based upon the 1885 test oath earlier used to completely disfranchise Mormon voters.[28]

Both political parties fully endorsed this sweeping language, and the delegates were in nearly unanimous agreement. Only Aaron Parker (D-Idaho) objected, in an obtuse way. He proposed that while anyone was disfranchised under the section, they were relieved of the obligation to pay taxes. Parker declared he offered the amendment "for the purpose of pinning this convention down to a consideration of the fundamental principles of human rights." He told the delegates he was surprised by men who would "assent to doctrines and principles and maintain them until they are hoarse," but who would repudiate them in practical operation. Parker believed "the cornerstone of American institutions [was] no taxation without representation," and cited the U.S. Constitution and Declaration of Independence. He concluded by stating what everybody knew. "This report is designed for no other purpose than to disfranchise a class of religious enthusiasts, who do not believe as you do, and who do not believe as I do. . . ." Parker was gaveled down before he was done, and his ideas quickly voted down (pp. 916–18).

Several other random suggestions sought to make the section even stronger. Robert Anderson (D-Bingham) was concerned about disfranchising voters only because they belonged to an organization and thought the same goal could be accomplished by simply requiring each voter to swear, "I do not hold any kind of obligation or supposed duty, or revelation to justify the violation of laws as interpreted by the courts" (p. 928). It was also suggested the following language be added: "or who claims to have direct revelation from God to commit those crimes" (pp. 928–30). These proposals were voted down without discussion, and the anti-Mormon clause was voted in without debate.

4. Suffrage and Saints

SECTION 4 of the suffrage committee Report was the lightning rod for the convention's most thunderous debate. A prolonged controversy in the committee over this section had delayed bringing a report to the convention, which in turn delayed the date of adjournment. Finally, the four Republican members of the committee, James Beatty, O. J. Salisbury (R-Custer), W. B. Heyburn, and Charles M. Hays (R-Oywhee), filed a majority report, and the three Democrats, George Ainslie (D-Boise), A. E. Mayhew (D-Shoshone), and F. W. Beane (D-Bingham), filed a minority report. The majority report proposed a section which read, "The legislature may prescribe qualifications, limitations and conditions for the right of suffrage additional to those prescribed in this article, but shall never annul any of the provisions in this article contained." The minority report objected to the entire section. (p. 943). The primary concern was about the Mormon voters of the future. The majority report wanted to empower the legislature so that Mormons could forever be disfranchised, regardless of changes in the church. The minority report sought to leave open the possibility of the church renouncing polygamy, and church members receiving the franchise and voting with the Democrats once again.

The majority report was finally read before the committee of the whole late in the morning session on July 25. James Beatty, the chairman of the suffrage committee, immediately offered a compromise amendment which he thought would satisfy the entire convention. "The legislature may prescribe qualifications, limitations and conditions for the right of suffrage concerning the classes and persons referred to in the immediately preceding section, additional to those prescribed therein, but shall never annul any provision in this article contained" (p. 930). Beatty optimistically related the majority report was changed "by agreement of both sides of the house," and stated the compromise was offered "for the very purpose of avoiding any discussion" and he hoped they would "all come to a unanimous conclusion upon this important question" (p. 931).

George Ainslie quickly accepted Beatty's proposal, and was willing to lay aside the minority report. He explained, "there was no violent difference of opinion between the minority and majority as to the restrictions to be placed in this constitution upon these bigamists and polygamists, or Mormons, if we are going to use the word for all of them, as to disfranchising them thoroughly." There had been disagreement because the Democrats feared the section "might be extended by the legislature further than the majority had contemplated; that it might be applied to some of the secret societies, Masons and Odd Fellows, and some were of the opinion that it might reach as far as Catholics" (p. 931).

Cries of "Question, question" were raised by the delegates, when William H. Clagett abruptly rose and cautioned, "I don't think we want to be rushed on this proposition" (p. 931). Clagett's credentials as an anti-Mormon were as impressive as those of any delegate at the convention. The first order of governmental business when Clagett, twenty-three years old, arrived in Nevada in 1861 was the dismantling of the Mormon government which preceded the miners. While serving as Montana Territory's delegate to the House, he supported the Edmunds Act and opposed Utah statehood with some of the strongest anti-Mormon speeches ever given.

Clagett warned the delegates, "The state is dealing with an adversary which does assume as many shapes as Proteus ever assumed of old, and can assume any shape it sees fit; can profess anything, and by virtue of its pretense that it receives revelations from on high, may relieve its members from the obligation of civil conduct." His advice was to "leave the power of the state as broad as the capacity of this sect, to change the front and manner of its attack and its defense." He sobered the delegates with this prediction, "If you put this substitute in here your Mormons will be in power in this territory inside a year" (pp. 931–33).

James Reid, the Democratic caucus leader and a gifted orator, defended Beatty's proposed compromise. Reid explained how the committee had "brooded on this matter for a week," and how the convention had delayed its debate for several days until finally all the committee and both party caucuses had come to an agreement. He maintained Clagett was alone in wanting to reopen the controversy. Reid assured the delegates "the question we are all agreed upon should be the downing of the Mormons." He argued that under Beatty's amendment, if "this prodigious monster, this hydra-headed monster, rears its head," the legislature had the power to "scotch that monster." Further, he contended the majority report was objectionable because it empowered the legislature to disfranchise foreigners, even though they had become United States citizens, as well Catholics and Freemasons (pp. 933–35).

Beatty was surprised by Clagett's objection, and was quick to defend his conduct in the matter. He explained that "influential gentlemen outside of the convention" had been responsible for the amendment, and that he had not assumed any personal authority at all on the matter. Still, he defended the amendment because he thought the amendment gave the legislature the power to deal with "that hateful church," but at the same time did not authorize disfranchisement of members of "the Masonic fraternity" or "Methodist society" (pp. 935–38). Suddenly someone called for an adjournment.

John Morgan quickly added, "I wish to make the announcement that the republicans meet in the council chamber immediately after adjournment." The delegates agreed, 35 to 16, and the convention floor was cleared. Either Reid erred when he claimed the Republican caucus had approved the amendment, or Clagett missed the meeting. Clagett was reading the proposal for the first time on the floor and such was his influence that when he alone objected, matters came to a sudden halt for reconsideration.

The afternoon of July 25, 1889, must have been one of the longest days in James Beatty's career, because he spent it eating crow. Beatty was apparently chosen to preside over the suffrage committee because he was a prominent Republican, not because he was a strong anti-Mormon. The makeup of the entire committee reflects this same consideration. There were four Republicans and three Democrats, but only two of the seven came from Mormon country and could therefore be expected to be a strong anti-Mormon. One was F. W. Beane from Bingham County, where railroaders exerted strong anti-Mormon influence. The other was Beatty from Alturas county, where miners were adamantly anti-Mormon. The immigration of these two groups in the early 1880s contributed significantly to the growth of anti-Mormonism in territorial government, and eventually lead to expulsion of Mormons from the political community.

Even though Beatty represented a county which had often gone on record against the Mormons, he was not strong enough in those convictions for the rest of the delegates. He was late returning to the convention after the caucus and lunch recess, and when he did arrive he announced, "I have instructions to withdraw that substitute, and in obedience to the instructions" he made his motion. Before making his withdrawal, however, he again defended himself. He gave more detail on the origins of the substitute he had offered. He explained there had been a meeting in the Overland Hotel involving Republican committee members and influential persons from outside the convention. Beatty steadfastly refused to name who was involved. He also assured the convention "I did not offer it as my own," but rather on behalf the those who met in the Overland Hotel who had assured him the substitute had the support of both parties (pp. 943–44, 952).

The Republican caucus had not only decided to withdraw Beatty's substitute, but to ram the majority report through the convention without a vote. The chair ruled the substitute could not be withdrawn, but it was quickly voted down 24 to 31. Democrats maneuvered to delay approval of the majority report by moving to report back to the convention, and to strike the section from the report. Both were voted down by the same margin, without debate. The delegates were on the verge of voting on the majority report when James Reid rose and demanded that debate not be cut off entirely (p. 946).

Reid did not argue the merits of the section, instead he addressed "some incidental questions." He argued that this treatment of the Mormons violated the United States Constitution. He argued it was a breach of the "rules and precedents that have become a part of the unwritten law commonly regulating deliberative assemblies" for the Republicans to breach an agreement that had been made between the chairman of the committee and the minority party (p. 947). A number of other delegates later repeated this theme in the debates.

Reid's most adamant contention was that withdrawing the substitute violated the bipartisan character of the convention. "The minority have some rights here, and I propose at this time to show where the minority has been treated with injustice." Then he listed his complaints about Republican partisanship. The Democrats had not objected when Republicans insisted upon controlling the Ada County delegation, even though it had been earlier agreed it would be evenly divided. Neither did they object when Clagett announced at a preliminary caucus that he had been authorized to preside over the convention. Then Republicans had taken all the offices at the convention, and chaired nearly all the important committees. In contrast, the minority had come to the convention in good faith and without partisan objectives. Reid claimed he was the first in the territory to draw resolutions in a public meeting calling for statehood, even though he came from a region which strongly favored annexation to Washington rather than statehood. He explained, "I joined in readily and made sacrifice of my business and other sacrifices . . . and I came under that proclamation which declared to this whole state that this was to be done by us as patriots, that we were to come here as men loving Idaho" (pp. 946–52).

Drew W. Standrod (D-Oneida) rose to meet Reid's challenge. Standrod followed Clagett as the second delegate to criticize Mormons and support the majority report, and he was probably second only to Clagett in anti-Mormon sentiments at the convention. Standrod's family were stockraisers, which made them part of a group long opposed to Mormon colonization in Idaho. Stockmen were already grazing cattle in the open valleys and plains of southeastern Idaho when the first Mormon settlements were established in Franklin and Malad. After the 1872 survey of the Idaho-Utah boundary, stockmen became an important part of the Oneida Independent Anti-Mormon party. Standrod was elected District Attorney in 1888, and and so was involved in prosecuting Mormons at the time he came to the convention.

Standrod began, "The great trouble in this convention, Mr. Chairman, is that there are too many members who have never lived in the community where this church predominates. They do not understand the question." He cautioned the delegates this was the one question "which we place above all other questions that have or will come before this convention," and stressed, "this is a question that comes directly to the fireside and to the home of every man in my section of the country" (pp. 954–56).

Standrod wanted to go even further than the majority report, and suggested providing that "the privilege of voting or holding office in this state shall be a franchise granted or withheld at the will of the legislature, giving them absolute power." He was worried about a "despotic theocracy," and cautioned against placing too much emphasis upon bigamy and polygamy. He argued, "the least evil existing in that church today is this practice. It is a theocracy that is used for the purpose of securing political influence in the country where it exists." Standrod wanted to make certain "no member of this Mormon organization should ever exercise the right of franchise or be permitted to vote in this state." To accomplish this end, he urged the delegates should the Mormons "by revelation renounce polygamy and bigamy and seem to abandon these practices that now exist in the church, then delegate to the legislature the power to provide against anything of that character" (pp. 953–55).

Standrod also rebutted Reid's arguments in opposition to the majority report. He first belittled Reid's reliance upon the U.S. Constitution. "I want to ask the gentlemen who have preached on this evil, day in and day out, about the great rights and the great safeguards we have had under the constitution of the United States—I ask them what aid has the constitution of the United States ever given in regard to the franchise? . . . They have left this question absolutely to the states until it came down to the Fifteenth Amendment" (p. 957). Standrod reassured the delegates there was little chance the legislature would ever disfranchise anybody but Mormons, because it had not done so during the territorial period. He conceded, "the democrats have not been treated fairly in a good many respects," but thought the question of Mormon suffrage was "a question that transcends all political feeling, or at least it should. . . ." (p. 956). In the end, Standrod urged the delegates to send a clear message to Congress which said, "We have got confidence in ourselves; we can control the matter. You leave the franchise to us and we will see that it is properly exercised and in a spirit of justice and right and against Mormonism" (p. 958).

Once Reid and Standrod spoke, the floodgates had been opened, and any hope the Republicans had of forcing their majority report quickly through the convention disappeared. All afternoon, and through an evening session, delegate after delegate took the floor to state his mind on the question. Speeches were long, and often rancorous; and for the most part they just repeated the basic themes of the controversy that had been outlined by Reid and Standrod in the initial exchange.

Orlando Batten (D-Alturas) joined Reid to argue the Democrats were "being treated in that rank bare-faced spirit of partisanship." He complained, "We do not so much object to the matter of this section as to the manner in which it has been forced upon us." Batten bluntly described the convention as he saw it. "We were invited here as to an unpartisan feast, but we discovered, I am sorry to say it—I hate to use such a harsh term—that we have been entrapped and decoyed into a regular partisan camp. . . . We have been flouted and outreached in this matter without having in any manner violated our faith. I do charge it upon the opposition that they have broken faith . . ." (pp. 974–76).

Aaron Parker went further than Reid and Batten, and claimed the entire Mormon question was one of politics. He argued, "the sole object of that test oath legislation in our legislatures has been for no other purpose than to disfranchise these people in southeastern Idaho, not because they were polygamists, not because they were Mormons, but because they voted the democratic ticket" (p. 1035). Peter J. Pefley (D-Ada) agreed with Parker and objected to "the granting of unheard of powers to the legislature in order to regulate the right of suffrage to suit the republican party and keep it in power forever" (p. 1016).

William Clagett was criticized by those opposing the majority report. During the debates Reid described Clagett as "a good and learned man," but also as "the wildest and most radical man in his notions" about innovations in the constitution (p. 987). In referring to Clagett's initial objection to the compromise, Batten lamented that "a fire-brand—an apple of discord," had interjected himself, broken the agreement, and caused discord. As might have been expected, Clagett defended his intervention with a back-fire, "[O]ur democratic friends had succeeded in entrapping our chairman into a well-considered scheme; but fortunately we have got out of the trap" (p. 982). Clagett described the trap in Beatty's proposed compromise. "Now if you adopt section 4 and limit the power of the legislature . . . inside of a year you would have the Mormon priesthood intrenched [sic] so strongly in the strong places in this state that nothing but an avalanche or a revolution would ever be able to dislodge them" (p. 983).

Clagett also defended the way in which he and the Republicans had run the convention. He thought there were nine important committees at the convention, and that he had tried to give half of them to the Democrats, in addition to four or five unimportant committees. Referring to the allegation of partisanship, he retorted, "I deny that charge in toto and in detail. It cannot under the facts of the record be sustained" (p. 977). Referring to the majority report he said, "[I]t is not because we would in any way expect to ever obtain any party advantage out of this matter, but it is because the republicans have been freely, each one for himself, acting upon this question" (p. 983).

Clagett explained to the delegates what was required for a nonpartisan convention. "Does a non-partisan convention require that both political parties shall be equally represented? Certainly not. . . . A non-partisan convention consists of a convention in which all parties shall be represented according to their voting strength, and so are represented on the floor of this house" (p. 977).

While Clagett claimed there were no politics in the Mormon question, other Republican delegates made party politics an explicit part of their argument. John Morgan declared to the convention, "within the last ten months the democratic party met in convention in the city of Boise and had in its organization, in its councils nominating candidates for office in this territory, a full-fledged Mormon" (p. 1038). He warned his Republican colleagues, "I say we may well fear that possibly somebody in the democratic party may hereafter desire to get these Mormons into their organization in order to vote for their candidates" (p. 1039).

Weldon Heyburn cynically responded to Reid. "All this talk, this nice palaver about constitutional conventions or any other political body—because this is a political body, convened here for policial purposes, for the purpose of forming a government—when you talk to me in this nice palaver about this body being non-political, non-partisan, I smile or let it pass by as a rule, because there is no such thing" (pp. 998–99). Heyburn proudly subscribed to the partisan's creed. "I have never at any period since my majority disclaimed or disguised the fealty I owe the party to which I belong. Whenever political principles are being discussed or supported, I am always found on the side of my political party, not because it is my party, but because I believe it is the right side . . ." (p. 998).

Like Reid, a number of other delegates were also distrustful of the legislature and concerned who might be disfranchised under the broad language supported by the

Republicans. Lycurgus Vineyard (D-Alturas) cautioned, "We know that legislatures are liable to act upon bias. . . . Ought not we to pause and consider the latitude which is thrown open to the legislature, that is always governed by the caprice that happens to pervade the community at that particular time and the 'isms' and 'schizms' that are prevalent throughout the commonwealth at the time the legislature is in session?" (p. 973). Alexander Mayhew wanted the right to vote firmly established "so that it could not every two years after an exciting political contest be left to the whims and caprices of a biennial mob of adventurers who seek places in the legislative assembly" (p. 1034).

J. W. Poe was concerned the American party, which took the position that only "American born citizens" had the right to vote, might get control of the legislature. He wanted to protect the rights of Methodists, Baptists, Catholics, and members of secret societies. He warned the convention, "[The legislature further] has the right to say that any man or set of men who unite themselves for the purpose of protecting themselves against capital . . . they have the right to say that any man who belongs to a union of this kind shall not exercise the right of franchise" (p. 962). Reid warned of railroads, which were "reaching out like an octopus with its arms, taking in your country. It has already got the farmers by the throat. How long will it take to control the legislatures?" (p. 989). If that happened, he warned, "If you belong to labor unions that are opposed to Chinese, or any great question," then you will be disfranchised (p. 989).

Republicans tried in several ways to dispell fears about whom the legislature might disfranchise. James Beatty asked rhetorically, "What possible objection can you make to that, save the single objection you have urged that the legislature will then have the power to disenfranchise [sic] good citizens? I admit that . . . but I ask, have you any fear that any legislature ever elected by the people of the state of Idaho will undertake to commit such an outrage as that?" (p. 967). In a comment that reflects great conceit and self-satisfaction, Weldon Heyburn assured the Democrats, "The legislatures that will control the destinies of this state will be drawn from the same body from which this august assemblage was drawn . . . when they are again sent here to make laws for the state, they will bring back with them the wisdom and integrity that has distinguished their deliberations in this body" (p. 997).

Just as Drew Standrod had done, the other supporters of the majority report not only addressed the concerns of the dissenters, but made a forceful argument for adoption by describing their fears of the Mormon church, and the reasons the legislature needed such broad authority. John Lewis, who only spoke at the convention on the Mormon question, was a "Josephite Mormon" and represented another Oneida County community which had been anti-Mormon from the beginning. After the death of Joseph Smith in Carthage, Illinois, Brigham Young and the main body of the Mormon church migrated west to the Great Salt Lake, where plural marriage became more widely practised. Those who remained, called Josephites, professed loyalty to Joseph Smith, rejected plural marriage, and formed the Reorganized Church of Jesus Christ of Latter Day Saints. The Josephites were successful in converting a number of people from the main church in Utah, and very early established a colony in Malad. Another group of apostates called the Morrisites had settled in Soda Springs. These groups combined with the stockmen and a few Mormons to govern Oneida County as the Liberal party during the 1870s. After the 1872 survey, the political lines became clearly drawn and the Liberal party evolved into the Independent Anti-Mormon party.

Lewis was referring to Oneida County's history when he rose and modestly began, "I am not in the habit of speaking before a convention of this kind, but inasmuch as the matter of Mormonism has come up, I beg to say that I have lived amongst that people for thirty-three years and I know a little about them" (p. 962). Lewis accused the Mormons of being "against the government, and will remain so until they have the supreme power, if they vote at all, of the country in the end" (p. 964). To make his point, Lewis told this story. "The Mormon people seem to me something like an Irishman—a red-headed Irishman, who landed once at Castle Garden; it happened to be on the day of election, and the republicans surrounded him the moment Pat got off, and the democrats came around too; look here, says they, come now, let's vote; no, says Pat, I won't vote for either of you. Well, they were all urging him; bejabbers, says he, I won't vote at all, but at last they urged him so hard, says he, is there any government in this country? Why, yes; well then, I vote against the government" (p. 964).

John Morgan from Bingham County gave the most damning descriptions of Mormons, and was most adamant in his opposition to them. Morgan had come to Idaho in 1879 when he was appointed chief justice of the territorial supreme court. He served on the court until 1885. Since he was assigned to the southeastern judicial district, he presided over a number of prosecutions of Mormons under the Edmunds Act.

Morgan strongly denounced the theocratic nature of the Mormon church. "George Cannon rules this church with a rod of iron. He has a despotism more tryannical and more despotic than the despotism of the czar of Russia today. He tells one man to go, and he goeth; another to come, and he cometh" (p. 1041). Morgan alleged church authorities used force to maintain their control. "The man who dares to raise his voice against this organization, either privately or publicly, if it is discovered, has the water cut off; his stacks are burned, his cattle are killed upon the range, his barn is burned, and perchance his house, and he is a ruined man. For this reason they dare not vote, they dare not talk, they dare not exercise any of the rights that an American citizen may exercise in this country" (p. 1045).

Another recurring theme in Morgan's argument was the subversive nature of the Mormons. He declared, "The whole intent and purpose of this organization is to overthrow the government of the United States. When the North and South were engaged in a death struggle only a few years ago, Brigham Young and other prophets of that church, in their public meetings hailed the day when these brothers were warring, and said the time would come when this government would be destroyed and they would be the ruling power, and they prayed God that the day might be hastened, might come soon" (p. 1040).

Morgan also indicted the Mormons for a litany of crimes. "They have been guilty of every crime in the calendar, murder, incest, arson. There is within the sound of my voice today, tonight in this hall, a man who had a son in the prime of manhood, full of the strength of youth, as good a man as has been raised in this country or any other country, who was within the last two years lured into the mountains and shot down and his carcass left to be devoured by carrion birds by this Mormon organization" (p. 1039).

The Democrats did not defend Mormons against these attacks. During the ten years before the convention they had learned that the cost of defending Mormons was the election. George Ainslie had been defeated for reelection as representative to Congress in the first territory-wide anti-Mormon campaign. Ainslie was forced to spend the entire campaign explaining why he had supported George Cannon when Congress had refused to seat Cannon as Utah's territorial representative in the previous session. By the time of the convention, Democrats were trying to to be as anti-Mormon as the Republicans. James Reid drew large applause at the convention when he summed up the opposition to the majority report. "I have done as much to suppress Mormonism as any other man on this floor; I voted for the law which protects you now; I voted for the law that gave you the right to pass that test oath. But when we stand up here and down Mormons, I don't propose to down Americans" (p. 991).

The only voice raised in defense of Mormons was that of Peter J. Pefley. "I am tired of sitting and thought I would get up awhile. I have been listening a long time to a great deal of eloquence. I have many times wished I was a great orator, and never more perhaps than on this occasion, from the fact that this is the time at which I think the very essence of the privilege of American citizens is endangered in this territory" (p. 1014).

Pefley continued, "Sir, American citizenship is the highest work that can exist; I honor our principles and government. With it a man can travel the wide world over and all the time be protected by the hues of the stars and stripes. And if any court, potentate, no matter what his power is, should attempt to infringe the rights and prerogatives of an American citizen, all the powers of this government would be brought to bear, if necessary to avenge his wrong and restore his liberty. . . . Yet if he landed the next day . . . in Idaho, and was a Mormon, and some of these statesmen should see him put a two-bit piece into a Moromon contribution box, he would be disfranchised and barred from holding office. . . ." (pp. 1015–16).

Pefley recalled the history of religious persecution in the United States. "Political and religious persecution are supposed to have died at the termination of the revolution; but it appears that Idaho is again an exception, and that the bloody history of two hundred years ago is about to repeat itself, in sentiment at least, with all its hideousness in this state, which should be one of the most liberal, tolerant and enlightened in the American Union" (p. 1017).

Pefley concluded his oration by asking the convention, "I have a request to make of a certain kind of people on this floor, and that is, when you shall reach that beautiful shore and look over the jasper rampart into that dark abyss, you will bear witness in heaven that Pefley did not vote on this occasion to punish the innocent with the guilty, and that I shall have credit at least for one righteous act on the great book" (p. 1018).

This was the second time Pefley had excited the convention by being the only voice to dissent from an otherwise unanimous passion. Early in the convention he proposed to delete the phrase "grateful to Almighty God" from the preface. For that motion he was labeled an "infidel" and had other delegates move to censor by striking his motion from the record of the proceedings. Pefley continued his lonesome resistance to the end. As the delegates were ready to sign the final document, Pefley took the floor, "I always think consistency is a jewel highly prized, and inasmuch as there are sections in there that I could not endorse when they passed as sections or articles, I cannot now conscientiously sign the constitution and therefore asked to be excused." Frank P. Cavanah (D-Elmore) immediately moved to deny Pefley his pay if he refused to sign. It was the same Cavannah who had moved to expunge from the record Pefley's motion to remove the reference to "God Almighty." There were many clashes between the strong personalities at the convention, like Clagett and Reid, and McConnell and Ainslie. Perhaps because religion was involved, none appear as personal and deeply-felt as the problems between Pefley and Cavanah. Clagett ruled Cavanah out of order, but Pefley had the last word, his last words at the convention: "I do not ask any pay, and I would not have it, and the gentleman can save his motion" (p. 2043).

As many others had, Morgan warned the delegates of the threat they faced. "And if we adopt a constitution here that will permit these Mormons by any hook or crook to come into this territory to vote, we can be overwhelmed and voted down within six months" (p. 1041).

These dire warnings, and the Republican advantage to be gained, had their effect when the final votes were taken late Saturday night. Beatty's substitute was still on the floor and the first to be voted on. It was defeated 16 to 36. All 16 votes in favor were Democrats. Three Democrats (Anderson, Beane, Kinport) from Bingham County, where anti-Mormon sentiments were high, apparently voted with their party rather than their constituents. Opposing the compromise were thirty-two Republicans and four Democrats. Two of the Democrats were Standrod and Samuel Taylor. Their experiences in the Oneida Independent Anti-Mormon Party and their speeches at the convention made it clear they were anti-Mormon first and foremost, and belonged to a party only incidentally. The other two Democrats were Myer from Boise County and A. J. Pierce from Custer. A vote then was immediately taken on the majority report granting extensive power to the legislature. It passed 42 to 10. Pefley did not vote on either motion.

The Mormon revelation concerning polygamy, so often referred to on the floor of Idaho's Constitutional Convention, was announced by Mormon President Wilford Woodruff on September 26, 1890, just one week before Idaho's first state election. President Woodruff assured the world that there had been nothing done during his administration to encourage polygamy. Woodruff referred to federal anti-polygamy statutes and cases upholding them, and said, "I hereby declare my intention to submit to those laws and to use my influence with the members of the church over which I preside to have them do likewise." Woodruff's manifesto was the key to the door which brought Mormons back into Idaho politics. President Benjamin Harrison accepted the declaration, and agreed to amnesty for any polygamous relations established prior to the revelation. Idaho politicians soon fell in line, and on February 3, 1893, the legislature repealed the test oath and Mormons once again were franchised.[29]

The Mormon question was like a thunderstorm sweeping across Idaho's politcal landscape a century ago. The storm was intense and violent in the halls of the 1889 constitutional convention, then it quickly passed and the skies cleared. However, it left permanent changes in the country it passed through. Idaho became a state because of it. Had Idaho Republicans not been able to disfranchise the Mormons and break the Democratic control, the territory would not have suddenly been made into a state by a Republican-controlled Congress looking for ways to strengthen its hold. On the other side, the same storm of controversy permanently changed the Mormon church, not only in Idaho but in Salt Lake City. The practice of polygamy was abandoned. Even more fundamentally, the controversy led the Mormons to discontinue their practice of bloc voting, in favor of local communities dividing themselves between the parties according to their own interests. The Mormons left Idaho as Democratic but returned primarily Republican. All things considered, these changes may have been more important in the affairs of the world than Idaho's statehood.

Notes

1. See chapter 2 above.

2. The debates at the Idaho Constitutional Convention are reported in Hart, I. W., ed. *Proceedings and Debates of the Constitutional Convention of Idaho 1889.* 2 vols. Caldwell: Caxton Printers, Ltd., 1912. These volumes are paginated consecutively, and all page references in the text of this chapter are to them.

3. The opening of the reservations refers to the allotment policy adopted by Congress with the passage of the Dawes Act in 1887. Under this policy, each Indian was to receive an allotment of 160 acres or less. The lands remaining after the allotments were declared surplus lands, and the reservation was opened for settlement by non-Indians. Otis, Delos S. *The Dawes Act and the Allotment of Indian Lands.* Norman: University of Oklahoma Press, 1973.

4. *Pioneer Irrigation Dist. v. Walker,* 20 Idaho 605, 119 P. 304 (1911).

5. *Bissett v. Pioneer Irrigation Dist.,* 21 Idaho 98, 120 P. 461 (1912).

6. *Ferbrache v. Drainage Dist. No. 5,* 23 Idaho 85, 128 P. 553 (1912).

7. 1931 Idaho Sess Laws 462, H.J.R. No. 2, ratified at the general election in 1932.

8. *City of Phoenix v. Kolodziejski,* 399 U.S. 204, 90 S.Ct. 1990, 26 L.Ed. 2d 523 (1970).

9. *Muench v. Paine,* 94 Idaho 12, 480 P.2d 196 (1971).

10. An Act Relative to Elections, 1864 Idaho Sess Laws 560.

11. An Act Relative to Elections, 1874–75 Idaho Sess Laws 684.

12. See Larson, T. A. "The Woman's Rights Movement in Idaho." *Idaho Yesterdays* 16 (Spring 1972):2–15, 18–19.

13. Beeton, Beverly. *Women Vote in the West: The Woman Suffrage Movement, 1869–1896.* New York: Garland Publishing Co., 1986, p. 118.

14. *Idaho Tri-Weekly Statesman* (Boise), January 10, 1872.

15. An Act to Establish a Public School System, 1879 Idaho Sess Laws 21.

16. An Act to Amend an Act to Establish a Public School System, 1885 Idaho Sess Laws 194.

17. *Boise City Republican* 16 October 1886, p. 4, col. 2.

18. An Act to Remove the Disqualifications of Persons Elected to the Office of County Superintendant of Public Schools, 1889 Idaho Sess Laws 13–14.

19. Moynihan, Ruth Barnes. *Rebel for Rights, Abigail Scott Duniway.* New Haven: Yale University Press, 1983; Smith, Helen Krebs. *The Presumptious Dreamers: A Sociological History of the Life and Times of Abigail Scott Duniway.* Lake Oswego, Oregon: Smith, Smith and Smith Publishing Co., 1974.

20. 1895 Idaho Sess Laws 232, S.J.R. No. 2, ratified in November, 1896.

21. Beal, Merrill D. and Wells, Merle W. *History of Idaho.* 3 vols. New York: Lewis Historical Publishing Company, 1959, pp. 577–80.

22. Ch. 126, §14, 22 Stat. 61 (1882).

23. 1961 Idaho Sess Laws 1073, S.J.R. No. 1, ratified at the general election November 6, 1962.

24. U.S. Const. Art. I. § 2, cl. 3.

25. The story of Nez Perce allotment is told in Gay, E. Jane. *With the Nez Perces.* Lincoln: University of Nebraska Press, 1981.

26. 43 Stat. 253, 8 U.S.C.A. § 1401(a)2).

27. 1949 Idaho Sess Laws 597, H.J.R. No. 2, ratified in November, 1950.

28. See Chapter 2, § 2.

29. 1895 Idaho Sess Laws, 37–39.

9.
Water

1. Territorial Water Development

WATER AND THE RIGHT TO USE IT have always been fundamental features of life for Idaho's inhabitants. Indians residing in the region when whites arrived had elaborate customs relating to water. For example, the more permanent Nez Perce villages were located at critical sites on the rivers, and political organization was often based on the river's drainage. Hereditary and customary rights to fishing sites were recognized. The intensive use of the Snake River by the Shoshone and Bannock tribes has also been documented.[1]

The first recorded irrigation within the country that became Idaho was done by Reverend Henry Harmon Spaulding. In 1838 he dug ditches at Lapwai to provide water for his Presbyterian mission.[2] He abandoned his labors in 1847. The second irrigation project was at the early Mormon settlement in the Lemhi Valley.[3] While this colony was able to secure water, they could not secure themselves from grasshoppers or local Indians so were forced to retreat. In 1860 a second, and permanent Mormon community was established in Idaho at Franklin.

A new water use, mining, came to Idaho in 1860 when Elias D. Pierce's party discovered gold in the Clearwater drainage.[4] Mining quickly spread to the Boise Basin and eventually to every corner of the state. If there was suitable land, irrigation came soon after mining. Inevitably, some disappointed miner would turn his hand to irrigated farming.

William McConnell, who represented Latah County at the constitutional convention, was just such a person. In 1863 he was raising a truck garden in the Payette

Valley to supply the miners in the region. In the summer of 1889, on the convention floor, he recalled, "I believe I had the first irrigating ditch that was ever taken out of the waters of this or Boise county for irrigating purposes. . . . " (p. 1137).[5] McConnell sold green onions at $1.00 per bunch of twelve, and $2.00 per dozen for cucumbers and corn. He later reflected about these early farming ventures. "They were the first monopolists in Idaho, and I am willing to testify that we enjoyed it."[6]

While Idaho farmers did not enjoy their monopoly for long, irrigated agriculture developed steadily. In the Boise, Payette, and Weiser valleys, and in the region around Lewiston, most of this was accomplished by individual enterprise. The first to locate on a river were able to find land that could be watered with relatively little difficulty. In contrast, most development in the southeastern region was accomplished by the cooperative effort of a Mormon colony. By 1880, in all parts of the territory, the lands that could be developed by individual enterprise had been taken, and a new approach was needed if irrigation development was to continue.[7]

That new approach was the ditch company, whose objective was to profit by constructing a canal and selling the water to others. Perhaps the first of these enterprises was begun by W. D. Morris in 1878. He planned a canal eight feet wide at the bottom and twelve feet at the top to irrigate bench lands in the Boise valley. After Morris died, the project was enlarged and finished by W. Ridenbaugh. The Settlers' Ditch near Meridian began as a cooperative venture, but evolved into a ditch company when taken over by John Lemp, Idaho's "Boss Brewer," who represented Ada County at the constitutional convention.

Little formal water law developed during Idaho's territorial period. In most regions settlement was sparse and irrigation projects small, so there was plenty of water for all. The two exceptions were the mining camps and the Mormon colonies, where specialized legal systems developed for resolving conflicts. Most Idaho miners came from California and brought with them the mining codes used in the California mining fields, which had been inherited from early Spanish miners. These codes were based on the principle of prior appropriation, which recognized a water right whenever water was diverted and put to a beneficial purpose. Water law in the Mormon colonies was based on the Mormon theology that had been developed in the Great Salt Lake Basin. These principles emphasized the community nature of water use and the duty to share, and the absolute authority of the bishop to apportion water and resolve disputes.

The first territorial water statute coincided with the emergence of the ditch companies. In 1881 the territorial legislature passed two general water statutes. The last and longest section of the first statute protected settlers from ditch company power. Any settler along a ditch was entitled to water, and if that right were interfered with, the owners of the ditch were personally liable for damages, and a lien was placed on the canal. Farmers were only entitled to that amount of water "good husbandry shall require," and they were liable for damages caused by waste.[8]

In the first section of the statute, the legislature granted a right to acquire water by appropriation and provided that first in line was first in right. This general principle was qualified in several important ways. All water rights existing before the statute were recognized. Further, courts were required to recognize any custom and practice of common right that might have developed over the years. Finally, there was a section that granted to any landowner on or in the vicinity of a stream a right to use the water to irrigate. On the surface the statute appears to contradict itself by adopting a general prior appropriation principle *and* the riparian principle, in which all landowners on the stream have a common right. However, as the events at the constitutional convention reveal, this was not a principle of riparian rights but a preference for irrigation.

In addition to establishing these general water rights, the legislature in 1881 provided for the securing and administration of the rights. Posting and developing were necessary to acquire a right.[9] Further, water districts were authorized upon a majority vote of the users of a common water right.[10] Districts were authorized to select a water master who was empowered to supervise the water system and to distribute the water.

These statutes played an important role in the development of the water article of the Idaho Constitution. The first principal water law case to make its way to the Idaho territorial supreme court also influenced the convention. That case, *Drake v. Earhart*,[11] had been tried and taken under advisement by the time the delegates gathered for the convention. The case involved the water in Quigley Gulch, near Hailey. The plaintiffs based their claim on prior use, while the defendants claimed a riparian right. Several delegates to the convention were involved in the case, and were well aware that regardless of the outcome of the litigation, the convention would fashion its own solution for the new state. That solution was first developed in the manufactures, agriculture and irrigation committee.

2. The Manufactures, Agriculture, and Irrigation Committee

THERE WERE TWO GREAT DEBATES about water at the Idaho Constitutional Convention. The first related to private takings under Article I, Section 14. After a heated debate and a conference meeting of the irrigation and mining committees, the convention provided for taking of easements for water development by a private person over the land of another. While the delegates acknowledged these private takings were novel in constitutional and property law, they also thought they were absolutely necessary to develop irrigation on the Snake River plains.

The second great water debate was provoked by Article XV, "Water Rights." The timing of the debate on this article is important. It occurred immediately after the convention had spent itself in the debate over suffrage and the Saints. As a result, some of the passion and controversy had gone. There was not a single partisan quibble between the Democrats and Republicans. There were no duels between Clagett and Reid, the parties' two great orators. Even more amazing, there was no anti-Mormon sentiment expressed. This is one of the few significant debates where the Mormons were not denounced. There were fifty-two delegates present on the Mormon question, but only thirty-nine one day later, when the water article was considered. The debate on the water article marked the convention's beginning to wind down.

The committee that drafted the water rights article was misnamed. Instead of "Manufactures, Agriculture and Irrigation," a better choice would have been "Irrigation, Irrigation and Irrigation." The committee was made up almost entirely of delegates from the irrigation counties: Bingham (Beane, Taylor, Harkness); Logan (Allen); Elmore (Stull); Ada (Costin, Moss); and Washington (Jewell). The only committee member from north of the Salmon River was William McConnell, and since he dug one of the territory's earliest ditches, even his water credentials were in good order. By a quirk of circumstance, this north Idaho delegate became the principal advocate for Idaho's water rights article. When the article came to the convention floor, Cavanah (who had earlier replaced Stull) was absent, and McConnell stepped forward to speak for the committee (pp. 1115, 1119–20).

The article reported by the committee clearly reflected the dominance of irrigation interests. Six sections were proposed. Section 1 declared all water appropriated or to be appropriated a public use and subject to regulation and control by the state. Three sections dealt with the sale of water: § 2 declared the right to sell water was a franchise subject to authority of the state; § 4 protected a purchaser of water with developed agricultural property by declaring the seller could never deprive the buyer of annual water; and, § 6 granted the legislature the authority to set reasonable maximum rates for the sale of water.

The remaining two sections reported by the committee provided for the priority of water rights. Section 5 spoke to settlers in a water district, and provided for priority according to the date of settlement, except that the legislature was empowered to limit that priority in the interest of subsequent settlers.

Section 3 was the most general priority section, and it created a great debate at the convention. As reported by the committee, the section read:

> The right to divert and appropriate the unappropriated waters of any natural stream to beneficial uses, shall never be denied. Priority of appropriation shall give the better right as between those using the water; *but when the waters of any natural stream are not sufficient for the service of all those desiring the use of the same, those using the water for domestic purposes shall (subject to such limitations as may be prescribed by law) have the preference over those claiming for any other purpose; and those using the water for agricultural purposes shall have preference over those using the same for manufacturing purposes* (p. 1117) [emphasis added].

The first portion of the section states the priority principle, first-in-time, first-in-right. However, the underlined portion qualified that principle by establishing preferred uses, regardless of the date the use began. Domestic use was favored over all other uses, and agriculture was preferred over manufacturing.

The irrigation committee had gone far beyond the 1881 statute in attempting to secure a preference for irrigation settlers. While one section of the statute put limitations on ditch companies, and another granted a right to irrigate to riparian owners, every section of the committee report was devoted to these objectives. The committee was proposing a "modified priority" or "agricultural preference" principle.

The committee encountered two competing theories of water rights on the convention floor. The strongest opposition was from those who favored a pure priority system. John T. Morgan (R-Bingham) moved to amend § 3 of the committee's report as follows: "The right to divert and appropriate the unappropriated waters of any natural stream to beneficial uses, shall never be denied, and those prior in time shall be superior in right" (p. 1122).

The second competing theory was the common-law riparian doctrine, advanced by Lycurgus Vineyard (D-Alturas), a lawyer and newcomer to the territory. Under a riparian system, rights to water accrue by virtue of ownership of land through which the stream flows rather than by virtue of appropriation of it. Vineyard wanted to amend § 3 by adding, "but no appropriations shall defeat the right to a reasonable use for irrigation of said water by a riparian owner of the land through which said water may run" (p. 1131).

This chapter examines the debates over these principles that took place on the floor of the Idaho Constitutional Convention. The conflict between agricultural priority and pure priority will be examined first, followed by the conflict between agricultural priority and riparian rights. The committee's agricultural priority prevailed in these debates, but the committee was not able to block two important amendments (just compensation and mining districts), which are discussed in the next section. The chapter concludes by looking at the water rights article after one hundred years.

3. Agricultural Priority vs. Pure Priority

WILLIAM MCCONNELL stepped forward to speak in defense of the committee's proposal for a modified or agricultural priority system in § 3, but his advocacy was not particularly effective. His arguments did not address the objections raised on the floor of the convention. Either he did not understand those objections, or chose to ignore them. Either way, he was not persuasive.

Several times McConnell argued in favor of § 3 by explaining the evil the committee sought to extinguish. As he related it, committee members were concerned about a manufacturer who first appropriated the water, then sold or leased it to settlers who established farms, and then sought to return the water to manufacturing purposes and shut the water off to the farms. McConnell argued the manufacturer could "crush those farmers by turning the water again on to his wheels" (p. 1137), because "he might conclude at any time after those farms were in a high state of cultivation, that he could use this water temporarily for such a time as should compel those men to abandon their properties or sell them out for a mere nothing" (pp. 1120–21). As a result, the manufacturer-speculator could, "throw that country, which is now attempting to be brought under cultivation, and some of which is already blooming as a garden, out again into a waste" (p. 1125). McConnell was afraid of the ditch company.

James Beatty (R-Alturas), a Hailey lawyer, and others pointed out this argument was not relevant to § 3 of the committee report, and did little to support it. They explained § 3 established a general principle of allocation, applicable to all water users, not just conflicts between manufacturers and speculators and the settlers they sold water to. They argued the committee had adequate protections in § 2, which declared the sale of water a franchise, § 4 which prohibited keeping water from settlers in the circumstances described by McConnell, and § 6 which granted the legislature power to set rates for water sales.

McConnell's argument may not have been the most relevant, but it was passionate. He concluded. "Let us not place anything in this constitution, which will place those agriculturalists, who are necessarily poor people, in the power of any incorporation which brings out a ditch" (p. 1324). His argument was also political. "It is to your interests, gentlemen, who live in the southern part of the territory, to see that the eloquence of those men, who perhaps may be paid and perhaps not, for their eloquence, does not prevail in this convention" (p. 1342).

Isaac Coston (D-Ada) was the first committee member to give a strong and direct defense of the special preferences in § 3. He argued that domestic use of water was the most "sacred purpose to which water could be applied" (p. 1124), and "that all using water to drink, for cooking and for the ordinary domestic purposes, have the best right by nature" (p. 1122).

Coston's argument supporting the preference of agriculture over manufacturing was based on hardship and necessity. "Now, the question is which will suffer the most; the orchards that are located along this stream for which the water has been used to irrigate them, or those manufacturing plants" (p. 1123).

For him, the answer was clear, the farmer's loss, "would be irreparable, it could not be remedied, there is no substitute for it; and I claim there is good logic, and anyone having due regard for the public interests will recognize that right and preference." At the same time, "all manufacturing establishments can substitute power in case of unusual scarcity of water or drouth" (p. 1123).

Coston closed by arguing Idaho needed a preference for agriculture if it was to flourish. "If the water power of this country can be used to prevent irrigation of the country, if it can be held by virtue of a prior right, good-bye to all the prosperity that we expect to come from the use of the water in irrigating our plains and developing this country" (p. 1123).

John Gray (R-Ada) had a more basic argument in support of irrigation. "Suppose there may be upon the stream farmers and manufacturers, and in ordinary years there is water for them all, but in some years there is not. Then I want the farmer to have it, because his are the products I live on; I can't live on cotton or wool or anything of that kind; I want something to eat. . . . " (p. 1142).

James Beatty was the principal opponent of the committee's report. His first contention was that the Committee was violating private property: "I don't believe such a law as that would be constitutional, it would be taking away the priority right of one man and giving it to another; and I do not see how it is possible that we could make such a law as that" (p. 1118).

Beatty assumed prior appropriation was the law, and he favored it. "[Section 3] proposes to disregard entirely priority of right. . . . I know of but one way to regulate it, and that is that the parties first in time hold the water; the parties who come and take up the water for any purpose should be entitled to the use of that water" (p. 1117).

At another time he argued the claimant of water had a natural right. "He takes up that water right, being the first man there. He certainly under all laws of nature would be entitled to it, because he is the first man there, and so far by our laws he would be entitled to it" (p. 1138).

Beatty also thought manufacturing was as important to Idaho's future as agriculture. He pointed out, "Here you will give the farmer, we claim, more preference right to all the water of that stream, and shut down a manufacturing establishment that may employ a hundred families in carrying on its business. You will destroy the interests and rights of a hundred families in order to benefit one agriculturalist" (p. 1117).

James Shoup (R-Custer) also argued the importance of manufacturing, "Agriculture only gives employment to the strong; for those who can go into the fields and do hard work. While manufacturing establishments give employment to everybody; they give employment to the strong men, they give employment to women" (p. 1130).

Even though a strong case for the irrigation preference was not made, the delegates were willing to support it. The vote was not counted the first time the report was approved, but in the final vote it was twenty-six for agricultural priority and sixteen for pure priority (p. 1364). The convention had approved a principle that said, "when the waters of any natural stream are not sufficient for the service of all those desiring the use of the same," (which of course is the only time a water right really matters) domestic users had preference over all others, and irrigation a preference over all but domestic uses.

4. Agricultural Priority vs. Riparian Doctrine

LYCURGUS VINEYARD moved to put the doctrine of riparian rights into the Idaho Constitution by amending § 3 of Article XV. He offered this description of riparian rights, "The owner of land through which a natural stream of water flows is the riparian owner; and according to the doctrine of the common law he has the right to use of the waters of that stream . . . provided he turns it back into the stream so that the riparian owner below him may enjoy the use of the water of the stream without any diminution thereof. . . . (p. 1132)."

Vineyard agreed with the majority of the delegates that agriculture should be protected, but thought riparian rights the best means of protection. He said, "I maintain it in all sincerity and candor, if you propose to protect agriculture in this territory . . . I think this is the first step towards their protection" (p. 1132).

Perhaps the most striking assertion by Vineyard was the contention that riparian rights prevailed in Idaho at the time. He declared, "There is no question about this doctrine, and it is admitted here in this territory. I tried a case upon this proposition here not a month ago in Alturas County . . ." (p. 1132). Was he correct? Did the riparian doctrine prevail in the territory? Vineyard referred to *Drake v. Earhart*. Vineyard defended Earhart and others on the theory that as riparian owners, they had superior claim to Drake, the Oregon Short Line and other plaintiffs, whose claim dated back to an appropriation of all the water, made in 1879 by Quigley. The case had not been decided by the time of the convention, so Vineyard was merely optimistically predicting the outcome of the case when he argued before the convention.

Many delegates rose to take issue with Vineyard's claim about riparian rights. W. C. B. Allen said that following Vineyard's suggestion would "throw aside all the experience of California, Utah and Colorado and go back to the primitive age when the riparian doctrine was first established" (p. 1134). John S. Gray said, "Let the first man who goes and blazes a trail into the country and finds a ranch and cultivates it, let him have his rights because he is prior to me, and I shall not go above him or below him or any other place and say 'it is riparian, I must have it' " (p. 1136).

The convention rejected Vineyard's riparian rights by such a large voice vote there was no count taken. The same thing happened in the district court when its opinion was issued after Vineyard returned from the convention, so he appealed to the territorial supreme court. The case was decided March 6, 1890, just a few months before statehood. Unfortunately for Vineyard, by then James Beatty had been appointed to the court. Beatty was the strongest pure priority advocate at the convention, and he wrote the opinion denying Vineyard's appeal.

Judge Beatty's opinion in *Drake v. Earhart* was to become a landmark in Idaho water law and in the western states in general. Just as he had championed pure prior appropriation at the convention, Judge Beatty favored it in his opinion. He was surprised there was an issue, for it had always been decided "the same way by almost every appellate court between Mexico and the British possessions, and from the shores of the Pacific to the eastern slope of the Rocky Mountains, as well as by the supreme court of the United States."[12] He rejected this "phantom of riparian rights" and held "the maxim, 'first in time, first in right,' should be considered the settled law here."[13]

Judge Beatty took the opportunity in his opinion to review for Idaho the history of the prior appropriation doctrine. He wrote, "When, from among the most energetic and enterprising classes of the east, that enormous tide of emigration poured into the west, this was found an arid land . . . [t]he new inhabitants were without law, but they quickly recognized that each man should not be a law unto himself. . . . Instead of attempting to divide it among all, thus making it unprofitable to any, or instead of applying the common-law riparian doctrine, to which they had been accustomed, they disregarded the traditions of the past, and established as the only rule suitable to their situation that of prior appropriation."[14]

Recent historians have taken issue with the history described by Judge Beatty. Prior appropriation law in the West is no longer seen as a product of the ingenious American settler faced with conditions of necessity. Instead, the roots of the doctrine are now traced to the mining codes in California, which in turn were based upon the mining codes of the Mexicans and Chileans, who were the first to arrive in the California gold fields. These codes can be traced back to medieval mining codes and ultimately to Roman law.[15]

Whatever the roots of prior appropriation doctrine, the *Drake* opinion firmly planted it in territorial law. However, the opinion was stillborn. Some six months before it was even written, the Idaho Constitutional Convention had adopted a provision significantly modifying prior appropriation by giving a preference to domestic and agriculture uses. But would these preferences have a significant impact?

5. *Just Compensation and Mining*

EVEN THOUGH THE IRRIGATION COMMITTEE won its battles with the pure priority and riparian theories, it was unable to block a critical amendment proposed by George Ainslie (D-Boise). Ainslie was an Idaho pioneer, and often argued on behalf of Idaho's earliest settlers at the convention. He staunchly tried to protect their water rights by supporting prior appropriation, but when it appeared irrigation was to get preference, he moved to amend § 3 by adding, "But the usage by such subsequent appropriators shall be subject to such provisions of the law regulating the taking of private property for public and private use, as referred to in Section 14 of Article I of the constitution" (p. 1145). The two most important guarantees provided by § 14 are the right to just compensation and the right to due process of law as provided by the legislature.

A number of delegates agreed with Ainslie and objected to the committee report because it was an unconstitutional taking. James Beatty adamantly said, "I don't believe such a law as that would be constitutional; it would be taking away the priority rights of one man and giving it to another" (p. 1118). He thought the prior appropriator at least had to be paid, and repeatedly returned to the theme, "The man who first goes there and takes possession is the man entitled to it, and if somebody else wants that right and can make better use of it than the man who first took possession of it, let him buy it from him" (p. 1119).

There is evidence the irrigation committee accepted the proposition that preferred users must pay if they displace prior users. W. C. B. Allen, a member of the committee, said, "I will say that the committee accepted that very view in conference with the committee on Mines and Mining, and the committee on Irrigation and the committee on Bill of Rights . . . It is subordinate to that proposition in the Bill of Rights" (p. 1344).

However, there is also strong evidence some thought the subsequent agricultural appropriator was to get the water without having to pay for it or to adhere to standard condemnation procedures. Several delegates claimed there was nothing in the section allowing the taking of prior rights. S. F. Taylor (A.M.D-Bingham) argued, "I don't understand this section gives anybody any right to appropriate any water that has already been appropriated" (p. 1143).

J. W. Poe from Nez Perce County argued while there "might appear to be a taking of vested rights," read in the "proper light" there was in fact none. He explained there was "no such thing as property in water" since users had only a "usufructuary right." He thought the effect of the section was to limit the manufacturer to the purposes for which the water was taken, "but the moment the manufacturer might conceive of the time when he could make the water more profitable for irrigating purpose[s] than for manufacturing purposes, then he loses his priority right as a manufacturer" (p. 1129).

William Clagett also argued no rights were being taken. "The language of this section . . . does not propose to take away the prior right of the manufacturer at all. It simply says that when there is a scarcity of water for those desiring to make use of it in that shape, as in the case of a dry year, then for that year the power shall yield to the interest of agriculture" (p. 1350).

Other delegates admitted vested rights might be affected, but argued the law of necessity prevailed over the principle of prior appropriation. Isaac Coston repeatedly emphasized the section was applicable only "in time of scarcity." He explained, "The legislature has power in an emergency, and when the water of any natural stream is not sufficient for the service of all those desiring to use the same—the legislature is granted the power to step in and regulate the questions which may arise under that emergency" (p. 1350).

Perhaps Edgar Wilson from Ada County was the agriculturalists' most passionate and bold advocate. He pleaded, "But God does not sprinkle these plains, and so they are an absolutely barren waste, and without water never can be used" (p. 1359).

Clagett asked, "Do you propose to take that man's right away from him without paying him for it, under the preferred right of agriculture?" (p. 1359).

Wilson shot back, "Yes, of necessity. We exist under peculiar circumstances, and it is necessary that be done; it requires a heroic remedy" (p. 1359).

When the time arrived for the vote on Ainslie's motion to require compensation and due process, not many heroes were there to be counted. Only twenty-five delegates, about one-third of the total, were present to hear the count and find that Ainslie's motion had passed 13 to 12 (p. 1163). This narrow margin meant the agriculturalists had gotten only a paper preference. While they could displace manufacturing in time of scarcity, they would have to pay for it and adhere to due process. These conditions would make the preference impossible to enjoy.

A second important amendment related to mining was added to Article XV, § 3, before it secured the approval of the convention. It is unclear whether the manufactures, agriculture and irrigation committee intended to provide for priority between agriculture and mining. The proposed article did not mention mining. Some delegates, like Edgar Wilson, thought there was no reason to provide for it because there was in fact no competition. He explained, "There will never be any controversy between those desiring water for mining purposes and those desiring water for agricultural purposes, unless perhaps in some of the placer mines on the Snake river, because where they use water for mining purpose in those mountain streams, it is not necessary to irrigate, the altitude is so great that little agriculture is carried on" (p. 1358).

William McConnell disagreed with Wilson, and argued § 3 covered the problem and, of course, gave agriculture the highest priority. When the section was first read James Shoup asked whether it gave agriculture priority over mining. McConnell said he thought it did, "If it had been during the season for irrigation, and also for use for mining, and the water failed to such an extent that there would not be enough to carry on both purposes, then agriculture should take the precedence over mining. That was the object of the committee" (p. 1116).

Wilson interrupted McConnell with a different reading. He said, "mining is not manufacturing by any means." When Shoup queried, "You manufacture bullion, don't you?," Wilson shot back, "No sir. I don't take it that the word manufacture includes mining. I am certain I am right about that" (p. 1116).

The mining interests at the convention were powerful and came forward to protect their own water rights, which had been left ambiguous under the section. Weldon B. Heyburn (R-Shoshone), a lawyer successful at representing large mining interests, moved to add the following language to the section: "and in any organized mining district those using the water for mining purposes or for milling purposes connected with mining shall have preference over those using the same for manufacturing and agricultural purposes" (p. 1156).

Heyburn explained he was concerned about "those little Italian ranchers, who settle along our mining streams to raise their truck, without professing to have any title to the land at all." He declared, "We do not want any such class of people to acquire a prior right to the use of our streams in the mountains, which we need for the primary industry of the country, which is mining" (p. 1164). No one spoke against the motion and it passed 21 to 6 (p. 1166), making it clear that the convention delegates did not think mining and irrigation were competing uses of water.

A second Heyburn amendment did cause controversy, but among miners rather than between miners and farmers. Heyburn proposed a new section to the water article to read, "Where land has been located along or covering any natural stream for any purpose, which contemplates the use of the water of such stream, then no person shall be permitted to take the water from said stream at a point above the land so located to the exclusion of such locator after such location" (p. 1166).

Heyburn complained about newcomers and "an evil that has grown up in the mining camps." He explained, "The first thing the modern prospector, a certain class of prospectors, does when he goes into the mountains is to acquire all the water in the canyons, and when he has got it the gulches are worth nothing for mining purposes." He stated that he had recently investigated a water problem and found, "thirty-two locations inside of ten miles, and there was not a ditch in connection with one of them, and they were all posted and recorded in that county." All of this was done for "the express purpose of embarrassing" the first miner and "compelling him to buy the water" (p. 1172).

No one supported Heyburn and strong voices spoke against him. John Gray argued that prior appropriation law protected the first locator. William Clagett agreed, and further argued Heyburn's section would prevent subsequent locators who made discoveries on the hillsides from developing their mines. George Ainslie thought the section was "reintroducing this old claim of riparian proprietorship that is dead on the Pacific Coast and always will be" (p. 1170). Even Willis Sweet (R-Latah), often an ally of Heyburn, said at the end of the discussion, "I do not see my way clear to support the additional section offered by Mr. Heyburn" (p. 1176). The amendment failed by a wide margin and no vote count was taken (p. 1176).

6. Water in the Constitution Today

IS THE GENERATION OF ELECTRICITY considered manufacturing under the Idaho Constitution? If so, the battle between irrigation and manufacturing at the convention was the first in a century-long war. Competition between these two uses for the Snake River has dominated the development of the water rights article of the constitution during the entire period of statehood.

Hydroelectric power came to Idaho just before the constitutional convention, and the delegates debated whether generating electricity was manufacturing within the preference sections of Article 15, § 3. In arguing for irrigation, McConnell posed a hypothetical question that was a premonition of what was to come. "You have here [in Boise], as I understand it, quite a large irrigation canal on this river. Part of the waters of that canal are used today for manufacturing purposes, in generating electricity to light this town. It might occur, as the science and use of electricity become more fully developed in this country, that it will pay the proprietors of that ditch better to use the water entirely for the generation of electricity, and . . . throw that country . . . already blooming as a garden, out again into a waste" (p. 1125).

Edgar Wilson immediately moved to add "power or motor" after manufacturing in Section 3. He wanted to make certain agriculture had a preference over power generation, and was afraid "this word manufacturing would not include it. They don't manufacture anything; they generate electricity. . . . Suppose they want to run an electric motor car in this town some time. You are not manufacturing anything there; you are generating electricity for the purpose of running that car" (p. 1126).

McConnell said it was a distinction without a difference, but was willing to second the motion. Another delegate asserted, "They manufacture light" (p. 1126). When the vote was taken, only four were cast in favor of the amendment (p. 1148). While the result of the vote was clear, its interpretation is difficult. Did the delegates defeat the amendment because they thought power generation was included in manufacturing or did they think irrigation should not have a preference over power generation?

Both irrigation and hydroelectric development accelerated on the Snake River after statehood. The private ditch companies, which promised large-scale development at the time of the convention, were so heavily burdened by the article passed at the convention and so damaged by the financial crash of 1893 that they disappeared from Idaho shortly after the turn of the century.[16] Development languished for awhile. Then the United States government became involved in irrigation construction on a large scale, and a new era of development began. In the years that followed, the Bureau of Reclamation developed the Minidoka, Boise-Payette, American Falls, Milner-Gooding, Palisades and other large projects.[17] The first power generation plant on the main Snake River was constructed at Swan Falls in 1901 to service Silver City mines.[18] Five small regional companies with "run-of-the-river" developments merged in 1915 to form Idaho Power Company, and the potential for large-scale hydroelectric development was created.

By the late 1920s, residents in the Upper Snake Valley became worried that power generation rights downstream would prevent future upstream development. In 1928 they were able to amend the critical priority sentence of Section 3 to read, "The right to divert and appropriate the unappropriated waters of any natural stream to beneficial uses shall never be denied *except that the state may regulate and limit the use thereof for power purposes*" (amendment italicized).[19] Irrigators sought to bring the river under control of the state, and thus themselves.

At about the same time, the federal government was asserting jurisdiction over the river. The first federal license was granted to the Swan Falls facility in 1928. Thus began the struggle between Idaho and the federal government for jurisdiction and control over the upper Snake River, which has become an important subplot in Idaho's water drama.

The 1930s brought new development, and an attempt by the Idaho legislature to exert a stronger influence on management of the river. In 1935 the legislature created the State Water Conservation Board and empowered it with administrative and governmental authority, such as the power to make surveys and investigations concerning water supply, waste, and loss.[20] These powers were sustained in *State Water Conservation Board v. Enking*.[21] The State Water Conservation Board was also authorized to condemn water rights and appropriate unappropriated public waters. However, the opinion in *State Water Conservation Board* held these powers were unconstitutional because they violated the right to appropriate water guaranteed in Article XV, § 3. Federal power licenses issued during this period tended to protect the licensee from subsequent development while state licenses subordinated the power license to subsequent development.

The controversy between irrigation and power erupted again in the 1950s, when Idaho Power Company proposed three dams in Hells Canyon. At the same time, the federal government was proposing a large single-dam project for the same area. As part of its campaign to gain approval for its projects, Idaho Power Company agreed to subordinate the rights being acquired to subsequent upstream consumptive uses. Those who participated in this process apparently thought Idaho Power had agreed to subordinate all of its water rights on the Snake River, rather than only the rights associated with the Hells Canyon complex.[22]

In 1963 the Los Angeles Department of Water and Power suggested 2.4 million acre feet should be diverted every year from the Snake River near Twin Falls to the Colorado River system to increase the supply of water to southern California and Arizona. Idaho reacted quickly to prevent the diversion by putting the water to work for Idaho. To accomplish this, Article XV of the Idaho Constitution was amended in 1964 by adding a seventh section. The new section created the Water Resource Agency, and empowered it to "formulate and implement a state water plan for optimum development of water resource in the public interest." The amendment also conferred particular powers upon the agency, such as developing water projects, issuing revenue bonds, generating hydroelectric power, appropriating public waters as trustee for agency projects, and control over water projects on state lands.[23] The 1965 legislature created the Idaho Water Resource Board to implement the amendment.[24] The creation of the agency and its power to issue revenue bonds were held constitutional in *Idaho Water Resource Bd. v. Kramer.*[25]

Development of a water plan was more controversial than creation of the agency or board. The board issued its plan in three parts, in 1972, 1974, and 1976. Policy 32 of the plan set minimum stream flows, which would limit future irrigation appropriations. A statute passed in 1977 stipulated the plan would not become effective until it had been submitted to the legislature.[26] In 1978 the legislature adopted fourteen of the Board's policies, modified nineteen of them and rejected four. It also passed implementing statutes.[27]

The director of the department of water resources requested an opinion from the attorney general on the constitutionality of the legislative approval. He wondered whether the legislature had authority for the statute since the department was empowered by the 1964 amendment to formulate and implement a plan. The attorney general found no "glaring problem" to rebut the normal presumption of validity accorded to statutes.[28] However, the Idaho supreme court did find glaring problems and in *Idaho Power Co. v. Idaho*[29] held the Water Resources Board had exclusive authority to formulate the state water plan.[30]

Not to be denied authority over the state water plan, the legislature proposed an amendment to Article XV, § 7, which was passed in 1984. It provides, "The Legislature of the State of Idaho shall have the authority to amend or reject the state water plan . . . any change in the water plan shall be submitted to the Legislature. . . . "[31]

While this intergovernmental struggle over who would have power over Idaho's waters went on, the conflict between irrigation and power generation became more intense. In 1977 Matthew Mullaney and other Idaho Power rate payers filed a complaint with the Public Utilities Commission. They alleged Idaho Power had wasted its water right at Swan Falls by failing to protect it, and that as a consequence the company's capital investment was overstated and ratepayers were being overcharged.

Idaho Power responded by filing objections against a number of pending water permit requests. It also filed suit in the Idaho district court, seeking to adjudicate its water right at Swan Falls, which it claimed dated from 1900. The Department of Water Resources, the Public Utilities Commission, rate payers, ditch companies, and individuals were named as defendants. They contended the state could limit hydropower rights, and that Idaho Power had agreed to subordinate its priority rights. The defendants also argued Idaho Power had lost any rights it had by adverse possession, forfeiture, abandonment, laches, subordination, waiver and quasi-estoppel.

The district court ruled that the subordination clause in the license for the Hell's Canyon complex subordinated all of Idaho Power's rights on the Snake River and its tributaries. In *Idaho Power Co. v. State*,[32] the Supreme Court reversed and held, "the language of the subordination clause affects the operation of the three dams in the Hells Canyon project only and does not extend to the other dams on the river, and specifically does not subordinate the water rights of Idaho Power at Swan Falls."[33]

Lawyers familiar with the case observed, "With that ruling, the State of Idaho went from a partially appropriated to an over-appropriated water system on the Snake River."[34] No longer were future appropriations at issue; recent appropriations were now threatened. The case was remanded to the district court for further hearings on other affirmative defenses, and perhaps ultimately on the dates and amounts of Swan Falls water use.

Rather than return to court, the parties decided to sit down at the bargaining table and on October 25, 1984, they ended the litigation by signing the Swan Falls Agreement. Under the agreement, Idaho Power got a protectable water right to 3900 cubic feet per second during the irrigation season and 5600 cubic feet per second during winter. The agreement also set policy on important related matters. Idaho agreed to a general adjudication of all rights on the Snake in order to better manage the water and to protect Idaho Power's rights. Some of the 600 cubic feet per second remaining available was set aside for domestic, commercial, municipal and industrial use, with the rest allocated by a permit system which will be evaluated on a "public interest" standard. All of the remaining water will be held in trust by the state, and a marketing system established for the transfers of existing rights.[35]

The Idaho legislature indicated its approval of the Swan Falls Agreement by passing the legislation necessary to implement it.[36] Congress has agreed to proceed in a manner consistent with the agreement.[37] The adjudication of the Snake River has begun. The scope of these proceedings has been expanded to include all water in the Snake River drainage used in Idaho, from Lewiston to the uppermost tributaries.[38] The importance of the adjudication can hardly be overestimated. It will be the final allocation of the Snake River. The estimated cost of this process is $28 million.

These contemporary developments are dramatic, and they bristle with constitutional issues. The Swan Falls Agreement and the supporting legislation avoided immediate litigation, but the far-reaching and novel provisions will inevitably become fodder for more constitutional controversy. As the adjudication begins to affect how Idahoans use their water, many questions will be raised.

One of the clearest features of Idaho's first century of constitutional water law is the basic struggle between irrigation (today allied with other consumptive users) and power generation (today allied with other in-stream advocates). The conflict between manufacturing and agriculture was the greatest water issue at the convention, and it is still the dominant issue. No one knows how the story might have changed had the convention not cast that 13 to 12 vote in favor of Ainslie's requirement for just compensation.

Another significant feature of these one hundred years of conflict is that the controversy always has a constitutional dimension. The competing users try to establish their rights and reach accommodation in and through the constitution. These tactics reflect the fact that the Idaho Constitution is the fundamental water law in the land.

Notes

1. Walker, Deward E., Jr. *Indians of Idaho*. Moscow, University of Idaho Press, 1978; Josephy, Alvin M. Jr. *The Nez Perce Indians and the Opening of the Northwest*. New Haven: Yale University Press, 1965, pp. 3–40; Clark, Scott. "Nineteenth Century Shoshone-Bannock Riparian Adaption." Master's thesis, Idaho State University, 1986; Turner, Allen. "The Realm of the Sacred." *In* Holmer, Richard N., ed. *Shoshone-Bannock Cultural History*. Pocatello: Swanson-Crabtree Anthropological Laborary, Idaho State University, Publication #85–16, 1986.

2. Drury, Clifford Merrill. *Henry Harmon Spalding*. Caldwell, Idaho: Caxton Printers, Ltd., 1936, p. 226.

3. Beal, M. D. *A History of Southeastern Idaho*. Caldwell, 1942, pp. 136–152; 168–170.

4. Burcham, Ralph Jr. "Elias Davidson Pierce, Discoverer of Gold in Idaho: A Biographical Study." Master's Thesis, University of Idaho, 1950.

5. Hart, I. W., ed. *Proceedings and Debates of the Constitutional Convention of Idaho 1889*. 2 vols. Caldwell: Caxton Printers, Ltd., 1912. These volumes are paginated consecutively, and all page references in the text of this chapter are to them.

6. McConnell, W. J. *Early History of Idaho*. Caldwell: Caxton Printers, Ltd., 1913, p. 122.

7. Lewis, Mary Gunnell. "History of Irrigation Development in Idaho." Master's thesis, University of Idaho, 1924.

8. Stat. L. 1881, pp. 267–73.

9. Ibid.

10. Stat. L. 1881, pp. 273–75.

11. 2 Idaho 750, 23 P. 541 (1890).

12. Ibid. at p. 753, 542.

13. Ibid.

14. Ibid.

15. August, Raymond S. "Law in the American West: A History of its Origins and Its Dissemination." Ph.D. dissertation, University of Idaho, 1987, pp. 238–64.

16. Lewis, *History of Irrigation Development in Idaho*, pp. 50–51.

17. Beal, Merrill D. and Wells, Merle W. *History of Idaho*. 3 vols. New York: Lewis Historical Publishing Company, 1959. Vol. 2, pp. 136–91.

18. For general history of power development and associated legal controversies in Idaho see Costello, Patrick D. and Kole, Patrick K. "Commentary on Swan Falls Resolution." WNRL Digest, Summer, 1985; Young, G. and Cochrane, F. *Hydro Era: The Story of Idaho Power Company*. Boise: Idaho Power Company, 1978; *Idaho Power Co. v. Idaho*, 104 Idaho 575, 661 P2d. 741 (1983).

19. 1927 Idaho Sess Laws 591, H.J.R. No. 13, ratified at the general election in November 1928.

20. 1935 Idaho Sess Laws 112.

21. 56 Idaho 722, 58 P.2d 779 (1936), overruled on other grounds *State, Dept. of Parks v. Idaho Dept. of Water Administration*, 96 Idaho 440, 530 P.2d 924 (1974), and *Idaho Water Resource Bd. v. Kramer*, 97 Idaho 535, 548 P.2d 35 (1976).

22. Costello, Patrick D. and Kole, Partick K. "Commentary on Swan Falls Resolution." WNRL Digest, Summer, 1985, p. 12.

23. Proposed by S.J.R. No. 1 (1964, 1st E.S.), S.L. 1965, p. 22, and ratified at the general election, November 3, 1964.

24. 1965 Idaho Sess Laws 901.

25. 97 Idaho 535, 548 P.2d 35 (1976).

26. An Act Relating to Legislative Approval of the State Water Plan, 1977 Id. Sess. Laws, p. 252.

27. House Concurrent Resolution No. 48, 1978 Id. Sess. Laws, at 1003, and chs. 306, 345 and 356.

28. Opinion of the Attorney General, No. 77–26 (1977).

29. 104 Idaho 570, 661 P.2d 736 (1983).

30. Grant, Douglas L. "The Idaho Water Plan: The Threshold Constitutional Problems and Suggested Solutions." *Idaho Law Review*. 15(1979):443.

31. Proposed by S.J.R. No. 117 (S.L. 1984, p. 689), and ratified at the general election of November 6, 1984.

32. 104 Idaho 575, 661, P2d.741(1983).

33. Ibid. at p. 586, 752.

34. Costello and Kole. "Commentary on Swan Falls Resolution." p. 13.

35. Ibid.

36. An Act Relating to the Adjudication of Water Rights, 1985 Id. Sess. Laws, p. 27.

37. 101 Stat. L. 1450.

38. *In re Snake River Water System*, 115 Idaho 1, 764 P.2d 78(1988).

10.

The Judicial Department

1. The Territorial Courts

THERE HAVE BEEN RADICAL CHANGES in Idaho's judicial system since its creation by the territorial Organic Act in 1863.[1] Then, as today, there were district courts of general jurisdiction exercising both common law and chancery jurisdiction, and appeals went from the district court to the Idaho supreme court and, in the proper case, on to the United States Supreme Court. However, there the similarities end.

The territorial supreme court, which consisted of three justices appointed by the president, held an annual session in the seat of government. The territory was divided into three judicial districts. Each supreme court justice presided as district judge in one of those districts and was required to maintain a residence there. This peculiar structure meant that a justice sat on the appeal of his own decision, which added considerably to the inherent problem of winning on appeal. Today Idaho is divided into seven judicial districts which are presided over by a total of thirty-three district judges.[2] In addition, there is an independent supreme court with five justices.[3] All these judges are elected today, rather than appointed.

There are also other important differences. The territorial courts had the jurisdiction of both the United States courts and the local or territorial courts. Today, there is a separate federal court system for the state. The territory also had justices of the peace and probate courts. Justices of the peace, in county or municipal courts, had criminal jurisdiction over misdemeanors and civil jurisdiction over cases involving small sums. The primary jurisdiction of the probate courts, which were established in each county, was the administration of estates, but they also shared concurrent civil jurisdiction with the justices of the peace. Today, probate courts and justices of the peace are gone,[4] replaced by a small claims court and magistrate's division of the district courts in a unified court system.[5]

Given that nearly half of the delegates to the Idaho Constitutional Convention were lawyers, it is not surprising to find the convention critical of the territorial judiciary. The address to the people written by the convention and issued to encourage ratification of the constitution argued that a new judiciary was one of the principal reasons for statehood:

> The most intolerable evil, however, under which we have lived for the past twenty-five years, has been the changing and shifting character of our judicial decisions, by which we have been deprived of the inestimable benefit of judicial precedents as a safeguard to our rights of person and property.
>
> Scarcely has one judge, sent to us from abroad, obtained even a slight insight into the laws and customs of the territory, before another coming in his room has undone the work of his predecessor, and this chronic condition of change has left all of our business and property interests in a constant state of doubt and uncertainty.
>
> To make confusion worse confounded, we have been denied an appeal from these raw and inexperienced decisions to an independent supreme court, under the territorial system of having the judge below review his own judgments on appeal, while the small judicial force of the territory (unable or incompetent to perform the duties devolving upon it) cause our calendars to be overburdened with causes, and such justice as we at last obtain to be delayed until litigants are ruined (p. 2092).[6]

The following list of appointments to the Idaho territorial supreme court makes vivid the "chronic condition of change"[7] the delegates were complaining about:

Chief Justices

Sidney Edgerton	3/10/1863
Silas Woodson	7/26/1864
John R. McBride	2/28/1865
Thomas J. Bowers	7/18/1868
David Noggle	4/9/1869
M. E. Hollister	1/14/1875
William G. Thompson	1/13/1879
John T. Morgan	6/10/1879
J. B. Hays	8/14/1885
H. W. Weir	9/29/1888
James H. Beatty	5/1889

Associate Justices

Alexander C. Smith	3/10/1863

Samuel C. Parks	3/10/1863
Milton Kelly	4/17/1865
John Cummins	5/29/1866
R. T. Miller	7/1/1868
J. R. Lewis	4/15/1869
William C. Whitson	7/12/1870
M. E. Hollister	3/20/1871
John Clark	1/14/1875
H. E. Prickett	1/19/1876
Norman Buck	1/27/1880
Case Broderick	5/1/1884
John L. Logan	/18/1888
C. H. Barry	8/13/1888
Willis Sweet	12/1889

The convention delegates complained about the lack of clear precedent and crowded judicial dockets caused by these changes, but there were other problems with the territorial judiciary. Salaries of the judges were always troublesome. The Organic Act set the salary at $2,500 (or later $3,000), greenback. During the 1870s, gold was the medium of trade in Idaho and greenbacks were discounted to forty cents on the dollar. In addition, the cost of living was high. Food and the amenities of civilization were costly, and the districts were large. Any conscientious judge was required to supplement his salary with personal resources.

This story of an early session of the Second District in Idaho City illustrates the problem. The first several days on the civil calendar were taken up with arguments on demurrer, that is, the defendants contended that even if the facts were as alleged by plaintiff, defendant was still entitled to dismissal on the law. After all the arguments were made, the judge proceeded to rule in the cases, first for the plaintiff, then the defendant, and alternating to the end. When questioned about the explanation for the decisions by one of the lawyers, the judge said:

> [I]f you think a man can be appointed from one of the eastern states, come out here and serve as a judge in Idaho on a salary of $3,000 a year, payable in greenbacks worth forty cents on the dollar, and give reasons for everything he does, you are greatly mistaken.[8]

The territorial legislatures addressed this problem by contributing to the annual salaries. This was justified because of the work the judges did in adjudicating local cases, but it put the judges at the mercy of the territorial legislature. The legislature also had the power to assign judges to the districts. The Second District was viewed as the hub of Idaho law and politics, and therefore as the prime assignment from the legislature. Assignments to the other two districts were considered less desireable.

The legislature used these powers during the territorial period to express its displeasure with the judiciary. For example, when Milton Kelly, a radical Republican, was appointed associate justice in 1865, the southern Democrats who controlled the legislature were angered. A Boise County delegate introduced a bill to assign Kelly to the northern district. He argued:

> Believing that the removal of Milton Kelly to the most thinly settled portions of our Territory, where matters of litigation are, comparatively speaking, of an unimportant nature, and of sufficient importance to require a stretch of what little legal ability he possesses, would meet with unqualified approval of a majority of the citizens of Idaho Territory, and be an act of justice to ourselves, we would respectfully recommend the early passage of the bill.[9]

Only Idaho County Democrat S. S. Fenn dissented from the majority report. He argued, futilely, that he did not want northern Idaho to become "a penal colony, to which to banish all weak and incompetent Federal officials." The same legislature passed a bill to remove the judicial and executive officers from the territorial payroll, which was signed into law after the governor negotiated a deal to have his own salary exempted.[10] The salaries were later restored after the passions of the moment had passed.

A final inherent problem with the territorial courts was the wild and rugged Idaho geography. On paper, Idaho district courts were organized by the points of the compass: northern, southern, and eastern. However, the courts were often difficult to reach due to river basins, mountain ranges and desert expanse. The creation of probate courts, justices of the peace, and requiring district judges to hold an annual term in each county in their district were attempts to solve the problem. Despite these efforts, parties, witnesses, and lawyers were often far from county seats, making litigation a slow, expensive process that impeded the forces of development.

These territorial experiences were on the minds of the delegates to the Idaho Constitutional Convention, especially the lawyers, as they made their way to Boise in the summer of 1889. The judiciary committee was assigned the task of finding solutions.

2. The Judiciary Committee and Its Work

ON JULY 31, the twenty-second day of the convention, the judiciary article finally reached the floor of the convention. The convention was almost over. The delegates were only five days away from adjourning, and the only major topics remaining to be considered were finance and revenue, county governments and apportionment.

There was a reason for the delay. The judiciary committee which produced the judiciary article had a difficult task to accomplish. It had fifteen members, more than any convention committee except apportionment, which had a delegate from each county. The judiciary committee began with nine members, but Alexander Mayhew (D-Shoshone) suggested early in the proceedings the committee be increased to fifteen because it would "have more labor to perform than any other committee." He argued that if the debates all took place before the committee it would not take the time of the convention (p. 58).

In addition to being large, the judiciary committee was evenly divided on two of the most important issues to come before it. Early in the convention president William H. Clagett (R-Shoshone) proposed to reform the common-law right to a unanimous jury verdict. The committee debated at length, but when the final vote was taken was evenly divided and did not recommend the section. Clagett was not discouraged, however, and took his innovation to the declaration of rights committee which was pleased to endorse it.[11] The second issue that split the judiciary committee down the middle was the method of selecting supreme court justices. Seven committee members favored electing the justices, and seven appointing them, so the committee proposed two sections to the convention.

The judicial article was also delayed because it was long. Its twenty-seven sections were more than any other article. The length of the article confirms an observation made early in the convention by Frank Steunenberg (D-Ada):

> A large majority of the members are lawyers, and as quibbling and priddling is a part of their training, if not of their nature, the chances of an extended session are favorable.[12]

The list of members on the judiciary committee would make a strong slate of nominees if one were starting an Idaho lawyers' hall of fame. The Chairman was Weldon B. Heyburn (R-Shoshone), a corporate mining lawyer in the Coeur d'Alenes who was later elected to the U.S. Senate.[13] Willis Sweet (R-Latah) was a young Moscow lawyer who converted his close connections with Fred T. Dubois into several favors for Latah County, a term in the House of Representatives, and several federal appointments. James Beatty (R-Alturas) served on the commission that codified the Idaho statutes in 1887, was briefly on the territorial supreme court and spent the last seventeen years of his career sitting as the federal district judge in Idaho. John T. Morgan (R-Bingham) had served on the territorial supreme court, and was later elected to the state supreme court. Edgar Wilson (R-Ada) had served as the Boise City attorney and prosecuting attorney, and after the convention served in Congress from 1893–95.

George Ainslie (D-Boise) was in the group of lawyers first sworn into the territorial bar and had served as the territory's representative to Congress. Alexander Mayhew was the Democratic workhorse in Shoshone County who served in the territorial council and the state senate and sat for many years as a local judge. James Reid (D-Nez Perce), who had served in Congress before coming to Idaho, was a popular speaker and elected to chair the Democratic caucus at the convention. While these were the most widely-known committee members, the remaining seven all had considerable reputations as lawyers in their local communities: J. M Howe (R-Nez Perce), W. W. Woods (D-Shoshone), Homer Stull (D-Elmore), Frank Harris (D-Washington), O. B. Batten (D-Alturas), H. S. Hampton (R-Cassia) and W. H. Savidge (R-Bingham).

Even though the judicial article had twenty-seven sections, it dealt with only three general topics. The first matter addressed was the distinction between law and equity and the pleading system (the manner in which lawyers present cases to the courts) to be used in the new state (§ 1). The second topic was the number and structure of the state's courts (§§ 2–12 and 14–24). The final subject was the interrelationship between the judicial and legislative departments on questions of salary, recommended changes in the law and related matters (§§ 13 and 25–27).

This chapter examines those sections of the committee report that generated the most controversy at the convention. The first and least dramatic controversy dealt with § 1, abolishing common-law pleading. A second and far more important debate was generated by § 6, providing the method of selection for supreme court justices. The third and last major controversy concerned the number of district courts and their apportionment. While these debates were important, the delegates at the convention were anxious to adjourn. As a consequence, they voted to consider the article only once, rather than first consider it in a committee of the whole and then again as a convention, as had been done with the other articles (pp. 1493–95).

3. Merger of Law and Equity and Code Pleading

THE FIRST SECTION of the judicial article adopts code pleading for Idaho. It provides, "The distinctions between actions at law and suits at equity, and the forms of all such actions, and suits, are hereby prohibited. . . ." All private actions are to be "denominated a civil action" and any action by the state for a public offense "shall be termed a criminal action." It is important to note the section modifies the common-law system inherited from England in two ways: forms of action are replaced with a few greatly simplified pleadings *and* the law and equity courts are merged.

This language originated in 1840 in the Republic of Texas.[14] As an adjustment between the two cultures living there, the Fourth Congress of the Republic adopted common law, but not the common-law system of pleading. Instead, it abolished the common-law forms of pleading, merged law and equity, and adopted the simple "petition and answer" system used in Spanish pleading. This was the second part of Idaho's Constitution with Spanish rather than common-law roots, the first being the prior appropriation doctrine.

New York made the novel adjustment in Texas into a reform movement. In 1848, New York adopted provisions similar to those in Texas at the recommendation of a commission headed by David Dudly Field. The new approach became known as the Field Code and was widely adopted in the United States, including Idaho, during the territorial period.[15]

When § 1 was read at the convention, William Clagett moved to amend it to read, "The distinctions *in form* between actions at law and suits in equity . . ." (amendment italicized) (p. 1498). Clagett wanted to make it clear that the substantive rules of law and equity were not being abolished, only the forms of the actions. He explained, "[O]n the plain letter of the language it is a prohibition of the substance of all distinction between actions at law and suits in equity . . . and that is not intended; it is simply intended to reach a distinction in the forms of actions . . ." (p. 1498).

George Ainslie opposed Clagett's amendment arguing the language was taken *verbatim* from the New York Constitution, "and in order to have the guidance of the decisions of the court of appeals and the highest courts of New York, we had better adopt their language" (p. 1498). He said, "I don't see the necessity of improving on the language of New York lawyers" (p. 1499). The convention agreed and defeated Clagett's motion.

Clagett proposed another amendment to a different section of the judiciary article also related to the unified court system. He proposed this amendment: "Each district judge shall have the power to appoint a master in chancery for each county in his district. . . . Such master shall have the power to issue temporary injunctions . . . but no temporary injunction or restraining order shall be issued . . . until the party affected has had an opportunity on reasonable notice to appear and resist such issuing" (pp. 1557–58). It eventually became clear Clagett proposed appointment of chancery masters on behalf of A. J. Pinkham (R-Alturas). Pinkham argued, "It is the common practice in every state to have a master in chancery" (p. 1570).

James Reid spoke against the appointment of a master because it would be inconsistent with the theory of a unified court system using code pleading. He said, "We used to have masters in chancery in our system when we had the old common law system, and the biggest fees ever paid to anybody were paid to those masters in chancery. . . . But we have abolished those systems, and now have the code practice" (p. 1571). Weldon Heyburn argued a judge should not be able to delegate his authority to a master. "I do not believe in a judge being empowered to delegate his power, the exercise of that judicial discretion with which he expects to act . . . . I want that power to issue from the court itself, and I want the court to be responsible for the exercise of that discretion" (p. 1560).

While Clagett spoke for Pinkham about the appointment of a master, he spoke forcefully for himself about the right to be heard before an injunction was issued against you. Clagett argued:

[T]he principal reason I offer [the amendment] is to get rid of that which has constituted the greatest standing abuse in the administration of justice in all these territories of the west, and under which more devilment has been wrought, if I may use the expression, than under all others combined; and that is the power of district judges to issue ex parte, without any notice whatever, injunctions tying up the possession and use of real property, particularly mining property, throwing upon the defendant the necessity of going to a large expense to move to dissolve the injunction, and in the meantime putting a stop to the entire operations that may be carried on (p. 1558).

Clagett was concerned his opponents sought "to befog the attention or minds" of the delegates, and so explained the practical application of his proposal. He described a miner in possession who had exhausted all his resources to make a mine productive, only to have another party with "some 'shingle' or pretended title" get an *ex parte* injunction from the district court. Clagett testified, "I have seen that thing done in Shoshone county to my personal knowledge, until man after man who had an undoubted legal title was frozen out and compelled to abandon his property." He alleged that the practice of injunctions without notice had "given rise to a set of blackmailers who are constantly prostituting and using these powers of the court for the purpose of extorting money from those against whom they perhaps trump up a pretended title" (pp. 1562–64).

Those who opposed Clagett's proposal cautioned the delegates not to be seduced by Clagett's oratory. James Beatty said, "I believe it is a rule among horse-racing men that when a horse distances all others he is ruled off the track; and I almost feel that my friend from Shoshone should be ruled out here, for like these wild storms that sweep over our mountains, now he, by his eloquence and zeal sweeps everything before him. He springs on us a proposition unexpected to me, and now he says we are befogging your minds by the suggestions we have made" (p. 1568). Weldon Heyburn cautioned, "I don't want to see the eloquence of the gentleman carry this convention away from reason, common sense and common honesty" (pp. 1564–65).

George Ainslie was critical because Clagett's proposal was never presented to the judiciary committee, which had worked for three weeks on the article (pp. 1567–68). Ainslie, Heyburn and Reid all argued Clagett's case was atypical, that in the usual case the party seeking the injunction was rightfully in possession and was trying to restrain a claim jumper. Beatty said, "That is an unnatural case. . . . The cases where we want this injunction are like this: some party comes along who has no title or right to mine a claim, and in the absence of the true owners he works upon it; and without their knowledge, as I have known numerous instances, gets out a large amount of ore" (p. 1568). Ainslie said, "I can give instances of some farmers in this house, where the man would be deprived of the right of injunction and irreparable harm would result to his farm" (p. 1567).

Clagett might have been like a storm sweeping the convention on this occasion, but the skies cleared. A vote was first taken upon the power to appoint a master. Upon its defeat, Clagett withdrew his amendment and did not propose it again (p. 1571).

The Idaho supreme court has been sensitive to Clagett's concern, and in *Dewey v. Schreiber Implement Co.*[16] held the principles of law and equity had not been abolished by the section. The court also has a series of cases which encourage the reforms the section embodied: simplified pleadings and the merger of law and equity.[17] There have been some difficulties in compartmentalizing all matters as either civil or criminal, and during Idaho's first century the court has decided that contempt in civil cases[18] and post-conviction proceedings[19] are civil in nature, and that traffic violations[20] are inherently criminal.

4. Selecting Supreme Court Justices

THE JUDICIARY COMMITTEE was evenly divided on the manner in which supreme court Justices should be selected (pp. 1500–01). Seven members favored § 6 of the committee report which provided for six-year terms and election at large; seven favored § 7 which provided for nomination by the governor and confirmation by the Senate, with the proviso that all three justices could not be from the same political party.

Those members of the committee who favored election came to the convention floor ready to make their case. Six influential delegates rose to champion election: Wilson, Heyburn, Mayhew, Morgan, Sweet and Reid. This group included four Republicans and two Democrats, and represented the largest delegations at the convention: Ada, Shoshone, Bingham and Latah counties.

The advocates of electing the supreme court justices offered their experiences as a principal line of argument. Edgar Wilson recounted his days in Pennsylvania and Michigan, and claimed those courts were made of "men of national reputation among the finest lawyers these United States have ever produced; and they have been elected by direct vote of the people" (p. 1502). Judge John T. Morgan claimed the very elective system being proposed had worked well during the thirty-five years he lived in Illinois. He also reminded the delegates of the English history of judicial selection and the American Revolution. "Under the original system as it was in England many years ago, everybody was appointed by the crown, and they were the servants of the crown; and in order to get rid of this tyranny and despotism the system of election was invented and was adopted" (p. 1511).

Alexander Mayhew said he had "taken a little pains" to find out what other states were doing. He reported there were thirty-eight states, with twenty-four electing judges and fourteen appointing them. He thought that since the large majority favored election, including some of the largest states, Idaho should follow the precedent (p. 1503).

The election proponents also pointed to the political evils of an appointive system. Willis Sweet argued, "It is a well-known fact that the supreme court of the United States has been packed two or three times within the last thirty years for the purpose of carrying certain questions" (p. 1516). Morgan illustrated the politics of a recent U.S. Supreme Court appointment by observing, "of this gentleman it was said that no man, not even his worst enemy, had ever accused him of being a lawyer at any time in his career" (p. 1510).

Only two delegates argued on behalf of appointment on the convention floor, but they were powerful figures. The first was James Beatty, who was on the judiciary committee, and the second was William Clagett. In rebuttal to the election advocates, they argued history and experience favored appointment of justices. Beatty said, "I believe that in earlier times when our judges were generally selected by some appointing power, we had better judges than we have now." He accused state supreme courts of "very strange political rulings" and concluded, "I think no judges in the world stand as high as the United States judges from the supreme court judges down; and those are all selected by the appointing power" (p. 1504).

Clagett agreed, and challenged the convention to "[c]ompare the federal judiciary with the state judiciary; take the august tribunal of the supreme court of the United States, and take all your district judges and size them up with these state judges, and see what the difference is." He asked why members of the state bar who were as learned as the federal judges were never selected, and answered his own question, "Simply because they are required to be elected by the people, and the whole question of their nomination and election is controlled by the interests of party conventions, and the haphazard result of an election" (p. 1509).

Clagett became more aggressive in his attack on party and elective politics. He claimed that "if you were to go from one office to another of every one of the great corporations" in the territory, "they would, without one single exception, all vote in favor of the electoral system. And why? Simply because they can control and manipulate in the background." Only after a judge is on the bench for several years can you tell "where the cat was that was in the meal-bag at the time of the nomination" (p. 1515). Appointments, on the other hand, were made in the light of day by the governor and subject to confirmation by the Senate. Beatty joined in the indictment of convention politics. "I believe it would be those who manipulate the conventions, rather than the people that would finally make the election" (p. 1504).

Clagett and Beatty's attack on political parties and elections provoked heated rebuttals. Willis Sweet thought the people of Idaho "would absolutely demand of this convention the right to select their own judges. . . . They claim the right to elect every officer that governs them by themselves; and that is a right they are going sooner or later to have for themselves, from president to constable" (p. 1512). Edgar Wilson agreed. "The people at large, of both political parties, are better judges than the governor or the legislature can be" (p. 1503).

John T. Morgan, who ironically came to Idaho as an appointed justice of the territorial supreme court, gave this stirring testament to rights of voters. "And we have been coming nearer and nearer universal suffrage, both in England and in this country, as the time goes by, and the nearer we get to universal suffrage, in my opinion, the better officers we shall get from the highest to the lowest in this country"[21](p. 1511).

Willis Sweet defended party politics, and argued they would produce good nominees. "[M]y understanding is that where political parties are struggling for supremacy in the state, they universally select their best men for the judgeship, with a view of having men of character and ability to fill those positions to assist in pulling the rest of the ticket through" (p. 1511).

The election proponents advanced arguments in addition to the lessons of history and the merits of universal suffrage. Weldon Heyburn contended appointment was a violation of the separation of powers principle. Because "the creator will be the master of the created," appointment would blend the executive and judiciary (p. 1513). James Reid argued against appointment, since smaller counties could not participate in the confirmation process because they were not assured a seat in the Senate (p. 1517).

Finally, the question was called and a roll call vote taken. Thirty-six delegates supported election and seven appointment. Included in those voting for election were eight members of the judiciary committee (Ainslie, Batten, Heyburn, Mayhew, Morgan, Reid, Sweet and Wilson). Since there were only seven votes for election in the committee, one of these delegates had switched his vote. The seven votes for appointment included three committee members, Beatty, Hampton and Harris. Apparently, the other supporters of appointment (Howe, Woods and Savidge) were not present for the debate, but would probably not have turned the tide against popular suffrage (pp. 1519–20).

Article 5, § 6, which embodies the convention's decision to elect justices, has been amended three times. A sentence was added in 1910 to permit calling a district judge to serve on any case where a supreme court justice is disqualified or unable to sit.[22] In 1920 the number of justices was increased from three to five.[23] Finally, in 1981 the manner of choosing the chief justice was amended. In the original section, the justice with the shortest term was chief. At present, the chief (who is also the executive head of the judicial system) is chosen for a four-year term by a majority vote of the justices.[24]

These three amendments have had minor impacts on the supreme court when compared to § 7, which was added to Article 6, suffrage and elections, in 1934. Clagett and Beatty had warned of the evils of party politics in the selection of judges and thought appointment was the cure. The citizens of Idaho came to see those evils in the first forty years of statehood,[25] but decided the cure was nonpartisan election rather than appointment. Article 6, § 7 provides:

> The selection of justices of the Supreme Court and district judges shall be nonpartisan. The legislature shall provide for their nomination and election, but candidates for the offices of justice of the Supreme Court and district judge shall not be nominated nor endorsed by any political party and their names shall not appear on any political party ticket, nor be accompanied on the ballot by any political party designation.[26]

This section makes it clear that Idaho favors popular but not partisan election of judges.

While in theory Idaho elects its supreme court justices, in fact appointment has been just as important during the state's first one hundred years. Forty-three men have served as a justice of the Idaho supreme court during the first century. Twenty-four of them won their first term on the court in an election. However, the other nineteen were first appointed to complete the term of a justice who had either died in office or resigned.[27] These incumbent appointees typically have won reelection. An initial appointment has been particularly important during the last thirty-five years. During that period only Justices Donaldson (1963) and Shepherd (1968) have won their way onto the court through an election, and eight justices have joined the court by appointment:

McQuade (1956), McFadden (1959), Spear (1966), Bakes (1971), Bistline (1976), Huntley (1982), Johnson (1988), McDeavitt (1989), and Boyle (1989).[28]

The delegates at Idaho's Constitutional Convention were adamantly in favor of electing their justices. They would have been shocked to find all five of Idaho's centennial justices would be first appointed, and by the same governor.[29]

5. The District Courts

DURING THE TERRITORIAL PERIOD, three judges handled all the work of the district courts and supreme court. Each of the three sat as a district judge, and they sat together as the supreme court. They exercised the jurisdiction of local or territorial courts and of federal courts.

The judiciary committee proposed to expand the number of judges from three to eight, first by creating a three-judge supreme court in § 6 and second by recommending the following, § 11:

> The state shall be divided into five (5) judicial districts, for each of which a judge shall be chosen by the qualified electors thereof, whose term of office shall be four (4) years. And there shall be held a district court in each county, at least twice in each year, to continue for such times in each county as may be prescribed by law. But the legislature may reduce or increase the number of districts, district judges and district attorneys. This section shall not be construed to prevent the holding of special terms under such regulations as may be provided by law.

While the judiciary committee unanimously agreed on this section, the delegates did not. William McConnell (R-Latah) moved to amend by reducing the number of districts from five to three "in the interest of economy." With tongue in cheek, McConnell explained the reason for his motion. "I do it out of consideration for the attorneys purely. Because the number of judges provided in this article is so large and the expense so great which the people will have to bear, I am satisfied we will have many explanations to make to the people. . . . Of course, if the attorneys can make us see that it is to the interest of the people to have eight judges in this territory where we now have but three, I am will to acquiesce in it." He thought the territorial judges "manage in a kind of way to keep the work done" and that state district judges would have less work because they would not also sit as a supreme court and because there would be fewer retrials with the new provisions for less than unanimous jury verdicts (pp. 1528–30).

McConnell feigned timidity when he said, "[M]en on the floor like myself have a delicacy about opposing these legal gentlemen, who are trained on the rostrum." He rather quickly adapted to the rostrum, and was soon accusing attorneys of being the root of the problem of court delays: "It is a notorious fact that the reason why the business of our county is behind is on account of the dilatory proceedings of the attorneys in not attending upon court" (p. 1532).

Aaron Parker (D-Idaho) supported McConnell. He said there was no congestion in Idaho County, and that Shoshone County had a backlog during the time he lived there because "the late judge there was an imbecile." He told the delegates that dockets in Oneida and other counties could be cleared if "you do away with your efforts to make criminals out of law-abiding citizens" by prosecuting Mormons for perjury (pp. 1537–38).

Orlando Batten (D-Alturas) shared the concerns of McConnell and Parker, but he argued there should be four districts. He accused the lawyer-delegates of following the Philander Greene principle. He explained that Philander Greene was a delegate to a national convention who said, "What are we here for, if not for the offices?" Batten said the lawyers should be "honest and candid . . . and rightly charge ourselves with a good deal of the blame" for delays in judicial proceedings (pp. 1550–52).

Members of the judiciary committee staunchly defended their proposal for five districts and eight judges, just as they had the election of supreme court justices. Weldon Heyburn interrupted McConnell for cross-examination. He asked, "What is the condition of the business of the district court in the county from which the gentleman comes, as to being behind or not?" Then he followed up with, "I will ask the gentleman what is the condition of the court calendar in Shoshone county?" Heyburn spoke to the other delegates and explained his motives: "Mr. President, my object in asking questions of the gentleman was to see whether he knew anything about the facts relating to this matter, or whether he was simply going on buncombe" (pp. 1528–29). Heyburn claimed he knew the answer. "There isn't a district in this territory that is not months and months behind in its business" (p. 1531). Judge Morgan supported Heyburn's assessment and reviewed the circumstances in Alturas, Elmore and Logan counties, describing cases being under advisement for up to a year and cases being half-tried and then delayed until the next term (pp. 1546–47).

The judiciary committee members further argued there would be more litigation and court business after statehood. Railroad and mining development were sure to come hand in hand after statehood, and with them litigation that would need to be resolved. Judge Morgan argued there was a "kind of human pirate" in every mining camp who was willing to jump claims and trump up titles. He concluded, "If those men can keep those questions in litigation for months or a year, you must buy them out to get rid of them and that is all they want" (p. 1548).

The delegates who wanted five districts argued that lawyers were not to blame for delays. Judge Morgan declared, "It is to the interest of the attorneys to push the business through and get rid of it. I have been a practicing attorney for thirty-three years, and I think I know what the interest of an attorney is" (p. 1537). James Reid agreed, "I have always found that when the clients wanted the cases tried the lawyers are willing to try them" (p. 1549).

To the committee members, the real economics of the decision involved more than just the cost of the judges. Reid summed it up, "Cheap justice is generally injustice"

(p. 1537). Judge Morgan elaborated, "It is ruinous, absolutely ruinous to men to have cases for trial in these courts" because the subject of litigation becomes worthless after such a long time or because they have great amounts of money invested (p. 1549).

James Reid then tried to explain why the increased expense of three supreme court and five district court judges made good sense. The increase was significant, and so the explanation was complicated. During the last territorial years, the federal government paid most of the annual salaries of the three justices, so the expense to the territory was small.

By contrast, the judiciary committee recommended an annual salary of $3,000 for the eight supreme and district court judges, for a total of $24,000. In addition, the committee recommended that a prosecuting attorney be elected in each district and paid an annual salary of $2,500. That brought the total salaries for the judicial department to $31,500. The convention delegates were proposing a "cadillac" judiciary. In their proposed budget for the first year of statehood, the delegates recommended spending $38,220 for the judiciary department. This was over twenty-seven percent of Idaho's total projected state budget of $138,125. The figure for the judiciary was over $15,000 larger than the next line item in the budget which was the penitentiary at $23,075 (p. 2093).

Reid conceded the dramatic increase, but explained that it was covered by a greater scheme that would in fact result in great savings to Idaho taxpayers. The greater scheme first involved adopting Article V, § 18, which eliminated the eighteen county attorneys provided under the territorial statutes, and replaced them with five district attorneys, one for each judicial district. Reid estimated this would save $36,000 per year, and argued that was only half the plan. The really big savings were to be found in the article on county organization, where §§ 7 and 8 provided for the salaries of the county sheriff, clerk of the district court, probate judge, county assessor, county treasurer, coroner, county surveyor, justices of the peace and constables. It was the plan of the convention to pay each of these officers on a user fee basis, rather than a salary paid from tax revenues. The tax savings to result from moving these officers from salaries to fees was estimated by Reid to be $110,000 to $120,000. He summed up his claim that the judiciary under statehood could be cheaper than that as a territory. "[Y]ou will find your county and state expenses will be $40,000 or $50,000 less than the territorial expense is now, if you adopt the two systems proposed" (p. 1535).

There was some interest at the convention in a compromise of four judicial districts. Four districts had been proposed during the territorial period but rejected by Congress. Orlando Batten argued for four districts on the convention floor. According to comments by Clagett, the scheme of four districts was once even approved by the judiciary committee. In the end, the debates reveal that a four-district compromise was not possible because of the terrain in the new state. The geographical landscape determined the judicial landscape.

Batten said, "I honestly believe four judges will be sufficient," but summed up the difficulty in this fashion. "[O]wing to the peculiar condition of things, the fact that there is an almost impassible or a difficult range of mountains that divides us in twain, we cannot adjust this matter nicely." He wanted to defy the mountains, "I don't think we should raise this barrier of mountains as a sort of obstacle in the way" (pp. 1551–52).

Early in the debate over judicial districts, Clagett had supported creating four districts, two north of the Salmon and two south. With respect to the north he said emphatically, "you must have judges enough to have them within reasonable striking distance of the litigants; and for that reason it requires two men in north Idaho" (p. 1539). Clagett's argument provoked protest from lawyers in the south, especially Edgar Wilson, who began, "[T]o say that two judges in south Idaho shall attend to thirteen counties and that northern Idaho shall have two judges, is so manifestly unjust that I don't think the convention would adopt it" (p. 1539). Sol Hasbrouck thought Clagett's proposal "so manifestly unfair, that I don't suppose anyone in this convention will have the courage to maintain the proposition" (p. 1549).

Wilson also stated the argument in terms of dollars and cents. "The valuation as shown by our assessment of the taxable property in southern Idaho is $16,431,799. The taxable property of the five northern counties was $5,192,948. In other words, in southern Idaho, south of the Salmon River mountains we pay more than three times the amount of taxes they pay in northern Idaho" (p. 1553).

There was some talk of having four districts with counties north and south of the Salmon River combined, for example Nez Perce, Idaho, Washington, Ada and Owyhee counties in a single district. Wilson explained the difficulties for an Ada county litigant in such a district who needed an injunction at the time the judge was sitting in Idaho County. "Then the litigant and his attorney would have to go 1,200 or 1,500 miles by rail, 200 miles on the back of a mule or 200 miles on snowshoes probably to get his injunction" (p. 1552). Of course, the route Wilson described was similar to that traveled by the convention delegates from north Idaho; each of them had to leave the territory on their way to the state constitutional convention.

Wilson finally summed up for the convention. "The question is either three or five judges." Idaho's rivers and mountains dictated the answer. The delegates voted so overwhelmingly for five districts the votes weren't even counted (p. 1557).

The debate on the number of judicial districts was one of the rare occasions at the convention when the acrimony between northern and southern Idaho surfaced. Even though dividing Idaho at the Salmon River was the major issue during the entire territorial period, the regions were persuaded by the promise of statehood to set their differences aside. If statehood was a shotgun marriage, then the last territorial legislature was the exchange of wedding gifts. In a mood of reconciliation, that legislature located the university at Moscow and the asylum at Blackfoot. It also tried to strengthen the bonds between the two regions by connecting them with the first wagon road in the White Bird Hill area.

At the Constitutional Convention there was even more harmony between northern and southern delegates than in the last territorial legislature. At no time before or since the convention have the relations between the two regions been so amicable. The number of districts adopted by the convention is good evidence of this. During the territorial period, thirty-three percent (1 of 3) of the district judges sat north of the

Salmon River. The constitutional convention increased the share of the north to forty percent (2 of 5) of the total. That same convention, however, provided that the legislature had the power to alter the organization of the district courts. As a result, during the first one hundred years of statehood the percentage of district judges with residences north of the Salmon has eroded to twenty-four percent (8 of 33).

Just as the northern Idaho judiciary has never been treated so well as in Idaho's original constitution, Idaho's lawyers and judges have never been so blessed, before or since. The convention delegates recommended a budget for the first year of statehood which allocated over twenty-seven percent to the judiciary. In fact, twenty-three percent of that first state budget went to the judiciary.

Just as Idaho citizens have disagreed with the convention delegates about the amount to be spent on the judiciary, they have also disagreed about how to pay for what is spent. The delegates proposed to eliminate county attorneys, and have a prosecuting attorney for each judicial district. After experimenting with this system for a few years, the counties demanded their county attorneys back and the constitution was amended in 1896.[30] The plan of the delegates to pay for the judiciary by compensating local officials with fees rather than salaries did not survive much longer. In 1898 the constitution was amended to provide for an annual salary rather than fees.[31]

Perhaps no article of Idaho's Constitution has changed more during Idaho's first century than the judicial article. Gone are the probate courts, the justices of the peace, the partisan election of judges, the district prosecutors, the user fees, and the generous budget for the judiciary. Forces of history have no doubt caused many of these changes, but many have also been brought about by those who inherited the constitution. Idaho's lawyers designed the original judiciary at the constitutional convention; Idaho citizens have designed their centennial judiciary in the voting booths.

Notes

1. 12 Stat. L. 808, ch. 117; see also S.L. 1864, pp. 192–97.

2. Id. Stat. 1–801 *et.seq.*

3. Id. Const. Article V, § 6.

4. 1961 Idaho Sess Laws 1077, H.J.R. No. 10, ratified at the general election November 6, 1962.

5. Id. Code §§ 1–2301 to 1–2315.

6. Hart, I. W., ed. *Proceedings and Debates of the Constitutional Convention of Idaho 1889.* 2 vols. Caldwell: Caxton Printers, Ltd., 1912. These volumes are paginated consecutively, and all page references in the text of this chapter are to them. 7. Hawley, James H. *History of Idaho: The Gem of the Mountains.* 5 vols. Chicago: S. J. Clarke, 1920. Vol. 1, p. 590.

8. Hawley, *History of Idaho,* vol. I, p. 590.

9. Limbaugh, Ronald Hadley. "The Idaho Spoilsman: Federal Administration and Idaho Territorial Politics, 1863–1890." Ph.D. diss., University of Idaho, 1966, p. 37.

10. Limbaugh, "Idaho Spoilsman," p. 38.

11. See chapter 3 above, pp. 000–000.

12. "The Ship of State," *Caldwell Tribune,* 13 Jy. 1889, p. 3, col. 2.

13. See Ch. 1 § 2 above for biographical information about each of the committee members.

14. August, Raymond S. "Law in the West A History of the Origins and Distribution of Western American Law." Ph.D. diss., University of Idaho, 1987, 2 vols. Vol. I, pp. 41–104; Millar, Robert W. "The Old Regime and the New in Civil Procedure." In *Law A Century of Progress 1835–1935*. New York, New York University Press, 1937. Vol. I, pp. 207–73.

15. "There is in this Territory but one form of civil actions for the enforcement or protection of private rights and the redress or prevention of private wrongs. . . ." 1887 Rvsd. Idaho Stat. § 4020.

16. 12 Idaho 280, 85 P. 921 (1906).

17. *Murphy v. Russell*, 8 Idaho 133, 67 P. 421 (1901); *City of Pocatello v. Murray*, 21 Idaho 180, 120 P. 812, aff'd, 226 U.S. 318 (1912); *Carroll v. Hartford Fire Ins. Co.*, 28 Idaho 466, 154 P.2d 985 (1916); *Addy v. Stewart*, 69 Idaho 357, 207 P.2d 498 (1949).

18. *Nordick v. Sorensen*, 81 Idaho 117, 338 P.2d 766 (1959).

19. *Clark v. State*, 92 Idaho 827, 452 P.2d 54 (1969); *State v. Goodrich*, 104 Idaho 469, 660 P.2d 934 (1983).

20. *State v. Bennion*, 112 Idaho 32, 730 P.2d 952 (1986).

21. According to today's understanding, instead of "universal suffrage," Morgan meant to say "popular sovereignty or suffrage," which is the belief that the people and not some select elite have the right to decide political questions. Universal suffrage refers to granting the right to vote to all members of the community, something Idaho's Constitutional Convention clearly did not believe in.

22. Proposed by 1909 Idaho Sess Laws 441, S.J.R. No. 7, and ratified at the general election in November 1910.

23. Proposed by 1919 Idaho Sess Laws 618, H.J.R. No. 6, and ratified at the general election in November 1920.

24. Proposed by 1981 Idaho Sess Laws 776, H.J.R. No. 2 and ratified at the general election November 2, 1982.

25. Pursuant to a state statute, Supreme Court justices were elected on a non-partisan ballot between 1913 and 1918.

26. Proposed by 1933 Idaho Sess Laws 469, S.J.R. No. 2, and ratified at the general election in November, 1934.

27. Judicial appointments are governed by Article 4, §5 and Article 5, §19 of the Idaho Constitution.

28. *Idaho Blue Book*. 1989–1990 edition. Boise: Office of the Secretary of State, 1989.

29. Justices Bakes (1971), Bistline (1976), Johnson (1988) McDeavitt (1989) and Boyle (1989) have all been appointed by Democratic Governor Cecil Andrus.

30. 1895 Idaho Sess Laws 236, S.J.R. No. 5, ratified at the general election in November 1896.

31. 1897 Idaho Sess Laws 185, H.J.R. No. 10, ratified at the general election in November 1898.

11.

Local Government

1. Introduction

FOUR COMMITTEES REPORTED SECTIONS dealing with local government at the Idaho Constitutional Convention. The legislative committee proposed a section prohibiting the legislature from passing special or local laws affecting a variety of local government questions. The public indebtedness committee reported three sections limiting the power of local government to incur indebtedness. One section required a special election to approve any expenditures beyond current revenues. Another limited the total amount of debt that could be incurred to five percent of the assessed value of the property subject to tax. A third section prohibited any unit of local government from pledging credit to aid any private person.

Two committee reports dealt exclusively with local government. The municipal corporations committee proposed a bill with four sections providing for city government. Section 1 empowered the legislature to make general laws for the government of cities and § 2 granted to counties and cities an inherent local police power to pass any ordinance that did not conflict with state law. Section 3 prohibited the state government from assuming the debts of a local government. Finally, § 4 prohibited local governments from becoming stockholders in any joint stock companies or corporations.

The county organization committee reported the longest and most detailed article on local government. It recommended eleven sections covering two basic topics: (1) the establishment of counties, and (2) the creation of county offices. With respect to the establishment of counties, the committee proposed to recognize the existing counties and to require that in the creation of future counties, none could be smaller in size than 400 square miles. It was also recommended that the voters in the county should locate the county seat, and that any decision to sever a portion from one county and attach it to another be made by the voters in the area to be severed. The committee recommended creating the following county offices: commissioners, sheriff, treasurer, probate judge, assessor, coroner and surveyor. The committee went on to set the salaries of these officers, and to provide that they should be paid by commissions and fees charged for the services rendered.

James W. Reid (D-Nez Perce) chaired the committee on county organization. Reid was important at the constitutional convention for the role he played as the leader of the Democratic caucus and a principal spokesman for Democratic causes. He was also an important representative of the conservative members of the legal profession. Perhaps Reid's most lasting contribution to Idaho was his work as the "Founder of Idaho Counties." Not only did Reid chair the county organization committee, he headed up the campaign to have counties recognized in the apportionment of the legislature. Reid staunchly defended the importance of county governments, and his influence is still clearly visible one hundred years later.

Predictably, the Idaho constitutional debates on local government were dominated by local issues. For the most part, these provisions were not debated on their merits. The delegates were more concerned about the impact upon their constituents, and this concern led to three major debates. First, two counties were concerned about debt limitations, Shoshone because it was already so heavily indebted and Ada because Boise City was anxious to become more heavily indebted. The second debate was caused by Shoshone County's desperate need to change the location of its county seat. In the third debate, Alturas County was concerned about the division of counties because it very much needed to acquire more area from another county in order to survive. This essay describes the debates on these three issues.

2. Local Government Indebtedness

MANY CONVENTION DELEGATES wanted to severely limit the ability of local governments to incur indebtedness. An Address to the People written by the convention to accompany the constitution assured Idaho voters that "[T]he business and tax-paying portion of our people was especially prominent and watchful of every interest of vital concern" (p. 2095).[1] Nowhere is the evidence of the watchful interest of the taxpayers more obvious than in the limitations on local indebtedness. The limitations were so popular, both the public indebtedness and municipal corporations committees independently recommended three identical sections. The public indebtedness article came to the convention floor first and as a result that is where the limitations finally appear in the constitution (pp. 585–86).

Sections 1 and 2 of the public indebtedness article limited the state's power to incur debt and to pledge its credit. Section 3 prohibited local governments from incurring debt beyond the revenue expected for the year without approval of two-thirds of the voters at a special election. In addition to an election, the section also required that at the time the debt was incurred it was necessary to establish an annual tax sufficient to pay the interest and principal on the debt.

The purpose of this section was to put county government on a cash basis, except for special indebtedness. It was a common practice in many of the counties at the time to issue scrip to pay current expenses. The scrip was then frequently bought up at a discount by speculators who would later redeem the scrip at a handsome profit when tax receipts became available. Ironically, the convention that was trying to curtail the use of scrip was itself being financed by scrip. Neither Congress nor the Idaho Legislature provided a budget for the Idaho Convention. The delegates were expected to advance their expenses and accept scrip as reimbursement. Typically, speculators purchased much of the scrip which was ultimately redeemed by Congress.[2]

A number of delegates objected to the section because it went too far in limiting local government. One of these was the president of the convention, William H. Clagett (R-Shoshone). He proposed to amend the section by adding, "Provided, that this section shall not be construed to apply to ordinary indebtedness created under the general laws of the state" (p. 586). Clagett explained his concern. "We all know that in the practical administration of county government, that there sometimes will be extraordinary expenses, I mean extrordinary expenses in the ordinary administration of affairs" (p. 586)." Clagett gave witness fees as an example.

Other lawyers joined in opposition to the section. James W. Reid drew a distinction between permanent indebtedness and current expenses, such as juror fees, and argued the committee apparently wanted to limit only permanent debt, not ordinary debt (p. 590). Weldon Heyburn (R-Shoshone) pointed out that his county depended heavily upon a license tax which fluctuated in revenue from fourteen to twenty thousand dollars per year, and that in some years "there may be an unusual number of capital cases to be tried in the criminal court" (p. 590). He declared, "We don't want to have any part of our court expenses in doubt; we don't want to leave any part of the ordinary legitimate expenses of running county government in doubt, and we don't want to call a county election for the purpose of making up a deficit of four or five hundred dollars at the end of the year . . ." (p. 591). W. C. B. Allen (R-Logan) thought the Committee had not "thoroughly digested" the fact that it was "a necessity to issue scrip at different times in case of any emergency court expenses, or any emergency" (p. 587).

The lawyers were joined in opposition to the limitation by Peter J. Pefley (D-Ada), a former mayor speaking on behalf of Boise City. He said there were streams and ditches running adjacent to the city that were always liable "to break away and run down through the city, and if we had to wait to hold an election and get two-thirds of the voters to ratify another levy, the whole city might be ruined before it could be abated" (p. 592).

Only two delegates defended the section. George Ainslie (D-Boise) complained about Clagett's amendment, "That absolutely nullifies the section, destroys the whole life of it" (p. 587). Orlando Batten (D-Alturas), a member of the public indebtedness committee, cautioned the convention, "Let's not do as did Rip Van Winkle when he made a resolution not to drink anything—keep on drinking and say each drink did not count" (p. 589). This was not enough to save the section, and Clagett's amendment was adopted by a confusing but near unanimous vote (p. 594).

The delegates then took up the fourth section recommended by the public indebtness committee. This section limited the amount of debt that could be incurred by any local taxing authority to five percent of the assessed property value subject to taxation.

Edgar Wilson (R-Ada) was the first to object. He proposed amending the section by adding, "provided, that in any city or town of over 2,000 inhabitants by consent of the qualified electors thereof expressed at a special election held for such purpose, such limit shall be not to exceed 15 per centum of the assessed valuation of such city or town" (pp. 594–95).

Wilson was concerned about Boise City. He explained the city's balance sheet to the convention. It had a floating indebtedness of $40,000, and the assessed value of its property was "between eleven and twelve hundred thousand dollars." He also explained Boise City's aspirations. The city council had succeeded in getting a memorial to Congress from the territorial legislature. The memorial requested authorization for a $150,000 debt limit for the purpose of refinancing the current debt and constructing a sewer and water system. The memorial was pending, and without an exception to the committee's section, it was "absolutely impossible to provide for a sewerage system or water works in Boise City" (pp. 595–96).

Wilson also offered a philsophical argument for his amendment, a debtor's manifesto:

> As you all know, these western towns cannot grow except by contracting a large indebtedness. There has not been a western town within the last ten years that has increased to any extent unless they incur large indebtedness. I think, as well shown by writers on political economy, that municipal indebtedness is absolutely necessary for municipal prosperity and making the municipal improvements that call for indebtedness, and I make the assertion that with indebtedness the debtors are those who make vastly more wealth—the borrowers are the towns that acquire it (pp. 595–96).

J. W. Poe (R-Nez Perce) supported Wilson. He argued local people should have the authority to make the decision. "I say, leave it to the people who are to reap the benefit or the damage . . . This is a republican form of government and the people of the municipality or county ordinarily know their business" (p. 601).

Weldon Heyburn was less philosophical and more blunt in his argument against the section. He began, if the section "is not stricken out, as far as the members of this convention from Shoshone county are concerned, they can just go home, because they will have no interest in the state government whatever" (pp. 599–600). He explained Shoshone County had a bonded indebtedness of $150,000, a floating indebtedness of

$65,000, and an assessed valuation of a little over a million dollars. Since this debt was already several times the limit provided, unless it was struck "[T]he wheels of their government will be stopped . . . right there." He pleaded, "We have a government that must be kept in motion. We have courts that must be held, officers that must perform their duty, processes that must be served in order to maintain good government and peace and order in our community" (pp. 599–600).

Heyburn concluded his argument by moving to strike the five percent limitation entirely, and the delegates adopted his suggestion (p. 601). The convention then adopted without amendment the next section, which prohibited local governments from pledging its credit to any private interest. The floor debates on these three debt limitations made it clear the convention as a whole was not as conservative and restrictive as the committees that wrote the public indebtedness and municipal corporations articles.

Article VIII, §§ 3 and 4, the two local debt limitation sections adopted at the Idaho Constitutional Convention, survived the first sixty years of statehood without amendment. However, the Idaho supreme court frequently interpreted them during this period, especially § 3 requiring a special election for permanent indebtedness. The court sometimes concluded the limitations did not apply. For example, they did not limit municipalities from levying special assessments against particular properties benefited because such an assessment was not an indebtedness or liability.[3] The Board of Regents of the University of Idaho was not limited because it was not named.[4] A number of expenditures were defined as "ordinary and necessary" and therefore not limited, including work on streets,[5] repair of damage caused by accident or casualty,[6] and the salaries of public school teachers.[7] Obligations imposed by law were not limited by the sections.[8]

The court more often, however, rigorously applied the limitations. In the early years it had to remind local governments the debt limitations were mandatory.[9] A number of special expenditures had to be submitted to the voters, including construction of a bridge[10] and wagon road,[11] acquisition of a courthouse site,[12] construction of a school house addition and acquisition of furniture,[13] and acquisition of an electrical system.[14]

Even though often litigated, Article 8, § 3 was not first amended until 1950. This amendment weakened the limitations on indebtedness by permitting revenue bonds to be issued for construction of water and sewer systems and treatment plants as well as off street parking facilities.[15] Revenue bonds are repaid from the rates and charges assessed against users of the facilities constructed rather than from assessed taxes.

Amendments have become more frequent in recent years. In 1964 port districts were allowed to issue revenue bonds and were excused from the special election calling for passage by two-thirds.[16] The period for payment of normal indebtedness was also extended from twenty to thirty years. A 1966 amendment permitted revenue bonds for public recreation facilities[17] and a 1968 amendment permitted air navigation facilities.[18] In 1972 the vote requirement to approve revenue bonds for water or sewer projects was lowered from two-thirds to majority.[19] A special section was added in 1974 to authorize revenue bonds for environmental pollution control facilities.[20] Rehabilitation of existing electrical generating facilities was added to the list of projects eligible for majority-approved revenue bonds in 1976.[21] Port districts received expanded authority for projects in a another section added in 1978.[22]

The most recent amendment, in 1982, continued the trend away from the Idaho Constitution's original limitations on indebtedness. The most troublesome limitation has been the requirement that a special tax be levied and a sinking fund established for each debt. Every amendment, beginning in 1950, has avoided this limitation by authorizing revenue bonds. In the latest amendment a new section was added to Article 8 to authorize issuance of nonrecourse revenue bonds for industrial development facilities.[23] The legislature was given broad authority over these bonds, including power to authorize local governments to form public corporations. This trend away from strict debt limitations is likely to continue as local governments struggle to provide basic services to their residents when financial support from both state and federal governments is declining.

3. Local Laws and County Seats

AT THE TIME OF STATEHOOD most Idaho citizens did not live in the towns and villages. To these people the county was the closest and most important unit of government. Police protection, voting, courts, land titles, and education were some of the more important functions of the counties. Given these conditions it is not surprising that drawing county lines and locating county seats were difficult and contentious local issues, especially since settlement patterns often produced rapid population shifts.

The Organic Act of the territory of Idaho vested authority over these county decisions in the territorial legislature. The Act stated that county officers were to be elected or appointed by the governor, all as provided by laws passed by the legislature.[24] The Washington territorial legislature had similar authority during the period Idaho was a part of Washington Territory, and had created Shoshone, Nez Perce, Idaho and Boise counties by 1863.[25] By 1889 the Idaho territorial legislature had created another fourteen counties.

Territorial legislatures were often consumed by controversies over county lines and county seats, and other local issues. Congress responded in 1886 by enacting the Symms Bill. The first section of the bill prohibited passage by territorial legislatures of any "local or special laws" in enumerated areas. Included in the list of prohibited subjects were bills "locating or changing county seats."[26] Congress clarified the bill two years later. While ratifying the creation of San Juan County by New Mexico, Congress stipulated the Symms Bill did not prohibit "the creation by Territorial legislatures of new counties and the location of the county seats thereof."[27]

The legislative committee at the Idaho Constitutional Convention recommended incorporating the provisions of the Symms Bill into the constitution. It proposed this section. "The legislature shall not pass local or special laws in any of the following enumerated cases." One of those cases was the "changing of county seats."[28]

William Clagett immediately objected to the limitation because of the impact it would have on Shoshone County. He proposed striking the limitation, or adding "unless the law authorizing the change shall require that three-fifths of the legal votes cast at a special or general election shall designate the place to which the county seat shall be changed" (p. 1239). His objective was to authorize the legislature to pass a special law for the change of his county seat, but to still let the local people choose the new location in an election.

Clagett explained Shoshone County's needs. Population shifted dramatically in mining districts, always moving to the newest discovery. As a result, Murray, where the county seat was established in the early 1880s, turned out to be in the wrong place by the end of the decade. The population was now far away, and was causing an unnecessary expenditure of $15,000 per year in operating the county government. Claggett complained, "we have to pass over two ranges of mountains to get to the county seat and are being bankrupted by this proposition" (p. 1233).

In earlier territorial days this problem would have been cured with a special statute from the legislature. However, after 1886 the Symms Bill prohibited such a statute. While the legislature had authority to pass a general statute governing the subject uniformly in all the counties, it had been unable to do so during the 1886 and 1888 sessions. As a result, Shoshone County had been unable to get a special or a general statute, and was in dire need of relief. Clagett argued for his amendment, "There is no possible objection to passing a special law for the removal of a county seat, provided it is required in the law to be submitted to the vote of the people in the county" (p. 1233).

Alexander Mayhew (D-Shoshone) supported his colleague's amendment. He too explained that county business was expensive, especially litigation, because his county seat was twenty miles from the newly-arrived railroad and the majority of the residents. He recalled as an example the need to move the Shoshone county seat to Murray. Until the mining discoveries in the Coeur D'Alene's, the county seat was in Pierce where it had been located during Idaho's first mining rush in the Clearwater country in the 1860s. Mayhew concluded by declaring he was "somewhat opposed to the legislature having the right to pass special acts for the removal of county seats," but thought there were times when "absolute necessity" made it acceptable (pp. 1242–43).

James Shoup (R-Custer) opposed Clagett's suggestion. He asked, "If the legislature will not agree with a general law, is it probable they can agree upon any act for any one particular county?" (p. 1240). Edgar Wilson also raised questions because he wanted to generally discourage changing county seats. He explained, "This question of changing county seats is one of the most vexing questions that ever disturbed this or any other people. It has caused more trouble in new countries than any other question . . . and in some of the western states . . . has led to insurrections, to little rebellions and small civil wars . . . ." (pp. 1241–42). John T. Morgan (R-Bingham) thought the amendment would create problems because there were at least a dozen counties in positions similar to Shoshone County. "If you keep these counties forever pulling and hauling between county seats or between one place and another, you will forever be having elections at great expense and bitter feeling" (p. 1245). John S. Gray (R-Ada) accused Clagett, "If I understand the gentleman, it is this, that he wants to legislate for Shoshone county . . . And if they cannot get a general law that hits, then he wants a special law" (p. 1247).

Clagett was successful in getting his amendment passed. As a concession to those who opposed him, he then moved to add a provision to his amendment which would permit special acts only when there was no general law on the subject.[29] The section has never been amended, and has never been important even to Shoshone County. Shoshone got its solution in May of 1890 when Congress authorized an election on the county seat question at the next general election,[30] at which time the county voters moved the county seat from Murray to Wallace.

While Clagett's special exception for county seats has not been significant in Idaho's first century, the general prohibition against special or local legislation has. There has always been difficulty distinguishing between a general law on the one hand, and a local or special law on the other. At the convention J. W. Poe, an attorney from Lewiston, said, "I understand then that if a man by the name of Smith wants his name changed it would affect every man in the state whose name is Smith; it would have to reach all the Smiths" (p. 1228).

John Morgan, who had served on the territorial supreme court, was impatient with Poe. He said, "It seems to me strange that gentlemen do not understand this section. That same proposition has been presented to me two or three times." Still, he did not provide a definition of the difference and explained only by pointing to statutes then on the books authorizing district courts to change names (pp. 1228–29).

The Idaho supreme court has said a statute is general if its terms apply to, and its provisions operate upon, all persons and subjects in a like situation.[31] On the other hand, local or special laws are those that apply to one individual, to individuals out of a class or to a special locality.[32]

The most difficult statutes are those that create a class of one. A good example was provided at the convention during the debate on the proposal to limit local government indebtedness to five percent of the assessed property. Edgar Wilson, from Boise City, proposed that any city over 2,000 be permitted a debt limit of fifteen percent, all the time acknowledging there was only one city in the class and that he was trying to solve the problems of that locality (pp. 595–96).

The supreme court has held a statute is not special simply because it has only a local application or applies only to a special class, if it actually applies to all such classes and all similar localities and to all belonging to the specified class to which the law is applicable.[33] The legislature is given considerable discretion, and can define different classes or distinguish between different situations so long as it is not arbitrary, capricious or unreasonable.[34]

A number of important Idaho statutes have survived an attack alleging they were local or special legislation, including an ad valorem tax with agricultural and other exemptions,[35] a State Water Conservation Board,[36] a state insurance fund,[37] a Health Facilities Authority,[38] the creation of new counties,[39] the Prohibition Law (even though it operated differently in wet and dry territories),[40] amendments to special local government charters existing at statehood,[41] apportioning state license plates,[42] the Public Assistance Act,[43] establishing state parks,[44] Sunday closing laws,[45] Workmen's Compensation laws,[46] and most recently a resort city tax.[47]

Other statues have been declared a local or special law and declared unconstitutional, including creating a corporation in effect,[48] making gambling a misdemeanor in one part of the state and not a crime in another,[49] an appropriation to pay the members of the legislature their expenses,[50] an appropriation to Lemhi County to construct and repair Williams Creek Road,[51] and authorizing water adjudication to proceed against all claimants without notice or attempt to serve them.[52]

These cases are evidence that, just as during territorial days, local interests continue to lobby the state legislature for local legislation. The legislature often cannot resist giving aid, and the litigation that often follows reflects the bitterness caused by the intervention.

4. *Dividing and Creating Counties*

POPULIST POLITICS were popular in the Rocky Mountain states in 1889, making government more responsive to the citizens.[53] The delegates at the Idaho Constitutional Convention sought to empower the voters in many ways. For example, all principal officers in the state, including supreme court justices, were to be elected rather than appointed. Another provision was that local voters should decide local questions. The county organization committee reported several sections that empowered local voters at the expense of the legislature. One of those sections, borrowed from the Colorado Constitution, provided:

> No part of the territory of any county shall be stricken off and added to an adjoining county without first submitting the question to the qualified voters of the county from which the territory is proposed to be stricken off; nor unless a majority of all the qualified voters of said county voting on the question vote therefore (p. 1880).

This section came before the convention late in the afternoon on Friday, August 2, the twenty-fifth and nearly last day in session. James Beatty (R-Alturas) immediately objected. Predictably, he was concerned with the local impact of the section. Beatty was straightforward about it. "[T]his section is to me, and to the people I represent, of more interest that any other question in this constitution. . . . Now, I tell you, Mr. President, where this shoe fits very closely, for I have nothing to conceal" (pp. 1780–81).

Beatty began his argument by analyzing the practical effect of the section. He concluded that no part of a county would ever be divided. "Now, I ask you in all honesty, where can you in this territory get a majority of the voters of any county to consent that they shall lose one foot of their sacred soil? . . . I claim you cannot get a county in this territory, by a majority of the voters of that county, to consent to losing any portion of its territory" (p. 1781).

Beatty explained to the convention why this result would be disastrous for Alturas County. "The last legislature of Idaho territory, to its shame be it said, made a division of Alturas county, which is the most outrageous in my opinion of any that ever was enacted. They have left what was once a princely domain, a county of too large dimension I admit, but a county of about $4,000,000 worth of property, reduced to a little pitiable $750,000 worth of property . . . and included in that is three or four hundred thousand dollars worth of burned property recently destroyed by the fire at Hailey" (pp. 1781–82).

The division of Alturas County in 1888 that Beatty was complaining about was an extraordinary event, even for the Idaho legislature. Even though the particular legislation dividing Alturas was unusual, the general story of that division is but another example of the usual pattern of settlement in the territory. In the beginning, there were a few large, and sparsely populated counties. Then a new mining discovery or other settlement would occur, and the new residents and their politicians would begin a campaign to get the county seat, or perhaps another new county altogether. After a few bitter sessions, the legislature would be persuaded and a new county created. The legislation would end the current struggle, but also be the seed of another cycle of controversy which would inevitably accompany new changes in settlement patterns.[54]

Alturas County was created in 1864 by Idaho's first territorial legislature.[54] It included all the territory which today lies in Custer, Blaine, Elmore, Gooding, Camas, Jerome, Minidoka and part of Power counties. The county seat of Alturas was originally located at Esmeralda. Then came the opening of the mines in the Wood River and the settlement of Hailey, Ketchum, and Bellevue, which began a campaign to move the county seat. An election was held, and despite allegations of fraud and irregularities Hailey was chosen as the new county seat.

The Wood River mines flourished in the 1880s, aided by the arrival of the Oregon Short Line. A group of lawyers and politicians derisively known as the "Hailey Ring" not only dominated affairs in Alturas County, they became one of the most powerful delegations in the territorial legislature. The Ring made many enemies in its drive for power and influence. Representatives from Rocky Bar, Mountain Home and Pine Grove lobbied the 1886 legislature for division but had little success. By 1888 these forces were able to elect an Alturas delegate to the lower house of the legislature. He hoped to gain the support of delegates from other counties who would have their own reasons to divide the county, and greatly reduce the influence of Alturas in the legislature.

In early January 1889 D. L. Bradley from Ada County introduced an act to divide Alturas and create Elmore County. At the same time George P. Wheeler from Bingham County proposed to carve off a piece of Alturas and annex it to Bingham. Both acts were referred to committee, where the Hailey Ring tried to keep them bottled. Repeated rumors of bribery attempts prompted a special investigating committee, which finally reported evidence of political logrolling but no bribery.

In a desperate attempt to save their county, the Hailey forces set a procedural backfire. They introduced an omnibus division bill that would create Elmore and Logan counties and leave Alturas with Hailey, Ketchum, Bullion, and a small portion of the Camas Prairie. The expectation was that this would divide the division sentiment, because even the most ardent divisionist would not want to leave Alturas with so little. However, rather than saving themselves by this strategy, the Hailey forces found their plan produced the opposite effect from that intended.

The house committee on counties reported favorably on the omnibus bill. Antidivisionists fought the bill at every step, before the committee and before the House. For example, at 2:00 a.m. on January 31 the House finally decided it was ready to vote on the bill. The representatives looked around for J. A. Bruner of Boise County because he had the only copy of the bill. They were angered and frustrated to discover that Bruner, who opposed division, had retired for the evening. The vote was delayed another twelve hours, but when it finally came the division bill was passed 13 to 10.

The process was much the same in the Council. A special committee created to consider the division bill was not able to report back to the Council until the day before adjournment. J. P. Clough, president of the Council and sympathetic to the Hailey interests, tried to help them by declaring the session would officially end at midnight on the sixtieth day of the session. Sixty days was the maximum session permitted under federal statute, and the sooner the deadline arrived, the better the chances of survival for Alturas County. Filibuster continued through the evening and at the stroke of midnight Clough hammered the gavel down and declared the Council adjourned *sine die* without taking a vote on the omnibus bill. Clough left the chambers with Brigham, Campbell and Perkins. However, a quorum of seven remained in the Council chambers. They proceeded to elect S. F. Taylor president *pro tem* and passed the omnibus bill by a 7 to 0 vote. A similar thing happened with other bills in the House after Speaker Burkhart adjourned at midnight and left. These irregular proceedings earned this legislative session a reputation as Idaho's most notorious "rump" session.

When word reached Mountain Home a huge sagebrush pile was fired to light up the newborn Elmore County. But the tenacious Alturas partisans were unwilling to acknowledge the birth. Edward L. Curtis, who served both as clerk of the Council and secretary of state, sided with the division advocates. He certified as official a copy of the Council journal which had three pages and Clough's adjournment cut from it. The actions taken after Clough left were recorded, and the journal was signed by the president *pro tem* instead of Clough. When Curtis refused Clough's demand to correct the journal, Clough filed an original action in the territorial supreme court seeking a writ of mandamus ordering Curtis to produce and correct the journal. Burkhart pursued a similar course with respect to the House journal.

On March 11, just over one month after the session adjourned, the Idaho supreme court denied Clough and Burkhart their writs of mandamus in a 2 to 1 decision.[55]

Chief Justice Weir, with Logan concurring, held the courts were bound to accept the legislative journals as certified and could not go behind them to inquire into what was actually done. Secretary Curtis was bound by statute to accept the journals forwarded by the clerks, and the court did not have the power to expand his duties and compel him to accept a journal offered by one who was only a member of the body. If there were improprieties or delinquencies, the people would act as the final tribunal and apply the corrective at the ballot box. Justice Berry dissented, arguing the journals were on their face improper because the session had extended beyond the sixty days allowed by Congress.

Clough and Burkhart immediately appealed to the United States Supreme Court. In the meantime there was great confusion and antagonism in Alturas County, or Elmore, Logan and Alturas counties. Was Alturas County to pay to maintain prisoners and hospital patients from the Elmore and Logan regions? The new officers of Elmore and Logan were served restraining papers by the Alturas sheriff. Elmore responded by arresting Alturas Deputy Sheriff John E. Harris when he tried to summons jurors at Rocky Bar.

The organizers of the Idaho Constitutional Convention recognized the validity of the division statute and apportioned three delegates to both Logan and Elmore counties. Alturas County had six delegates. Had Alturas not been divided it would have been represented by twelve delegates, three more than Ada County's nine, which would have been the next largest delegation.

Because of these circumstances, the Hailey forces were fighting for their lives at the constitutional convention. In an irony that could only be produced by politics, James Beatty argued for striking the section from the constitution so that the legislature that had treated Hailey with such injustice the session before would have the power to give back the life it had taken.

Beatty explained Alturas's needs. "I say in all frankness, we do expect and hope that some future legislation will remedy this evil, will grant us some relief, at least, and put us upon some respectable basis by which we can exist as a county, instead of going out of existence or going into bankruptcy. And I am not talking for mere talk. I say, that unless relief of that kind is granted, the territory of Idaho has one county that will be virtually bankrupt,[56] and we cannot help ourselves" (p. 1783).

Lycurgus Vineyard (D-Alturas), also from Hailey, supported Beatty and revealed Alturas hoped to get legislation taking from Logan and annexing to Alturas "that immense stretch to the west of Hailey known as Camas prairie, . . . a farming community, generally understood to be in sympathy with old Alturas county" (p. 1789).

Beatty's charges against the 1888 legislature were strong, and his rhetoric sharp. Several delegates who had served in that legislature and the delegates from Elmore and Logan counties took the floor of the convention to defend themselves, and to fire countercharges at Beatty. These debates give some indication of what it must have been like in the last days of the 1888 legislative session.

Alexander Mayhew originally seconded Beatty's motion to strike, but became convinced by Beatty's argument the section should remain. Mayhew was member of the

Council in 1888. He had served on the special committee that considered the division bill, and he was one of the seven who remained to pass the bill after the session had been adjourned by Clough. Mayhew was offended by Beatty's charge of an injustice done by an "infamous legislature."

Mayhew explained to the convention delegates what had really happened. The problem in 1888 was not the legislature in general, but the delegation from Alturas. Two House members of that delegation favored division and two opposed it. One Council member favored division and one opposed it. The division bill that ultimately passed was introduced in both houses by members of the Alturas delegation. He concluded "the dissension and discord in the last legislature was caused by the members from Alturas County" (p. 1786).

His argument then was directed at Beatty in particular. "[I]f I recollect right, the gentleman was here on the outside of that legislature, figuring and working as a lobbyist either to prevent or foster the division. . . . *You* (Mr. Beatty) were the first man who threw the fire-brand into the legislature. *You* (Mr. Beatty) were the first man who introduced this discord and this dissension—" (p. 1786). At this point Mayhew was called to order by the chair and protested bitterly when the chair insisted.

Beatty defended himself, "It is true, I was here, my friend Mayhew, but did very little, and I was an advocate of Elmore county, cutting Elmore county off, and tried for one to avoid this trouble, and finally got disgusted and went home. That is the truth about it" (p. 1795).

Other delegates went beyond defending the 1888 legislature, and made other arguments why the section should remain. Frank P. Cavanah (R-Elmore) accused Alturas of paying "ridiculous salaries. . . . You pay more to your officers than all of Elmore county's salaries—nearly a thousand dollars more." Beatty admitted the salaries were too high but defended them saying "the county commissioners had no other choice or rule to go by but to take the assessment which had been returned [before division], and allow those officers the salaries they were entitled to at the time they were elected" (p. 1788).

John S. Gray (R-Ada) argued in favor of the committee's report, because if the question of dividing counties was not kept out of the legislature, "the legislature amounts to nothing. You commence from the first day you come into the legislature; it is trade here and trade there; stand by me and I will stand by you. Let such be the case, and your legislatures, when they have got through, have amounted to nothing at all" (p. 1785). In an irony that can only be produced in the practice of law, Gray had just four months earilier defended the work of the 1888 legislature and Secretary of State Curtis in the Supreme Court in the actions brought by Clough and Burkhart.

J. S. Whitton (R-Logan) challenged Beatty's argument that Alturas County was overburdened with debt. He pointed to the provisions of the division bill which apportioned the debts of old Alturas to the new counties by a commission of experts. Alturas had refused to cooperate and refused to appoint a commissioner so "it is only the fault of Alturas county that it has not been adjusted" (p. 1788). Beatty claimed no adjustment could be made until the appeal pending before the United States Supreme Court had been decided.[57]

James Reid, who chaired the five-person committee which recommended the local voting provision, defended it. He assured Beatty "when we drew that section, no thought of Alturas ever entered our heads, and it was only after the section was agreed upon that we understood it would affect that county" (p. 1792). He also illustrated the operation of the section with an example from his own county. The legislature had recently annexed a northern part of Nez Perce County to Latah County for school purposes. This section would make division more difficult, "It means, if my friend in Latah county wants to take that country up there from Nez Perce and leave her emasculated, that Nez Perce shall have something to say about it" (p. 1793).

Only two other delegates joined Beatty and Vineyard from Alturas to argue for striking the section. James Shoup wanted to strike because of his own local circumstances. "Where I live in the Pahsimeroi valley, the county line runs right through the center of the valley. The ranches are divided. My own ranch is half in one county and half in the other, and the result is it cannot have any school districts, any roads running across the valley, or anything of that kind" (p. 1794). William Clagett also supported Beatty because he thought the section "cured no evil" (p. 1797). The legislature would have to become involved in calling the special election under the section as it was written and at the same time was deprived of the power to alter county boundaries as necessary from time to time.

Even though few delegates were willing to speak with Beatty, there were many willing to vote for him. On a roll call vote Beatty's motion to strike was narrowly defeated 22 to 24 (p. 1802). Two Alturas delegates, Ballentine and McMahon were absent. Their presence would presumably have produced at least a tie vote, and perhaps a victory if the chair broke the tie by voting in their favor.

The section was taken up for reconsideration the next day, Saturday, August 3, the twenty-sixth day in session (pp. 1874–96). Beatty had not convinced the convention to strike the section, but he had clearly demonstrated the section made new counties in the future impossible. Beatty managed to make his argument again and get another vote on a motion to strike during the reconsideration but again was narrowly defeated, this time 24 to 28. Upon reconsideration, three portions of the section were changed to make it workable. First, the electors qualified to vote were changed from the whole county, which would never approve a division, to those electors living in the area to be cut off. Second, the percentage of vote needed for passage was reduced from two-thirds to majority. Finally, a sentence was added making it clear the section did not apply to the formation of new counties. The power of the ballot box triumphed when the section as reconsidered was adopted. The section remains unchanged to this day.

Like Idaho's territorial legislature and its supreme court, its constitutional convention had handed Alturas County another defeat, its third straight. The fourth came in March 1890 when the United States Supreme Court affirmed the decision of the territorial court in the Clough and Burkhart cases.[58]

Despite these many defeats, the Hailey interests continued their struggle. They pursued their strategy of a legislative solution in the first state legislature, even though James Beatty had not been able to eliminate the section that took the necessary power from the legislature and vested it in the local voters. The first state legislature apparently decided the constitution should not stand in the way of justice, and on March 3, 1891, passed an act creating Alta and Lincoln counties.[59] The new Alta County was the area previously in Alturas County, and the larger half of the area previously in Logan County. The new Lincoln County was composed of what remained of Logan County.

The elected officials of Logan County refused to recognize the new statute and the issue came before the Idaho supreme court for a second time. In a 2 to 1 decision, the court spoiled the brief moment of victory enjoyed by Hailey partisans and held the act was unconstitutional. John T. Morgan wrote the opinion for the majority. Morgan had attended Idaho's Constitutional Convention as a delegate from Bingham County, and he was anxious to vindicate the intention of the delegates. He wrote, "It is evident that the whole intent and object of the act was to cut this body of territory from the county of Logan, and attach it to the county of Alturas. . . . But the constitution says this cannot be done except by a vote of the people."[60]

Despite this setback by the court, the Hailey interests continued to work for a legislative solution. They had no choice. A new statutory scheme to bypass the constitution was suggested, and enacted by the legislature in March 1895. The legislature first passed a statute that abolished Alturas and Logan counties and put all of the region in new Blaine County.[61] Several weeks later another act was passed creating Lincoln County out of Blaine County, with the county seat established at Shoshone.[62] This plan was designed to make it appear the legislature was exercising its power to create new counties, rather than annexing a part of one county to another, which had to be approved by the voters.

By 1895 there had been a change of attitude by Logan County officials for they recognized the new statute, rather than defy it as they had done in 1891. However, there were others who refused to acknowledge the change and once again the matter came before the Idaho supreme court. Apparently, Chief Justice Morgan had also experienced a change of sentiment about the Alturas issue. While reviewing the 1891 statute, he had looked closely at the whole intent and object of the legislature and concluded the constitution had been violated. His attitude toward the 1895 statute was quite different, for he wrote, "[T]he motives that actuated the two houses of the legislature in the passage of these acts, and of the governor in approving of them, cannot in any manner . . . be brought in question."[63] In a unanimous opinion, Morgan held the statutes constitutional.

By this final adjustment, Alturas County, one of the most colorful and important counties on the eve of statehood, passed into Idaho's history. Even though Alturas County became part of the past, Hailey became a part of Idaho's future because of its dogged struggle to remain the county seat of a region large enough to be a viable county. James Beatty left Hailey soon after statehood to begin his long tenure as judge of the federal district court in Idaho. However, those who followed him were finally able to accomplish in the Idaho legislature what he had not been able to do at the constitutional convention.

Notes

1. Hart, I. W., ed. *Proceedings and Debates of the Constitutional Convention of Idaho 1889*. 2 vols. Caldwell: Caxton Printers, Ltd., 1912. These volumes are paginated consecutively, and all page references in the text of this chapter are to them.

2. 26 Stat 217.

3. *McGilvery v. City of Lewiston*, 13 Idaho 338, 90 P. 348 (1907); *Byrns v. City of Moscow*, 21 Idaho 398, 121 P. 1034 (1912); *Elliott v. McCrea*, 23 Idaho 524, 130 P. 785 (1913).

4. *State ex rel. Miller v. State Bd. of Educ.*, 56 Idaho 210, 52 P.2d 141 (1935).

5. *Thomas v. Glindeman*, 33 Idaho 394, 195 P. 92 (1921).

6. *Hickey v. City of Nampa*, 22 Idaho 41, 124 P. 280 (1912).

7. *Corum v. Common School Dist.*, 55 Idaho 725, 47 P.2d 889 (1935).

8. *Independent School Dist. No. 12 v. Manning*, 32 Idaho 512, 185 P. 723 (1919).

9. *Dunbar v. Board of Comrs.*, 5 Idaho 407, 49 P. 409 (1897); *Gem Irrigation Dist.*, 56 Idaho 29, 48 P.2d 1099 (1935).

10. *County of Ada v. Bullen Bridge Co.*, 5 Idaho 79, 47 P. 818 (1896).

11. *McNutt v. Lemhi County*, 12 Idaho 63, 84 P. 1054 (1906).

12. *Bannock County v. C. Bunting & Co.*, 4 Idaho 156, 37 P. 277.

13. *Petrie v. Common School Dist. No. 5*, 44 Idaho 92, 255 P. 318 (1927).

14. *Miller v. City of Buhl*, 48 Idaho 668, 284 P. 843 (1930); *Washington Water Power Co.v. City of Coeur d'Alene*, 9 F.Supp. 263 (D. Idaho 1934).

15. 1949 Idaho Sess Laws 598, J.J.R. No. 9, ratified at the general election in 1950.

16. 1963 Idaho Sess Laws 1149, H.J.R. No. 5, ratified at the general election in 1964.

17. 1966 Idaho Sess Laws (2nd Ex. Sess.) 86, ratified at the general election in 1966.

18. 1967 Idaho Sess Laws 1577, J.J.R. No. 7, ratified at the general election in 1968.

19. 1972 Idaho Sess Laws 1251, J.J.R. No. 73, reatified at the general election in 1972.

20. S.J.R. No. 114 (S.L. 1974, p. 1888), ratified at the general election in 1974.

21. S.J.R. 109 (S.L. 1976, p. 1269), ratified at the general election in 1976.

22. S.J.R. No. 102 (S.L. 1976, p. 978), ratified at the general election in 1978.

23. 1982 Idaho Sess Laws 933, H.J.R. No. 17, ratified at the general election in 1982.

24. 12 Stat 808.

25. Bancroft, Hubert H. *History of Washington, Idaho, and Montana, 1845–1889*. San Francisco: The History Company, 1890. Vol. 31, p. 404.

26. 24 Stat 170.

27. 25 Stat 336.

28. Article III, § 19.

29. Ibid.

30. 26 Stat 111.

31. *Gillesby v. Board of Comm'rs.*, 17 Idaho 586, 107 P. 71 (1910); *Jones v. Power County*, 27 Idaho 656, 150 P. 35 (1915); *Ada County v. Wright*, 60 Idaho 394, 92 P.2d 134 (1939).

32. *Ada County v. Wright*, 60 Idaho 394, 92 P.2d 134 (1939).

33. *Neilson v. Lindstrom*, 68 Idaho 226, 191 P.2d 1009 (1948).

34. *School Dist. No. 25 v. State Tax Comm'n*, 101 Idaho 283, 612 P.2d 126 (1980); *Sun Valley Co. v. City of Sun Valley*, 109 Idaho 424, 708 P.2d 147 (1985); *Twin Falls Clinic & Hosp. Bldg. Corp. v. Hamill*, 103 Idaho 19, 644 P.2d 341 (1982).

35. *Leonardson v. Moon*, 92 Idaho 796, 451 P.2d 542 (1969).

36. *State Water Conservation Bd. v. Enking*, 56 Idaho 722, 58 P.2d 779 (1936); overruled on other grounds, *State Dep't of Parks v. Idaho Dep't of Water Administration*, 96 Idaho 440, 530 S.W.2d 924 (1974) and *Idaho Water Resources Bd. v. Kramer*, 97 Idaho 535, 548 P.2d 35 (1976).

37. *State ex rel. Williams v. Musgrave*, 84 Idaho 77, 370 P.2d 778 (1962).

38. *Board of County Comm'rs v. Idaho Health Facilities Auth.*, 96 Idaho 498, 531 P.2d 588 (1975).

39. *Sabin v. Curtis*, 3 Idaho 662, 32 P. 1130 (1893); *Bannock County v. C. Bunting & Co.*, 4 Idaho 156, 37 P. 277 (1894), overruled on other grounds, *Veatch v. Moscow*, 18 Idaho 313, 109 P. 722 (1910); *Leach v. Nez Perce County*, 24 Idaho 322, 133 P. 926 (1913); *Jones v. Power County*, 27 Idaho 656, 150 P.35 (1915).

40. *Ex parte Crane*, 27 Idaho 671, 151 P. 1006 (1915), aff'd sub nom. *Crane v. Campbell*, 245 U.S. 304, 38 S.Ct. 98, 62 L.Ed. 304 (1917).

41. *Boise City Nat'l Bank v. Boise City*, 15 Idaho 792, 100 P. 93 (1908); *Howard v. Independent School Dist.*, 17 Idaho 537, 106 P. 692 (1910); *Bagley v. Gilbert*, 63 Idaho 494, 122 P.2d 227 (1942); *State v. Romich*, 67 Idaho 229, 176 P.2d 204 (1946).

42. *Ada County v. Wright*, 60 Idaho 394, 92 P.2d 134 (1939).

43. *Nielson v. Lindstrom*, 68 Idaho 226, 191 P.2d 1009 (1948).

44. *State ex rel. Idaho State Park Bd. v. City of Boise*, 95 Idaho 693, 92 P. 995 (1907).

45. *State v. Dolan*, 13 Idaho 693, 92 P. 995 (1907).

46. *Wanke v. Ziebarth Constr. Co.*, 69 Idaho 64, 202 P.2d 384 (1948); *Brock v. City of Boise*, 95 Idaho 630, 516 P.2d 189 (1973).

47. *Sun Valley Co. v. City of Sun Valley*, 109 Idaho 424, 708 P.2d 147 (1985).

48. *Jackson v. Gallet*, 39 Idaho 382, 228 P. 1068 (1924).

49. *In re Ridenbaugh*, 5 Idaho 371, 49 P. 12 (1897).

50. *Peck v. State*, 63 Idaho 375, 120 P.2d 820 (1941).

51. *Board of County Comm'rs v. Swensen*, 80 Idaho 198, 327 P.2d 361 (1958).

52. *Bear Lake County v. Budge*, 9 Idaho 703, 75 P. 614 (1904).

53. Bakken, Gordon. *Rocky Mountain Constitution Making, 1850–1912*. Westport, Greenwood Press, 1987, pp. 37–49.

54. 1863–64 Idaho Sess Laws 628–30. For the story of Alturas and Blaine counties, see Hawley, James H. *History of Idaho: The Gem of the Mountains*. 5 vols. Chicago: S. J. Clarke, 1920. Vol. I, pp. 601–02; 614–17.

55. *Clough v. Curtis*, 2 Idaho 488 (1889); *Burkhart v. Reed*, 2 Idaho 470 (1889).

56. The debt of Alturas County was somewhere between $290,000 and $325,000. *In re Counties v. County of Alturas*, 4 Idaho 145, 152, 37 P. 349, 350 (1894).

57. Alturas County officials continued to refuse to participate in the allocation long after the appeal was decided by the U.S. Supreme Court. They resisted until finally ordered to participate in May 1894 by the Idaho Supreme Court. Ibid.

58. *Clough v. Curtis*, 134 U.S. 361 (1890).

59. 1890–91 Idaho Sess Laws 120–124.

60. *People v. George*, 3 Idaho 72, 26 P. 983 (1891).

61. 1895 Idaho Sess Laws 31–34.

62. 1895 Idaho Sess Laws 170–74.

63. *Wright v. Kelley*, 4 Idaho 624, 633, 45 P. 565, 567 (1895).

12.
Adoption and Adaptation

1. Ratification

THE IDAHO CONSTITUTIONAL CONVENTION began to wrap up its work on August 2 appointing the committee of ten to prepare an address to the people. Its purpose was introduce the constitution and point out its advantages. The committee included some of the most prominent men of the convention, including president William H. Clagett, William J. McConnell, George Ainslie, James W. Reid, and Frank P. Cavanah (p. 1701).[1]

The address, written by Ainslie, was divided into two parts. The first half stated the complaints of Idaho Territory, much in the same way the Declaration of Independence had listed the grievances of the colonies over one hundred years earlier. The address complained of "no voice" in the selection of local, territorial and national authorities. The people were held "in a state of political vassalage," in direct conflict "with the spirit of republican and democratic institutions." Congress could annul any territorial statute; no great pubic works projects could be undertaken; the Alien Land Act passed by Congress prevented investment of foreign capital within the territory; the school lands were unsold and unoccupied and therefore not making a contribution towards the support of education; and there had been "an abuse of the veto power [by] alien governors" (pp. 2991–92).

Even worse, according to the address, "The most intolerable evil . . . under which we have lived for the past twenty-five years, has been the changing and shifting character of our judicial decisions. . . ." The judicial decisions had been shifting because none of the judges were in Idaho long enough to obtain "even a slight insight into the

laws and customs of the territory," and because, since each district judge also sat on
the territorial supreme court, there was no "independent supreme court" (p. 2092).

The second half of the address was written because "[s]ome objection has been
urged against statehood on the ground that the cost of government will be greatly
increased." The committee of ten projected the following budget for the new state:

Executive Department	$20,220	($22,820)
Judiciary Department	38,220	(45,219)
Legislative Department	15,110	(18,998)
Insane Asylum	20,000	(51,873)
Penitentiary	23,075	(26,000)
Interest on outstanding bonds	10,200	(*)
State University	11,000	(0)
All other	300	(31,539)
TOTAL	$138,125	($196,449)[2]

* no information available

Compared with the actual appropriations of the first legislature, the committee of
ten budget was wildly optimistic. They were twelve percent low on the executive
department and penitentiary, sixteen percent low on the judiciary department and
twenty-one percent low on the legislative department. The legislature made no appropriation to the state university, even though a statewide property tax was established to
create a building fund. However, the legislative expenditure for the insane asylum and
for other items greatly exceeded the projections. Costs of acquiring lands and construction more than doubled the budget for the asylum. The largest miscellaneous
expenditure was $10,000 for Idaho's display at the Columbian Exposition.

The committee of ten projections totaled $138,125, an increase of $53,760 over
the cost of territorial government, which was $84,365 (p. 2093). Despite this increase,
the Committee wrote "it affords us great satisfaction to announce to the taxpayers of
Idaho that the aggregate cost of the state and county governments under the proposed
constitution will be $55,290 *less* annually than under the present territorial government"
(emphasis added). The increase was to be turned into savings "[b]y changing the system of county government now in vogue," to a system "by which officers are to be paid
fees instead of salaries." Sheriffs, auditors, recorders, probate judges, district attorneys,
superintendents of public instruction, and clerks of the district courts were all to be
paid by the fees they charged. The address optimistically claimed, "in many instances
the fees of officers will amount annually to a sum greater than the maximum compensation allowed them," and the excess would go into the treasury for the benefit of the
taxpayers (p. 2094).

School taxes would also be reduced by statehood. Idaho would receive 3,340,000
acres of school lands from the United States, valued at $10 per acre. Twenty-five sec-
tions, or 16,000 acres, would be sold annually, and the interest earned on the proceeds
of the sales would go to reduce school taxes. In ten years, this annual sum would be

$96,000. In addition, the lands sold would be immediately subject to taxation. Idaho would get an additional 668,160 acres to provide a location and support for a university, penitentiary, agricultural college, scientific school, normal school, charitable institutions, and public buildings.

The address concluded by arguing the new constitution had a broad base of support. The convention had been "in no sense a partisan one," since both political parties were represented by delegates from every county. "This happy combination of political forces was reflected in the spirit which at every stage of its deliberations animated the convention." Every material, industrial and professional interest was represented, and "[t]he business and tax-paying portion of our people was especially prominent and watchful of every interest of vital concern." The new constitution was "a conservatively progressive one,"[3] which would, "cause an immediate and wonderful increase in population, and in the wealth and happiness of the people" (p. 2095).

George Ainslie, author of the address, and the most prominent of the several delegates who had been in Idaho since the creation of the territory, closed with the territorial pioneers' sentiments. "For a quarter of a century the pioneers of Idaho have been patiently laying the foundations of the future state. They have at all times upheld the power and dignity of the nation. . . . They have partly redeemed the wilderness which they found, and by their heroic sacrifices paved the way for the higher civilization upon which they are entering. . . . and long to be again restored to the full rights of citizenship under the constitution of the United States" (p. 2095).

While the committee of ten made an eloquent argument supporting the constitution, neither it nor the convention itself provided for an election to ratify it.[4] Just as there was no congressional or territorial legislative authority or money for the convention, there was no authority or money for such an election.

On October 2, 1889, Governor Shoup issued a proclamation calling for an election on November 5, in much the same manner as he had called for the convention itself. Governor Shoup's proclamation stated the county commissioners should provide resources to conduct the election. Some opponents of the constitution were unwilling to accept the authority of the proclamation. "Governor Shoup . . . knows that the county commissioners have no legal authority to appropriate one dollar of the people's money for the purpose of defraying the expense of an election wholly unauthorized by law."[5] Logan, Alturas and Cassia counties did not appoint the necessary officials until the last minute, while Ada, Washington, Owyhee, Elmore, Oneida, Bingham, and Kootenai counties moved quickly to organize an election.

It took some time to organize the ratification election, but the ratification debate began as soon as the convention adjourned. The "boomers," or strong statehood supporters, organized a campaign of newspaper support headed by John R. French and the *Idaho Daily Statesman*. Outside the Mormon communities, the only papers in the south to oppose the constitution were the *Idaho Democrat* (Boise), *Ketchum Keystone*, and *Wood River News Miner*. Aaron Parker's *Idaho County Free Press* in Grangeville was the only northern paper opposed, even though the *Palouse News* from Washington spoke against it on behalf of die-hard annexationists.

The boomers built their promotion for statehood around the promise of development. They estimated that three-quarters of Idaho's mines were idle, lying undeveloped for lack of capital. Foreign capital was prohibited from investment by the Alien Land Act which Congress had passed some years earlier to prevent foreign purchase of large tracts of grazing lands in the western territories. Statehood offered a way to avoid the Alien Land Act restrictions. Statehood would also give Idaho two senators and a representative in Congress, who could work on statutes of special concern to Idaho. Idaho's mining interests were anxious for Congress to issue paper money (silver certificates), backed by silver bullion, the most abundant mineral in the territory. They also wanted Congress to restrict importation of Mexican lead in order to relieve a depression in prices. Southern Idaho wanted Congress to finance the large irrigation projects on the Snake River that were essential to stimulate growth on the plains. The *Idaho Daily Statesman* stated every congressman from Idaho should know there was "such a public sentiment here at home as will compel every man, by whatever party elected, to vote first, last, and all the time, for IRRIGATION, SILVER and LEAD, the three pillars of Idaho'[s] prosperity."[6]

There was no general territory-wide organization opposing the constitution. There were, however, regional pockets of resistance. Few people actually opposed statehood, but some did oppose particular aspects of the constitution. The Mormon communities objected to the constitutional test oath, which continued their disfranchisement. After the convention, Aaron Parker continued to object that the test oath disfranchised worthy, law-abiding citizens, and their unborn descendants, and said the convention delegates had been guilty of inaugurating "a regime of restricted suffrage, with themselves as the censors and arbiters of who is and who is not qualified to vote."[7]

Alturas County had gotten little relief at the convention from the division done in the last territorial legislature and as a result had little enthusiasm for its work. Annexationists in the north still preferred gaining statehood by joining Washington rather than southern Idaho. There were Democrats in Boise who were opposed because the boomers and the convention were controlled by Republicans, and many new political offices would be filled by Republicans. Stockmen were concerned about losing the public range to new settlers and the fences that were sure to appear soon after statehood.

These dissidents criticized numerous sections of the proposed constitution. Aaron Parker used his *Idaho County Free Press* to continue his arguments against the private takings clause, and against the legislative apportionment provisions. Parker argued each county should have a senator, and justly complained that Idaho County had to share a senator with Nez Perce County, and was also underrepresented in the House, while counties of similar population and property enjoyed their own representatives in each house of the legislature. The judiciary was criticized because of the eight judgeships created and the article on county organization was criticized for making salaries of county officers payable from fees rather than tax revenues.

Opponents also argued Idaho did not have a large enough population to become a state or pay the costs of running a state government. Congress had specified that

60,000 people were necessary for statehood in the Northwest Ordinance of 1787. While this figure was often referred to as the standard, Illinois, Colorado, and Oregon had all been admitted with fewer. As a result, there was some uncertainty about how many people were actually needed. There was even more uncertainty about how many people there were in the territory. The 1880 census counted 32,610.[8] The boomers claimed there were 100,000 by 1889. Governor Shoup estimated 113,777 when stating the argument for admission in his annual report to Congress. The debate was ultimately resolved one year later by the 1890 census which reported Idaho was home to 84,385 residents.[9]

As the ratification election approached, it became apparent support for the constitution and statehood was overwhelming. Organizers then became concerned about apathy and a low voter turnout, which would not make a good showing to Congress. Democratic and Republican state committees prepared and distributed guidelines for conducting the election to be used by local leaders in counties where the commissioners had failed to act. Meetings were organized around the state to stimulate interest. Many convention delegates spoke at these meetings, including John T. Morgan, I. N. Coston, Charles A. Clark, Weldon B. Heyburn, Willis Sweet, William J. McConnell, Alexander E. Mayhew, William H. Clagett and James W. Reid.

When the ratification election was finally held on November 5, both the procedure and the turnout were irregular. The outcome was clear, however, as the constitution was approved by a 7 to 1 margin, with 12,333 voters in favor and 1,776 voters against.

Some important precincts in the territory, like Genesee in Latah County, did not open the polls. In many others, polls were opened by community leaders selected on election day by the voters. At most polls, every male resident of age was encouraged to vote. One observer commented, "The system of conducting the polls was of such an informal character that anything wearing hide, hair, feathers or boots could vote, and the result is such that no one believes half the returns sent in."[10]

The results varied as much from county to county as the election process itself.[11] Latah distinguished itself during the election as one of the counties most in favor of the constitution. It cast a total of 2,640 votes, more than 600 votes larger than any other county. In addition, ninety-five per cent of the Latah votes favored the constitution. There was strong support in other counties too. In Shoshone County, ninety-seven per cent of the 1,862 votes favored the constitution, while in Kootenai county ninety-eight percent of the 1,056 voters were in favor. In Ada County seventy-five percent of the 1,774 votes were in favor. These counties cast a higher percentage of their votes for the constitution than other counties, and their total votes were also high when compared to the 1888 general election.[12]

While a majority favored the constitution in every county, the total votes were low and the margin of passage narrow in some. Only 83 votes were cast in Bear Lake County, the heart of Mormon country, and only fifty-three percent of them favored the constitution. Only 215 votes were cast in Nez Perce County with fifty-two percent voting yes. Annexationist sentiment was strongest here, and it appears many voters stayed away from the polls since 635 votes had been cast in 1888. Fifty-eight percent of the 222 Cassia County votes were yes while in Idaho County, home of Aaron Parker, one of the constitution's strongest critics, fifty-nine percent - 199 voters - were in favor. The Mount Idaho precinct in Idaho County cast 33 votes in favor and 33 opposed, and noted at the bottom of the return was this summary assessment of local sentiment, "This mossback outfit is a standoff."[13]

While the boomers were pleased that eighty-seven percent of the votes cast favored the constitution, and statehood, they were a little disappointed that only 14,109 votes had been cast. The vote total for the 1888 territorial delegate election had been 16,053. Nevertheless, the drama of Idaho's statehood movement shifted to Congress, and the lead role was played by Fred T. Dubois.

2. Admission

FRED T.DUBOIS[14] was born in 1851 into an Illinois family with many political friends, including Abraham Lincoln. He and his brother graduated from Yale together in 1872 and came to Idaho together in 1880 to work at the Fort Hall Agency. Fred was appointed U.S. marshal (and ex-officio warden of the penitentiary) for Idaho in 1882. He was an ardent anti-Mormon and was active in prosecuting them under the Edmunds Act. By 1886 he was able to organize a successful campaign for territorial representative to Congress, and in 1888 won reelection.[15]

The ratification vote had been important, but the vote in Congress on Idaho's statehood bill was critical. Dubois was expected to get approval, and if successful was to rewarded by election as Idaho's first full-term Senator.[16] The bill would have to be reported favorably by both House and Senate committees on the territories, and be supported by a majority vote in both the House and Senate. Dubois expected the most difficulty from Democrats in the House. He had several strategies to overcome their objections. The bill would be first introduced in the Senate, where approval was more likely. Dubois himself would secure appointment to the House committee on territories so he would have an effective position from which to work. President Harrison was asked to deliver a special message to Congress calling for approval of Idaho's statehood bill.

Dubois worked diligently to implement his strategies. He met with important committee members in both houses, and was assured of their support. He argued Idaho's cause with great enthusiasm before the committees, and to President Harrison. He secured appointment to the House committee on territories. All was going well, when unexpected opposition suddenly appeared. Idaho was just one of many territories seeking statehood in the Fifty-first Congress. Frederick Jackson Turner has called our attention to the importance of 1890 and the close of the American frontier.[17] But closing the frontier was just half the story. The other half was making the frontier territories into states. Four new states had been admitted before Dubois reached Washington: North and South Dakota, Montana and Washington. Like Idaho, these territories held constitutional conventions in the summer of 1889. However, unlike Idaho, their paths to statehood had been cleared because Congress had authorized their conventions and petitions in an Omnibus Act passed in February 1889. As a result, Idaho found itself allied with Wyoming, which also had created a constitution without legislative or congressional authority during the summer of 1889.

Democrats, especially in the House, became concerned about the number of Republican states suddenly being admitted. Their strategy was to condition admission of Idaho and Wyoming upon simultaneous admission of two Democratic territories, New Mexico and Arizona. They also sought to delay consideration of Idaho's admission. The first delay was the wait for the Supreme Court opinion in *Davis v. Beason*. Samuel D. Davis was a member of the Mormon church who took the test oath and voted in the 1888 general elections. He was indicted for perjury in 1889, tried, convicted, and sentenced to a jail term. The territorial supreme court affirmed the conviction, and Davis appealed to the United States Supreme Court, contending he had committed no crime, and that the test oath violated the First Amendment of the U.S. Constitution.

If the Supreme Court did not affirm the conviction, Idaho's ambition for statehood was ended. Dubois wrote to Aaron F. Parker, referring to the Supreme Court: "If their decision is adverse, of course we are done. If not, it ends all objection on that score. I shall not ask for statehood unless we can keep the Mormons out of our politics. In fact I would oppose it."[18]

On December 8, 1889, Senator Orville H. Platt (R-Conn.) introduced Idaho's first admission bill. It was referred to the committee on territories, which heard arguments in support of the bill from Dubois on December 16 and 18. Dubois also introduced his own statehood bill in the House on the 18th. It was becoming apparent that Democratic opposition to statehood was developing, under the leadership of Congressman William H. Springer of Illinois. Most of the Democratic members of the Senate Territorial Committee did not attend a meeting to consider Idaho on December 27. Alexander Mayhew and other Idaho Democrats lobbied their national leaders in an attempt to change their opposition.

A January 6 Senate territorial committee hearing was postponed for a week in hopes the *Davis* opinion would be issued, and Congressman Springer introduced an omnibus bill calling for admission of Wyoming, Idaho, New Mexico and Arizona. On January 13, Isaac S. Struble from Iowa introduced another Idaho statehood bill in the House. On the same day, Mormon spokesmen appeared before the Senate territorial committee to oppose Idaho's statehood. While the Idaho Convention had denied the Mormons a right to speak, the Democrats in Congress wanted to hear them out. J. W. Wilson, the attorney representing Davis in his appeal to the Supreme Court, and William Budge, a prominent Mormon bishop, argued Idaho should not be admitted because it lacked sufficient population, proposed to pay its state officials extravagant salaries, and disfranchised Mormons. Dubois made a detailed rebuttal, and Governor Shoup and ex-Governor Stevenson also spoke in favor of statehood. Bishop Budge spoke before the Senate committee again on the 14th, and again Dubois offered a rebuttal.

Similar debates took place before the House committee on territories. And in both committees Mormon arguments, Democratic opposition, and the pending decision in *Davis* delayed a decision on Idaho's fate. That decision came on February 3, 1890, with Justice Field affirming Davis's conviction. He wrote, "Laws are made for the government of actions, and while they can not interfere with mere religious belief and opinions they may with practices. . . . requiring every voter to take an oath that he does not belong to an order that advises a disregard of the criminal law of the Territory, is not open to any valid legal objection . . . "[19]

The *Davis* opinion was a definitive rebuttal of the Mormon contentions that Idaho's proposed constitution infringed upon individual religious freedoms. Final arguments were then heard in both the Senate and House committees. The Senate committee on territories reported favorably on Idaho's statehood bill on February 18. Congressman Springer continued to support his omnibus bill in the House committee, until a compromise was worked out. It was finally agreed that each of the four proposed territories would be taken up in the order originally listed. The territories were to be discussed without interruption until a decision was reached, and Springer and the Democrats agreed not to filibuster or otherwise impede discussion.

In the meantime, Dubois had secured passage of a House resolution which called for taking up consideration of the proposed new states at any time, with preference over other items on the calendar. Once the compromise had been reached in committee, the bills soon came onto the floor of the House. The Wyoming bill passed on March 26, 139 in favor and 127 opposed. On April 2, the Idaho bill was taken up. George W. Dorsey (R-Nebraska), Dubois, and Marcus A. Smith (D-Arizona) spoke in favor of admission. Charles H. Mansur (D-Missouri), J. Logan Chipman (D-Michigan) and William C. Oates (D-Alabama) objected, contending that while states could make bigamy and polygamy crimes, the Idaho Constitution went too far in infringing upon the natural right of suffrage that belonged to every citizen.

The debate was carried over onto April 3, and became more acrimonious. John D. Stewart (D-Georgia) accused Springer of having earlier supported the Edmunds Act and then reversing his position. Charles R. Buckalew (Pennsylvania) defended Springer, and argued there was a fundamental difference between the Edmunds Act and Idaho's Constitution. Springer also defended himself, and attacked Idaho's Constitution because there was no enabling statute authorizing the convention and because Idaho's legislative apportionment was "the most stupendous fraud of the kind that I have ever seen. . . . In this constitution the Republican leaders have so gerrymandered the districts . . . as to perpetuate the power of the Republican party in that State indefinitely."[20]

So the debate continued, mostly concerning the Mormon question. When the vote was finally taken, 129 favored Idaho's admission while only 1 voted against. Sixty-seven of the Democrats present abstained. Springer and others on the House committee had written a minority report favoring the four-state Omnibus Bill without consulting other members of the House who had already assured Idaho's promoters they would favor admission. Rather than embarrass Springer's leadership by voting against him, Democrats decided not to vote at all. Ironically, even though Dubois correctly anticipated the strongest opposition would come from the House, the House was first to pass his bill.

The House bill reached the Senate on April 5, but it was tabled because silver, and not statehood, had the highest priority on the Senate calendar. For two months the Senate debated monetary policy and the silver question, and when June arrived Dubois and others became concerned the Senate would adjourn and Idaho would be denied statehood at the last minute. Finally, on June 27, the Senate approved the Wyoming bill 29 to 18. Three days later the Idaho bill was taken up. Shelby N. Cullom (Illinois) the bill's strongest supporter, and Zebulon B. Vance (North Carolina) the strongest opposition voice. For the most part, they repeated the debates that had already taken place in the House and in the two committees. Similarly, the final Senate vote resembled previous votes on the question. The support for Idaho was clearly there, and admission was granted without a roll call vote.

Dubois wanted to have President Harrison sign the bill on July 4. However, when he found out that would delay adding Idaho's star for a whole year, he arranged to have it signed on July 3. To announce the happy moment of statehood, Dubois immediately telegraphed to Idaho: "Turn the Eagle Loose."

3. Amendments

IDAHO'S FOUNDERS WERE CAREFUL in Article XX to provide Idaho citizens with two methods of changing their constitution. Sections 1 and 2 provide for amendments, while §§ 3 and 4 provide for revisions.

Under § 1, amendments may be proposed in either house of the legislature. If two-thirds of both houses agree to submit the amendment to the people, an election is held. If a majority of the electors ratify the amendment, it becomes part of the constitution. Section 2 requires that all amendments be submitted separately on the ballot so that voters can vote on each independently.

These amendment procedures have been used often in Idaho's first one hundred years. They have even been used to amend themselves. The original Section 1 required the legislature to conduct the ratification election on any proposed amendment, and instructed it to publish the amendment for six consecutive weeks in at least one paper of general circulation in each county. In 1974 the section was amended to require publication at least three times in every paper qualified to publish legal notices and to require a statement of the arguments proposing and opposing the amendment.[21]

Idaho citizens ratified their first amendment in 1894, when Article XVIII, § 6, providing for county officers, was changed to create an independent county superintendent of public instruction, rather than have the probate judge serve as ex-officio superintendent as provided in the original section.[22] They ratified their most recent amendment in 1988 when the prohibition of lotteries in Article III, § 20 of the original constitution was repealed, and a state-operated lottery was authorized.[23]

Idaho's Constitution has been amended one hundred eight times during its first one hundred years.[24] The legislature has always provided for ratification elections to be held in conjunction with even-numbered, biennial general elections. Since statehood, thirty-seven general elections have produced amendments, and only eleven opportunities have not. The longest period without an amendment was from 1922 through 1926. The longest run of consecutive amendments was the thirteen elections between 1960 and 1984. Seventeen amendments were passed between 1910 and 1920, more than in any other decade. Amendments have tended to come in pairs. Two amendments have been passed in twelve elections, while one and three amendments have been passed in eight elections, four amendments passed in five elections, and five amendments passed in two elections.

Idaho citizens have changed their constitution dramatically in two elections by passing eight amendments at one time. Demands for popular government in 1912 ratified amendments to: create the referendum to permit the people to approve or reject any legislative act; to create the initiative so the people could pass legislation; to make membership on the Board of Education subject to legislative control; to make all state officers subject to recall election; to make the county treasurer rather than the assessor the tax collector; to relax debt limitations on the state government; to permit the use of convict labor; and to guarantee each county the senator the constitutional convention had denied.[25]

Eight amendments were also passed in 1982. Unlike 1912, when all eight amendments related to a common political movement, the demand for more popular government, the 1982 amendments changed unrelated sections in many parts of the constitution. Amendments provided for election of the chief justice of the supreme court by the other justices; removed the language meant to legitimize the Mormon test oath in the original constitution; deleted the requirement for cumulative voting of corporate stock; permitted waiver of a jury trial in all criminal cases; reduced the voting age to eighteen; extended county prosecutor's terms to four years; authorized nonrecourse revenue bonds approved by the legislature; and required that state lands be managed for maximum long-term financial return.

Not only have the constitution's amendment sections been used to change the constitution, they have been litigated often. On two occasions, the supreme court has invalidated amendments passed by the electors. In 1909 the court struck down an amendment that made a number of changes in the judiciary department, including raising the salaries and reshaping the district courts and their jurisdictions.[26] The amendment was void because it involved separate amendments and was not submitted properly to permit separate ballots, and because the ballots did not state the salary was being raised as called for in the legislation. In 1929 the court invalidated an amendment extending the term of elected state officials to four years because the ballot stated the term was to be "limited to four years" instead of "four years."[27] A number of other complaints about the validity of the process of amending have reached the supreme court; but in each instance the validity of the amendment was sustained.[28]

4. Revision

EVEN THOUGH THE IDAHO CONSTITUTION has often been amended, it has never been revised. Article XX, § 3 provides that when two-thirds of both houses deem it necessary to revise the constitution, they may submit the question of calling a convention to the electors. If a majority of the electors vote for a convention, the legislature is authorized at its next session to organize a convention which will have, at a minimum, twice as many delegates as there are in the most numerous branch of the legislature.

Attempts to revise Idaho's Constitution have been made. In 1965, during the diamond anniversary of the state, an effort to recreate the constitution was launched by the legislature. Five years later when the new constitution was put to a vote, Idaho citizens soundly rejected it and in effect, reratified the 1890 document.

In the early 1960s many states were revising and modernizing their constitutions. The spirit of reform made its way into Idaho, and the League of Women Voters and others began to study the constitution and make recommendations for change. The pressure continued to build and in 1964, and again in 1965, Governor Robert E. Smylie recommended to the legislature that a constitutional convention be called under Article XX, § 3, for the purpose of writing a revision. He said the constitution was "filled with cobwebs of bigotry and suspicion and restraint that are not useful to the people in the conduct of this, their government." He complained, "There are so many restrictions in the document that it sometimes seems more to resemble the results of a tangled skein of political intrigue, rather than the tablets of law on which a government is built." (Of course the constitution was the result of some political intrigue, and the purpose of this book has been to unravel part of the tangled skein.) Governor Smylie warned, "If we are to stay the hand of centralized government then our governmental institutions at the local level need to be strong and effective." Despite this broad call for reform, Governor Smylie mentioned just two specific items. He encouraged adoption of an amendment that would create "a strong, independent action agency" that could "move effectively to protect, conserve and promote in every way the utilization of both the quality and the quantity of Idaho's priceless water resources," and he was in favor of extending the term of office for county sheriffs, and perhaps other county officers, from two to four years, because it would have a stabilizing influence.[29]

The legislature responded to Governor Smylie's call and issued a call for a convention to "conduct a thorough study and review" and to "consider and adopt proposed revisions or amendments to the constitution." It fixed the number of delegates at twice the number in the Idaho House of Representatives, and called for a nonpartisan election of delegates. The convention was to convene within fourteen months of the election at which the electors approved of it, at a time and place specified by the governor, and was to remain in session no longer than sixty days.[30]

The legislature also created a fifteen-member Idaho Commission on Constitutional Revision, which was instructed to "conduct a thorough study and review of the constitution," to hold hearings and do research, and to "make recommendations for proposed revisions or amendments." The commission was also to organize the convention in the event the electors approved its calling. Five members of the commission were to be appointed by the governor, five by the chief justice of the supreme court and five by the legislative council.[31]

A number of prominent citizens were appointed to the constitution revision commission, and as with the original convention delegates, lawyers played a prominent role. Appointed from the legal community were Raymond L. Givens (Boise) who served as chair, Carl Burke (Boise), Russell Randall (Lewiston), James E. Schiller (Nampa), Judge Lloyd J. Webb (Burley), Robert C. Strom (Craigmont) and State Senator James A. McClure (Payette). Other commission members were Mrs. Eugene H. Smith (Idaho Falls) who served as vicechair; state senators Don G. Frederickson (Gooding) and Perry Swisher (Pocatello); state representatives Orval Hansen (Idaho Falls) and Darrell Manning (Pocatello); Douglas D. Kramer (Twin Falls); Dr. Boyd A. Martin (Moscow); and Dr. Frank Seeley (Pocatello).[32]

The commission began its work with addresses by Governor Smylie and Chief Justice McQuade at the organization meeting on June 24, 1965. It divided into three committees: executive, legislative, and judicial, assigning each existing article to a committee.[33] As the commission's work progressed it became apparent that many of the articles were not so objectionable. At the organizational meeting, the entire constitution was read, and the articles classified into those that needed change, those that needed study, and those that needed no change. There appeared to be limited support for a broad revision, but some enthusiasm for revising particular articles.

However, there was no efficient way under the existing constitution to revise it article by article. Section 1 of Article XX provided for amendments, but § 2 required that each section be voted on separately. Piecemeal voting would inevitably lead to piecemeal revision and almost certainly produce a document that was less, not more, satisfactory. Section 3 of Article XX provided for revision but seemed to require a constitutional convention where the entire document, rather than particular articles, would be subject to change.

Reformers sought to find a solution to this problem by amending Article XX to authorize article by article amendments. Article V, providing for the judiciary department, was perhaps the article most often targeted for revision. Even before the creation of the constitution revision commission the legislative council had been authorized to study and make recommendations for judicial reform. Even though the judiciary sub-committee of the commission and the council committee met and consulted, the commission announced its own proposed revisions in its 1966 report.[34] Upon the recommendation of the revision commission, the 1967 legislature voted to ask the electors whether Article XX, § 2 should be amended to read, " . . . if any proposed amendment is submitted to the legislature by a duly authorized constitutional Revision Commission . . . it may embrace as one question any or all subjects contained within any Article of the Constitution and related subjects within any other Articles . . . ."[35] The Idaho voters soundly rejected the idea. In retrospect, this vote was a clear signal of the citizens' ultimate attitude towards revision. Having been denied the authority to amend article by article, the commission continued to work on a general revision. Studies were conducted and committee meetings held every three months. Drafts were written and released, and public hearings held, and then revisions and adjustments made. The commission's final draft was completed in the fall of 1969, and sent to the legislature which conducted hearings on every article and made several important changes.

Finally, the legislature produced a final draft. It liked the draft so much, in fact, it did not want to refer it to a convention for further revision as called for by its 1965 statute. Instead, the legislature passed a bill amending the 1965 statute by removing the call for a constitutional convention.[36] However, Governor Samuelson vetoed it. The legislature responded with a joint resolution declaring, "The Legislature of the state of Idaho does not deem it necessary to call a Constitutional Convention for the purpose of submitting a revised Constitution to the electors . . ." The resolution also put the entire revised constitution on the November ballot.[37]

The power of the legislature to submit a revision without a convention was challenged when Raymond L. Smith filed suit against Secretary of State Pete T. Cenarrusa seeking a declaratory judgment that the election was unconstitutional and an order enjoining it. The district court ordered the judgment requested, and Cenarrusa appealed. On September 9, just two months before the election, a majority of three members of the supreme court issued an opinion reversing the lower court. The two remaining justices filed a dissent one month later.

Justice Shephard wrote the opinion for the majority, and concluded § 3 of Article XX merely set out one way, not the exclusive way, of revising the constitution. Justice Shephard put great emphasis upon Article I, § 2, which provides, "All political power is inherent in the people," and goes on to guarantee the right of the people to "alter, reform or abolish" the government when they deem it necessary. He also emphasized "the fundamental concept of our republican and representative form of government wherein the legislative branch of government is elected by the people to represent them and put forward their desires and needs in the form of legislative action." Since state constitutions are restrictions on power, rather than grants of it, and since Article III on the legislative department stated no applicable restraints, Justice Shephard reasoned that the legislature could submit the revised constitution without calling a convention.[38]

Chief Justice McQuade dissented, arguing a convention was the only permissible way of revision. He thought the inherent power of the legislature, which could be exercised unless explicitly restrained in the constitution, existed only "in the area of *legislative action*" and that the "area of *constitutional amendment* or *revision* is not an *ordinary* legislative action." He wrote, "The grant of legislative power in the constitution did not transfer from the people to the legislature all the legislative power inhering in the former," and concluded that the requirement of a convention was a fundamental check on the legislature that was "being set aside in the name of expediency and by means of tenuous interpretation."[39]

With the *Smith* case resolved, and the legislature able to submit a revision without calling a convention, attention turned to the merits of the commission's proposed constitution. It now became important to ask what changes had been made and why. The chairman of the commission, retired Supreme Court Justice Raymond L. Givens summarized the commission's answers. He identified three important changes. The first was the "short ballot," which was favored by "a universal tendency throughout the United States" and which accomplished the goal of "solidifying executive responsibility." Under the short ballot proposal, the governor and lieutenant governor would be elected from the same party, and the attorney general, comptroller, supreme court justices, district court judges and others would be appointed. The second important change was the deletion of those sections that specified and limited the kinds of taxes that could be levied, and the prohibition on extension of the state's credit. The proposed amendments would restrict "taxation to governmental purposes, but otherwise remove[s] the hampering restriction." Finally, explained Chairman Givens, "provision is made for amendment to the constitution by convention as at present or by the legislature when recommended by legislative commission direct to the people."[40]

Chairman Givens did mention one suggested amendment that was not made. He conceded, "There is too much government, both state and national, and that there should be fewer boards, bureaus, departments and elective official with consequent curtailment of state expenditures of money." However, the commission concluded these offices and expenditures had been brought about by the urging of the people. Referring to the public hearings, Chairman Givens said, "it is perfectly apparent that the real complaint on the part of those vociferous dissidents in this area is because they have not been able to elect to the legislature their candidates." Since "nothing in the constitution can insure the election of members of the legislature which will be satisfactory to all of the constituents"[41], no recommendation was made to reduce the number of state offices, or the amount of tax revenues necessary to sustain them.

Judge Henry S. Martin of the seventh judicial district was one of the most outspoken opponents of the commission's revision, and he responded to Chairman Givens. He complained the short ballot would reduce the number of elected state and district officials from thirty-six to two, and deprive the people of "the constitutional right to elect them." Appointing instead of electing all judges would create a "going through the chairs deal" where judges worked their way up through the system and "a good man from the practice would scarcely have a chance." He was also critical of revisions in the judiciary article, which provided for a chief justice appointed for life who presided over all of the state's courts. Appointment of district judges and supervision from above threatened the independence of the local courts. Judge Martin defended Idaho's restrictive constitution, arguing the restrictions "are made to make a state run for a while at least with incompetent or even corrupt legislators, and until the people can do something about it at the next election." The prohibition against extending the state's credit was necessary because "[t]his restriction has kept the State out of much controversy and financial difficulty in the past."

Judge Martin also aroused fears about the security of water rights under the new constitution. He observed that the existing constitution had been approved by Congress in the Idaho Statehood Act, and that the new constitution would not have specific Congressional blessing. He reasoned this "would make quite a difference in federal respect for our water rights." He concluded his criticisms by pointing out that the "thousands of hours of lawyers' and litigants' time and hundreds of thousands of dollars" that had been spent "clearing the meaning" of the present constitution would be wasted by the adoption of the revision.

There was no grassroots political structure animating the entire revision project, or campaigning for it as election day approached. The task of promoting the revision fell upon the revision commission itself. A "Proposed Revision of the Idaho Constitution" showing and explaining the changes section by section was published.[42] Public meetings were organized in communities throughout the state to provide Commission members a forum for explaining and advocating the constitutional changes they thought necessary for a modern Idaho.

The voters were not convinced. They went to the ballot box on November 3, 1970 to reratify their original constitution by casting 220,204 (66%) votes against the revision and a mere 75,138 (34%) votes for it. Only two counties voted in favor. Latah County showed the greatest support for the revision by casting fifty-seven percent of its votes in favor, just as it had shown great support for the 1890 constitution. The revision also received just over fifty percent of the vote in Bannock County, but failed to pass in the remaining forty-two counties. Jefferson County showed itself most strongly opposed by casting eighty-nine percent of its votes against the revision.

The rejection of these general revisions viewed together with the various amendments passed during the first one hundred years of statehood reveal the fundamental themes of Idaho's constitutional heritage. Article I, § 2 declares "All political power is inherent in the people," and Idaho's people have insisted upon guarding and exercising their power, especially the power to elect their state and local government officials. Idaho's founders overwhelmingly voted for electing rather than appointing judges and most other government officers, and the voters have always soundly rejected any attempts at change.

The founders distrusted legislators and elected local officials, especially when it came to spending money. State and county government was put on a cash basis, special indebtedness could be incurred only by special elections that also passed special taxes, and the state's credit could not be pledged. These restrictions have, for the most part, survived to celebrate their one hundredth birthday.

Local, and especially county governments, have always been important units of government. They have an inherent police power, unless preempted by the state. Counties are entitled to representation in the Senate, and their officers and their duties are subject to constitutional, but not legislative, control.

While these principles have survived the test of time, a few parts of the constitution have not. There have been radical changes. The most obvious has been the extension of the right to vote and other rights of citizenship to more residents. Mormons were the first to be welcomed into the new political community, then women, Indians and Chinese.

Despite these exceptions, the story of Idaho's Constitution has been one of stability. Amending the constitution over one hundred times averages an amendment a year, but each amendment deals with only one section, and more amendments have been defeated than passed. In particular, amendments designed to make amendments easier have been defeated. Idahoans apparently have too much reverence for the text to tolerate much revision. As a result, it is safe to predict that when Idaho reaches its bicentennial, its constitution will look very much like it does today.

Notes

1. The other committee members were A. J. Pinkham, Charles M. Hays, Henry Armstrong, S. F. Taylor and Charles A. Clark. Hart, I. W., ed. *Proceedings and Debates of the Constitutional Convention of Idaho 1889*. 2 vols. Caldwell: Caxton Printers, Ltd., 1912. These volumes are paginated consecutively, and all page references in the text of this chapter are to them.

2. The figures in parenthesis are the actual appropriations made by the first legislature. The numbers have been compiled from various acts passed, and arranged for comparison with the committee of the budget. *General Law of The State of Idaho passed at the First Session of the State Legislature*. Boise City, Idaho: Statesman Publishing Company, 1891, pp. 3, 7, 8, 19, 43–5, 164, 171, 189, 215, 229–33, 250.

3. Ainslie emphasized the progressive nature of the constitution again before the ratification election was held. He refuted opposition to the constitution because of increased costs of state government by saying the taxation argument was "the last resort of demagogues and political cranks, who always oppose anything and everything of a progressive nature." *The Elmore Bulletin*, November 2, 1889, p. 2, col. 2.

4. For the general history of the ratification process, see Graff, Leo W. Jr. "The Idaho Statehood Movement, 1888–1890." Master's thesis, University of Idaho, 1960; Wells, Merle W. "The Admission of the State of Idaho." *Secretary of State Twenty-Seventh Biennial Report* 1944:56–57.

5. *Keystone*, 12 Oct. 1889, p. 2., col. 1.

6. *Idaho Daily Statesman*, 21 Sept. 1889, p. 2, col. 1.

7. *Idaho County Free Press*, 27 Sept. 1889, p. 4, cols. 1–2.

8. *Statistics of the Population of the United States at the Tenth Census (June 1, 1880)*. Washington, D.C.: Government Printing Office.

9. The population figure was 88,385 if reservation Indians are included. *Compendium of the Eleventh Census: 1890*, 52 Cong., 1 Sess., House Misc. Doc. No. 340, Part 6. Washington, D.C.: Government Printing Office, 1892, p. 2.

10. *News-Miner*, 15 Nov. 1889, p. 2, col. 2.

11. Official Returns of Idaho Territory, 6 Nov. 1888, State Archives, Idaho State Historical Society:

COUNTY	YES	NO	TOTAL
Ada	1,331	443	1,774
Alturas	290	51	341
Bear Lake	44	39	83

Bingham	716	171	887
Boise	539	80	619
Cassia	130	92	222
Custer	477	33	510
Elmore	95	26	821
Idaho	199	137	336
Kootenai	1,032	24	1,056
Latah	2,523	117	2,640
Lemhi	890	30	920
Logan	334	65	399
Nez Perce	112	103	215
Oneida	280	94	374
Owyhee	388	37	425
Shoshone	1,811	51	1,862
Washington	442	173	615
Totals	12,333	1,776	14,109

12. In the 1888 general election, Shoshone County cast 1,805 votes, Kootenai County 613 votes, and Ada County 1,670 votes.

13. Idaho State Historical Society, Boise, Box 5, File 519.

14. *Autobiography of Fred T. Dubois*. Microfilm No. 47 in University of Idaho Library; Boise: Idaho State Historical Society Microfilm Service, 1959; Graff, Leo W. "The Senatorial Career of Fred T. Dubois of Idaho, 1890–1907." Ph. D. diss., University of Idaho, 1968; Wells, Merle W. "Fred T. Dubois and the Idaho Progressives." *Idaho Yesterdays* 4(Summer 1960):24–31.

15. Dubois received 8,191 votes in 1888; Hawley, the Democratic candidate, 6,404; and Norman Buck 1,458. Official Returns of Idaho Territory, November 6, 1888, State Archives, Idaho State Historical Society, Boise.

16. Dubois was able to win the election for Idaho's first full-term senator, but not without a bitter fight with William H. Clagett. The first Idaho state legislature elected Dubois in December, but in February reversed itself and elected Clagett. Under the U.S. Constitution, the Senate itself has the power to decide who should be seated. Dubois was the favorite, and Clagett the challenger, in the fight that followed. The matter was referred to the priviledges and elections committee, which recommended Dubois be seated. Clagett and his friends had several opportunities to protest the committee report in front of the full Senate but lost in a final vote of 55 to 5. Dubois was defeated for reelection by Henry Heitfeld in 1897. He later became a Democrat and was elected to serve another term in the Senate from 1901–1907.

17. Turner, Frederick Jackson. *The Frontier in American History*. New York: Holt, Rinehart & Winston, 1920.

18. Quoted in the *Ketchum Keystone*, 28 Dec. 1889, p. 2, cols. 3–4.

19. *Davis v. Beason*, 133 U.S. 333, at 334(1890).

20. *Cong. Record*, 51st Cong., 1st Sess., p. 2999.

21. S.J.R. No. 10, (1974 Idaho Sess Laws 1890), ratified on November 5, 1974.

22. Amended as proposed by 1893 Idaho Sess Laws 224, and ratified at the general election in November, 1894.

23. Proposed 1987, 1987 Idaho Sess Laws 801, H.J.R. No. 3, ratified November 8, 1988.

24. The information in this paragraph has been compiled from the Table of Amendments to Constitution of Idaho, 1 Idaho Code pp. 393–99, 1989 Cumulative Pocket Supplement, p. 63.

25. See chapter 5 above on the legislative apportionment debate.

26. *McBee v. Brady*, 15 Idaho 761, 100 P. 97 (1908).

27. *Lane v. Lukens*, 48 Idaho 517, 283 P. 532 (1929).

28. 29. *Green v. State Bd. of Canvassers*, 5 Idaho 130, 47 P. 259 (1896); *Hays v. Hays*, 5 Idaho 154, 47 P. 732 (1897); *Utter v. Moseley*, 16 Idaho 274, 100 P. 1058 (1909); *Mundell v. Swedlund*, 58 Idaho 209, 71 P.2d 434 (1937); *State ex rel. Kinyon v. Enking*, 62 Idaho 649, 115 P.2d 97 (1941); *Keenan v. Price*, 68 Idaho 423, 195 P.2d 662 (1942); *Penrod v. Crowley*, 82 Idaho 511, 356 P.2d 73 (1960); and, *Idaho Water Resource Board v. Kramer*, 97 Idaho 535, 548 P.2d 35 (1976).

29. Governor's Message to the Legislature of Idaho, Thirty-eighth Session, pp. 8–9.

30. H.B. No. 280, 1965 Idaho Sess. Laws 891–95.

31. Ibid., pp. 895–97.

32. Roster of Members, Idaho Constitution Revision Commission, Manuscript Group 105, Box 1, 1965–66 Correspondence File, University of Idaho Special Collections.

33. The executive committee was assigned the articles on the executive department, finance and revenue, public indebtedness and subsidies, education and school lands, public institutions and militia. The legislative committee was assigned the article on the legislative department, suffrage and elections, immigration and labor, live stock, state boundaries, county organizations and apportionment. The judicial committee was assigned the articles on declaration of rights, distribution of powers, the judicial department, public and private corporations, municipal corporations, water rights, amendments and schedule and ordinance.

34. Report of Constitution Revision Commission to His Excellency Don R. Samuelson, Governor of the State of Idaho, and Members of the 39th Session of the Legislature of the State of Idaho, convening January 2, 1967, December 1, 1966, Raymond L. Givens, Chairman. Idaho Constitutional Revision Commission, Manuscript Group 102, Box 1, 1965–66 Correspondence File, University of Idaho Special Collections.

35. S.J.R. No. 3, 1967 Idaho Sess Laws 1569.

36. Senate Bill No. 1599.

37. A Joint Resolution Proposing a Revised Constitution for the State of Idaho, 1970 Idaho Sess Laws 739–68.

38. *Smith v. Cenarrusa*, 93 Idaho 818–25, 475 P.2d 11–18 (1970).

39. Ibid., at 825–29, at 18–22.

40. 7 Idaho L. Rev., pp. 88–89.

41. Ibid., at 88.

42. *Proposed Revision of the Idaho Constitution*. Published by Pete T. Cenarrusa, Secretary of State, Boise, Idaho (1970).

Appendix A.
Roster of Delegates

Ada		
John S. Gray	Rep	
John Lemp	Rep	
William C. Maxey	Rep	
A. B. Moss	Rep	
Edgar Wilson	Rep	
Charles A. Clark	Dem	
Isaac N. Coston	Dem	
Peter J. Pefley	Dem	
Frank Steunenberg	Dem	

Alturas		
J. W. Ballentine	Rep	
James H. Beatty	Rep	
A. J. Pinkham	Rep	
Orlando B. Batten	Dem	
Patrick McMahon	Dem	
Lycurgus Vineyard	Dem	

Bear Lake		
J. L. Underwood	Rep	
James M. Shoup	Rep	
A. J. Pierce	Dem	

Bingham		
Robert Anderson	Dem	
Frank W. Beane	Dem	
H. B. Kinport	Dem	
S. F. Taylor	A.M.-Dem	
H. O. Harkness	Rep	
John T. Morgan	Rep	
William H. Savidge	Rep	

Boise		
George Ainslie	Dem	
J. H. Myer	Dem	
Fred Campbell	Rep	

Cassia		
H. S. Hampton	Rep	
J. W. Lamoreau	Dem	

Custer		
A. J. Crook	Rep	
O. J. Salisbury	Rep	
J. S. Whitton	Rep	
Henry Armstrong	Labor	

Elmore			*Nez Perce*	
Frank P. Cavanah	Dem		J. W. Poe	Dem
Homer Stull	Dem		J. W. Reid	Dem
A. M. Sinnott	Rep		J. M. Howe	Rep
Idaho			*Oneida*	
T. F. Nelson	Dem		John Lewis	A.M.-Rep
Aaron F. Parker	Dem		Drew W. Standrod	Dem
Robert Larimer	Rep			
			Owyhee	
Kootenai			Charles M. Hays	Rep
W. A. Hendryx	Rep		Samuel J. Pritchard	Rep
Henry Melder	Rep		J. I. Crutcher	Dem
Albert Hagan	Dem			
			Shoshone	
Latah			William H. Clagett	Rep
J. W. Brigham	Rep		S. S. Glidden	Rep
William J. McConnell	Rep		W. W. Hammell	Rep
W. D. Robbins	Rep		Weldon B. Heyburn	Rep
Willis Sweet	Rep		A. D. Bevan	Dem
H. B. Blake	Dem		G. W. King	Dem
A. S. Chaney	Dem		Alexander E. Mayhew	Dem
			W. W. Woods	Dem
Lemhi				
N. I. Andrews	Rep		*Washington*	
Thomas Pyeatt	Rep		Frank Harris	Dem
John Hogan	Dem		E. S. Jewell	Dem
			Solomon Hasbrouck	Rep
Logan				
W. C. B. Allen	Rep			

Appendix B.
Committee Rosters

[The first person listed chaired the committee.]

Ways and Means

Sol Hasbrouck	Rep	Washington
Egar Wilson	Rep	Ada
J. M. Shoup	Rep	Custer
J. I. Crutcher	Dem	Owyhee
Frank Harris	Dem	Washington
H. B. Blake	Dem	Latah

Executive Department

George Ainslie	Dem	Boise
I. N. Coston	Dem	Ada
J. W. Poe	Dem	Nez Perce
John S. Gray	Rep	Ada
W. H. Savidge	Rep	Bingham
W. C. B. Allen	Rep	Logan
H. S. Hampton	Rep	Cassia

Legislative Department

John T. Morgan	Rep	Bingham
A. J. Pinkham	Rep	Alturas
W. D. Robbins	Rep	Latah
John Lewis	A.M.-Rep	Oneida
S. S. Glidden	Rep	Shoshone

H. B. Blake	Dem	Latah
P. J. Pefley	Dem	Ada
A. J. Pierce	Dem	Custer
Homer Stull	Dem	Elmore

Judiciary

W. B. Heyburn	Rep	Shoshone
Willis Sweet	Rep	Latah
James H. Beatty	Rep	Alturas
Edgar Wilson	Rep	Ada
J. M. Howe	Rep	Nez Perce
H. S. Hampton	Rep	Cassia
John T. Morgan	Rep	Bingham
W. H. Savidge	Rep	Bingham
A. E. Mayhew	Dem	Shoshone
George Ainslie	Dem	Boise
W. W. Woods	Dem	Shoshone
J. W. Reid	Dem	Nez Perce
Homer Stull	Dem	Elmore
Frank Harris	Dem	Washington
O. B. Batten	Dem	Alturas

Preamble and Bill of Rights

James M. Shoup	Rep	Custer
John T. Morgan	Rep	Bingham
D. W. Standrod	Dem	Oneida
W. W. Hammell	Rep	Shoshone
Charles A. Clark	Dem	Ada
Frank Steunenberg	Dem	Ada

Names, Boundaries and Organization of Counties

J. W. Reid	Dem	Nez Perce
G. W. King	Dem	Shoshone
E. S. Jewell	Dem	Washington
A. J. Crook	Rep	Custer
Sol Hasbrouck	Rep	Washington

Seat of Government, Public Institutions, Buildings and Grounds

Frank P. Cavanah	Dem	Elmore
J. I. Crutcher	Dem	Owyhee
H. B. Kinport	Dem	Bingham
P. M. McMahon	Dem	Alturas
John S. Gray	Rep	Ada

| W. J. McConnell | Rep | Latah |
| H. Melder | Rep | Kootenai |

Education, Schools, and University Lands

O. B. Batten	Dem	Alturas
A. S. Chaney	Dem	Latah
John Hogan	Dem	Lemhi
A. D. Bevan	Dem	Shoshone
James M. Shoup	Rep	Custer
A. J. Pinkham	Rep	Alturas
H. O. Harkness	Rep	Bingham
Henry Armstrong	Rep	Logan
W. J. McConnell	Rep	Latah

Election and Right of Suffrage

James H. Beatty	Rep	Alturas
O. J. Salisbury	Rep	Custer
W. B. Heyburn	Rep	Shoshone
Charles M. Hays	Rep	Owyhee
George Ainslie	Dem	Boise
A. E. Mayhew	Dem	Shoshone
F. W. Beane	Dem	Bingham

Revenue and Finance

Charles M. Hays	Rep	Owyhee
Willis Sweet	Rep	Latah
Sol Hasbrouck	Rep	Washington
A. J. Crook	Rep	Custer
S. L. Glidden	Rep	Shoshone
H. B. Blake	Dem	Latah
John Hogan	Dem	Lemhi
J. W. Lamoreaux	Dem	Cassia
F. Steunenberg	Dem	Ada

Legislative Apportionment

James M. Shoup	Rep	Custer
J. L. Underwood	Rep	Bear Lake
W. B. Heyburn	Rep	Shoshone
J. W. Ballentine	Rep	Alturas
Thomas Pyeatt	Rep	Lemhi
W. A. Hendryx	Rep	Kootenai
J. S. Whitton	Rep	Logan
J. W. Brigham	Rep	Latah

Charles M. Hays	Rep	Owyhee
W. C. Maxey	Rep	Ada
J. H. Myer	Dem	Boise
H. B. Kinport	Dem	Bingham
A. F. Parker	Dem	Idaho
Homer Stull	Dem	Elmore
J. W. Poe	Dem	Nez Perce
J. W. Lamoreaux	Dem	Cassia
D. W. Standrod	Dem	Oneida
E. S. Jewell	Dem	Washington

Militia and Military Affairs

W. W. Hammell	Rep	Shoshone
Thomas Pyeatt	Rep	Lemhi
Fred Campbell	Rep	Boise
A. J. Pinkham	Rep	Alturas
C. A. Clark	Dem	Ada
J. H. Myer	Dem	Boise
John Hogan	Dem	Lemhi

Public and Private Corporations

A. E. Mayhew	Dem	Shoshone
H. B. Kinport	Dem	Bingham
A. S. Chaney	Dem	Latah
A. D. Bevan	Dem	Shoshone
J. W. Ballentine	Rep	Alturas
N. I. Andrews	Rep	Lemhi
W. H. Savidge	Rep	Bingham
S. S. Glidden	Rep	Shoshone
S. J. Pritchard	Rep	Owyhee

Federal Relations

Willis Sweet	Rep	Latah
O. J. Salisbury	Rep	Custer
A. B. Moss	Rep	Ada
T. F. Nelson	Dem	Idaho
Robert Anderson	Dem	Bingham

Municipal Corporations

W. W. Woods	Dem	Shoshone
Albert Hagan	Dem	Kootenai
A. J. Pierce	Dem	Custer
P. J. Pefley	Dem	Ada

L. Vineyard	Dem	Alturas
James H. Beatty	Rep	Alturas
H. O. Harkness	Rep	Bingham
A. J. Crook	Rep	Custer
Edgar Wilson	Rep	Ada

Labor

Henry Armstrong	Labor	Logan
A. M. Sinnott	Rep	Elmore
J. M. Howe	Rep	Nez Perce
W. B. Heyburn	Rep	Shoshone
W. D. Robbins	Rep	Latah
G. W. King	Dem	Shoshone
J. W. Lamoreaux	Dem	Cassia
P. McMahon	Dem	Alturas
P. J. Pefley	Dem	Ada

Schedule

John S. Gray	Rep	Ada
Willis Sweet	Rep	Latah
J. M. Howe	Rep	Nez Perce
W. H. Savidge	Rep	Bingham
H. S. Hampton	Rep	Cassia
W. W. Woods	Dem	Shoshone
F. W. Beane	Dem	Bingham
H. B. Blake	Dem	Latah
L. Vineyard	Dem	Alturas

Manufactures, Agriculture, and Irrigation

Homer Stull	Dem	Elmore
I. N. Coston	Dem	Ada
E. S. Jewell	Dem	Washington
F. W. Beane	Dem	Bingham
S. F. Taylor	A.M-Dem	Bingham
W. C. B. Allen	Rep	Logan
W. J. McConnell	Rep	Latah
H. O. Harkness	Rep	Bingham
A. B. Moss	Rep	Ada

Mines and Mining

J. I. Crutcher	Dem	Owyhee
F. P. Cavanah	Dem	Elmore
A. D. Bevan	Dem	Shoshone

G. W. King	Dem	Shoshone
D. W. Standrod	Dem	Oneida
S. S. Glidden	Rep	Shoshone
J. W. Ballentine	Rep	Alturas
O. J. Salisbury	Rep	Custer
Chas. M. Hays	Rep	Owyhee

Livestock

H. O. Harkness	Rep	Bingham
J. L. Underwood	Rep	Bear Lake
Thomas Pyeatt	Rep	Lemhi
J. H. Myer	Dem	Boise
A. J. Pierce	Dem	Custer

Printing and Binding

W. C. B. Allen	Rep	Logan
Chas. M. Hays	Rep	Owyhee
John Lemp	Rep	Ada
A. M. Sinnott	Rep	Elmore
C. A. Clark	Dem	Ada
A. F. Parker	Dem	Idaho
F. Steunenberg	Dem	Ada

Revision and Enrollment

James H. Beatty	Rep	Alturas
W. W. Hammell	Rep	Shoshone
John T. Morgan	Rep	Bingham
James M. Shoup	Rep	Custer
J. M. Howe	Rep	Nez Perce
Albert Hagen	Dem	Kootenai
L. Vineyard	Dem	Alturas
Frank Harris	Dem	Washington
D. W. Standrod	Dem	Oneida

Salaries of Public Officers

J. W. Poe	Dem	Nez Perce
I. N. Coston	Dem	Ada
J. W. Reid	Dem	Nez Perce
Edgar Wilson	Rep	Ada
Sol Hasbrouck	Rep	Washington

Public Indebtedness and Subsidies

| A. Hagan | Dem | Kootenai |

O. B. Batten	Dem	Alturas
S. F. Taylor	A.M.-Dem	Bingham
W. J. McConnell	Rep	Latah
H. O. Harkness	Rep	Bingham

Appendix C.
Constitution of the State of Idaho

Approved July 3, 1890
(Amendments through July 3, 1990 indicated in bold.)

Article I. Declaration of Rights
§ 1. Inalienable right of man. § 2. Political power inherent in the people. § 3. State inseparable part of Union. § 4. Guaranty of religious liberty. § 5. Right to habeas corpus. § 6. Right to bail - Cruel and unusual punishments prohibited. § 7. Right to trial by jury. § 8. Prosecutions only by indictment or information. § 9. Freedom of speech. § 10. Right of assembly. § 11. Right to keep and bear arms. § 12. Military subordinate to civil power. § 13. Guaranties in criminal actions and due process of law. § 14. Right of eminent domain. § 15. Imprisonment for debt prohibited. § 16. Bills of attainder, etc., prohibited. § 17. Unreasonable searches and seizures prohibited. § 18. Justice to be freely and speedily administered. § 19. Right of suffrage guaranteed. § 20. No property qualification required of electors - Exceptions. § 21. Reserved right not impaired.

Article II. Distribution of Powers
§ 1. Departments of government.

Article III. Legislative Department
§ 1. Legislative power - Enacting clause - Referendum - Initiative. § 2. Membership of house and senate. § 3. Term of office. § 4. Apportionment of legislature. § 5. Senatorial and representative districts. § 6. Qualifications of members. § 7. Privilege from arrest. § 8. Sessions of legislature. § 9. Powers of each house. § 10. Quorum, adjournments and organization. § 11. Expulsion of members. § 12. Secret sessions prohibited. § 13. Journal. § 14. Origin and amendment of bills. § 15. Manner of passing bills. §

243

16. Unity of subject and title. § 17. Technical terms to be avoided. § 18. Amendments to be published in full. § 19. Local and special laws prohibited. § 20. Gambling not to be authorized. § 21. Signature of bills and resolutions. § 22. When acts take effect. § 23. Compensation of members. § 24. Promotion of temperance and morality. § 25. Oath of office. § 26. Power and authority over intoxicating liquors. § 27. Continuity of state and local governmental operations.

Article IV. Executive Department
§ 1. Executive officers listed - Term of office - Place of residence - Duties. § 2. Election of officers. § 3. Qualifications of officers. § 4. Governor is commander of militia. § 5. Supreme executive power vested in governor. § 6. Governor to appoint officers. § 7. The pardoning power. § 8. Governor may require reports - Message to legislature. § 9. Extra sessions of legislature. § 10. Veto power. § 11. Disapproval of appropriation bills. § 12. Lieutenant governor to act as governor. § 13. Lieutenant governor is president of senate. § 14. President pro tempore to act as governor. § 15. Great seal of the state. § 16. Grants and permissions. § 17. Accounts and reports of officers. § 18. Board of examiners. § 19. Salaries and fees of officers. § 20. Departments limited.

Article V. Judicial Department
§ 1. Forms of action abolished. § 2. Judicial power - Where vested. § 3. Impeachments - Where and how tried. § 4. Impeachments - Where and how tried - Conviction - Impeachment of governor. § 5. Treason defined and limited. § 6. Supreme Court - Number of justices - Term of office - Calling of district judge to sit with court. § 7. Justices prohibited from holding other offices. § 8. Terms of supreme court. § 9. Original and appellate jurisdiction of supreme court. § 10. Jurisdiction over claims against the state. § 11. District courts - Judges and terms. § 12. Residence of judges - Holding court out of district - Service by retired justices and judges. § 13. Power of legislature respecting courts. § 14. Special courts in cities and towns. § 15. Clerk of supreme court. § 16. Clerks of district courts - Election - Term of office. § 17. Salaries of justices and judges. § 18. Prosecuting attorneys - Term of office - Qualifications. § 19. Vacancies - How filled. § 20. Jurisdiction of district court. § 21. Jurisdiction of probate courts. [Repealed.] § 22. Jurisdiction of justices of the peace. [Repealed.] § 23. Qualifications of district judges. § 24. Judicial districts enumerated. § 25. Defects in laws to be reported by judges. § 26. Court procedure to be general and uniform. § 27. Change in compensation of officers. § 28. Removal of judicial officers.

Article VI. Suffrage and Election
§ 1. Secret ballot guaranteed. § 2. Qualifications of electors. § 3. Disqualification of certain persons. § 4. Legislature may prescribe additional qualifications. § 5. Residence for voting purposes not lost or gained. § 6. Recall of officers authorized. § 7. Nonpartisan selection of supreme and district judges.

Article VII. Finance and Revenue
§ 1. Fiscal year. § 2. Revenue to be provided by taxation. § 3. Property to be defined and classified. § 4. Public property exempt from taxation. § 5. Taxes to be uniform -

Exemptions. § 6. Municipal corporations to impose their own taxes. § 7. State taxes to be paid in full. § 8. Corporate property must be taxed. § 9. Maximum rate of taxation. § 10. Making profit from public money prohibited. § 11. Expenditure not to exceed appropriation. § 12. State tax commission, members, terms, appointment, vacancies, duties, powers - County board of equalization, duties. § 13. Money - How drawn from treasury. § 14. Money - How drawn from county treasuries. § 15. Legislature to provide system of county finance. § 16. Legislature to pass necessary laws. § 17. Gasoline taxes and motor vehicle registration fees to be expended on highways.

Article VIII. Public Indebtedness and Subsidies
§ 1. Limitation on public indebtedness. § 2. Loan of state's credit prohibited - Holding stock in corporation prohibited - Development of water power. § 3. Limitations on county and municipal indebtedness. § 3A. Environmental pollution control revenue bonds - Election on issuance. § 3B. Port district facilities and projects - Revenue bond financing. § 4. County, etc. not to loan or give its credit. § 5. Special revenue financing.

Article IX. Education and School Lands
§ 1. Legislature to establish system of free schools. § 2. Board of education. § 3. Public school fund to remain intact. § 4. Public school fund defined. § 5. Sectarian appropriations prohibited. § 6. Religious test and teaching in school prohibited. § 7. State board of land commissioners. § 8. Location and disposition of public lands. § 9. Compulsory attendance at schools. § 10. State university - Location, regents, and lands. § 11. Loaning permanent endowment funds.

Article X. Public Institutions
§ 1. State to establish and support institutions. § 2. Seat of government. § 3. Seat of government - Change in location. § 4. Property of territory becomes property of state. § 5. State prisons - Control over. § 6. Directors of insane asylum. [Repealed.] § 7. Change in location of institutions.

Article XI. Corporations, Public and Private
§ 1. Certain grants and charters invalidated. § 2. Special charters prohibited. § 3. Revocation and alteration of charters. § 4. Shares of stock - How voted. § 5. Regulation and control of railroads. § 6. Equal transportation rights guaranteed. § 7. Acceptance of constitution by corporations. § 8. Right of eminent domain and police power reserved. § 9. Increase in capital stock. § 10. Regulation of foreign corporations. § 11. Constructing railroad in city or town. § 12. Retroactive laws favoring corporations prohibited. § 13. Telegraph and telephone companies. § 14. Consolidation of corporations with foreign corporations. § 15. Transfer of franchises. § 16. Term "corporation" defined. § 17. Liability of stockholders - Dues. § 18. Combinations in restraint of trade prohibited.

Article XII. Corporations, Municipal
§ 1. General laws for cities and towns. § 2. Local police regulations authorized. § 3. State not to assume local indebtedness. § 4. Municipal corporations not to loan credit.

Article XIII. Immigration and Labor
§ 1. Bureau of immigration - Commissioner. § 2. Protection and hours of labor. § 3. Restrictions on convict labor. [Repealed.] § 4. Child labor in mines prohibited. § 5. Aliens not to be employed on public work. § 6. Mechanics' liens to be provided. § 7. Boards of arbitration. § 8. Duties and compensation of commissioner.

Article XIV. Militia
§ 1. Persons subject to military duty. § 2. Legislature to provide for enrollment of militia. § 3. Selection and commission of officers. § 4. Preservation of records, banners, and relics. § 5. National and state flags only to be carried. § 6. Importation of armed forces prohibited.

Article XV. Water Rights
§ 1. Use of waters a public use. § 2. Right to collect rates a franchise. § 3. Water of natural stream - Right to appropriate - State's regulatory power - Priorities. § 4. Continuing rights to water guaranteed. § 5. Priorities and limitation on use. § 6. Establishment of maximum rates. § 7. State water resource agency.

Article XVI. Livestock
§ 1. Laws to protect livestock.

Article XVII. State Boundaries
§ 1. Name and boundaries of state.

Article XVIII. County Organization
§ 1. Existing counties recognized. § 2. Removal of county seats. § 3. Division of counties. § 4. New counties - Size and valuation. § 4A. Consolidation of counties. § 5. System of county government. § 6. County officers. § 7. County officers - Salaries. § 8. County officers - How paid. § 9. County officers - Liability for fees. § 10. Board of county commissioners. § 11. Duties of officers.

Article XIX. Apportionment
§ 1. Senatorial districts. [Superseded.] § 2. Representative districts. [Superseded.]

Article XX. Amendments
§ 1. How amendments may be proposed. § 2. Submission of several amendments. § 3. Revision or amendment by convention. § 4. Submission of revised constitution to people.

Article XXI. Schedule and Ordinance
§ 1. Judicial proceedings continued. § 2. Laws continued in force. § 3. Territorial fines and forfeitures accrue to state. § 4. Territorial bonds and obligations pass to state. § 5.

Territorial officers to continue in office. § 6. Submission of constitution to electors. § 7. When constitution takes effect. § 8. Election proclamation to be issued. § 9. Election to be ordered - Conduct of election. § 10. Canvass of election returns. § 11. Certificates of election. § 12. Qualifications of officers. § 13. Tenure of office. § 14. Convention of first legislature. § 15. Legislature to pass necessary laws. § 16. Transfer of cases to state courts. § 17. Seals of courts. § 18. Transfer of probate matters. § 19. Religious freedom guaranteed - Disclaimer of title to Indian lands. § 20. Adoption of federal Constitution.

Signatures.

Preamble

We, the people of the state of Idaho, grateful to Almighty God for our freedom, to secure its blessings and promote our common welfare do establish this Constitution.

Article I. Declaration of Rights

§ 1. *Inalienable rights of man.* All men are by nature free and equal, and have certain inalienable rights, among which are enjoying and defending life and liberty; acquiring, possessing and protecting property; pursuing happiness and securing safety.

§ 2. *Political power inherent in the people.* All political power is inherent in the people. Government is instituted for their equal protection and benefit, and they have the right to alter, reform or abolish the same whenever they may deem it necessary; and no special privileges or immunities shall ever be granted that may not be altered, revoked, or repealed by the legislature.

§ 3. *State inseparable part of Union.* The state of Idaho is an inseparable part of the American Union, and the Constitution of the United States is the supreme law of the land.

§ 4. *Guaranty of religious liberty.* The exercise and enjoyment of religious faith and worship shall forever be guaranteed; and no person shall be denied any civil or political right, privilege, or capacity on account of his religious opinions; but the liberty of conscience hereby secured shall not be construed to dispense with oaths or affirmations, or excuse acts of licentiousness or justify polygamous or other pernicious practices, inconsistent with morality or the peace or safety of the state; nor to permit any person, organization, or association to directly or indirectly aid or abet, counsel or advise any person to commit the crime of bigamy or polygamy, or any other crime. No person shall be required to attend or support any ministry or place of worship, religious sect or denomination, or pay tithes against his consent; nor shall any preference be given by law to any religious denomination or mode of worship. Bigamy and polygamy are forever prohibited in the state, and the legislature shall provide by law for the punishment of such crimes.

§ 5. *Right of habeas corpus.* The privilege of the writ of habeas corpus shall not be suspended, unless in case of rebellion or invasion, the public safety requires it, and then only in such manner as shall be prescribed by law.

§ 6. *Right to bail - Cruel and unusual punishments prohibited.* All persons shall be bailable by sufficient sureties, except for capital offenses, where the proof is evident or the presumption great. Excessive bail shall not be required, no excess fines imposed, nor cruel and unusual punishments inflicted.

§ 7. *Right to trial by jury.* The right of trial by jury shall remain inviolate; but in civil actions, three-fourths of the jury may render a verdict, and the legislature may provide that in all cases of misdemeanors five-sixths of the jury may render a verdict. A trial by jury may be waived in all criminal cases, by the consent of all parties, expressed in open court, and in civil actions by the consent of the parties, signified in such manner as may be prescribed by law. In civil actions the jury may consist of twelve or of any number less than twelve upon which the parties may agree in open court. **Provided, that in cases of misdemeanor and in civil actions within the jurisdiction of any court inferior to the district court, whether such case or action be tried in such inferior court or in district court, the jury shall consist of not more than six.**

§ 8. *Prosecutions only by indictment or information.* No person shall be held to answer for any felony or criminal offense of any grade, unless on presentment or indictment of a grand jury or on information of the public prosecutor, after a commitment by a magistrate, except in cases of impeachment, in cases cognizable by probate courts or by justices of the peace, and in cases arising in the militia when in actual service in time of war or public danger; provided, that a grand jury may be summoned upon the order of the district court in the manner provided by law, and provided further, that after a charge has been ignored by a grand jury, no person shall be held to answer, or for trial therefor, upon information of the public prosecutor.

§ 9. *Freedom of speech.* Every person may freely speak, write and publish on all subjects, being responsible for the abuse of that liberty.

§ 10. *Right of assembly.* The people shall have the right to assemble in a peaceable manner, to consult for their common good; to instruct their representatives, and to petition the legislature for the redress of grievances.

§ 11. *Right to keep and bear arms.* The people have the right to **keep and** bear arms, which right shall not be abridged; but this provision shall not prevent the passage of laws to govern the carrying of weapons concealed on the person nor prevent passage of legislation providing minimum sentences for crimes committed while in possession of a firearm, nor prevent the passage of legislation providing penalties for the possession of firearms by a convicted felon, nor prevent the passage of any legislation punishing the use of a firearm. No law shall impose licensure, registration, or special taxation on the ownership or possession of firearms or ammunition. Nor shall any law permit the confiscation of firearms, except those actually used in the commission of a felony.

§ 12. *Military subordinate to civil power.* The military shall be subordinate to the civil power; and no soldier in time of peace shall be quartered in any house without the consent of its owner, nor in time of war except in the manner prescribed by law.

§ 13. *Guaranties in criminal actions and due process of law.* In all criminal prosecutions, the party accused shall have the right to a speedy and public trial; to have the process of the court to compel the attendance of witnesses in his behalf, and to appear and defend in person and with counsel.

No person shall be twice put in jeopardy for the same offense; nor be compelled in any criminal case to be a witness against himself; nor be deprived of life, liberty or property without due process of law.

§ 14. *Right of eminent domain.* The necessary use of lands for the construction of reservoirs or storage basins, for the purpose of irrigation, or for rights of way for the construction of canals, ditches, flumes or pipes, to convey water to the place of use for any useful, beneficial or necessary purpose, or for drainage; or for the drainage of mines, or the working thereof, by means of roads, railroads, tramways, cuts, tunnels, shafts, hoisting works, dumps, or other necessary means to their complete development, or any other use necessary to the complete development of the material resources of the state, or the preservation of the health of its inhabitants, is hereby declared to be a public use, and subject to the regulation and control of the state.

Private property may be taken for public use, but not until a just compensation, to be ascertained in the manner prescribed by law, shall be paid therefor.

§ 15. *Imprisonment for debt prohibited.* There shall be no imprisonment for debt in this state except in cases of fraud.

§ 16. *Bills of attainder, etc., prohibited.* No bill of attainder, ex post facto law, or law impairing the obligation of contracts shall ever be passed.

§ 17. *Unreasonable searches and seizures prohibited.* The right of the people to be secure in their persons, houses, papers and effects against unreasonable searches and seizures shall not be violated; and no warrant shall issue without probable cause shown by affidavit, particularly describing the place to be searched and the person or thing to be seized.

§ 18. *Justice to be freely and speedily administered.* Courts of justice shall be open to every person, and a speedy remedy afforded for every injury of person, property or character, and right and justice shall be administered without sale, denial, delay or prejudice.

§ 19. *Right of suffrage guaranteed.* No power, civil or military, shall at any time interfere with or prevent the free and lawful exercise of the right of suffrage.

§ 20. *No property qualification required of electors - Exceptions.* No property qualifications shall ever be required for any person to vote or hold office except in school elections, or elections creating indebtedness, **or in irrigation district elections, as to which last-named elections the legislature may restrict the voters to land owners.**

§ 21. *Reserved rights not impaired.* This enumeration of rights shall not be construed to impair or deny other rights retained by the people.

Article II. Distribution of Powers

§ 1. *Departments of government.* The powers of the government of this state are divided into three distinct departments, the legislative, executive and judicial; and no person or collection of persons charged with the exercise of powers properly belonging to one of these departments shall exercise any powers properly belonging to either of the others, except as in this constitution expressly directed or permitted.

ARTICLE III. Legislative Department

§ 1. *Legislative power – Enacting clause – Referendum – Initiative.* The legislative power of the state shall be vested in a senate and house of representatives. The enacting clause of every bill shall be as follows: "Be it enacted by the Legislature of the State of Idaho."

The people reserve to themselves the power to approve or reject at the polls any act or measure passed by the legislature. This power is known as the referendum, and legal voters may, under such conditions and in such manner as may be provided by acts of the legislature, demand a referendum vote on any act or measure passed by the legislature and cause the same to be submitted to a vote of the people for their approval or rejection.

The people reserve to themselves the power to propose laws, and enact the same at the polls independent of the legislature. This power is known as the initiative, and legal voters may, under such conditions and in such manner as may be provided by acts of

the legislature, initiate any desired legislation and cause the same to be submitted to the vote of the people at a general election for their approval or rejection.

§ 2. *Membership of house and senate.* Following the decennial census of 1990 and in each legislature thereafter, the senate shall consist of not less than thirty nor more than thirty-five members. The legislature may fix the number of members of the house of representatives at not more than two times as many representatives as there are senators. The senators and representatives shall be chosen by the electors of the respective counties or districts into which the state may, from time to time, be divided by law.

§ 3. *Term of Office.* The senators and representatives shall be elected for the term of two (2) years, from and after the first day of December next following the general election.

§ 4. *Apportionment of legislature.* The members of the legislature following the decennial census of 1990 and each legislature thereafter shall be apportioned to not less than thirty nor more than thirty-five legislative districts of the state as may be provided by law.

§ 5. *Senatorial and representative districts.* A senatorial or representative district, when more than one county shall constitute the same, shall be composed of contiguous counties, and a county may be divided in creating districts only to the extent it is reasonably determined by statute that counties must be divided to create senatorial and representative districts which comply with the constitution of the United States. A county may be divided into more than one legislative district when districts are wholly contained within a single county. No floterial district shall be created. Multi-member districts may be created in any district composed of more than one county only to the extent that two representatives may be elected from a district from which one senator is elected. The provisions of this section shall apply to any apportionment adopted following the 1990 decennial census.

§ 6. *Qualifications of members.* No person shall be a senator or representative who, at the time of his election, is not a citizen of the United States, and an elector of this state, nor anyone who has not been for one year next preceding his election an elector of the county or district whence he may be chosen.

§ 7. *Privilege from arrest.* Senators and representatives in all cases, except for treason, felony, or breach of the peace, shall be privileged from arrest during the session of the legislature, and in going to and returning from the same, and shall not be liable to any civil process during the session of the legislature, nor during the ten days next before the commencement thereof; nor shall a member, for words uttered in debate in either house, be questioned in any other place.

§ 8. *Sessions of legislature.* The sessions of the legislature shall be held **annually** at the capital of the state, commencing on the **second** Monday of January **of each year**, unless a different day shall have been appointed by law, and at other times when convened by the governor.

§ 9. *Powers of each house.* Each house when assembled shall choose its own officers; judge of the election, qualifications and returns of its own members, determine its own rules of proceeding, and sit upon its own adjournments; but neither house shall, without the concurrence of the other, adjourn for more than three (3) days, nor to any other place than that in which it may be sitting.

§ 10, *Quorum, adjournments and organization.* A majority of each house shall constitute a quorum to do business; but a smaller number may adjourn from day to day, and may compel the attendance of absent members in such manner and under such penalties as such house may provide. A quorum being in attendance, if either house fail to effect an organization within the first four (4) days thereafter, the members of the house so failing shall be entitled to no compensation from the end of the said four (4) days until an organization shall have been effected.

§ 11. *Expulsion of members.* Each house may, for good cause shown, with the concurrence of two-thirds (2/3) of all the members, expel a member.

§ 12. *Secret sessions prohibited.* The business of each house, and of the committee of the whole shall be transacted openly and not in secret session.

§ 13. *Journal.* Each house shall keep a journal of its proceedings; and the yeas and nays of the members of either house on any question shall at the request of any three (3) members present, be entered on the journal.

§ 14. *Origin and amendment of bills.* Bills may originate in either house, but may be amended or rejected in the other, except that bills for raising revenue shall originate in the house of representatives.

§ 15. *Manner of passing bills.* No law shall be passed except by bill, nor shall any bill be put upon its final passage until the same, with the amendments thereto, shall have been printed for the use of the members; nor shall any bill become a law unless the same shall have been read on three several days in each house previous to the final vote thereon: provided, in case of urgency, two-thirds (2/3) of the house where such bill may be pending may, upon a vote of the yeas and nays dispense with this provision. On the final passage of all bills, they shall be read at length, section by section, and the vote shall be by yeas and nays upon each bill separately, and shall be entered upon the journal; and no bill shall become a law without the concurrence of a majority of the members present.

§ 16. *Unity of subject and title.* Every act shall embrace but one subject and matters properly connected therewith, which subject shall be expressed in the title; but if any subject shall be embraced in an act which shall not be expressed in the title, such act shall be void only as to so much thereof as shall not be embraced in the title.

§ 17. *Technical terms to be avoided.* Every act or joint resolution shall be plainly worded, avoiding as far as practicable the use of technical terms.

§ 18. *Amendments to be published in full.* No act shall be revised or amended by mere reference to its title, but the section as amended shall be set forth and published at full length.

§ 19. *Local and special laws prohibited.* The legislature shall not pass local or special laws in any of the following enumerated cases, that is to say:

Regulating the jurisdiction and duties of justices of the peace and constables.

For the punishment of crimes and misdemeanors.

Regulating the practice of the courts of justice.

Providing for a change of venue in civil or criminal actions.

Granting divorces.

Changing the names of persons or places.

Authorizing the laying out, opening, altering, maintaining, working on, or vacating roads, highways, streets, alleys, town plats, parks, cemeteries, or any public grounds not owned by the state.

Summoning and impaneling grand and trial juries, and providing for their compensation.

Regulating county and township business, or the election of county and township officers.

For the assessment and collection of taxes.

Providing for and conducting elections, or designating the place of voting.

Affecting estates of deceased persons, minors, or other persons under legal disabilities.

Extending the time for collection of taxes.

Giving effect to invalid deeds, leases or other instruments.

Refunding money paid into the state treasury.

Releasing or extinguishing, in whole or in part, the indebtedness, liability or obligation of any person or corporation in this state, or any municipal corporation therein.

Declaring any person of age, or authorizing any minor to sell, lease or incumber his or her property.

Legalizing as against the state the unauthorized or invalid act of any officer.

Exempting property from taxation.

Changing county seats, unless the law authorizing the change shall require that two-thirds (2/3) of the legal votes cast at a general or special election shall designate the place to which the county seat shall be changed; provided, that the power to pass a special law shall cease as long as the legislature shall provide for such change by general law; provided further, that no special law shall be passed for any one county oftener than once in six (6) years.

Restoring to citizenship persons convicted of infamous crimes.

Regulating the interest on money.

Authorizing the creation, extension or impairing of liens.

Chartering or licensing ferries, bridges or roads.

Remitting fines, penalties or forfeitures.

Providing for the management of common schools.

Creating offices or prescribing the powers and duties of officers in counties, cities, townships, election districts, or school districts, except as in this constitution otherwise provided.

Changing the law of descent or succession.

Authorizing the adoption or legitimization of children.

For limitation of civil or criminal actions.

Creating any corporation.

Creating, increasing or decreasing fees, percentages, or allowances of public officers during the term for which said officers are elected or appointed.

§ 20. *Gambling not to be authorized.* No game of chance, lottery, gift enterprise or gambling shall be authorized under any pretense or for any purpose whatever, except for the following: (a) A state lottery which is authorized by the state if conducted in conformity with law; and (b) Pari-mutuel betting if conducted in conformity with law; and (c) Charitable games of chance which are operated by qualified charitable organizations in the pursuit of charitable purposes if conducted in conformity with law.

§ 21. *Signature of bill and resolutions.* All bills or joint resolutions passed shall be signed by the presiding officers of the respective houses.

§ 22. *When acts take effect.* No act shall take effect until sixty days from the end of the session at which the same shall have been passed, except in case of emergency, which emergency shall be declared in the preamble or in the body of the law.

§ 23. *Compensation of members.* The legislature shall have no authority to establish the rate of its compensation and expense by law. There is hereby authorized the creation of the citizens' committee on legislative compensation, which shall consist of six (6) members, three (3) to be appointed by the governor and three (3) to be appointed by the supreme court, whose terms of office and qualifications shall be as provided by law. Members of the committee shall be citizens of the state of Idaho other than public officials holding an office to which compensation is attached. The committee shall, on or before the last day of November of each even-numbered year, establish the rate of compensation and expenses for the services to be rendered by members of the legislature during the two-year period commencing on the first day of December of such year. The compensation and expenses so established shall, on or before such date, be filed with the secretary of state and the state auditor. The rates thus established shall be the rates applicable for the two-year period specified unless prior to the twenty-fifth legislative day of the next regular session, by concurrent resolution, the senate and house of representatives shall reject or reduce such rates of compensation and expenses. In the event of rejection, the rates prevailing at the time of the previous session, shall remain in effect.

The officers of the legislature, including committee chairmen, may, by virtue of the office, receive additional compensation as may be provided by the committee. No change in the rate of compensation shall be made which applies to the legislature then in office except as provided herein.

When convened in extra session by the governor, no such session shall continue for a period longer than twenty (20) days.

§ 24. *Promotion of temperance and morality.* The first concern of all good government is the virtue and sobriety of the people, and the purity of the home. The legislature should further all wise and well directed efforts for the promotion of temperance and morality.

§ 25. *Oath of office.* The members of the legislature shall, before they enter upon the duties of their respective offices, take or subscribe the following oath or affirmation: "I do solemnly swear (or affirm, as the case may be) that I will support the constitution of the United States and the constitution of the state of Idaho, and that I will faithfully discharge the duties of senator (or representative, as the case may be) according to the best of my ability." And such oath may be administered by the governor, secretary of state, or judge of the Supreme Court, or presiding officer of either house.

§ 26. *Power and authority over intoxicating liquors.* **From and after the thirty-first day of December in the year 1934, the legislature of the state of Idaho shall have full power and authority to permit, control and regulate or prohibit the manufacture, sale, keeping for sale, and transportation for sale, of intoxicating liquors for beverage purposes.**

§ 27. *Continuity of state and local governmental operations.* The legislature, in order to insure continuity of state and local governmental operations in periods of emergency resulting from disasters caused by enemy attack or in periods of emergency resulting from the imminent threat of such disasters, shall have the power and the immediate duty (1) to provide for prompt and temporary succession to the powers and duties of public offices, of whatever nature and whether filled by election or appointment, the incumbents of which may become unavailable for carrying on the powers and duties of such offices, and (2) to adopt such other measures as may be necessary and proper for so insuring the continuity of governmental operations. In the exercise of the powers hereby conferred, the legislature shall in all respects conform to the requirements of this constitution except to the extent that in the judgment of the legislature so to do would be impracticable or would admit of undue delay.

Article IV. Executive Department

§ 1. *Executive officers listed* – *Term of office* – *Place of residence* – *Duties.* The executive department shall consist of a governor, lieutenant governor, secretary of state, state auditor, state treasurer, attorney general and superintendent of public instruction, each of whom shall hold his office for **four years** beginning on the first Monday in January next after his election, **commencing with those elected in the year 1946**, except as otherwise provided in this Constitution.

The officers of the executive department, excepting the lieutenant governor, shall, during their terms of office, reside within the county where the seat of government is located, where they shall keep the public records, books and papers. They shall perform such duties as are prescribed by this Constitution and as may be prescribed by law.

§ 2. *Election of officers.* The officers named in section 1 of this article shall be elected by the qualified electors of the state at the time and places of voting for members of the legislature, and the persons, respectively, having the highest number of votes for the office voted for shall be elected; but if two (2) or more shall have an equal and the highest number of votes for any one (1) of said offices, the two (2) houses of the legislature at its next regular session, shall forthwith, by joint ballot, elect one (1) of such persons for said office. The returns of elections for the officers named in section 1 shall be made in such manner as may be prescribed by law, and all contested elections of the same, other than provided for in this section, shall be determined as may be prescribed by law.

§ 3. *Qualifications of officers.* No person shall be eligible to the office of governor or lieutenant governor unless he shall have attained the age of thirty (30) years at the time of his election; nor to the office of secretary of state, state auditor, or state treasurer, unless he shall have attained the age of twenty-five (25) years; nor to the officer of attorney general unless he shall have attained the age of thirty (30) years, and have been admitted to practice in the Supreme Court of the state or territory of Idaho, and be in good standing at the time of his election. In addition to the qualifications above described each of the officers named shall be a citizen of the United States and shall have resided within the state or territory two (2) years next preceding his election.

§ 4. *Governor is commander of militia.* The governor shall be commander-in-chief of the military forces of the state, except when they shall be called into actual service of the United States. He shall have power to call out the militia to execute the laws, to suppress insurrection, or to repel invasion.

§ 5. *Supreme executive power vested in governor.* The supreme executive power of the state is vested in the governor, who shall see that the laws are faithfully executed.

§ 6. *Governor to appoint officers.* The governor shall nominate and, by and with the consent of the senate, appoint all officers whose offices are established by this constitution, or which may be created by law, and whose appointment or election is not otherwise provided for. If during the recess of the senate, a vacancy occurs in any state or district office, the governor shall appoint some fit person to discharge the duties thereof until the next meeting of the senate, when he shall nominate some person to fill such office. If the office of a justice of the supreme or district court, secretary of state, state auditor, state treasurer, attorney general, or superintendent of public instruction shall be vacated by death, resignation or otherwise, it shall be the duty of the governor to fill the same by appointment, **as provided by law,** and the appointee shall hold his office until his successor shall be selected and qualified in such manner as may be provided by law.

§ 7. *The pardoning power.* **Such board as may hereafter be created or provided by legislative enactment** shall constitute a board to be known as the board of pardons. Said board, or a majority thereof, shall have power to remit fines and forfeitures, and **only as provided by statute,** to grant commutations and pardons after conviction of a judgment, either absolutely or upon such conditions as they may impose in all cases of offenses against the state except treason or conviction on impeachment. The legislature shall by law prescribe the sessions of said board and the manner in which application shall be made, and regulate proceedings thereon, but no fine or forfeiture shall be remitted, and no commutation or pardon granted, except by a decision of a majority of said board, after a full hearing in open session, and until previous notice of the time and place of such hearing and the release applied for shall have been given by publication in some newspaper of general circulation at least once a week for four weeks. The proceedings and decision of the board shall be reduced to writing and with their reasons for their actions in each case, and the dissent of any member who may disagree, signed by him, and filed, with all papers used upon the hearing, in the office of the secretary of state.

The governor shall have power to grant respites or reprieves in all cases of convictions for offenses against the state, except treason or conviction on impeachment, but such respites or reprieves shall not extend beyond the next session of the board of pardons; and such board shall at such session continue or determine such respite or reprieve, or they may commute or pardon the offense, as herein provided. In cases of conviction for treason the governor shall have the power to suspend the execution of the sentence until the case shall be reported to the legislature at its next regular session, when the legislature shall either pardon or commute the sentence, direct its execution, or grant further reprieve.

§ 8. *Governor may require reports — Messages to legislature.* The governor may require information in writing from the officers of the executive department upon any subject relating to the duties of their respective offices, which information shall be given upon oath whenever so required; he may also require information in writing, at any time under oath, from all officers and managers of state institutions, upon any subject relating to the condition, management and expenses of their respective offices and institutions, and may, at any time he deems it necessary, appoint a committee to investigate and report to him upon the condition of any executive office or state institution. The governor shall at the commencement of each session, and from time to time, by message, give to the legislature information of the condition of the state, and shall recommend such measures as he shall deem expedient. He shall also send to the legislature a statement, with vouchers, of the expenditures of all moneys belonging to the state and paid out by him. He shall also, at the commencement of each session, present estimates of the amount of money required to be raised by taxation for all purposes of the state.

§ 9. *Extra sessions of legislature.* The governor may, on extraordinary occasions, convene the legislature by proclamation, stating the purposes for which he has convened it; but when so convened it shall have no power to legislate on any subject other than those specified in the proclamation; but may provide for the expense of the session and other matters incidental thereto. He may also, by proclamation, convene the senate in extraordinary session for the transaction of executive business.

§ 10. *Veto power.* Every bill passed by the legislature shall, before it becomes a law, be presented to the governor. If he approve, he shall sign it, and thereupon it shall become a law; but if he do not approve, he shall return it with his objections to the house in which it originated, which house shall enter the objections at large upon its journals and proceed to reconsider the bill. If then two-thirds (2/3) of the members present agree to pass the same, it shall be sent, together with the objections, to the other house, by which it shall likewise be reconsidered: and if approved by two-thirds (2/3) of the members present in that house, it shall become a law, notwithstanding the objections of the governor. In all such cases the vote of each house shall be determined by yeas and nays, to be entered on the journal. Any bill which shall not be returned by the governor to the legislature within five (5) days (Sundays excepted) after it shall have been presented to him, shall become a law in like manner as if he had signed it, unless the legislature shall, by adjournment, prevent its return, in which case it shall be filed, with his objections, in the office of the secretary of state within ten (10) days after such adjournment (Sundays excepted) or become a law.

§ 11. *Disapproval of appropriation bills.* The governor shall have power to disapprove of any item or items of any bill making appropriations of money embracing distinct items, and the part or parts approved shall become a law and the item or items disapproved shall be void, unless enacted in the manner following: If the legislature be in session, he shall within five (5) days transmit to the house within which the bill originated a copy of the item or items thereof disapproved, together with his objections thereto, and the items objected to shall be separately reconsidered, and each item shall then take the same course as prescribed for the passage of bills over the executive veto.

§ 12. *Lieutenant governor to act as governor.* In case of the failure to qualify, the impeachment, or conviction of treason, felony, or other infamous crime of the governor, or his death, removal from office, resignation, absence from the state, or inability to discharge the powers and duties of his office, the powers, duties and emoluments of the office for the residue of the term, or until the disability shall cease, shall devolve upon the lieutenant governor.

§ 13. *Lieutenant governor is president of senate.* The lieutenant governor shall be president of the senate, but shall vote only when the senate is equally divided. In case of the absence or disqualification of the lieutenant governor from any cause which applies to the governor, or when he shall hold the office of governor, then the president pro tempore of the senate shall perform the duties of the lieutenant governor until the vacancy is filled or the disability removed.

§ 14. *President pro tempore to act as governor.* In case of the failure to qualify in his office, death, resignation, absence from the state, impeachment, conviction of treason, felony or other infamous crime, or disqualification from any cause, of both governor and lieutenant governor, the duties of the governor shall devolve upon the president of the senate pro tempore, until such disqualification of either the governor or lieutenant governor be removed, or the vacancy filled; and if the president of the senate, for any of the above named causes, shall become incapable of performing the duties of governor, the same shall devolve upon the speaker of the house.

§ 15. *Great seal of the state.* There shall be a seal of this state, which shall be kept by the secretary of state and used by him officially, and shall be called "The great seal of the state of Idaho." The seal of the territory of Idaho, as now used, shall be the seal of the state until otherwise provided by law.

§ 16. *Grants and permissions.* All grants and permissions shall be in the name and by the authority of the state of Idaho, sealed with the great seal of the state, signed by the governor, and countersigned by the secretary of state.

§ 17. *Accounts and reports of officers.* An account shall be kept by the officers of the executive department and of all public institutions of the state of all moneys received by them severally, from all sources, and for every service performed, and of all moneys disbursed by them severally, and a semi-annual report thereof shall be made to the governor, under oath; they shall also, at least twenty days preceding each regular session of the legislature, make full and complete report of their official transactions to the governor, who shall transmit the same to the legislature.

§ 18. *Board of Examiners.* The governor, secretary of state, and attorney general shall constitute a board of examiners, with power to examine all claims against the state, except salaries or compensation of officers fixed by law, and perform such other duties as may be prescribed by law: **provided, that in the administration of moneys in cooperation with the federal government the legislature may prescribe any method of disbursement required to obtain the benefits of federal laws.** And no claim against the state, except salaries and compensation of officers fixed by law, shall be passed upon by the legislature without first having been considered and acted upon by said board.

§ 19. *Salaries and fees of officers.* The governor, secretary of state, state auditor, state treasurer, attorney general, and superintendent of public instruction shall, **monthly** as due, during their continuance in office, receive for their services compensation, which, for the term next ensuing after the adoption of this constitution, is fixed as follows: Governor, three thousand dollars ($3,000) per annum; secretary of state, one thousand eight hundred dollars ($1,800) per annum; state auditor, one thousand eight hundred dollars ($1,800) per annum; state treasurer, one thousand dollars ($1,000) per annum; attorney general, two thousand dollars ($2,000) per annum; and superintendent of public instruction, one thousand five hundred dollars ($1,500) per annum. The lieutenant governor shall receive the same per diem as may be provided by law for the speaker of the house of representatives, to be allowed only during the sessions of the legislature. The compensations enumerated shall be in full for all services by said officers respectively, rendered in any official capacity or employment whatever during their respective terms of office.

No officer named in this section shall receive, for the performance of any official duty, any fee for his own use; but all fees fixed by law for the performance by either of them, of any official duty, shall be collected in advance and deposited with the state treasurer quarterly to the credit of the state. The legislature may, by law, diminish or increase the compensation of any or all of the officers named in this section, but no such diminution or increase shall affect the salaries of the officers then in office during their term; provided, however, the legislature may provide for the payment of actual and necessary expenses to the governor, lieutenant governor, secretary of state, attorney general, and superintendent of public instruction, while traveling within the state in the performance of official duty.

§ 20. *Departments limited.* **All executive and administrative officers, agencies, and instrumentalities of the executive department of the state and their respective functions, powers, and duties, except for the office of governor, lieutenant governor, secretary of state, state auditor, state treasurer, attorney general and superintendent of public instruction, shall be allocated by law among and within not more than twenty (20) departments by no later than January 1, 1975. Subsequently, all new powers or functions shall be assigned to departments, divisions, sections or units in such manner as will tend to provide an orderly arrangement in the administrative organization of state government. Temporary agencies may be established by law and need not be allocated within a department; however, such temporary agencies may not exist for longer than two (2) years.**

Article V. Judicial Department

§ 1. *Forms of action abolished.* The distinctions between actions at law and suits in equity, and the forms of all such actions and suits, are hereby prohibited; and there shall be in this state but one form of action for wrongs, which shall be denominated a civil action; and every action prosecuted by the people of the state as a party, against a person charged with a public offense, for the punishment of the same, shall be termed a criminal action.

Feigned issues are prohibited, and the fact at issue shall be tried by order of court before a jury.

§ 2. *Judicial power — Where vested.* The judicial power of the state shall be vested in a court for the trial of impeachments, a Supreme Court, district courts, and such other courts inferior to the Supreme Court as established by the legislature. **The courts shall constitute a unified and integrated judicial system for administration and supervision by the Supreme Court. The jurisdiction of such inferior courts shall be as prescribed by the legislature. Until**

provided by law, no changes shall be made in the jurisdiction or in the manner of the selection of judges of existing inferior courts.

§ 3. *Impeachments — Where and how tried.* The court for the trial of impeachments shall be the senate. A majority of the members elected shall be necessary to a quorum, and the judgment shall not extend beyond removal from, and disqualification to hold office in this state; but the party shall be liable to indictment and punishment according to law.

§ 4. *Impeachments — Where and how tried — Conviction — Impeachment of governor.* The house of representatives solely shall have the power of impeachment. No person shall be convicted without the concurrence of two-thirds (2/3) of the senators elected. When the governor is impeached, the chief justice shall preside.

§ 5. *Treason defined and limited.* Treason against the state shall consist only of levying war against it, or adhering to its enemies, giving them aid and comfort. No person shall be convicted of treason unless on the testimony of two witnesses to the same overt act, or on confession in open court. No conviction of treason or attainder shall work corruption of blood or forfeiture of estate.

§ 6. *Supreme Court — Number of justices — Term of office — Calling of a district judge to sit with court.* The Supreme Court shall consist of **five** justices, a majority of whom shall be necessary to make a quorum or pronounce a decision. **If a justice of the Supreme Court shall be disqualified from sitting in a cause before said court, or be unable to sit therein, by reason of illness or absence, the said court may call a district judge to sit in said court on the hearing of such cause.**

The justices of the Supreme Court shall be elected by the electors of the state at large. The terms of office of the justices of the Supreme Court, except as in this article otherwise provided, shall be six years.

The justices of the Supreme Court shall, immediately after the first election under this constitution, be selected by lot, so that one shall hold his office for the term of two years, one for the term of four years, and one for the term of six years. The lots shall be drawn by the justices of the Supreme Court, who shall, for that purpose, assemble at the seat of government, and they shall cause the result thereof to be certified to by the secretary of state and filed in his office.

The chief justice **shall be selected from among the justices of the Supreme Court by a majority vote of the justices. His term of office shall be four years. When a vacancy in the office of chief justice occurs, a chief justice shall be selected for a full four year term. The chief justice shall be the executive head of the judicial system.**

§ 7. *Justices prohibited from holding other offices.* No justice of the Supreme Court shall be eligible to any other office of trust or profit under the laws of this state during the term for which he was elected.

§ 8. *Terms of Supreme Court.* At least four (4) terms of the Supreme Court shall be held annually; two (2) terms at the seat of state government, and two (2) terms at the city of Lewiston, in Nez Perce county. In case of epidemic, pestilence, or destruction of court houses, the justices may hold the terms of the Supreme Court provided by this section at other convenient places, to be fixed by a majority of said justices. After six (6) years the legislature may alter the provisions of this section.

§ 9. *Original and appellate jurisdiction of Supreme Court.* The Supreme Court shall have jurisdiction to review, upon appeal, any decision of the district courts, or the judges thereof, **and any order of the public utilities commission, and any order of the industrial accident board: the legislature may provide conditions of appeal, scope of appeal, and procedure on** appeal from orders of the public utilities commission and of the industrial accident board. On appeal from orders of the industrial accident board the court shall be limited to a review of questions of law. The Supreme Court shall also have original jurisdiction to issue writs of mandamus, certiorari, prohibition, and habeas corpus, and all writs necessary or proper to the complete exercise of its appellate jurisdiction.

§ 10. *Jurisdiction over claims against the state.* The Supreme Court shall have original jurisdiction to hear claims against the state, but its decision shall be merely recommendatory; no process in the nature of execution shall issue thereon; they shall be reported to the next session of the legislature for its action.

§ 11. *District courts — Judges and terms.* The state shall be divided into five (5) judicial districts, for each of which a judge shall be chosen by the qualified electors thereof, whose term of office shall be four (4) years. And there shall be held a district court in each county as may be prescribed by law. But the legislature may reduce or increase the number of districts, district judges and district attorneys. This section shall not be construed to prevent the holding of special terms under such regulations as may be provided by law.

§ 12. *Residence of judges — Holding court out of district — Service by retired justices and judges.* Every judge of the district court shall reside in the district for which he is elected. A judge of any district court, **or any retired justice of the Supreme Court or any retired district judge,** may hold a district court in any county at the request of the judge of the district court thereof, and upon the request of the governor, **or of the chief justice, and when any such request is made or approved by the chief justice** it shall be his duty to do so; but a cause in the district court may be tried by a judge pro tempore, who must be a member of the bar, agreed upon in writing by the parties litigant, or their attorneys of record, and sworn to try the cause. **Any retired justice or district judge may sit with the Supreme Court and exercise the authority of a member thereof in any cause in which he is requested by that court so to do, and when requested by the chief justice shall perform such other duties pertaining to the judicial department of government as directed. Compensation for such service shall be as approved by the legislature.**

§ 13. *Power of legislature respecting courts.* The legislature shall have no power to deprive the judicial department of any power or jurisdiction which rightly pertains to it as a coordinate department of the government; but the legislature shall provide a proper system of appeals, and regulate by law, when necessary, the methods of proceeding in the exercise of their powers of all the courts below the Supreme Court, so far as the same may be done without conflict with this Constitution; **provided, however, that the legislature can provide mandatory minimum sentences for any crimes, and any sentence imposed shall be not less than the mandatory minimum sentence so provided. Any mandatory minimum sentence so imposed shall not be reduced.**

§ 14. *Special courts in cities and towns.* The legislature may provide for the establishment of special courts for the trial of misdemeanors in incorporated cities and towns, where the same may be necessary.

§ 15. *Clerk of Supreme Court.* The clerk of the Supreme Court shall be appointed by the court, and shall hold his office during the pleasure of the court. He shall receive such compensation for his services as may be provided by law.

§ 16. *Clerks of district courts — Election — Term of office.* A clerk of the district court for each county shall be elected by the qualified voters thereof at the time and in the manner prescribed by law for the election of members of the legislature, and shall hold his office for the term of four (4) years.

§ 17. *Salaries of justices and judges.* The salary of the justices of the Supreme Court, until otherwise provided by the legislature, shall be three thousand dollars ($3,000) each per annum, and the salary of the judges of the district court, until otherwise provided by the legislature, shall be three thousand dollars ($3,000) each per annum, and no justice of the Supreme Court, or judge of the district court, shall be paid his salary, or any part thereof, unless he shall have first taken and subscribed an oath that there is not in his hands any matter in controversy not decided by him which had been finally submitted for his consideration and determination, thirty (30) days prior to the taking and subscribing such oath.

§ 18. *Prosecuting attorneys — Term of office — Qualifications.* **A prosecuting attorney shall be elected for each organized county in the state,** by the qualified electors **of such county, and shall hold office for the term of two years, and commencing with the general election in 1984** shall hold office for the term of four years, and shall perform such duties as may be prescribed by law; he shall be a practicing attorney at law, and a resident and elector of the **county for which he is elected.** He shall receive such compensation for services as may be fixed by law.

§ 19. *Vacancies — How filled.* All vacancies occurring in the offices provided for by this article of the Constitution shall be filled as provided by law.

§ 20. *Jurisdiction of district court.* The district court shall have original jurisdiction in all cases, both at law and in equity, and such appellate jurisdiction as may be conferred by law.

§ 21. *Jurisdiction of probate courts.* [Repealed.]

§ 22. *Jurisdiction of justices of the peace.* [Repealed.]

§ 23. *Qualifications of district judges.* No person shall be eligible to the office of district judge unless he be learned in the law, thirty (30) years of age, and a citizen of the United States, and shall have resided in the state or territory at least two (2) years next preceding his election, nor unless he shall have been at the time of his election, an elector in the judicial district for which he is elected.

§ 24. *Judicial districts enumerated.* Until otherwise provided by law, the judicial districts shall be five (5) in number, and constituted of the following counties, viz:

First District — Shoshone and Kootenai.

Second District — Latah, Nez Perce, and Idaho.

Third District — Washington, Ada, Boise, and Owyhee.

Fourth District — Cassia, Elmore, Logan, and Alturas.

Fifth District — Bear Lake, Bingham, Oneida, Lemhi, and Custer.

§ 25. *Defects in laws to be reported by judges.* The judges of the district courts shall, on or before the first day of July in each year, report in writing to the justices of the Supreme Court, such defects or omissions in the laws as their knowledge and experience may suggest, and the justices of the Supreme Court shall, on or before the first day of December of each year, report in writing to the governor, to be by him transmitted to the legislature, together with his message, such defects and omissions in the Constitution and laws as they may find to exist.

§ 26. *Court procedure to be general and uniform.* All laws relating to courts shall be general and of uniform operation throughout the state, and the organized judicial powers, proceedings, and practices of all the courts of the same class or grade, so far as regulated by law, and the force and effect of the proceedings, judgments, and decrees of such courts, severally, shall be uniform.

§ 27. *Change in compensation of officers.* The legislature may by law diminish or increase the compensation of any or all of the following officers, to wit: governor, lieutenant governor, secretary of state, state auditor, state treasurer, attorney general, superintendent of public instruction, commissioner of immigration and labor, justices of the Supreme Court, and judges of the district courts and district attorneys; but no diminution or increase shall affect the compensation of the officer then in office during his term, provided, however, that the legislature may provide for the payment of actual and necessary expenses of the governor, secretary of state, attorney general, and superintendent of public instruction incurred while in performance of official duty.

§ 28. *Removal of judicial officers.* **Provisions for the retirement, discipline and removal from office of justices and judges shall be as provided by law.**

Article VI. Suffrage and Elections

§ 1. *Secret ballot guaranteed.* All elections by the people must be by ballot. An absolutely secret ballot is hereby guaranteed, and it shall be the duty of the legislature to enact such laws as shall carry this section into effect.

§ 2. *Qualifications of electors.* Every male **or female** citizen of the United States, **eighteen years old**, who has resided in this state and in the county where he **or she** offers to vote for **the period of time provided by law**, if registered as provided by law, is a qualified elector.

§ 3. *Disqualification of certain persons.* No person is permitted to vote, serve as a juror, or hold any civil office who is under guardianship, or who has, at any place, been convicted of a felony, and who has not been restored to the rights of citizenship, or who, at the time of such election, is confined in prison on conviction of a criminal offense.

§ 4. *Legislature may prescribe additional qualifications.* The legislature may prescribe qualifications, limitations, and conditions for the right of suffrage, additional to those prescribed in this article, but shall never annul any of the provisions in this article contained.

§ 5. *Residence for voting purposes not lost or gained.* For the purpose of voting, no person shall be deemed to have gained or lost a residence by reason of his presence or absence while employed in the service of this state, or of the United States, nor while engaged in the navigation of the waters of this state or of the United States, nor while a student of any institution of learning, nor while kept at any alms house or other asylum at the public expense.

§ 6. *Recall of officers authorized.* **Every public officer in the state of Idaho, excepting the judicial officers, is subject to recall by the legal voters of the state or of the electoral district from which he is elected. The legislature shall pass the necessary laws to carry this provision into effect.**

§ 7. *Nonpartisan selection of Supreme and district judges.* **The selection of justices of the Supreme Court and district judges shall be nonpartisan. The legislature shall provide for their nomination and election, but candidates for the offices of justice of the Supreme Court and district judge shall not be nominated nor endorsed by any political party and their names shall not appear on any political party ticket, nor be accompanied on the ballot by any political party designation.**

Article VII. Finance and Revenue

§ 1. *Fiscal year.* The fiscal year shall commence on the second Monday of January in each year, unless otherwise provided by law.

§ 2. *Revenue to be provided by taxation.* The legislature shall provide such revenue as may be needful, by levying a tax by valuation, so that every person or corporation shall pay a tax in proportion to the value of his, her, or its property, except as in this article hereinafter otherwise provided. The legislature may also impose a license tax, both upon natural persons and upon corporations, other than municipal, doing business in this state; also a per capita tax: provided the legislature may exempt a limited amount of improvements upon land from taxation.

§ 3. *Property to be defined and classified.* The word "property" as herein used shall be defined and classified by law.

§ 4. *Public property exempt from taxation.* The property of the United States, **except when taxation thereof is authorized by the United States,** the state, counties, towns, cities, **villages, school districts,** and other municipal corporations and public libraries shall be exempt from taxation.

§ 5. *Taxes to be uniform – Exemptions.* All taxes shall be uniform upon the same class of subjects within the territorial limits, of the authority levying the tax, and shall be levied and collected under general laws, which shall prescribe such regulations as shall secure a just valuation for taxation of all property, real and personal: provided, that the legislature may allow such exemptions from taxation from time to time as shall seem necessary and just, and all existing exemptions provided by the laws of the territory, shall continue until changed by the legislature of the state: provided further, that duplicate taxation of property for the same purpose during the same year, is hereby prohibited.

§ 6. *Municipal corporations to impose their own taxes.* The legislature shall not impose taxes for the purpose of any county, city, town, or other municipal corporation, but may by law invest in the corporate authorities thereof, respectively, the power to assess and collect taxes for all purposes of such corporation.

§ 7. *State taxes to be paid in full.* All taxes levied for state purposes shall be paid into the state treasury, and no county, city, town, or other municipal corporation, the inhabitants thereof, nor the property therein, shall be released or discharged from their or its proportionate share of taxes to be levied for state purposes.

§ 8. *Corporate property must be taxed.* The power to tax corporations or corporate property, both real and personal, shall never be relinquished or suspended, and all corporations in this state or doing business therein, shall be subject to taxation for state, county, school, municipal, and other purposes, on real and personal property owned or used by them, and not by this constitution exempted from taxation within the territorial limits of the authority levying the tax.

§ 9. *Maximum rate of taxation.* The rate of taxation of real and personal property for state purposes shall never exceed ten (10) mills on each dollar of assessed valuation, unless a proposition to increase such rate, specifying the rate proposed and the time during which the same shall be levied, shall have been submitted to the people at a general election, and shall have received a majority of all the votes cast for and against it at such election.

§ 10. *Making profit from public money prohibited.* The making of profit, directly or indirectly, out of state, county, city, town, township or school district money, or using the same for any purpose not authorized by law, by any public officer, shall be deemed a felony, and shall be punished as provided by law.

§ 11. *Expenditure not to exceed appropriation.* No appropriation shall be made, nor any expenditure authorized by the legislature, whereby the expenditure of the state during any fiscal year shall exceed the total tax then provided for by law, and applicable to such appropriation or expenditure, unless the legislature making such appropriation shall provide for levying a sufficient tax, not exceeding the rates allowed in section nine of this article, to pay such appropriation or expenditure within such fiscal year. This provision shall not apply to appropriations or expenditures to suppress insurrection, defend the state, or assist in defending the United States in time of war.

§ 12. *State tax commission, members, terms, appointment, vacancies, duties, powers – County boards of equalization, duties.* There shall be a state tax commission consisting of four (4) members, not more than two (2) of whom shall belong to the same political party. The members of said commission shall be appointed by the governor, by and with the consent of the senate; the first commission to consist of one (1) commissioner appointed for a term of two (2) years, one (1) commissioner appointed for a term of four (4) years and two (2) commissioners appointed for a term of six (6) years, and appointments thereafter to be for a term of six (6) years; each commissioner to serve until his successor is appointed and qualified. If during the recess of the senate a vacancy occurs in said commission, it shall be the duty of the governor to fill such vacancy by appointment, and the appointee shall hold office for the unexpired term of his predecessor. The duties heretofore imposed upon the state board of equalization by the Constitution and laws of this state shall be performed by the state tax commission and said commission shall have such other powers and perform such other duties as may be prescribed by law, including the supervision and coordination of the work of the several county boards of equalization. The board of county commissioners for the several counties of the state, shall constitute boards of equalization for their respective counties, whose duty it shall be to equalize the valuation of the taxable property in the county, under such rules and regulations of the state tax commission as shall be prescribed by law.

§ 13. *Money – How drawn from treasury.* No money shall be drawn from the treasury, but in pursuance of appropriations made by law.

§ 14. *Money – How drawn from county treasuries.* No money shall be drawn from the county treasuries except upon the warrant of a duly authorized officer, in such manner and form as shall be prescribed by the legislature.

§ 15. *Legislature to provide system of county finance.* The legislature shall provide by law, such a system of county finance, as shall cause the business of the several counties to be conducted on a cash basis. It shall also provide that whenever any county shall have any warrants outstanding and unpaid, for the payment of which there are no funds in the county treasury, the county commissioners, in addition to other taxes provided by law, shall levy a special tax, not to exceed ten (10) mills on the dollar, of taxable property, as shown by the last preceding assessment, for the creation of a special fund for the redemption of said warrants; and after the levy of such special tax, all warrants issued before such levy, shall be paid exclusively out of said fund. All moneys in the county treasury at the end of each fiscal year, not needed for current expense, shall be transferred to said redemption fund.

§ 16. *Legislature to pass necessary laws.* The legislature shall pass all laws necessary to carry out the provisions of this article.

§ 17. *Gasoline taxes and motor vehicle registration fees to be expended on highways.* On and after July 1, 1941, the proceeds from the imposition of any tax on gasoline and like motor vehicle fuels sold or used to propel motor vehicles upon the highways of this state and from any tax or fee for the registration of motor vehicles, in excess of the necessary costs of collection and administration and any refund or credits authorized by law, shall be used exclusively for the construction, repair, maintenance and traffic supervision of the public highways of this state and the payment of the interest and principal of obligations incurred for said purposes; and no part of such revenues shall, by transfer of funds or otherwise, be diverted to any other purposes whatsoever.

Article VIII. Public Indebtedness and Subsidies

§ 1. *Limitation on public indebtedness.* The legislature shall not in any manner create any debt or debts, liability or liabilities, which shall singly or in the aggregate, exclusive of the debt of the territory at the date of its admission as a state, **and exclusive of debts or liabilities incurred subsequent to January 1, 1911, for the purpose of completing the construction and furnishing of the state capitol at Boise, Idaho, and exclusive of debt or debts, liability or liabilities incurred by the eleventh session of the legislature of the state of Idaho,** exceed **in the aggregate the sum of two million dollars ($2,000,000),** except in case of war, to repel an invasion, or suppress an insurrection, unless the same shall be authorized by law, for some single object or work, to be distinctly specified therein, which law shall provide ways and means, exclusive of loans, for the payment of the interest on such debt or liability as it falls due, and also for the payment and discharge of the principal of such debt or liability within twenty (20) years of the time of the contracting thereof, and shall be irrepealable until the principal and interest thereon shall be paid and discharged. But no such law shall take effect until at a general election it shall have been submitted to the people, and shall have received a majority of all the votes cast for or against it at such election, and all moneys raised by the authority of such laws shall be applied only to specified objects therein stated or to the payment of the debt thereby created, and such law shall be published in at least one newspaper in each county or city, and county, if one be published therein, throughout the state for three (3) months next preceding the election at which it is submitted to the people. The legislature may at any time after the approval of such law, by the people, if no debts shall have been contracted in pursuance thereof, repeal the same.

§ 2. *Loan of state's credit prohibited – Holding stock in corporation prohibited – Development of water power.* The credit of the state shall not, in any manner, be given, or loaned to, or in aid of any individual, association, municipality or corporation; nor shall the state directly or indirectly, become a stockholder in any association or corporation, **provided, that the state itself may control and promote the development of the unused water power within this state.**

§ 3. *Limitations on county and municipal indebtedness.* No county, city, board of education, or school district, or other subdivision of the state, shall incur any indebtedness, or liability, in any manner, or for any purpose, exceeding in that year, the income and revenue provided for it for such year, without the assent of two thirds (2/3) of the qualified electors thereof voting at an election to be held for that purpose, nor unless, before or at the time of incurring such indebtedness, provisions shall be made for the collection of an annual tax sufficient to pay the interest on such indebtedness as it falls due, and also to constitute a sinking fund for the payment of the principal thereof, within **thirty (30)** years from the time of contracting the same. Any indebtedness or liability incurred contrary to this provision shall be void: Provided, that this section shall not be construed to apply to the ordinary and necessary expenses authorized by the general laws of the state **and provided further that any city may own, purchase, construct, extend, or equip, within and without the corporate limits of such city, off street parking facilities, public recreation facilities, and air navigation facilities, and for the purpose of paying the cost thereof may, without regard to any limitation herein imposed, with the assent of two thirds (2/3) of the qualified electors voting at an election to be held for that purpose, issue revenue bonds therefor, the principal and interest of which to be paid solely from revenue derived from rates and charges for the use of, and the service rendered by, such facilities as may be prescribed by law, and provided further, that any city or other political subdivision of the state may own, purchase, construct, extend, or** equip, within and without the corporate limits of such city or political subdivision, water systems, sewage collection systems, water treatment plants, sewage treatment plants, and may rehabilitate existing electrical generating facilities, and for the purpose of paying the cost thereof, may, without regard to any limitation herein imposed, with the assent of a majority of the qualified electors voting at an election to be held for that purpose, issue revenue bonds therefor, the principal and interest of which to be paid solely from revenue derived from rates and charges for the use of, and the service rendered by such systems, plants and facilities, as may be prescribed by law; and provided further that any port district, for the purpose of carrying into effect all or any of the powers now or hereafter granted to port districts by the law of this state, may contract indebtedness and issue revenue bonds evidencing such indebtedness, without the necessity of the voters of the port district authorizing the same, such revenue bonds to be payable solely from all or such part of the revenues of the port district derived from any source whatsoever excepting only those revenues derived from ad valorem taxes, as the port commission thereof may determine, and such revenue bonds not to be in any manner or to any extent a general obligation of the port district issuing the same, nor a charge upon the ad valorem tax revenue of such port district.

§ 3A. *Environmental pollution control revenue bonds – Election on issuance.* Counties of the state may in the manner prescribed by law issue revenue bonds for the purpose of acquiring, constructing, installing and equipping facilities designed for environmental pollution control, including the acquisition of all technological facilities and equipment necessary or convenient for pollution control, to be financed for, or to be sold, leased or otherwise disposed of to, persons, associations, or corporations other than municipal corporations or other political subdivision; provided, that such revenue bonds are issued with the assent of a majority of the qualified electors of the county voting at an election to be called and held for that purpose; and provided further, that such revenue bonds shall not be secured by the full faith and credit or the taxing power of the state or any political subdivision thereof. No provision of this constitution, including, but not limited to sections 3 and 4 of article 8 and section 4 of article 12, shall be construed as a limitation upon the authority granted under this section. Nothing herein contained shall authorize any county of the state to operate any industrial or commercial enterprise.

§ 3B. *Port district facilities and projects – Revenue bond financing.* Port districts may acquire, construct, install, and equip facilities or projects to be financed for, or to be leased, sold or otherwise disposed of to persons, associations or corporations other than municipal corporations and may in the manner prescribed by law issue revenue bonds to finance the costs thereof; provided that any such revenue bonds shall be payable solely from charges, rents or payments derived from the facilities or projects financed thereby and shall not be secured by the full faith and credit or the taxing power of the port district, the state, or any other political subdivision. No provision of this Constitution, including, but not limited to Sections 3 and 4 of Article 8 and Section 4 of Article 12, shall be construed as a limitation upon the authority granted under this section.

§ 4. *County, etc. not to loan or give its credit.* No county, city, town, township, board of education, or school district, or other subdivision, shall lend, or pledge the credit or faith thereof directly or indirectly, in any manner, to, or in aid of any individual, association or corporation, for any amount or for any purpose whatever, or become responsible for any debt, contract or liability or any individual, association or corporation in or out of this state.

§ 5. *Special revenue financing.* **The legislature may enact laws authorizing the creation of public corporations by counties or cities to issue nonrecourse revenue bonds or other nonrecourse revenue obligations and to apply the proceeds thereof in the manner and for the purposes heretofore or hereafter authorized by law, subject to the following limitations.**

Nonrecourse revenue bonds and other nonrecourse obligations issued pursuant to this section shall be payable only from money or other property received as a result of projects financed by the nonrecourse revenue bonds or other nonrecourse revenue obligations and from money and other property received from private sources.

Nonrecourse revenue bonds and other nonrecourse revenue obligations issued pursuant to this section shall not be payable from or secured by any tax funds or governmental revenue or by all or part of the faith and credit of the state or any political subdivision.

Nonrecourse revenue bonds or other nonrecourse revenue obligations issued pursuant to this section may be issued only if the issuer certifies that it reasonably believes that the interest paid on the bonds or obligations will be exempt from income taxation by the federal government.

Nonrecourse revenue bonds or other nonrecourse revenue obligations may only be used to finance industrial development facilities consisting of manufacturing, processing, production, assembly, warehousing, solid waste disposal, recreation and energy facilities, excluding facilities to transmit, distribute or produce electrical energy.

The counties or cities shall never exercise their respective attributes of sovereignty including, but not limited to, the power to tax, the power of eminent domain, and the police power on behalf of any industrial development project authorized pursuant to this section.

Sections 2, 3 and 4 of Article 8 shall not be construed as a limitation upon the authority granted by this section. The proceeds of revenue bonds and other revenue obligations issued pursuant to this section for the purpose of financing privately owned property or loans to private persons or corporations shall be subject to audit by the state but shall not otherwise be deemed to be public money or public property for purposes of this constitution. The section is supplemental to and shall not be construed as a repeal of or limitation on any other authority lawfully exercisable under the constitution and laws of this state, including, among other, any existing authority to issue revenue bonds.

Article IX. Education and School Lands

§ 1. *Legislature to establish system of free schools.* The stability of a republican form of government depending mainly upon the intelligence of the people, it shall be the duty of the legislature of Idaho, to establish and maintain a general, uniform and thorough system of public, free common schools.

§ 2. *Board of education.* The general supervision of the **state educational institutions and** public school system of the state **of Idaho,** shall be vested in **a state** board of education, **the membership, powers and duties of which shall be prescribed by law. The state superintendent of public instruction shall be ex officio member of said board.**

§ 3. *Public school fund to remain intact.* The public school fund of the state shall forever remain inviolate and intact; the interest thereon only shall be expended in the maintenance of the schools of the state, and shall be distributed among the several counties and school districts of the state in such manner as may be prescribed by law. No part of this fund, principal or interest, shall ever be transferred to any other fund, or used or appropriated except as herein provided. The state treasurer shall be the custodian of this fund, and the same shall be securely and profitably invested as may be by law directed. The state shall supply all losses thereof that may in any manner occur.

§ 4. *Public school fund defined.* The public school fund of the state shall consist of the proceeds of such lands as have heretofore been granted, or may hereafter be granted, to the state by the general government, known as school lands, and those granted in lieu of such; lands acquired by gift or grant from any person or corporation under any law or grant of the general government; and of all other grants of land or money made to the state from the general government for general educational purposes, or where no other special purpose is indicated in such grant; all estates or distributive shares of estates that may escheat to the state; all unclaimed shares and dividends of any corporation incorporated under the laws of the state; and all other grants, gifts, devises, or bequests made to the state for general educational purposes.

§ 5. *Sectarian appropriations prohibited.* Neither the legislature nor any county, city, town, township, school district, or other public corporation, shall ever make any appropriation, or pay from any public fund or moneys whatever, anything in aid of any church or sectarian or religious society, or for any sectarian or religious purpose, or to help support or sustain any school, academy, seminary, college, university or other literary or scientific institution, controlled by any church, sectarian or religious denomination whatsoever; nor shall any grant or donation of land, money or other personal property ever be made by the state, or any such public corporation, to any church or for any sectarian or religious purpose; **provided, however, that a health facilities authority, as specifically authorized and empowered by law, may finance or refinance any private, not for profit, health facilities owned or operated by any church or sectarian religious society, through loans, leases or other transactions.**

§ 6. *Religious test and teaching in school prohibited.* No religious test or qualification shall ever be required of any person as a condition of admission into any public educational institution of the state, either as teacher or student; and no teacher or student of any such institution shall ever be required to attend or participate in any religious service whatever. No sectarian or religious tenets or doctrines shall ever be taught in the public schools, nor shall any distinction or classification of pupils be made on account of race or color. No books, papers, tracts or documents of a political, sectarian or denominational character shall be used or introduced in any schools established under the provisions of this article, nor shall any teacher or any district receive any of the public school moneys in which the schools have not been taught in accordance with the provisions of this article.

§ 7. *State board of land commissioners.* The governor, superintendent of public instruction, secretary of state, attorney general **and state auditor** shall constitute the state board of land commissioners, who shall have the direction, control and disposition of the public lands of the state, under such regulations as may be prescribed by law.

§ 8. *Location and disposition of public lands.* It shall be the duty of the state board of land commissioners to provide for the location, protection, sale or rental of all the lands heretofore, or which may hereafter be granted to or acquired by the state by or from the general government, under such regulations as may be prescribed by law, and in such manner as will secure the maximum **long term financial return to the institution to which granted or to the state if not**

specifically granted; provided, that no state lands shall be sold for less than **the appraised price**. No law shall ever be passed by the legislature granting any privileges to persons who may have settled upon any such public lands, subsequent to the survey thereof by the general government, by which the amount to be derived by the sale, or other disposition of such lands, shall be diminished, directly or indirectly. The legislature shall, at the earliest practicable period, provide by law that the general grants of land made by congress to the state shall be judiciously located and carefully preserved and held in trust, subject to disposal at public auction for the use and benefit of the respective object for which said grants of land were made, and the legislature shall provide for the sale of said lands from time to time and for the sale of timber on all state lands and for the faithful application of the proceeds thereof in accordance with the terms of said grants; provided, that not to exceed **one hundred sections of state** lands shall be sold in any one year, and to be sold in subdivisions of not to exceed **three hundred and twenty acres of land** to one individual, company or corporation. **The legislature shall have power to authorize the state board of land commissioners to exchange granted or acquired lands of the state on an equal value basis for other lands under agreement with the United States, local units of government, corporations, companies, individuals, or combinations thereof.**

§ 9. *Compulsory attendance at schools.* The legislature may require by law that every child shall attend the public schools **of the state**, throughout the period between the ages of six and eighteen years, unless educated by other means, **as provided by law.**

§ 10. *State university—Location, regents, and lands.* The location of the University of Idaho, as established by existing laws, is hereby confirmed. All the rights, immunities, franchises, and endowments, heretofore granted thereto by the territory of Idaho are hereby perpetuated unto the said university. The regents shall have the general supervision of the university, and the control and direction of all the funds of, and appropriations to, the university, under such regulations as may be prescribed by law. No university lands shall be sold for less than ten dollars per acre, and in subdivisions not to exceed one hundred and sixty acres, to any one person, company or corporation.

§ 11. *Loaning permanent endowment funds.* The permanent **endowment** funds other than funds arising from the disposition of university lands belonging to the state, shall be loaned on United States, state, **county, city, village, or school district bonds or state warrants or on such other investments as may be permitted by law under such regulations as the legislature may provide.**

Article X. Public Institutions

§ 1. *State to establish and support institutions.* Educational, reformatory, and penal institutions, and those for the benefit of the insane, blind, deaf and dumb, and such other institutions as the public good may require, shall be established and supported by the state in such manner as may be prescribed by law.

§ 2. *Seat of government.* The seat of government of the state of Idaho shall be located at Boise City for twenty years from the admission of the state, after which time the legislature may provide for its relocation, by submitting the question to a vote of the electors of the state at some general election.

§ 3. *Seat of government — Change in location.* The legislature may submit the question of the location of the seat of government to the qualified voters of the state at the general election, then next ensuing, and a majority of all the votes upon said question cast at said election shall be necessary to determine the location thereof. Said legislature shall also provide that in case there shall be no choice of location at said election, the question of choice between the two places for which the highest number of votes shall have been cast shall be submitted in like manner to the qualified electors of the state at the next general election.

§ 4. *Property of territory becomes property of state.* All property and institutions of the territory, shall, upon the adoption of the constitution, become the property and institutions of the state of Idaho.

§ 5. *State prisons — Control over.* **The state legislature shall establish a nonpartisan board to be known as the state board of correction, and to consist of three (3) members appointed by the governor, one (1) member for two (2) years, one (1) member for four (4) years, and one (1) member for six (6) years. After the appointment of the first board the term of each member appointed shall be six (6) years. This board shall have the control, direction and management of the penitentiaries of the state, their employees and properties, and of adult probation and parole, with such compensation, powers, and duties as may be prescribed by law.**

§ 6. *Directors of insane asylum.* [Repealed.]

§ 7. *Change in location of institutions.* The legislature for sanitary reasons may cause the removal to more suitable localities of any of the institutions mentioned in section one of this article.

Article XI. Corporations, Public and Private

§ 1. *Certain grants and charter invalidated.* All existing charters or grants of special or exclusive privileges, under which the corporations or grantees shall not have organized or commenced business in good faith at the time of the adoption of this Constitution, shall thereafter have no validity.

§ 2. *Special charters prohibited.* No charter of incorporation shall be granted, extended, changed or amended by special law, except for such municipal, charitable, educational, penal, or reformatory corporations as are or may be, under the control of the state; but the legislature shall provide by general law for the organization of corporations hereafter to be created: provided, that any such general law shall be subject to future repeal or alteration by the legislature.

§ 3. *Revocation and alteration of charters.* The legislature may provide by law for altering, revoking, or annulling any charter of incorporation, existing and revocable at the time of the adoption of this Constitution, in such manner, however, that no injustice shall be done to the corporators.

§ 4. *Cumulative voting.* **The Legislature shall not prohibit corporations from electing directors by cumulative voting.**

§ 5. All railroads shall be public highways, and all railroad, transportation, and express companies shall be common carriers, and subject to legislative control, and the legislature shall have power to regulate and control by law, the rates of charges for the transportation of passengers and freight by such companies or other common carriers, from one point to another in the state. Any association or corporation organized for the purpose, shall have the right to construct and operate a railroad between any designated points within this state, and to connect within or at the state line, with railroads of other states and territories. Every railroad company shall have the right with its road, to intersect, connect with, or cross any other railroad, under such regulations as may be prescribed by law, and upon making due compensation.

§ 6. *Equal transportation rights guaranteed.* All individuals, associations, and corporations, similarly situated, shall have equal rights to have persons or property transported on and over any railroad, transportation, or express route in this state, except that preference may be given to perishable property. No undue or unreasonable discrimination shall be made in charges or facilities for transportation of freight or passengers of the same class, by any railroad, or transportation, or express company, between persons or places within this state; but excursion or commutation tickets may be issued and sold at special rates, provided such rates are the same to all persons. No railroad, or transportation, or express company shall be allowed to charge, collect, or receive, under penalties which the legislature shall prescribe, any greater charge or toll for the transportation of freight or passengers, to any place or station upon its route or line, than it charges for the transportation of the same class of freight or passengers to any more distant place or station upon its route or line within this state. No railroad, express, or transportation company, nor any lessee, manager, or other employee thereof, shall give any preference to any individual, association, or corporation, in furnishing cars or motive power, or for the transportation of money or other express matter.

§ 7. *Acceptance of Constitution by corporations.* No corporation other than municipal corporations in existence at the time of the adoption of this Constitution, shall have the benefit of any future legislation, without first filing in the office of the secretary of state an acceptance of the provisions of this Constitution in binding form.

§ 8. *Right of eminent domain and police power reserved.* The right of eminent domain shall never be abridged, nor so construed as to prevent the legislature from taking the property and franchises of incorporated companies, and subjecting them to public use, the same as the property of individuals; and the police powers of the state shall never be abridged or so construed as to permit corporations to conduct their business in such manner as to infringe the equal rights of individuals, or the general well being of the state.

§ 9. *Increase in capital stock.* No corporation shall issue stocks or bonds, except for labor done, services performed, or money or property actually received; and all fictitious increase of stock or indebtedness shall be void. The stock of corporations shall not be increased except in pursuance of general law, nor without the consent of the persons, holding a majority of the stock **of the class to be increased**, first obtained at a meeting, **held pursuant to such notice as is provided by the legislature.**

§ 10. *Regulation of foreign corporations.* No foreign corporation shall do any business in this state without having one or more known places of business, and an authorized agent or agents in the same, upon whom process may be served; and no company or corporation formed under the laws of any other country, state, or territory, shall have or be allowed to exercise or enjoy, within this state any greater rights or privileges than those possessed or enjoyed by corporations of the same or similar character created under the laws of this state.

§ 11. *Constructing railroad in city or town.* No street, or other railroad, shall be constructed within any city, town, or incorporated village without the consent of the local authorities having the control of the street or highway proposed to be occupied by such street or other railroad.

§ 12. *Retroactive laws favoring corporations prohibited.* The legislature shall pass no law for the benefit of a railroad, or other corporation, or any individual, or association of individuals retroactive in its operation, or which imposes on the people of any county or municipal subdivision of the state, a new liability in respect to transactions or consideration already passed.

§ 13. *Telegraph and telephone companies.* Any association or corporation, or the lessees or managers thereof, organized for the purpose, or any individual, shall have the right to construct and maintain lines of telegraph or telephone within this state, and connect the same with other lines; and the legislature shall by general law of uniform operation provide reasonable regulations to give full effect to this section.

§ 14. *Consolidation of corporations with foreign corporations.* If any railroad, telegraph, express, or other corporation, organized under any of the laws of this state, shall consolidate, by sale or otherwise, with any railroad, telegraph, express, or other corporation, organized under any of the laws of any other state or territory, or of the United States, the same shall not thereby become a foreign corporation, but the courts of this state shall retain jurisdiction over the part of the corporate property within the limits of the state in all matters that may arise, as if said consolidation had not taken place.

§ 15. *Transfer of franchises.* The legislature shall not pass any law permitting the leasing or alienation of any franchise so as to release or relieve the franchise or property held thereunder from any of the liabilities of the lessor or grantor, or lessee or grantee, contracted or incurred in the operation, use, or enjoyment of such franchise, or any of its privileges.

§ 16. *Term "corporation" defined.* The term "corporation" as used in this article, shall be held and construed to include all associations and joint stock companies having or exercising any of the powers or privileges of corporations not possessed by individuals or partnerships.

§ 17. *Liability of stockholders — Dues.* Dues from private corporations shall be secured by such means as may be prescribed by law, but in no case shall any stockholder be individually liable in any amount over or above the amount of stock owned by him.

§ 18. *Combinations in restraint of trade prohibited.* That no incorporated company or any association of persons or stock company, in the state of Idaho, shall directly or indirectly combine or make any contract with any other incorporated company, foreign or domestic, through their stockholders or the trustees or assignees of such stockholders, or in any manner whatsoever, for the purpose of fixing the price or regulating the production of any article of commerce or of produce of the soil, or of consumption by the people; and that the legislature be required to pass laws for the enforcement thereof, by adequate penalties, to the extent, if necessary for that purpose, of the forfeiture of their property and franchise.

Article XII. Corporations, Municipal

§ 1. *General laws for cities and towns.* The legislature shall provide by general laws for the incorporation, organization and classification of the cities and towns, in proportion to the population, which laws may be altered, amended, or repealed by the general laws. Cities and towns heretofore incorporated, may become organized under such general laws, whenever a majority of the electors at a general election, shall so determine, under such provisions therefore as may be made by the legislature.

§ 2. *Local police regulations authorized.* Any county or incorporated city or town may make and enforce, within its limits, all such local police, sanitary and other regulations as are not in conflict with its charter or with the general laws.

§ 3. *State not to assume local indebtedness.* The state shall never assume the debts of any county, town, or other municipal corporation, unless such debts shall have been created to repel invasion, suppress insurrection or defend the state in war.

§ 4. *Municipal corporations not to loan credit.* No county, town, city, or other municipal corporation, by vote of its citizens or otherwise, shall ever become a stockholder in any joint stock company, corporation or association whatever, or raise money for, or make donation or loan its credit to, or in aid of, any such company or association: provided, that cities and towns may contract indebtedness for school, water, sanitary and illuminating purposes: provided, that any city or town contracting such indebtedness shall own its just proportion of the property thus created and receive from any income arising therefrom, its proportion to the whole amount so invested.

Article XIII. Immigration and Labor

§ 1. *Bureau of immigration — Commissioner.* There shall be established a bureau of immigration, labor and statistics, which shall be under the charge of a commissioner of immigration, labor and statistics, who shall be appointed by the governor, by and with the consent of the senate. The commissioner shall hold his office for two years, and until his successor shall have been appointed and qualified, unless sooner removed. The commissioner shall collect information upon the subject of labor, its relation to capital, the hours of labor and the earnings of laboring men and women, and the means of promoting their material, social, intellectual and moral prosperity. The commissioner shall annually make a report in writing to the governor of the state of the information collected and collated by him, and containing such recommendations as he may deem calculated to promote the efficiency of the bureau.

§ 2. *Protection and hours of labor.* Not more than eight (8) hours actual work shall constitute a lawful day's work, on all state and municipal works, **and the legislature shall pass laws to provide for the health and safety of employees in factories, smelters, mines and ore reduction works.**

§ 3. *Restrictions on convict labor.* [Repealed.]

§ 4. *Child labor in mines prohibited.* The employment of children under the age of fourteen (14) years in underground mines is prohibited.

§ 5. *Aliens to be employed on public work.* No person, not a citizen of the United States, or who has not declared his intention to become such, shall be employed upon, or in connection with, any state or municipal works.

§ 6. *Mechanic's liens to be provided.* The legislature shall provide by proper legislation for giving to mechanics, laborers, and material men an adequate lien on the subject matter of their labor.

§ 7. *Boards of arbitration.* The legislature may establish boards of arbitration whose duty it shall be to hear and determine all differences and controversies between laborers and their employers which may be submitted to them in writing by all the parties. Such boards of arbitration shall possess all the powers and authority in respect to administering oaths, subpoenaing witnesses, and compelling their attendance, preserving order during the sittings of the board, punishing for contempt, and requiring the production of papers and writings, and all other powers and privileges, in their nature applicable, conferred by law on justices of the peace.

§ 8. *Duties and compensation of commissioner.* The commissioner of immigration, labor and statistics shall perform such duties and receive such compensation as may be prescribed by law.

Article XIV. Militia

§ 1. *Persons subject to military duty.* All able-bodied male persons, residents of this state, between the ages of eighteen and forty-five years, shall be enrolled in the militia, and perform such military duty as may be required by law; but no person having conscientious scruples against bearing arms, shall be compelled to perform such duty in time of peace. Every person claiming such exemption from service, shall, in lieu thereof, pay into the school fund of the county of which he may be a resident, an equivalent in money, the amount and manner of payment to be fixed by law.

§ 2. *Legislature to provide for enrolment of militia.* The legislature shall provide by law for the enrolment, equipment and discipline of the militia, to conform as nearly as practicable to the regulations for the government of the armies of the United States, and pass such laws to promote volunteer organizations as may afford them effectual encouragement.

§ 3. *Selection and commission of officers.* All militia officers shall be commissioned by the governor, the manner of their selection to be provided by law, and may hold their commissions for such period of time as the legislature may provide.

§ 4. *Preservation of records, banners and relics.* All military records, banners, and relics of the state, except when in lawful use, shall be preserved in the office of the adjutant general as an enduring memorial of the patriotism and valor of the soldiers of Idaho; and it shall be the duty of the legislature to provide by law for the safekeeping of the same.

§ 5. *National and state flags only to be carried.* All military organizations under the laws of this state shall carry no other device, banner or flag, than that of the United States or the state of Idaho.

§ 6. *Importation of armed forces prohibited.* No armed police force, or detective agency, or armed body of men, shall ever be brought into this state for the suppression of domestic violence except upon the application of the legislature, or the executive when the legislature can not be convened.

Article XV. Water Rights

§ 1. *Use of waters a public use.* The use of all waters now appropriated, or that may hereafter be appropriated for sale, rental or distribution; also of all water originally appropriated for private use, but which after such appropriation has heretofore been, or may hereafter be sold, rented, or distributed, is hereby declared to be a public use, and subject to the regulations and control of the state in the manner prescribed by law.

§ 2. *Right to collect rates a franchise.* The right to collect rates or compensation for the use of water supplied to any county, city, or town, or water district, or the inhabitants thereof, is a franchise, and can not be exercised except by authority of and in the manner prescribed by law.

§ 3. *Water of natural stream — Right to appropriate — State's regulatory power — Priorities.* The right to divert and appropriate the unappropriated waters of any natural stream to beneficial uses, shall never be denied, **except that the state may regulate and limit the use thereof for power purposes.** Priority of appropriations shall give the better right as between those using the water; but when the waters of any natural stream are not sufficient for the service of all those desiring the use of the same, those using the water for domestic purposes shall (subject to such limitations as may be prescribed by law) have the preference over those claiming for any other purpose; and those using the water for agricultural purposes shall have preference over those using the same for manufacturing purposes. And in any organized mining district those using the water for mining purposes or milling purposes connected with mining, shall have preference over those using the same for manufacturing or agricultural purposes. But the usage by such subsequent appropriators shall be subject to such provisions of law regulating the taking of private property for public and private use, as referred to in section 14 of article 1 of this Constitution.

§ 4. *Continuing rights to water guaranteed.* Whenever any waters have been, or shall be, appropriated or used for agricultural purposes, under a sale, rental, or distribution thereof, such sale, rental, or distribution shall be deemed an exclusive dedication to such use; and whenever such waters so dedicated shall have once been sold, rented or distributed to any person who has settled upon or improved land for agricultural purposes with the view of receiving the benefit of such water under such dedication, such person, his heirs, executors, administrators, successors, or assigns, shall not thereafter, without his consent, be deprived of the annual use of the same, when needed for domestic purposes, or to irrigate the land so settled upon or improved, upon payment therefor, and compliance with such equitable terms and conditions as to the quantity used and times of use, as may be prescribed by law.

§ 5. *Priorities and limitations on use.* Whenever more than one person has settled upon, or improved land with the view of receiving water for agricultural purposes, under a sale, rental, or distribution thereof, as in the last preceding section of this article provided, as among such persons, priority in time shall give superiority of right to the use of such water in the numerical order of such settlements or improvements; but whenever the supply of such water shall not be sufficient to meet the demands of all those desiring to use the same, such priority of right shall be subject to such reasonable limitations as to the quantity of water used and times of use as the legislature, having due regard both to such priority of right and the necessities of those subsequent in time of settlement or improvement, may by law prescribe.

§ 6. *Establishment of maximum rates.* The legislature shall provide by law, the manner in which reasonable maximum rates may be established to be charged for the use of water sold, rented, or distributed for any useful or beneficial purpose.

§ 7. *State Water Resource Agency.* **There shall be constituted a Water Resource Agency, composed as the Legislature may now or hereafter prescribe, which shall have power to construct and operate water projects; to issue bonds, without state obligation, to be repaid from revenues of projects; to generate and wholesale hydroelectric power at the site of production; to appropriate public waters as trustee for Agency projects; to acquire, transfer and encumber title to real property for water projects and to have control and administrative authority over state lands required for water projects; all under such laws as may be prescribed by the Legislature. Additionally, the State Water Resource Agency shall have power to formulate and implement a state water plan for optimum development of water resources in the public interest. The Legislature of the State of Idaho shall have the authority to amend or reject the state water plan in a manner provided by law. Thereafter any change in the state water plan shall be submitted to the Legislature of the State of Idaho upon the first day of a regular session following the change and the change shall become effective unless amended or rejected by law within sixty days of its admission to the Legislature.**

Article XVI. Livestock

§ 1. *Laws to protect livestock.* The legislature shall pass all necessary laws to provide for the protection of livestock against the introduction or spread of pleuro pneumonia, glanders, spenetic or texas fever, and other infectious or contagious diseases. The legislature may also establish a system of quarantine or inspection and such other regulations as may be necessary for the protection of stock owners and most conducive to the stock interests within the state.

Article XVII. State Boundaries

§ 1. *Name and boundaries of state.* The name of this state is Idaho, and its boundaries are as follows: Beginning at a point in the middle channel of the Snake river where the northern boundary of Oregon intersects the same; then follow down the channel of Snake river to a point opposite the mouth of the Kooskooskia or Clearwater river; then due north to the forty-ninth parallel of latitude; then east along that parallel to the thirty ninth degree of longitude west of Washington; thence south along that degree of longitude to the crest of the Bitter Root mountains; thence southward along the crest of the Bitter Root mountains till its intersection with the Rocky mountains; thence southward along the crest of the Rocky mountains to the thirty-fourth degree of longitude west of Washington; thence south along that degree of longitude to the forty-second degree of north latitude; these west along that parallel to the eastern boundary of the state of Oregon; thence north along that boundary to the place of beginning.

Article XVIII. County Organization

§ 1. *Existing counties recognized.* The several counties of the territory of Idaho, as they now exist, are hereby recognized as legal subdivisions of this state.

§ 2. *Removal of county seats.* No county seat shall be removed unless upon petition of a majority of the qualified electors of the county, and unless two-thirds (2/3) of the qualified electors of the county, voting on the proposition at a general election, shall vote in favor of such removal. A proposition of removal of the county seat shall not be submitted in the same county more than once in six (6) years, except as provided by existing laws. No person shall vote at any county seat election who has not resided in the county six (6) months, and in the precinct ninety (90) days.

§ 3. *Division of counties.* No county shall be divided unless a majority of the qualified electors of the territory proposed to be cut off, voting on the proposition at a general election, shall vote in favor of such division: provided, that this section shall not apply to the creation of new counties. No person shall vote at such election who has not been ninety (90) days a resident of the territory proposed to be annexed. When any part of a county is stricken off and attached to another county, the part stricken off shall be held to pay its ratable proportion of all then existing liabilities of the county from which it is taken.

§ 4. *New counties – Size and valuation.* No new counties shall be established which shall reduce any county to an area of less than four hundred (400) square miles, **nor the valuation of its taxable property to less than one million dollars ($1,000,000)**; nor shall any new county be formed which shall have an area of less than four hundred (400) square miles, **and taxable property of less than one million dollars ($1,000,000), as shown by the last previous assessment.**

§ 4A. *Consolidation of counties.* **Counties of the state of Idaho as they now exist, or may hereafter be created or exist, may be consolidated in such manner as shall be prescribed by law; provided, no county may be consolidated with another county, except upon approval of a two-thirds (2/3) majority vote in each county, of the qualified electors thereof voting upon the question, and the limitations and provisions of sections 2, 3 and 4 of Article 18 of the Constitution of the state of Idaho shall have no application to the question of consolidating counties.**

§ 5. *System of county government.* The legislature shall establish, subject to the provisions of this article, a system of county governments which shall be uniform throughout the state; and by general laws shall provide for township or precinct organization.

§ 6. *County officers.* The legislature by general and uniform laws shall, **commencing with the general election in 1986,** provide for the election biennially, in each of the several counties of the state, of county commissioners and for the election of a sheriff, a county assessor, a county coroner and a county treasurer, who is ex-officio public administrator, **every four years in each of the several counties of the state. All taxes shall be collected by the officer or officers designated by law.** The clerk of the district court shall be ex-officio auditor and recorder. No other county offices shall be established, but the legislature by general and uniform laws shall provide for such township, precinct and municipal officers as public convenience may require, and shall prescribe their duties, and fix their terms of office. The legislature shall provide for the strict accountability of county, township, precinct and municipal officers for all fees which may be collected by them, and for all public and municipal moneys which may be paid to them, or officially come into their possession. The county commissioners may employ counsel when necessary. The sheriff, **county assessor, county treasurer, and ex-officio tax collector,** auditor and recorder and clerk of the district court shall be empowered by the county commissioners to appoint such deputies and clerical assistants as the business of their office may require, said deputies and clerical assistants to receive such compensation as may be fixed by the county commissioners.

§ 7. *County officers — Salaries.* **All county officers and deputies when allowed, shall receive, as full compensation for their services, fixed annual salaries, to be paid monthly out of the county treasury, as other expenses are paid.** All actual and necessary expenses incurred by any county officer or deputy in the performance of his official duties, shall be a legal charge against the county, and may be retained by him out of any fees which may come into his hands. All fees which may come into his hands from whatever source, over and above his actual and necessary expenses, shall be turned into the county treasury at the end of each quarter. He shall at the end of each quarter, file with the clerk of the board of county commissioners, a sworn statement, accompanied by proper vouchers, showing all expenses incurred and all fees received, which must be audited by the board as other accounts.

§ 8. *County officers — How paid.* The compensation provided in section seven for the officers therein mentioned shall be paid by fees or commissions, or both, as prescribed by law. All fees and commissions received by such officers in excess of the maximum compensation per annum provided for each in section seven of this article shall be paid to the county treasurer for the use and benefit of the county. In case the fees received in any one year by any one of such officers shall not amount to the minimum compensation per annum therein provided, he shall be paid by the county a sum sufficient to make his aggregate annual compensation equal to such minimum compensation.

§ 9. *County officers — Liability for fees.* The neglect or refusal of any county officer or deputy to account for and pay into the county treasury any money received as fees or compensation, **in excess of his actual and necessary expenses, incurred in the performance of his official duties, within ten (10) days after his quarterly settlement with the county** shall be a felony, and the grade of the crime shall be embezzlement of public funds, and be punishable as provided for such offenses.

§ 10. *Board of county commissioners.* The board of county commissioners shall consist of three (3) members. **Their terms of office shall be as follows: At the general election of 1936 two (2) members shall be elected for a term of two (2) years and one (1) member shall be elected for a term of four (4) years; at each biennial election thereafter one (1) member shall be elected for a term of two (2) years and one (1) for a term of four (4) years. The legislature shall enact the necessary measures to put this provision into effect and in so doing shall allot such four (4) year term to each commissioner's election district or like subdivision of the county which may be provided by law, in rotation.**

§ 11. *Duties of officers.* County, township, and precinct officers shall perform such duties as shall be prescribed by law.

Article XIX. *Apportionment*

§ 1. *Senatorial districts.* [Superseded.]

§ 2. *Representative districts.* [Superseded.]

Article XX. *Amendments*

§ 1. *How amendments may be proposed.* Any amendment or amendments to this Constitution may be proposed in either branch of the legislature, and if the same shall be agreed to by two-thirds (2/3) of all the members of each of the two (2) houses, voting separately, such proposed amendment or amendments shall, with the yeas and nays thereon, be entered on their journals, and it shall be the duty of the legislature to submit such amendment or amendments to the electors of the state at the next general election, and cause the same to be published for at least **three (3) times in every newspaper qualified to publish legal notices as provided by law. Said publication shall provide the arguments proposing and opposing said amendment or amendments as provided by law,** and if a majority of the electors shall ratify the same, such amendment or amendments shall become a part of this Constitution.

§ 2. *Submission of several amendments.* If two (2) or more amendments are proposed, they shall be submitted in such manner that the electors shall vote for or against each of them separately.

§ 3. *Revision or amendment by convention.* Whenever two-thirds (2/3) of the members elected to each branch of the legislature shall deem it necessary to call a convention to revise or amend this Constitution, they shall recommend to the electors to vote at the next general election, for or against a convention, and if a majority of all the electors voting at said election shall have voted for a convention, the legislature shall at the next session provide by law for calling the same; and such convention shall consist of a number of members, not less than double the number of the most numerous branch of the legislature.

§ 4. *Submission of revised constitution to people.* Any constitution adopted by such convention, shall have no validity until it has been submitted to, and adopted by, the people.

Article XXI. Schedule and Ordinance

§ 1. *Judicial proceedings continued.* That no inconvenience may arise from a change of the territorial government to a permanent state government, it is declared that all writs, actions, prosecutions, claims, liabilities, and obligations against the territory of Idaho, of whatsoever nature and rights of individuals, and of bodies corporate, shall continue as if no change had taken place in this government; and all process which may before the organization of the judicial department under this Constitution, be issued under the authority of the territory of Idaho, shall be as valid as if issued in the name of the state.

§ 2. *Laws continued in force.* All laws now in force in the territory of Idaho which are not repugnant to this Constitution shall remain in force until they expire by their own limitation or be altered or repealed by the legislature.

§ 3. *Territorial fines and forfeitures accrue to state.* All fines, penalties, forfeitures, and escheats accruing to the territory of Idaho shall accrue to the use of the state.

§ 4. *Territorial bonds and obligations pass to state.* All recognizances, bonds, obligations, or other undertakings heretofore taken, or which may be taken before the organization of the judicial department under this Constitution, shall remain valid, and shall pass over to and may be prosecuted in the name of the state; and all bonds, obligations, or other undertakings executed by this territory, or to any other officer in his official capacity, shall pass over to the proper state authority, and to their successors in office for the uses therein respectively expressed, and may be sued for and recovered accordingly. All criminal prosecutions and penal actions which have arisen or which may arise before the organization of the judicial department under this Constitution, and which shall then be pending, may be prosecuted to judgment and execution in the name of the state.

§ 5. *Territorial officers to continue in office.* All officers, civil and military, now holding their offices and appointments in this territory under the authority of the United States, or under the authority of this territory, shall continue to hold and exercise their respective offices and appointments until suspended under this Constitution.

§ 6. *Submission of Constitution to electors.* This Constitution shall be submitted for adoption or rejection, to a vote of the electors qualified by the laws of this territory to vote at all elections, at an election to be held on the Tuesday after the first Monday in November, A.D. 1889. Said election shall be conducted in all respects in the same manner as provided by the laws of the territory for general election, and the returns thereof shall be made and canvassed in the same manner and by the same authority as provided in cases of such general elections, and abstracts of such returns duly certified shall be transmitted to the board of canvassers now provided by law for canvassing the returns of votes for delegate in congress. The said canvassing board shall canvass the votes so returned, and certify and declare the result of said election in the same manner, as is required by law for the election of said delegate.

At the said election the ballots shall be in the following form: For the Constitution: Yes. No.

And as a heading to each of said ballots shall be printed on each ballot, the following instruction to voters:

All persons who desire to vote for the Constitution, or any of the articles submitted to a separate vote, may erase the word "no." All persons who desire to vote against the Constitution, or against any article submitted separately may erase the word "yes."

Any person may have printed or written on his ballot only the words, "For the Constitution," or "Against the Constitution," and such ballots shall be counted for or against the Constitution accordingly.

§ 7. *When Constitution takes effect.* This Constitution shall take effect and be in full force immediately upon the admission of the territory as a state.

§ 8. *Election proclamation to be issued.* Immediately upon the admission of the territory as a state, the governor of the territory, or in case of his absence or failure to act, the secretary of the territory, or in case of his absence or failure to act, the president of this convention, shall issue a proclamation, which shall be published, and a copy thereof mailed to the chairman of the board of county commissioners of each county, calling an election by the people of all state, district, county, township, and other officers, created and made elective by this Constitution, and fixing a day for such election, which shall not be less than forty (40) days after the date of such proclamation, nor more than ninety (90) days after the admission of the territory as a state.

§ 9. *Election to be ordered — Conduct of election.* The board of commissioners of the several counties shall thereupon order such election for said day, and shall cause notice to be given, in the manner and for the length of time provided by the laws of the territory in cases of general elections for delegate to congress, and county and other officers. Every qualified elector of the territory, at the date of said election, shall be entitled to vote thereat. Said election shall be conducted in all respects in the same manner as provided by the laws of the territory for general elections, and the returns thereof shall be made and canvassed in the same manner and by the same authority as provided in cases of such general election; but returns for all state and district officers and members of the legislature shall be made to the canvassing board hereinafter provided for.

§ 10. *Canvass of election returns.* The governor, secretary, controller and attorney general of the territory, and the president of this convention, or a majority of them, shall constitute a board of canvassers to canvass the vote at such elections for all state and district officers and members of the legislature. The said board shall assemble at the seat of government of the territory on the thirtieth day after the date of such election (or on the following day if such day fall on Sunday) and proceed to canvass the votes for all state and district officers and members of the legislature, in the manner provided by the laws of the territory for canvassing the vote for delegates to congress, and they shall issue certificates of election to the persons found to be elected to said offices severally, and shall make and file with the secretary of the territory an abstract certified by them, of the number of votes cast for each person for each of said offices and the total number of votes cast in each county.

§ 11. *Certificates of election.* The canvassing boards of the several counties shall issue certificates of election to the several persons found by them to have been elected to the several county and precinct offices.

§ 12. *Qualifications of officers.* All officers elected at such election shall, within thirty days after they have been declared elected, take the oath required by the Constitution and give the same bond required by the law of the territory to be given in case of like officers of the territory, district or county, and shall thereupon enter upon the duties of their respective offices; but the legislature may require by law all such officers to give other or further bonds as a condition of their continuance in office.

§ 13. *Tenure of office.* All officers elected at said election, shall hold their offices until the legislature shall provide by law, in accordance with this Constitution, for the election of their successors, and until such successors shall be elected and qualified.

§ 14. *Convention of first legislature.* The governor-elect of the state, immediately upon his qualifying and entering upon the duties of his office, shall issue his proclamation convening the legislature of the state at the seat of government on a day to be named in said proclamation and which shall not be less than thirty (30) nor more than sixty (60) days after the date of such proclamation. Within ten (10) days after the organization of the legislature, both houses of the legislature shall then and there proceed to elect, as provided by law, two (2) senators of the United States for the state of Idaho. At said election, the two (2) persons who shall receive the majority of all votes cast by said senators and representatives, shall be elected as such United States senators, and shall be so declared by the presiding officers of said joint session. The presiding officers of the senate and the house, shall issue a certificate to each of said senators, certifying his election, which certificates shall also be signed by the governor and attested by the secretary of state.

§ 15. *Legislature to pass necessary laws.* The legislature shall pass all necessary laws to carry into effect the provisions of this Constitution.

§ 16. *Transfer of cases to state courts.* Whenever any two (2) of the judges of the Supreme Court of the state, elected under the provisions of this Constitution, shall have qualified in their offices, the causes then pending in the Supreme Court of the territory, and the papers, records, and proceedings of said court, and the seal and other property pertaining thereto, shall pass into the jurisdiction and possession of the Supreme Court of the state; and until so superseded the Supreme Court of the territory and the judges thereof shall continue, with like powers and jurisdiction, as if this Constitution had not been adopted. Whenever the judge of the district court of any district elected under the provisions of this Constitution shall have qualified in office, the several causes then pending in the district court of the territory, within any county in such district, and the records, papers, and proceedings of said district court, and the seal and other property pertaining thereto, shall pass into the jurisdiction and possession of the district court of the state for such county; and until the district courts of this territory shall be superseded in the manner aforesaid the said district courts and the judges thereof shall continue with the same jurisdiction and power to be exercised in the same judicial districts respectively, as heretofore constituted under the laws of the territory.

§ 17. *Seals of courts.* Until otherwise provided by law, the seals now in use in the Supreme and district courts of this territory are hereby declared to be the seals of the Supreme and district courts, respectively, of the state.

§ 18. *Transfer of probate matters.* Whenever this Constitution shall go into effect, the books, records, and papers, and proceedings of the probate court in each county, and all causes and matters of administration and other matters pending therein, shall pass into the jurisdiction and possession of the probate court of the same county of the state, and the said probate court shall proceed to final decree or judgment, order, or other determination in the said several matters and causes as the said probate court might have done as if this Constitution had not been adopted.

§ 19. *Religious freedom guaranteed - Disclaimer of title to Indian lands.* It is ordained by the state of Idaho that perfect toleration of religious sentiment shall be secured, and no inhabitant of said state shall ever be molested in person or property on account of his or her mode of religious worship. And the people of the state of Idaho do agree and declare that we forever disclaim all right and title to the unappropriated public lands lying within the boundaries thereof, and to all lands lying within said limits owned or held by any Indians or Indian tribes; and until the title thereto shall have been extinguished by the United States, the same shall be subject to the disposition of the United States, and said Indian lands shall remain under the absolute jurisdiction and control of the congress of the United States; that the lands belonging to citizens of the United States, residing without the said state of Idaho, shall never be taxed at a higher rate than the lands belonging to the residents thereof. That no taxes shall be imposed by the state on the lands or property therein belonging, to, or which may hereafter be purchased by, the United States, or reserved for its use. And the debts and liabilities of this territory shall be assumed and paid by the state of Idaho. That this ordinance shall be irrevocable, without the consent of the United States and the people of the state of Idaho.

§ 20. *Adoption of federal Constitution.* That in behalf of the people of Idaho, we, in convention assembled, do adopt the Constitution of the United States.

Signatures. Done in open convention at Boise City, in the territory of Idaho, this sixth day of August, in the year of our Lord, one thousand eight hundred and eight-nine.

Wm. H. Clagett, President, Geo. Ainslie, W. C. B. Allen, Robt. Anderson, H. Armstrong, Orlando B. Batten, Frank W. Beane, Jas. H. Beatty, J. W. Ballentine, A. D. Bevan, Henry B. Blake, Frederick Campbell, Frank P. Cavanah, A. S. Chaney, Chas. A. Clark, I. N. Coston, Jas. I. Crutcher, Stephen S. Glidden, John S. Gray, Wm. W. Hammell, H. S. Hampton, H. O. Harkness, Frank Harris, Sol. Hasbrouck, C. M. Hays, W. B. Heyburn, John Hogan, J. M. Howe, E. S. Jewell, G. W. King, H. B. Kinport, Jas. W. Lamoreaux, John Lewis, Wm. C. Maxey, A. E. Mayhew, W. J. McConnell, Henry Melder, John H. Myer, John T. Morgan, A. B. Moss, Aaron F. Parker, A. J. Pierce, A.J. Pinkham, J. W. Poe, Thos. Pyeatt, Jas. W. Reid, W. D. Robbins, Wm. H. Savidge, Aug. M. Sinnot, James M. Shoup, Drew W. Standrod, Frank Steunenberg, Homer Stull, Willis Sweet, Sam. F. Taylor, J. L. Underwood, Lycurgus Vineyard, J. S. Whitton, Edgar Wilson, W. W. Woods, John Lemp, N. I. Andrews, Samuel J. Pritchard, J. W. Brigham.

Index